# THE ROOTS

# OF

# BALKANIZATION

*Eastern Europe C. E. 500-1500
...And its Impact to the Present*

ION GRUMEZA

Conclusive Books

Copyright " 2025 Ion Grumeza
Conclusive Books
9462 Brownsboro Road
Suite 274
Louisville, KY 40241
U.S.A.

All rights reserved. No part of this publication may be reproduced, stored in a retrieval system or transmitted in any form or by any means—electronic, mechanical, photocopying, recording or otherwise—without the written permission of the author/publisher.

Cover conceived by Ion Grumeza; created by Sarah Smith
Interior by Sarah Smith

*The Roots of Balkanization - Eastern Europe C. E. 500-1500 …And its Impact to the Present* / Ion Grumeza — 2nd Edition 2025.

Photos of Ion Grumeza in "A Note to the Reader", Chapter 1, and on the back cover are from the author's personal collection.

ISBN: 979-8-9863323-8-3 (Paperback)
LCCN: 2025915263

# TABLE OF CONTENTS

A NOTE TO THE READER..................................................................V

PREFACE.........................................................................................IX

1. THE LAST CRUSADER: PRINCE DRACULA................................1

2. FROM INVASION TO SETTLEMENT...........................................42

3. FROM TRIBES TO COUNTRY.....................................................73

4. VOLATILE ALLIANCES IN THE BALKAN PENINSULA........100

5. THE AREA'S SHIFTING BORDERS...........................................129

6. THE SOCIAL AND ECONOMIC LIFE OF THE MANOR..........177

7. SPIRITUAL AND CULTURAL LIFE..........................................215

8. IN THE NAME OF GOD...............................................................260

9. THE END OF AN EMPIRE...........................................................291

EPILOG...........................................................................................339

BIBLIOGRAPHY............................................................................381

# A NOTE TO THE READER

DEAR READER,

My book will take you into a world of hostile times like none other in history. The meaning of "Balkanization" has not changed much since the existence of the Byzantine Empire.

My study of Balkanization traces the creation of the present Balkan nations, and examines their influence from the past Eastern Europe. It investigates the origins of specific mixed populations, their habits and traditions, as well as their national identities. These all shaped the alliances and rivalries which ultimately produced surprising demographic and historical changes.

Many chapters take a fresh look at the pagan and nomadic tribes who for centuries roamed the vast lands of Eurasia, until they found the trade routes that led to the riches of the Byzantine Empire. Pushing each other in all directions, these savage migratory people ended up sacking the prosperous Byzantine settlements in the Balkan Peninsula. All of them were aiming to pillage Constantinople, but with no avail.

The period of the rise of the Byzantine Empire (C.E. 500 to 1000) was plagued by countless destructive events at all levels. The emperors from Constantinople tried hard to maintain their authority over their land and the invaders. They played each invading tribe against the other, bribed them, employed mercenary armies to force them back, and called on the power of the Orthodox Church to pacify them.

During this time the future nation of the Ottomans was testing its military might by attacking the overstretched empire. It was already shaken by royal feuds, and was not strong enough to discipline the swarms of savage tribes plundering the ancient native Balkan nations.

The Balkan region was never a harmonious melting pot of ethnic people with different languages, cultures and civilizations. Rather, from the very beginning, it was a boiling cauldron of ethnic rivalries. The wars and revolutions that took place never solved anything to make co-existence better. On the contrary, by changing borders often they merely generated a ferocious territorialism amongst them. Legends were generated about a glorious past that was fueled by the bad blood of perpetual feuds. These stories were often based merely on exaggerated myths.

The Orthodox Church hoped to establish a common peaceful and civilized ground for all of the diverse and adverse Balkan nations. This never happened because the predatory invaders refused to be assimilated into the Hellenistic values. Instead, they all shared the phenomenon of balkanization. The nationalism and local patriotism of each Balkan nation always ran supreme. It is normal that each historian or spokesman from each country within this concerned geographical area has their own version as to what happened in the Balkans.

The reader will note that some events and information overlap from chapter to chapter. This is because the same material is susceptible to being understood from diverse points of view. My book aims to be concise and to the point, and it was written with students studying history in mind.

However, the reader should note that each page contains information so condensed that it could easily be the subject of a chapter, or even another book.

Occasionally, I share my fascination with the role of accidents and their effects on the history of this geographical area we are focusing on. In doing my research, I am always excited when I stumble over historical accidents or blunders. I then examine their unexpected effects, especially if they have been overlooked or intentionally changed by other historians. To me to get beyond any accidental coincidence and their effects represents a different approach to the study of history.

This book on Balkanization is the product of many years of my scholarly research, and from my numerous documentary trips within the Balkan Peninsula. I have visited the historical sites of the Byzantine and Ottoman battlefields, including war monuments of the distant past.

If allowed, in museums I was thrilled to touch the masterfully made shining armor, fine swords, primitive cannons, and other weapons of those bloody times, just to feel their cold steel. If only these objects could speak, what stories they would tell! New questions stir up in me: "What if I were there?" All of this has inspired me to write about so many historical events, and the people who were involved in them.

I visited churches with their austere Byzantine mosaics and their two dimensional pictures. But, when I stood in the middle of Hagia Sophia, I felt as if all the saints were looking at me as I asked, "What really happened here?" This powerful need to re-live past events on a metaphysical level has inspired me to undertake research into the challenging records of the Balkan world. It has been much tempered by the vagaries of history.

You, dear reader, will witness how the magnificent Byzantine Empire collapsed after twelve centuries under the numerically superior barbarian invasions. Also, you will witness how the Ottomans conquered Constantinople the "Queen of Cities." It had never been conquered until the year 1453.

After reading my book, I believe that your vocabulary will contain the word "balkanization." I feel confident that you will appreciate my findings and my effort to write about these most turbulent times in the history of the Balkan Peninsula. Also, how this now relates to our modern current events. Hopefully, it will satisfy your curiosity by understanding how the magnificent Byzantine Empire collapsed and its historical importance.

Thank you, interested reader,
Ion Grumeza Ph.D.
Metaphysical Sciences

Author Ion Grumeza lecturing about Prince Vlad III Dracula.

# PREFACE

The idea for a book on The Roots of Balkanization came to me during the ethnic wars in former Yugoslavia (from 1991-2001). Five ethnically diverse groups of people with three major religions disputed frontiers and claimed lands, such as the Kosovo area. NATO air strikes and the punishment of modern warlords enforced a "peace" not too different from that imposed by Ottoman raids in the Byzantine Empire. It did little to solve the problems deeply rooted in medieval Balkan history. Inherited fears, suspicions, revenge, and religious fanaticism are as alive and volatile in this area today as they were hundreds of years ago, all due to the legacy of balkanization.

The term "Balkan powder keg" was introduced at the beginning of the last century. The word "Balkanization" appeared after the Balkan wars of 1912-1913. It describes the ethnic violence, political confusion, and arbitrary re-division of lands into new countries populated with unhappy people of different origins, cultures, and religions. It was at that point when the small nations declared themselves "great" by usurping neighboring lands. Major global powers became involved in nationalistic disputes they did not understand. This has often happened throughout the history of the Balkans after their borders shifted and homogeneous ethnic groups were separated against their will. These relentless problems continue to be reflected in today's Balkan geopolitics.

This began in the earlier Middle Ages when they were pressed to live in tight neighborhoods; even though they had different ethnic roots, religions, languages, and written alphabets. Having shifting borders, and with many ethnic people being trapped under foreign laws and rules caused them to constantly rebel.

The term Balkanization also refers to the endless territorial ownership that has taken place based on imperial decisions, and on agreements between rulers when land was transferred among royal heirs or as endowments to royal marriages. All of these have led to disputable settlements and the dislocation of people which caused their migrations. While these arrangements have solved immediate problems, they have also created complex demographic dynamics. People found themselves displaced and living within the boundaries of new countries or nations having different languages, cultures, and religions. The solutions for them proved to be only temporary, and the conflicts only re-emerged with a greater intensity.

✠

Furthermore, history books on this subject often were written from the perspective of the "eye of the beholder" and "the victors write history." However, many scholars have focused on specific events, personalities, or even words, and missed the larger and more obvious picture of human endeavors in the Balkans.

I am not an Albanian, Greek, or Hungarian, nor do I belong to any branch of the Slavic race. I consider myself politically neutral and capable of providing a dispassionate historical account of events. However, I do periodically inject personal observations to clarify something that may be ambiguous, support a probability, oppose a common and perhaps erroneous viewpoint, and offer a conclusion.

Since I am Romanian, I may focus on Dacia, the former land of Romania and the Daco-Roman people named Wallachians, Vlachs, Moldavians and Transylvanians. They have been much neglected by historians, but they have a proven importance for the barbarian invasions into the Balkans and in the history of the Byzantine Empire.

Mainly, I have tried diligently to shed more light on centuries of bitter controversy regarding who was who, and who did what. Doing so, I could provide answers to the questions of what makes sense as to what may have really happened. For five centuries each invading barbarian horde attacked Constantinople hoping to pillage and destroy it, but they failed to penetrate its massive protective walls. Nevertheless, they weakened the Byzantine military resistance, which made it possible for the Ottoman armies to move as far West as the straits of the Bosporus, just hundreds of yards from Constantinople. Ironically, the Golden Horde almost destroyed the Turks in Asia and annihilated the power of the Magyars and Slavs in Europe, thus unwittingly resulting in Constantinople's survival, being spared for the moment.

However, approximately one hundred years later, by the invitation of the two Byzantine quarreling royal brothers asking for help, the Turks occupied the Gallipoli Peninsula. This gave the Ottomans access to Eastern Europe and they brought along with them both the Gypsies and the Black Plague.

The Ottoman Empire kept extending its borders, and the crescent red flags came to be reflected in the waters of the Danube River. All of the main players in this human drama of balkanization were in place. They contributed to the irreversible survival phenomenon of Balkanization, which is the subject of this volume.

✥

While writing this book, the most provocative challenge of all rested in the old manuscripts, which sometimes provided confusing material concerning the process of Balkanization. Often, one must look elsewhere for better clues. An example is the account of the historian Niketas Choniatēs who called the Turks Persians; Hungarians called Paiones; the Serbs were Triballoi; and the Vlachs named Mysians (those living in the former Dacia Moesia). To him, French and

Germans had interchangeable names and could collectively be called Latins; and the Greeks he called Romans.

Furthermore, the English spelling of any names from the above-mentioned nations are so bastardized that they can scarcely be linked to their original. Confusing is how the English language took over the Balkan names. Pope Michael is Pope Μιχαήλ, Mihaila in Greek; Emperor Leo V is Emperor Leōn; Mihali Szilaggyi is Mihai Salajan; King Charles is King Karel, and so on. The same thing happened with the names of the twelve apostles in the New Testament with their original Greek names. They were renamed in English as Andrew, John, Matthew, Peter, as were the rest of them.

Another example is the controversy about the famous general Ioan de Hunedoara, with a Romanian original name of Ioan Corvin, but known under the Magyar name of Janos Hunyadi or in English as John Corvinus and in Latin Ioannus Corvinus. He is claimed by at least three nationalities, and his name is spelled in at least fifteen ways in different languages. What is for certain is that each of his military victories against the Ottoman armies made him the acclaimed Defender of Christendom.

✠

The most unreliable and even deceptive documents I encountered in this inquiry into the historic processes of Balkanization were texts from Communist authors. They were steeped in bias and propaganda and deliberately misread sources and revised history. Documents from the Stalinist Era claim that the Slavs originated and created everything in Eastern Europe. Incorrectly dated and misnamed archeological sites were provided as evidence for this, alongside distorted historiographies. Some historians deliberately misinterpreted documents or took snippets and quotes out of context; their subsequent speculations are saturated with romantic and chauvinistic views designed to please certain readers, or, better put their leaders.

✢

The many kings and emperors who ruled over the Eastern European lands which they had never seen before, together with their complicated family trees and Shakespearian intrigues, presented even more challenges. Inaccuracies and biased judgment also fill these historical records. Small nations with modest pasts created earthshaking legends for themselves in an effort to prove their importance. Skirmishes that had unclear winners were acclaimed as glorious wars won by each participant, all of whom grotesquely inflated the number of attacking enemy soldiers. In many instances, an ethnic group claimed its right to a patch of land that was also claimed by its neighbor having the identical pathos and fabricated proofs.

Equally puzzling were the centuries old theories and legends, often inaccurate from the beginning, which were blindly accepted and still go unchallenged today. The Bulgarians and Hungarians, for example, consider ancient and Roman archeological sites to be part of their heritage, even though they arrived in Europe hundreds of years later and had no historical connection to that distant past. The Serbians include Emperor Trajan in their legends as "Tsar Troyan," an obvious myth with no historical validity. The Romans could never have occupied those nations because they did not exist in Europe at that time. Many discoveries and other sources can throw a confusing light on such matters of dispute, but it can also happen that the results are again shown to be false.

✢

Such myriad points of historical confusion pose a serious problem when it comes to understanding modern Eastern Europe. There is, for example the linguistic issue: The Slovakians can barely understand the Czechs, even though they recently belonged to the same country, Czechoslovakia. The Czechs understand the Poles to some extent. The Poles, however, do not understand the Croats who scarcely understand the Serbs. However, the Croatians and Serbs understand the Slovenians, who have a population of two million and speak at least forty major dialects. The language of the Bulgarians has nothing in common with that of the Hungarians and Albanians, and all of these languages are different from the Greeks, the Turks and the Romanians. There are also two distant states that have confusingly similar names: Slovakia and Slovenia, they have similar-colored flags, but speak different Slavic languages that contain similar sounds.

In the midst of all of this, it is the Romanians alone who speak a Latin dialect inherited from the Romans' occupation of Transylvania. The Macedonians speak the languages of the nations that divided them, and not that of Alexander the Great. Many Slavic people claim different ancestors, northern and southern Slavs with eastern and western Slavic languages. The Jews and Gypsies have their own tongue that originated in the Near and Far East. Yiddish is rooted in the Middle Ages of the German language.

To complicate matters still further, two major religions with many denominations, Christianity and Islam, divide the ethnic groups in Albania, Bosnia, Herzegovina, and Montenegro.

✢

Maps of the medieval era found in old documents, atlases, and books reveal amazing discrepancies. This occurs when it comes to things like the locations of different tribal federations, directions of migration, first settlements, areas circumscribed by newly founded states, the size of empires, and the shifts in borders at various points in history.

Little attention has been given to the historical timeline and the geographic configuration of the Balkan states. Their land and accessibility ultimately united or separated cultures and societies.

Borders often incorporated populations that did not belong within them, and flags represented nationalities with conflicting ethnicities. This having been said, I have done my best to evaluate the topography of the past, and have sought to create maps that are illustrative of the texts available for a specific historical era.

As I write these lines, the Macedonians are living in different Balkan countries, and much of the independent Republic of Macedonia has been claimed by Greece. When the Skopje airport was named after Alexander the Great and displayed his sculptured head, the Greeks were outraged. They were angered even more when they learned that a seventy-foot tall statue of the ancient emperor would be placed in the middle of the Macedonian capital. There was an international campaign underway to stop the project of these "Slavic-speaking people." It is felt that they have no right to glorify someone whom the Greeks consider their legendary hero, never mind that young Alexander did not speak Greek, and was banned from the Greek Olympic Games. The Albanians also claim Alexander the Great.

☦

Moreover, the Hungarians believe they have a right to own Transylvania which is a region of Romania. It is the land of the ancient Dacians from Transylvania who once were occupied by the Romans in 106 A.D.. These are the same Dacians, not the Magyars, who are sculpted in marble on Trajan's Column shown fighting the legionnaires. The column was erected in 113 A.D. in the middle of Rome, to celebrate the emperor's victory. At that time, the Magyar tribes lived in the middle of Siberia for the next seven centuries, before invading Europe more than 3,000 miles from Transylvania.

Since then, the Daco-Romans have served as a genetic common denominator for the nation of today's Romanians, and for offshoots of millions of descendents, named Vlachs. They were living south of the Danube River. Also, they were known as Aromanians, the Megleno-

Romanians or Macedo-Romanians who were speaking a Latin dialect which even today is mostly understood by the Romanians.

☩

Often historians have denied any controversy that has already been debated. Each nation tries to look better than the next, and the information could be contradictory at the very least. The tendency to conform and write what is today considered politically correct is as damaging to the historical records as is revisionism. What is certain is that governments with their rulers, presidents, and leaders come and go, many borders are re-drawn, and their economies and the people both thrive and suffer.

Yet, human nature has changed very little over the past one thousand years. People remember their heritage and identify with specific habits and a precise land that may have been named differently at different times in the past. With this identity comes a way of relating to others, to "outsiders," the barbarians of the past or the "foreigners" who are now equally unwanted "neighbors" of the present. This ethnic amalgam, and overall nightmarish human situation that no one can solve, is called Balkanization.

Writing this book, I aimed to fill a gap with authoritative and verifiable materials on how the process of Balkanization came about. I separated fact from fiction and traced the patterns of ethnic and cultural life of the Balkan people that originated fifteen centuries ago. Nevertheless, they renew their habits with each successive generation, resulting in today's Balkanized demographics with its diverse political and specific socioeconomic dynamics.

☩

I already published *DACIA, The Land of Transylvania, Cornerstone of Ancient Eastern Europe*, published by Hamilton Books in 2009. It covers the history of the Roman Empire which, under Trajan, occupied the rich region of Transylvania. The content of DACIA stops at the year 500 A.D.. My Balkanization book picks up the history of the Eastern Roman Empire, renamed the Byzantine Empire, until Constantinople was conquered by the Ottomans in the year 1453.

In an effort to shed some new light on the past and present much tried history of this area of the world, my main interest was to track the origin of the various tribal people settled in the Balkan Peninsula. I follow their respective processes of evolution from being migratory barbarians to form societies, nations, countries, and empires. I have also devoted the chapters of this book to various aspects of Eastern European history: cultural and religious conflicts, crusades, and wars often conducted out of spite, and concluded with possibly wrongful victories with dubious heroes.

This volume describes the economic and social life of the various infantile societies that were subject to intrigues in the royal courts. These intrigues were often resolved by marriage, divorce, arrest, confinement to convents or dungeons, blinding, and assassination. All of this unfolded in an era of chivalry and governance from the manors and fortresses, alongside the development of the great Byzantine arts, and the new languages of these foreign societies with their unique alphabets.

The Ottomans marched their way into the Balkans and ended up occupying and owning the region. It showed how their use of firearms on battlefields would change the history of warfare forever. My intention is to bring to light certain points that have been neglected in previous histories, and to identify missing historical links. At the same time, I am challenging some popular concepts used for the continuation of the peninsula's history.

Included is the much overlooked role of balkanization. Finally, now in the 21st century how the Balkan people cope with the modern world of the capitalist system which was formerly totally unknown to them. At the same their balkanization spread into Western Europe and the United States of America.

✞

My book begins with a chapter about a character with whom most everyone is familiar, Prince Vlad III Dracula the Impaler. In the middle of the fifteenth century, he ruled three times the Romanian principality of Wallachia/Muntenia. During his reigns, he became famous for his cruel punishment by impaling his enemies. He was important in the political scheme at that time because he tried to limit the Turkish expansion above the Danube River, and the rest of Eastern Europe. Against all odds, he scored victories that he believed would trigger an international Crusade as he tried to force the Ottoman Empire out of the Balkans.

It just happens that I am a Romanian-born writer and a native of Campulung-Muscel of Walachia/Muntenia, which was Prince Vlad III's first capital of his realm. I grew up with popular legends about Dracula, who is much beloved by the Romanian people who consider him a national hero. None of these are related to the Hollywood movie versions of the famous Bram Stoker's book. My chapter reveals why Dracula was a good ruler for the Romanians, the Balkan people, and Christians due to his anti-Ottoman struggle to keep the Turks from invading and occupying Europe. Prince Vlad III Dracula was a true Christian knight and the last Crusader who was much admired by Pope Pius II.

✙

Over time, the Roots of Balkanization extended into Eastern Europe, the Middle East, and Western Europe. Today, it has reached the United States through the invasion of millions of unwanted and undocumented immigrants from around the world. Just like the Dark Age barbarians described in my book, they want to pillage the benefits available from the American taxpayers' money, defy the laws of the land, and behave in dangerous ways. Therefore, they do not belong, and do not fit into the society and culture of America, which does not want or need their balkanization.

I am a legal immigrant who waited in the Traiskirchen refugee camp to be interviewed and approved for the American visa from the American consulate in Vienna over 50 years ago. In 1978 I became a proud naturalized American citizen. I believe that each hopeful immigrant must enter this country legally, and earn the right to pursue the "American Dream."

# THE LAST CRUSADER: PRINCE DRACULA

On October 31, 1448, a teenage contender to the throne of Wallachia declared himself the ruler of that land. He was not born there but in Sighisoara town, Transylvania; he was not baptized in its Orthodox faith; his princely origin was disputable; he had no money; he had no army or supporters; and most strangely of all, he was dressed as an officer of the Turkish army he had just left. The seventeen year-old was the son of Vlad II Dracul, the two time *domnitor* (ruler) of Wallachia and the illegitimate son of Prince Mircea the Elder, an iconic figure for the Romanians. Dracul's son was named Vlad the Third, later called Dracula (Son of the Devil). His tumultuous life and three periods of rule show what it was like to rule a small country in medieval Eastern Europe. It also illustrates the nascent meaning of Balkanization.

The Wallachian state once belonged to the powerful kingdom of ancient Dacia (today Romania) that also included the lands of Pannonia, Transylvania, Moesia, Moldavia, and western Ukraine. Roman occupation of the first four of these regions resulted in the Daco-Roman race who spoke a Latin dialect used by the Wallachians and their cousins, the Vlachs, who lived all over Eastern Europe. In the beginning of the fifteenth century, the Romanian principalities of Wallachia (also known as Muntenia/the mountainous land) and Moldavia were still independent, unlike Pannonia and Transylvania which were governed by Saxons; Moesia was occupied by the Bulgarians and Turks; and Ukraine was ruled by Lithuania.

The central geographic position of Wallachia in Eastern Europe and its dominance of the last increment of the Danube River attracted the ever opportunistic Turks. Mircea the Elder (r. 1386-1418) pushed back this latest invader of the Balkan Peninsula who conquered Bulgaria in 1396. Finally, in the twilight years of his life, he agreed to buy his country's autonomy and peace by paying a yearly tribute of three thousand gold coins to the Ottoman Court. This set a pattern for his followers, including his son Vlad II Dracul and his grandson Vlad III Dracula.

The story of Dracula begins with the first ruler of Wallachia, Basarab the Founder (r. 1310-1352) whose royal house split into rival families of Danesti and Basarab, the latter producing Mircea the Elder whose illegitimate son Vlad II started the Draculesti clan. The name originated in Nuremberg at the court of Emperor Sigismund of the Holy Roman Empire when in 1431 Prince Vlad II who had been baptized in the Orthodox faith (like his first son, Mircea,) converted to Catholicism to please his German supporters. Winning a knightly tournament proved his military skills, and he was invited to join the secret order of the Dragon, a group of anti-Ottoman crusaders.

Since the Wallachian throne was hereditary and held now by his kin Dan II from the rival Danesti clan, the knighted prince returned from Nuremberg to the safety of Transylvania. The dragon insignia on Vlad's tunic caused him to be nicknamed Dracul (the Devil) by the superstitious Romanians, who thought of the dragon as a demon. That same year, 1431, his second son, named Vlad III, was born in the city of Sighisoara; five years later another son arrived, Radu (the Handsome). He would become Dracula's enemy and a bitter rival for the throne. Thus the Draculesti family, another splinter of the House of Basarab, entered history.

After his Turkophile half-brother Alexandru Aldea (son of Mircea the Old) died in 1436, Vlad Dracul became the next Wallachian *domnitor* with the help of the Germans of Transylvania, who trusted him to keep the Turks away. But Emperor Sigismund died, and without this powerful protector, Wallachia was invaded by a Turkish army. It forced the prince to sign a treaty of submission in exchange for his country's independence. One year later, based on the agreement he had signed in order to stay in power, Prince Dracul had no choice but to assist a Turkish expedition in Transylvania.

This angered John Hunyadi (Iancu de Hunedoara), the Wallachian born general who was serving the crown of Hungary as the official governor of Transylvania, because Dracul had willingly become his vassal. Caught between superior military powers, the troubled prince decided to remain neutral.

Hunyadi was called a hero for his exploits against the Turks while Vlad II was called to the Sublime Court for an explanation. The frightened prince went to Gallipoli, bringing along his sons Vlad and Radu to prove his good faith to Sultan Murad II. His oldest son Mircea was left to rule Wallachia in his absence. Upon their arrival, the prince was arrested and his two sons were sent to a fortress in Asia Minor to become loyal subjects to the Ottoman Empire. Having been thusly given a lesson in obedience, the Wallachian prince was allowed to return to his realm, only to find Mircea destitute and Basarab II from the Danesti family ruling the country. Prince Dracul was forced to flee.

In 1443, with support from Hunyadi, Vlad Dracul was able to regain the Wallachian throne, only to be assassinated in 1447 by his own Orthodox boyars (landowners) who did not want to serve under a Catholic ruler. Officially he was blamed for the Christian defeat at Varna at the hands of the Turks in 1444 and for briefly holding Hunyadi in custody while retreating through Wallachia. Prince Mircea, who had participated at Varna, was ambushed; he was blinded with hot irons and then buried alive. Seeking an ally he could trust, Hunyadi installed Vladislav II from the Danesti family to the throne of Wallachia.

Meanwhile, the two young princely hostages Vlad III and hid brother Radu, were educated in the same Muslim spirit as their playmate, the sultan's son Mehmed II, who would grow up to become the mighty Mehmed the Conqueror of Constantinople. Radu's attractive features made him the lover of Mehmed and his father, while the roughness and obstinacy of Vlad made him subject to brutal punishments that were never forgotten by the future Impeller. While he fearlessly resisted becoming a Muslim, he was praised for his soldierly qualities and distinguished himself in the elite Janissary Corps, the Praetorian Guard of the sultan.

In September 1448 the armies of Hunyadi and Vladislav II attacked the Turks south of the Danube and successfully besieged the Vidin fortress. But the campaign took an unexpected turn when the Turks almost captured Hunyadi on the way back to Hungary. One month later Hunyadi suffered a crushing defeat at Kosovo, and Prince Vladislav II went missing in action on the battlefield.

✢

Taking full advantage of this situation, the 17 year old Dracula entered Wallachia at the end of October with a mixed contingent of mercenary soldiers and seized the capital of Targoviste. But after a brief two months of rule, he had to run back to the sultan for protection while Petru II of Moldavia helped Vladislav II of the Danesti clan, regain the throne in 1448, ruling until 1456.

A year later Petru II was replaced by Prince Bogdan II, an old friend of the Draculesti family. Dracula deserted the Turkish camp and showed up in Moldavia, his mother's native land. There he cemented a friendship with his younger cousin Stefan, son of Prince Bogdan II. Each swore loyalty to the other until death. After Bogdan was murdered in 1451, the young cousins ran for their lives to Transylvania. There, Dracula was well received by Hunyadi and the Hungarian King Ladislas V, both were distressed at the fall of Constantinople in 1453. With the capital of Orthodoxy destroyed, the Balkan nations had no central Christian leadership that could oppose the Muslim invasion of the Balkans.

Squeezed between the meteoric rise of the Ottoman and Russian empires and facing the ever rapacious Hungarians, the Daco-Roman population (the future Romanians) struggled to remain free. They were now named according to their locations: Bessarabians, Dobrudgians, Oltenians, Moldavians, Muntenians, Transylvanians; in brief, Wallachians or Vlachs if they lived south of the Danube River, was a name that encompassed all of these Latin speaking people in the Balkans. A similar fate awaited the Albanians, Bosnians, Croatians, Serbians, and others who tried to maintain their independence after the fall of the Byzantine Empire. In the meantime, the Turks pushed their occupation beyond the Danube into the Crimean Peninsula, and the Black Sea became an Ottoman Lake. Just like the Romans considered the Mediterranean Sea to be a Roman Lake.

Under these imperialistic circumstances, in July 1456 the crescent of Islam clashed with the cross of Orthodoxy during a crusade. The Turks were defeated at Belgrade and forced to make a humiliating retreat to the South of the Danube River. The Hungarian army suffered great losses in men and materials, and soon faced the most devastating blow of all, Hunyadi's death from the plague. Exploiting the military vacuum left by the decimated armies and already encouraged by Hunyadi, a family friend and his tutor, Prince Dracula, who was in charge of securing the Transylvanian border, crossed it into Wallachia ahead of a small mercenary force.

He was opposed by an equally small army led by Vladislav II. The melee ended with a knightly duel between the man who tried to keep the throne and the one who aimed to occupy it. Dracula won. After killing his enemy he marched unopposed to Targoviste, the capital of Wallachia, where at the end of August 1456, he crowned himself as the *voievode* and sole *domnitor* of the country. His bold move was approved by Mikhail Szilagy, the brother-in-law of Hunyadi and an old friend of the Draculesti family, now a powerful Transylvanian voievode. Sultan Mehmed II was also pleased to see his childhood friend in power, but he still imposed the customary yearly tribute in exchange for the Wallachian independence.

A spectacular comet happened to light up the night sky (it would later be designated as a Halley-type comet); this was considered as divine confirmation of Dracula's right to the throne and a promise of good fortune for his reign. What followed next, catapulted Prince Dracula into history and the future Gothic literature.

☦

Losing no time, Dracula engaged in a domestic crusade that involved bold actions and reform measures. A man of impeccable discipline and honor, overlaid with a thirst for revenge, he consolidated his power by hiring his own uniformed private mercenary army. It immediately began to collect taxes from the astonished boyars. The previous rulers had depended on the benevolence of their boyars for money and a supply of fighting men, but that had changed under the new young master.

His second step was to eliminate the chronic situation of thieves, beggars, homeless, and plague-infested people who "polluted" Wallachia. He impaled thieves in the marketplaces and along the roads to set an example. He invited other handouts to a free feast, after which he burned them alive in the barns where the banquet had taken place. In his opinion, they had departed earthly suffering for a better afterlife. Within a year, the Wallachian roads were so safe that a lost pouch full of gold coins could remain untouched in the middle of a busy intersection.

Dracula's next major goal was to take care of the intrigue-infested Wallachian Court with its backstabbing boyars. The entirety of Wallachia was divided by the feuds of the rich and powerful landowners who tried to override the authority and rights of the Wallachian prince. Each landowner could pledge loyalty to different contenders to the throne, and even to foreign rulers. Dracula decided to punish the treacherous boyars who were responsible for killing his father and brother, those same aristocrats who had never wanted him in the first place and who now were plotting to impeach him. He pondered the best way to punish them.

In 1457 he offered a princely feast to celebrate Easter and invited the arrogant boyars to be his guests. They arrived with much pomp and circumstance, carried on liters by servants, only to be arrested during the banquet. After a long march from Targoviste, they found themselves in a remote mountain region of Arges. There, the formerly rich and powerful were forced to build a new castle for their merciless prince Dracula.

The younger ones were worked to death; the older ones, impaled; their properties were handed over to the new nobility he created, certain to be loyal to Dracula as its members came from the military ranks. Dracula's instant justice pleased the commoners who nicknamed him "the Impaler."[1]

Trusting in his future, Dracula began to centralize his realm by building royal palaces, fortresses, and churches. He extended the capital of Targoviste and other cities, and constructed roads to enhance domestic and international trade. He offered money to handymen to open their businesses and encouraged the middle class with tax enhancements.

Meanwhile, he continued to confiscate the estates of the boyars, whom he impaled, and founded royal villages. In exchange, he asked for peasant recruits to be trained during post-harvest months for military service, obviously to be ready for war.

After only one year in power, Dracula ruled his country with confidence and an iron fist, as indicated by his signing a letter in Latin addressed to the leaders of the Saxon merchants in June 1458 with, *Wlad, dei gracia parcium Transalpinarum wayvoda* (I, Vlad, by the grace of God I am voievode of Transalps[2] –Transalps meaning the Romanian Carpathians). That letter with its firm signature was not welcomed by the Saxons and Hungarians who certainly did not want a Wallachian dominating them.

Dracula's coat of arms and the Wallachian flag showed an eagle holding a cross in its beak; under his flag he raided the Transylvanian communities around the cities of Sibiu/Hermannstadt and Brasov/Kronstadt, which sheltered many of his rivals to the crown. He impaled hundreds of suspected traitors in full view of the residents of those cities and even attempted to burn the monumental Catholic Black Church of Brasov. Furthermore, to make it clear who was in charge of Ungaro-Wallachia, (today Muntenia and Dobruja) he installed custom posts at the borders and forced foreign merchants especially from Transylvania to pay taxes when they traveled to, or did business in, Wallachia. His 1458-1459 raids of carnage and mutilation convinced the affected Saxons of one thing: Dracula had to be eliminated as soon as possible.

But, he seemed unstoppable. He regained possession of Bran/Dietrichstein Castle, initially built with wood in year 1212 by the Teutonic Order and was once owned by his grandfather. There he produced a son, enabling him to establish a family tradition and incorporate the castle domain into the Draculesti heritage.

He also created a new princely Order by naming the best soldiers *Viteaz* (Brave); they became Wallachian knights, another new nobility who supported him. Sultan Mehmed II was happy to see that his protégé was at war with everyone; this surely meant that sooner or later the fearsome prince would reach a point where the support of the Ottoman Empire was needed.

In brief, Dracula was the master of his land as long as he paid the yearly tribute in gold to the sultan, and sent the required five hundred boys to be trained as Janissaries for the Ottoman army, as the tradition of vassalage required. These things he did, but when Turkish envoys arrived for an audience with Dracula, he nailed their turbans to their heads when they refused to uncover them in his royal presence. This ruler demanded recognition and respect from everybody and had no compunction about making that clear.

Since Mehmed II was occupied with his wars in Asia Minor and with moving his capital from Adrianople renamed Edirne to Constantinople, the young sultan chose to turn a blind eye to this incident. In fact, any ambassadors who came dressed inappropriately or behaved in an irritating way were promptly impaled by Dracula. The prince firmly stated to those who were not properly trained to face a "wise ruler, then your master sentenced you to death, and if you dare to be insulting, then you are responsible for your death!"[3] The higher the rank, the higher was the stake upon which the offender was impaled.

Confident in his power, Dracula agreed to provide military aid for Prince Stefan III who was attempting to occupy the throne of Moldavia. He dutifully kept the loyalty oath he had given his cousin, even as Dracula tried to build a new coalition against the Turkish expansionism.

✟

Meanwhile, he decided to leave his mark on history by building a new capital for Wallachia in the Danubian flat land at Bucureşti (Bucharest), a trade center founded by his grandfather Mircea the Elder. Located in the marshes of the Dambovitsa River, Dracula's capital was surrounded by a natural moat infested with leeches, snakes, and mosquitoes—a certain deterrent for the horse mounted Turks, heavily dressed people of the sandy desert who avoided fighting in wet lands, and they did not know how to swim.

Furthermore, by moving the capital near the Danube and counting on a crusade that would free the Balkans, the prince hoped to fulfill his secret ambition: to reunite all Wallachians and Vlachs, into one kingdom and rebuild the Dacian Empire that was once the second largest in ancient Europe. Then the empire's capital, Bucureşti, would be right in the middle of the Dacian land that he would recover from the Turks and Bulgars.

Dracula's confidence was boosted by the ascent of King Matthias born in Transylvania to the throne of Hungary and by the election of Pope Pius II; the latter called for a new crusade and asked Matthias to establish a military base in Hungary to serve as a collection point for the crusaders. But few knew that, unlike Dracula, the fifteen year-old monarch had no intention of joining any anti-Ottoman war.

Believing everything was going his way, Dracula confidently signed his documents and letters from Bucureşti with, *Din mila lui Dumnezeu, Io Vlad voievod si domn si fiul marelui Vlad voievod, stapanind si domnind peste toata tara Ungrovlahiei, Amlasului si Fagarasului herteg* (By the grace of God, I, Vlad, voievode and lord and the son of the great Vlad voievode, Vlad II Dracul, ruling over the entire country of Ungaro-Wallachia, Amlas, and Fagaras duchies).[4] This was certified by an endowment document he signed on September 20, 1459.

Thus he made clear that at least part of Transylvania was his. This self-entitlement was frowned upon by the Saxons and Hungarians living there, who certainly did not want Dracula to be their ruler. He had already done financial damage to their trade, not to mention the raids and horrifying killings in the domains that had once belonged to his father Vlad II. Now those dukedoms were under the Saxons, who continued to shelter Dracula's half- brother Vlad the Monk, Dan III, Laiota the Old, and other knights from rival families who aspired to the throne of Wallachia.

It was at this point that a Turkish army corps entered southern Wallachia and carried out a campaign of pillage and rape. Dracula's cavalry intercepted the retreating Turks whose pace had been slowed by the plunder and prisoners they were taking with them. Wallachian mounted warriors slaughtered the invaders; any survivors were pulled by horses into sharp stakes laid flat on the ground. The enslaved Vlachs were set free and rewarded with plunder taken from the Turks.

A few enemies were allowed to cross south of the Danube so they could tell their leaders about the horrors they had witnessed. Prince Dracula considered the raid a breach of the treaty he had with the sultan—sufficient reason to stop paying the tribute to the Porte.

One year later, irritated by the refusal of the Saxon merchants to pay taxes while trading in Wallachia, Dracula again stormed their Transylvanian communities. He plundered and destroyed them, focusing particularly on those who had sheltered his rivals for the throne. The Saxons of Brasov, Sibiu, and Barsa land, bitterly complained to King Matthias about the cruelty of the Wallachians, who certainly were not friends of the Hungarians and had gone too far with their Draculian punishments.

Seeking their own justice, the unhappy merchants decided to eliminate the troublemaking prince and replace him with Dan III (the brother of Vladislav II), who pretended that King Matthias urged him to take the throne of Wallachia. Before Easter in 1460, the eager contender crossed the Transylvanian border into Wallachia, leading a group of boyar dissidents and a military contingent paid for by the Brasovians. It was a doomed venture.

Dracula was informed in advance and intercepted the party with a well-planned ambush in the Carpathian Mountains. Once again the prince rose to the occasion and humiliated Dan III in a spectacular duel, while the trespassers were slaughtered by Wallachian soldiers. Dan, who was accused of killing Dracula's father and brother, was forced to dig his own grave and recite his own burial ceremony; then he was beheaded. His surviving followers were impaled at different heights according to their titles.

Only seven enemies returned to Transylvania to tell the gruesome story of their defeat. This was intended to serve as a warning for anyone else who might have similar ideas of taking over the Wallachian throne.

Prolonging the victory, Dracula and his cavalry laid to waste so much of the area around the city of Brasov that its Saxon residents agreed to never again plot against him. However, the duchies of Amlas and Fagaras, historically part of Wallachia and through inheritance the property of the Draculesti family, refused to surrender Dracula's rivals to him.

The vengeful ruler responded with a raid that confirmed his reputation as a blood-thirsty tyrant: according to German narrations, some thirty thousand people were massacred on Saint Bartholomew's Day. Thousands were impaled on the hill facing Brasov, again as a lesson to Dracula's defiant citizens.

This punitive expedition, which became a part of European folklore, greatly displeased King Matthias, who saw his Transylvanian province threatened by the unruly Wallachian voievode. Finally an agreement was reached with the Impeller: the merchants promised to return all anti-Dracula dissidents; pay 15,500 forints at once (only four thousand were ever paid); and supply four thousand soldiers (who were never sent) in case Prince Vlad needed to carry out a war against the Turks. In exchange, the Wallachian ruler promised to stop the Turks from entering Transylvania.

It was a deal that made Dracula confident that he would not be attacked from the northwest; also, it assured him that he did not need to fear another foreign plot against him. However, there was a significant problem remaining, one that he could do nothing about: the Ottoman Empire numbered over fifteen million people and had an army whose size equaled that of his entire Wallachian population of five hundred thousand.

That same year, Mihail Szilagy, Dracula's only ally and protector, was seized by the Turks. Since he was considered a spy, he was tortured and sawed in a half in Constantinople. Dracula knew that his refusal to pay the yearly tribute and to pledge vassalage to Mehmed the Conqueror put him next in line to be hacked to pieces.

Fortunately, he had just learned that Pope Pius had pledged one hundred thousand ducats to finance another crusade and already delivered forty thousand gold coins to King Matthias who had offered

Hungary as the host for the western armies. He had also promised that forty thousand Hungarian soldiers would be available at the time when the international crusade began.

In spite of his bloody raids in Transylvania, Dracula believed King Matthias to be his trusted ally and sent an ambassador of good will to Buda, capital of Hungary. He carried a letter in which Dracula professed his undivided commitment to fight the Turks. It was a weighty decision, considering what the Prince did not know about the Council of Mantua of 1459 resolution: the Venetians were reluctant to have their military and transport navy participate in a new crusade, the French were expecting a war with England, and the Poles were fighting German knights who also fought against each other. Worse yet, he did not know that his letter of loyalty to Matthias and his unabated commitment to the future crusade was intercepted by the Turks and handed over to Sultan Mehmed II. Instead of solving his country's problems, Dracula had become a problem for everyone, excepting Pope Pius II.

✢

Nevertheless, the pope was fully committed to the united military effort that would throw the Turks out of the Christian continent; he scheduled the crusade to begin in the spring of 1462. The best Dracula could do was strengthen his alliance with King Matthias with whom he signed a peace agreement. This news, along with Dracula's repeated refusal to pay the yearly tribute, infuriated Sultan Mehmed II who ordered Catavolinos, his trusted Greek diplomat, to go to Wallachia and bring the ungrateful Prince to Constantinople.

Dracula received Catavolinos with all the necessary honors, but was aware of one thing: if he went to Constantinople he would face a certain, horrible death. Using the pretext that if he left the country, the Saxons and the treacherous boyars would install one of his rivals on the throne, the prince offered instead to pay ten thousand ducats and deliver five hundred boys. Shortly thereafter, Hamza Pasha, the commander of the Nicopolis fortress entered Wallachia with a Turkish contingent to take over the transport. To Dracula, the contingent looked more like an invading army of ten thousand strong.

Suspecting that Hamza's real mission was to capture him, Prince Dracula charged the invaders with his cavalry and decimated the intruders. Then, to prove his anti-Turkish stand to the West, Dracula ordered all the Turkish prisoners, including Catavolinos, to be impaled around the capital of Targoviste. He decapitated Hamza and had his body impaled on the highest stake, which was painted in gold; the head was put in a honey jar and sent to King Matthias as proof of the Wallachian commitment to fight the Ottomans.

This placed the teenaged Hungarian monarch in an awkward position. He did not want to attract the fury of the sultan whose armies had just occupied Serbia and were about to attack Belgrade, which was held by the Hungarians at the time. Dracula received no reply from the Hungarian capital.

✜

Prince Dracula spent the rest of 1461 training his army for war, envisioning himself as the next Hunyadi. At the same time, he fortified the new capital of Bucureşti and transformed the marshland into a prosperous trade city. It was built on wooden platforms above the marshland, using trees from the next great Vlasia Forest which covers the entire southern Wallachia down to the Danube River.

It was an excellent buffer zone to defend the new capital of Prince Dracula, now surrounded by heavy palisades, and brick bastions defended by cannons. He had taken those cannons during Transylvanian punishing expeditions, and from Turkish forts he had sacked. He built a fortified church on the nearby island on Snagov Lake as his refuge and a place to keep the royal treasury. For now, Voievode Vlad III was the supreme ruler of Wallachia.

✜

Encouraged by his success and wanting to take advantage of the fact that Mehmed II and his armies were fighting in Asia Minor in order to conquer and rule Trebizond, Dracula prepared to raid the Turkish garrisons south of the frozen Danube. Knowing full well that the Turks sought to avoid to fighting in winter and being determined to jumpstart a crusade of his own that would give him the undisputed ownership of Dacian Moesia, Dracula led his cavalry to the fortress of Giurgiu, located on the last leg of the Danbian River. This prosperous port city had belonged to Wallachia since time immemorial; it had been rebuilt by his father Vlad Dracul, but the Turks had occupied it and transformed it into one of their strongest northern military bases, on the Danube River on the Wallachian land.

Dressed as a highly ranked Turkish officer and leading a Wallachian squadron wearing similar Turkish uniforms, Dracula approached the fortress on a snowy day and ordered the garrison commander to open the gates. The sentries believed the officer who spoke perfect Turkish to be an important messenger traveling with bodyguards, and let them in.

The intruders silenced the sentries at once and opened the gates wide for the rest of the Wallachian cavalry to rush in and take over the fortress. They killed the Turkish garrison and, after looting their quarters, set them afire. What followed would fuel the legend of Dracula: over the next two weeks his soldiers engaged in raids that covered 800 kilometers/500 miles along the frozen Danube River to almost the Black Sea.

Dracula's priority was to destroy the main bridgeheads the Turks used to cross the Danube into Wallachia. He went on a rampage and sacked many Turkish garrisons and non-Christian settlements on the Bulgarian river bank. His Wallachians hacked the Muslim inhabitants to bits, impaled their leaders, built pyramids of enemy heads in the middle of the plazas, and looted and then burned their dwellings. Yet, for the Vlachs (the future Aromanians) who had been living in Bulgaria since Dacian times, these were blessed days: they regained their freedom from the Turkish yoke of oppression.

Countless numbers of them joined the fight, either because they sought revenge or because they believed in Dracula's mission. A few Italian, Hungarian, and Moldavian travelers were detained by the Prince as witnesses; they were sent back to their leaders to report on the carnage resulting from Dracula's mini-crusade.

In his correspondence with King Matthias on February 11, 1462, Dracula asked for help to continue the fight; the Prince listed the names of important locations he had destroyed, among them Durostor, Giurgiu, Nicopolis, Orsova, Rahova Rusciuk, Turnu, and free northern Dobrudja. He chillingly estimated the number of killed Turks and their Bulgarian collaborators at 23,884 "without counting those we burned in homes or whose heads were not cut by our soldiers."

And aware that he reached the point of no return in his relations with Sultan Mehmed II he concluded, "Thus Your Highness must know that I have broken the peace with him …not for *our sake*, but for the sake of the honor of Your Highness…The Holy Cross, and for guarding all Christianity and strengthening the Catholic law."[5]

To substantiate his war report, he had the letter delivered with two large bags filled with the noses and ears of the dead Turks. Finally, he claimed to have avenged the memory of Szilagy, his protector who had been slain by the Turks, and of his grandfather Mircea the Elder, who was blamed for the defeat of the crusaders at Nicopolis in 1396.

Dracula fully enjoyed his victorious campaign; no doubt, he considered himself a true crusader. After all, Pope Pius II had expressed admiration for his extraordinary military exploits, even though they had resulted in the deaths of only some ten thousand Ottoman soldiers in isolated garrisons. The Bulgars, Greeks, Serbs, and other Turkish-occupied nations were likewise impressed by Dracula's successes, which encouraged them to rise up and fight to regain their independence.

A flood of Gypsies serving the Ottoman army as repair men, had already left Bulgaria and moved to welcoming Wallachia. For the moment, Dracula was the undisputed hero of the entire region; that news reached Mehmed in Asia Minor as he was victoriously concluding another military expedition there.

The sultan was not about to let this situation continue. Freeing troops no longer needed in Anatolia, he entrusted Grand Vizier Mahmud with an army of thirty thousand to restore order in the troubled lands and bring Dracula to Constantinople. The general regained control of the most devastated cities in Bulgaria and left twelve thousand men to garrison them; then he used eighteen thousand crack troops to invade southeastern Wallachia.

☦

In March they crossed the Danube River and sacked the port of Braila from whence the Turks began punishing raids of rape and plunder, taking captive many Vlachs. Dracula's cavalry counter-attacked so strongly that it forced the Turks to rush back into Bulgaria for shelter. Many were killed, a few thousand were captured on the left bank of the Danube, and only eight thousand escaped across the wide river.

The sultan was so upset that he slapped the humiliated Mahmud. The incident did more harm than good for the Turkish population who were in a panic because of Dracula's repeated victories and had begun retreating across the Straights of the Bosporus to the safety of Asia Minor.

This strengthened Mehmed's resolve that Kaziglu Bey (The Impaler Prince) must be stopped, and the sooner the better, since the Greek monks of Rhodes were tolling the church bells in Dracula's honor and the pope (properly informed by Pietro Tommasi, the Venetian ambassador at Buda) prayed for his final victory. At this crucial juncture, Mehmed, who had added to his sultan title the epithets "the Reformer," "The Great," "The Victorious," and "the Conqueror," was under added pressure to calm the rumor that the Kaziglu Bey was on his way to storm Constantinople.

The sultan, who had conquered two empires, twelve kingdoms, and four hundred cities, was being humiliated by a former child hostage, who used to sleep on the roofs of the military barracks out of fear of being sodomized by the Janissary officers.

The undefeated Mehmed decided to take matters into his own hands, and began preparing to invade Wallachia. After consulting his astrologers, the thirty year-old sultan resolved to personally lead the punitive expedition. His personal Janissary guard was larger than the entire army of the "lunatic" Dracula. Moreover, it was time for the sultan to show his recognition of his beloved Radu the Handsome, his loyal companion and lover who was now ready to replace his bloodthirsty brother on the throne of Wallachia.

✠

Fully aware that he could not continue to be victorious, Dracula considered the winter raids finished and went back to București with his army, prisoners, Vlachian refugees, Christians who had run away from Turks, and a long column of carts full of plunder. Most importantly, he brought with him many captured cannons of different sizes and paraded them together with the captives.

Among the captives were Gypsies who had volunteered to fight for Wallachia; Dracula considered them skilled blacksmiths and jewelry makers. Only highly ranked Turkish prisoners were impaled; the rest were taken to complete the building of the new capital of Wallachia. He indulged in a well-deserved respite marked by a chain of celebrations. It was, however, interrupted by incoming news about the sultan's war preparations.

Suddenly, Dracula realized that he had to single-handedly face a massive Ottoman army led by the angry sultan who was seeking revenge and wanted to humiliate him. Faced with the abysmal reality of not having any allies, Dracula's jubilation plunged into despair: his anti-Ottoman mission was at stake as were his throne and his life.

Others were likewise aware of the sultan's wrath and the ultimate futility of Dracula's intent to fight the mighty Ottoman armies. One was Pietro Tommasi, who had represented Venice at Buda and joined Dracula in his plea to the West for help. He had seen letters sent by the Wallachian prince to King Matthias, in which Dracula tried to claim that, "by helping us, you really help yourself by stopping their army far from your land and by not allowing them to destroy our land and harm and oppress us."[6]

Clearly, Dracula was holding onto the hope that the Hungarian king would come with all or part of his army, or, if he was unable to travel, would order the troops under his command to aid the crusaders. Dracula begged for any military help he could get, even from the closer Transylvania, and requested that it arrive no later than April. After that date, the ice on the Danube would melt and the Turkish fleets from Constantinople and Gallipoli could easily bring in massive military enforcements. Fully confident in his mission, he invoked the wish of Almighty God who "will give us victory over the Infidel, the enemies of the Cross and Christ."

In the meantime, Dracula tried to get help from the Transylvanians, Moldavians, Poles, Tartars, and others who so far had refused to join the crusade. Their reasoning was simple and sound: success would make Dracula too strong while failure would bring the punishing Turks into their lands which were currently peaceful. In addition, just like their Western allies who had promised to join the fight did not come, because they did not wish to contact the bubonic plague pandemic from the other infected "crusaders," and die un-heroically.

Diplomat Tommasi continued to read Dracula's messages to King Matthias and in turn sent many well documented letters urging his superiors to help Dracula, whom he called *the Vallchian* "who was better than can be imagined," in his fight against the Turks (Sultan Mehmed). Since he was fully aware of the limited military power of Wallachia and Transylvania to continue the war, the diplomat advised the doge of Venetia to contact the pope for immediate and sufficient help. That help, upon which Dracula's fate hung, never came. Again, the Black Death of 1346 to 1353 claimed the lives of some 50 million Europeans, and still rampaging in Eastern Europe, scared everyone from coming to aid the unpredictable Vallachian rebel prince.

✜

As Dracula had correctly predicted, the vanguard of the Ottoman punishing expedition reached the Danube at the end of spring in 1462. Mehmed II was so certain of his military success that he took along Tursun Bey, his personal secretary, to record descriptions of the victorious battles he would win against Dracula.

By June 1462 the Turkish fleet was lined up on the lower Danube River, but because of severe rain storms there, troops and supplies could not land. Searching for the best place to set anchor, the warships continued to sail up and down the river, forcing the mounted Wallachians to follow them to prevent a bridgehead. To the sultan's surprise, the Wallachians sank many ships using the cannons they had previously captured from the Saxons and Turks.

Another Ottoman fleet from the Morava River on the Danube brought the Sipahi cavalry and Janissary infantrymen to the Vidin fortress. Their 120 heavy cannons took random shots at the laughing Wallachians who made obscene gestures to them from the opposite bank of the Danube. But the Wallachians' fighting formations of thirty thousand were too few and far between to cover the Turkish attack line of 150,000 troops from Vidin to the Braila fortresses. Soon the rain stopped.

This enabled the invading army to attempt to cross the Danube at Nicopolis-Turnu. Following a cannon barrage over a Wallachian military camp that happened to be defended by Gypsy recruits (who fled the scene at once), the first sacrificial troops rushed in rowboats to land under the cover of night.

Daybreak revealed to Sultan Mehmed a surprising scene of horror: squadrons of Wallachian horsemen were hacking the Ottoman marines to bits who were exhausted from digging their defense lines all night. The last three hundred troops who landed were practically slaughtered in their boats by Dracula's cavalry which had just returned from punishing the revolting boyars of the Oltenia region of Wallachia.

At this point, the entire Turkish fleet rallied and initiated what would be a prolonged cannon fire on the defenseless cavalrymen who had to retreat. During the first week of June, the Turkish engineers succeeded in connecting the opposite banks of the second largest river of Europe with a pontoon bridge, and the Janissaries crossed the Danube River en masse.

Sultan Mehmed II and his protégé Radu who was brought along to replace on the throne his brother Dracula, crossed as well and rewarded the brave soldiers of Allah with thirty thousand gold coins. From there, the Turks marched north through the immense Vlasia forest, fully used by the Wallachians to carry out ambushes and successful hit-and-run tactics.

Facing an enemy at least three times more numerous than his own soldiers, Dracula was forced to retreat inland. There he adopted a scorched earth strategy so the animals and population were evacuated, crops were set afire, and the wells were poisoned. Still, the invaders cautiously made slow but steady progress toward the old capital of Targoviste.

Dracula was justifiably alarmed and again begged King Matthias for military help: could he at least send a few hundred Transylvanians as a token to the alliance he had with the Western Europe? The king did not lift a finger to help as he secretly hoped Dracula would loose. Matthias' ambition was to rule civilized Austria and Czechia; Bohemia was more important than primitive Wallachia; and King Frederick III of Hapsburg, not the distant Mehmed II, was his real adversary.

Mathias' dream was to become the new Holy Roman Emperor, not to help a needy but haughty Wallahian prince, already loosing a doomed anti-Ottoman crusade. As for the pope's money, Matthias needed sixty thousand ducats to buy the holy crown from Frederick and his next priority was to build his three hundred-room palace.

As far as the Turkish invasion was concerned, the king would win regardless of its outcome: if Dracula was victorious, Matthias would get the credit for being his boss; if the sultan won, then Hungary would be left alone because it hadn't helped the troublemaking Wallachians. In the meantime, Matthias could enjoy watching the two combatants slaughter each other, believing that Hungary, with its population of four million, was playing the role of superpower in Eastern Europe.

Dracula continued to write imploring letters to King Matthias and even to the khan of the Tartars in the Crimea, emphasizing, "Your land will be next to suffer the same misfortune." Still, no answer was forthcoming. As for the rest of the European crusaders, they were horrified by the Black Plague that infested the German lands and were unwilling to take a risk and travel into what they heard were also epidemic infested Balkans. To go there and fight was suicide. Moreover, none of them wanted to die defending a sadistic ruler who might decide to impale them as well.

In truth, the so-called crusaders were reduced to a status symbol, since the knights battled each other to rule mini estates in small kingdoms. The daring Voievode Vlad III was left to fight the Turkish invasion, alone.

✚

By this time, Pope Pius had learned about the massive Turkish invasion and delegated Pietro Tommasi to investigate what happened with the one hundred thousand of gold ducats sent to Matthias to organize a crusade and help Prince Dracula. In an attempt to save face, the annoyed king ordered a general inspection of his army prior to its being sent to Wallachia, 300 miles away, across the Carpathian Mountains and Transylvania.

Encouraged by this news, the prince renewed his hope and intensified his hit-and run attacks against the invaders whose famous discipline began to deteriorate. Turkish squadrons sent to find food and water never returned, only to be found impaled on the road ahead. In many cases their horses were impaled as well.

Marching across the open plains of Wallachia in the torrid summer heat, the heavily armored Turks sought shade for their steel armor plates that became hot enough to fry eggs on. The exhaustion of both men and animals led to the abandonment of cannons, which were promptly seized by the Wallachians and used against their former owners. Horses without fodder and water were also abandoned, only to find better masters who in a few days brought them back up to fighting shape.

The sultan, who was suffering from bleeding hemorrhoids, had to dismount his horse and be carried on a litter. Worst of all, the Turks had to keep at a distance from the countless lepers and plague infested people sent by Dracula to greet the invaders.

After two weeks of contending with these appalling marching conditions, Mehmed halted his troops before approaching Targoviste and ordered camps to be set up on the banks of the Ialomitsa River. Finally, his army could enjoy an endless supply of fresh water. To raise morale, the sultan ordered the musicians to play invigorating tunes; the pounding of drums produced the desired invigorating effects.

Encampments with thousands of tents were mounted and surrounded by the luggage, wagons, animals, and bivouacs of the auxiliary troops. All passages into each camp were guarded by sentinels and patrolled by Sipahi cavalrymen, while Janissary units cordoned off the green tents of the generals and the gold-red tent of their beloved sultan.

Oxen that were no longer useful were slaughtered. Soon the smell of steaks on the fires smothered the stench of the latrines. After the men ate well and prayed to Allah, the fires were allowed to die out. The darkness of night blanketed the smoky camps. All seemed to be under control and much-needed sleep could not have come at a better time. But the serenity would not last; a decisive battle took place during that Friday night, June 17, 1462 between the sleeping Sultan's army attacked by the Wallachian squadrons led prince Dracula.

Deciding to win with a risky strategy, Dracula had dressed himself as a high-ranking Turkish officer. As such, he approached the sentries and ordered them to let his horsemen enter the sultan's main camp. The sleeping guards were silently killed. Hundreds of Wallachians on horses with hooves covered in muffling cloth dashed into the camp. They followed their prince who was looking for the sultan's tent which he had identified earlier in the day while riding past.

More squadrons of Wallachian horsemen stormed the main camps to assist Dracula's first attackers. But due to anxiety and darkness, he charged the tents of the viziers Isaac fighting against the wrong bodyguards who screamed in terror. Their fearful noises caused the rest of the camp to wake up. As they began to jump and look for weapons, the Wallachians were cutting the ropes that anchored the canvas and leather tents, causing them to collapse on the sleepy soldiers and thus preventing them from joining the fight. When they managed to free themselves, running in the pitch black night, they tripped over the ropes and began to kill each other, suspecting everyone was the enemy dressed in Turkish uniforms.

Finally, Dracula found the sultan's tent which was marked with a standard of seven horses' tails; but he killed only the servants. The Great Mehmed the Conqueror, was inside another tent belonging to his lover. The surprise attack created the expected panic that was fully exploited by the seven thousand Wallachian raiders who slaughtered the enemy. The sleeping camps were transformed into a bloodbath. When it was time for reinforcements, Dracula blew into his ram's horn signaling Viteaz Gales, his second in command, to arrive with the rest of the army and finish off the Turks.

It just so happened that at the same moment, the thunder of drums sounded from nearby, calling the Janissaries to fight. They encircled the terrified sultan, and their double-headed pole-axes began to hack at the Wallachians whose horses were now entangled in the loose tent ropes. Soon the gruesome face-to-face and hand-to-hand combat began to tilt in favor of the more numerous defenders.

Vainly Dracula blew his horn; Gales could not hear it because military blunder that would almost change the history of Sultan Mehmed II and his empire. of the drumbeats. Believing the night attack was over, the viteaz commander ordered his men to turn around and gallop to the safety of the Targoviste walls. It was a military blunder that would change the history of Wallachia and Prince Dracula's life.

With the element of surprise now lacking and bleeding from a head wound, Dracula on his white Arabian horse dashed over the dead bodies and collapsed tents to join other Wallachians fighting their way out of the hellish encampment. The attacking survivors vanished in the night as fast as they came, yet the Turks continued to kill each other, while some gave chase to the departing attackers.

When the morning light shone over the camp, it revealed that the carnage had, for the most part, been inflicted by frightened Turks upon each other. Ironically, the sneak attack had been inspired by a similar night attack used by Mehmed II nine years earlier, when he conquered Constantinople.

✠

The next day, the Wallachians rounded up the Turks who had fled from their camps and the countless animals who broke loose during the fight. Most of the wounded raiders who had covered their prince's retreat succeeded in returning to Targoviste. From far away they heard the drums and the shouts of *at-Tawakkul 'ala Allah!* (Our full trust is in God-Allah!), while Sultan Mehmed II reviewed his troops to boost their confidence. Dracula did the same in his camp, looking for those soldiers who were wounded in the back; these he declared cowards and ordered them to be executed. He impaled Viteaz Gales for the same reason, a cardinal mistake he would later regret.

Some ten thousand Turks died in the night attack, another three thousand were taken prisoner, and one thousand Wallachians never returned to their camp. Despite this, the sultan ordered his secretary Tursun Bey to write about the raid on his army: "it was a drop of water that hit the ocean."[7] And so it was recorded in the history books. Above the sultan's camps, thousands of vultures, falcons, and black crows glided past, all looking for fresh carnage. More determined than ever to destroy Dracula's military power, the sultan ordered his army to continue the invasion and occupy Targoviste city.

Meanwhile, Radu the Handsome and his loyalists were campaigning on the Danubian plains for support to replace his brother Dracula. It was not difficult to convince them; he only had to promise the boyars that he would restore their privileges and assure the defectors from Dracula's camp that they would not be punished. But above and beyond this, he preached of a lasting peace, a gentle reign, and no revenge for any past wrong doings. Radu sent envoys to the Saxon cities hardest hit by Dracula, tempting them with old fashioned advantageous trade regulations and vouching for the sanctity of their families. Radu's good nature attracted instant allies, including the inhabitants of Bucureşti and Targoviste, who had had enough of the cruelty of his brother.

Happy to hear the good news, the Turks, under Sultan Mehmed's command, pressed forward. But Dracula was far from surrendering and offered the invaders yet another horrifying spectacle. Just before reaching Targoviste they came upon a forest of impaled Turkish prisoners and Wallachians who were suspected of being traitors; it covered an area two miles long and one mile wide.

According to Chalkondyles, a Byzantine chronicler who also described the war, some twenty thousand bodies were rotting in the sun and being eaten by birds and worms, the work of Dracula's well paid mercenaries. The Turks passed through the "forest" of impaled bodies and entered Targoviste unopposed, only to find the streets filled with people begging for food and dying of the plague.

By the end of June, having occupied a worthless city, afraid of the deadly epidemic, and wanting to avoid subjecting his army to further horrors and loss of morale the sultan ordered his troops, now reduced by half, to retreat.

In confirming this, Chalkondyles wrote that the Wallachians, whom he called "Dacians," instilled much fear in the invaders "who in a great hurry crossed Istru [Danube]" into Bulgaria.[8] Their disorderly retreat, without plunder, even without their horses, they were looking sick and dressed in ragged uniforms, it showcased their sad ordeal in the "country of Dacia." He also wrote,

> The emperor said that he could not take the land away from a man who does such marvelous things and can exploit his rule and his subjects in this way and that surely a man who had accomplished this is worthy of greater things.[9]

However this event was described, it was an outright defeat of a massive Ottoman army and an unforgettable humiliation for Mehmed the Conqueror.

Dracula, on the other hand, was optimistic and sent a happy message to King Matthias, promising to convert to Catholicism and have all of Wallachia do so as well, if the Hungarians helped him win the final crusade. Confident in his mission, the prince continued to inflict casualties on the enemy in their disorderly retreat, while all his messages to Matthias were never received as they were all intercepted by the anti-Dracula boyars.

As for the Hungarian army, it was moving at a snail's pace toward Transylvania, as ordered by the young king whose aim was to avoid a military confrontation with the Turks. Then unexpectedly, another army entered eastern Wallachia, but not to help Prince Dracula.

☩

Learning about the Turkish retreat along the Danube, Prince Stefan III of Moldavia decided to occupy Chilia, the northernmost Danubian port of Wallachia. Believing his cousin Dracula was finished, Voievod Stefan rushed to take over the rich city before the Turks or Hungarians could do so. Dracula had to dispatch seven thousand Wallachian warriors (practically half of his army) to defend the vital city, using cannons to repel the attacks of their co-nationalists. The new weapon was so efficient that on June 22 it severely wounded cousin Stefan in the leg; because of this, the siege was called off, and he retreated with his army to Moldavia.

This was a devastating blow for Dracula who had helped his friend and relative gain his Moldovian throne and now his cousin Stefan was behaving like an enemy. Suddenly, it was clear to Dracula that he was a lone crusader; he had not one single ally.

Defying the reality of defeat and determined to save face, on July 11 Mehmed II made a triumphal entrance into the city of Adrianople. He acted like a victor, and in a way, he was. Radu was already recognized as the Wallachian ruler by most of the boyars who had rallied around him and by the commoners who were fed up with the long war. Still worse for Dracula, whose already limited military power was now divided, a Turkish corps retaliated by sacking and burning part of Braila after they failed to capture Chilia.

Meanwhile King Matthias was told that monks from Greece were singing *Te Deum Laudamus* in honor of Dracula and that Pope Pius II was putting together a coalition he wanted to lead in person to bring this crusade to a total victory. Matthias rushed to please the pontiff, reporting that the Turkish army had been defeated. To back this up, on July 15 the reluctant king left Buda with his army. This was very good news to Dracula, and it restored his confidence.

With his increased energy and renewed determination to win, Dracula regrouped his scattered army. He chalked up two victories (July 26 and September 8) against Radu's Turkish-backed units while on a march to capture the cities of Giurgiu and București. Dracula's success was promptly reported by many. Domenico Balbi wrote on June 27 from Constantinople, describing the Turkish invasion of Wallachia and the numerous defeats of the Turks there. On August 3 Aloisio Gabriel from Candia (Crete) confirmed the pitiful retreat of the Turkish army from Wallachia to Adrianople, concluding a letter with: "The danger passed, praised be the Lord!"[10] For the time being, the Turks were licking their wounds.

On September 17, King Matthias reviewed his troops in the Transylvanian city of Turda, still more than 100 miles away from the Wallachian border. Two weeks later, Dracula scored his last major victory against enemy troops moving from Braila to regain control of the capital of București. After many skirmishes, the battle took place in the middle of the Danubian plain.[11] There, in spite of his being outnumbered and outgunned, Dracula's heroism was decisive in the defeat of Radu's forces. But, again he did something extremely damaging to his reputation: he impaled the Wallachians loyal to Radu, and, to everyone's astonishment, he freed all the Turkish prisoners. This was his peace token to Sultan Mehmed II, but it was a major tactical mistake with respect to his own people.

✜

Ironically, the peaceful Radu was more popular than his brother who had won one battle after another in knightly fashion but persisted in impaling his own people. Wallachia was now divided into two parts: Dracula ruled in the northeast and his brother in the southwest. The latter territory became larger with each passing day. By now the old boyars had taken over most of the lands where Dracula's soldiers were not present. Worried about the fact that their families would be facing famine and the harshness of the approaching winter, the soldiers began returning in droves to their homes to harvest their crops. It became clear that Dracula's concept of a conscript army did not work.

As for the Hungarians, Moldavians, Transylvanians, and Saxons, Dracula's heroics did only one thing and it was most unwelcome, he brought the Ottoman armies next to their borders. The old boyars saw in Dracula's crusade nothing but a thirst for absolute power, and they realized that it had brought an unwanted destruction to Wallachia.

Neither King Matthias, nor other Christian leaders wanted to see a victorious Dracula in control of half of the Danube commercial traffic. He had already made it clear that his desire was to unite all Wallachians into an idealized the Greater Dacian Kingdom. But this meant only one thing: when he was strong enough, Dracula would occupy the Balkans and torturously rule over its pro-Turkish population.

None of his neighbors jumped to help the lone crusader, and he lost his new capital of București to Radu's forces. Nevertheless, the nearby garrison on Snagov Lake, where he built a church and where part of the Wallachian treasury was stored, still repelled Turkish attacks using the large cannons Dracula had mounted on the shores of the island. When the island was finally conquered, the occupiers were blasted into smithereens by explosions of the gun powder depots. No treasure was ever found.

✟

Dracula's greatest fear materialized when he received the news that the former capital of Targoviste had also surrendered to Radu without a fight; at the same time, he learned that even his viteaz commanders did not want to spend a second Christmas away from their families. His own family was also far away in the Poienari Castle built with the slave labor of punished boyars.

Dracula decided to head to Campulung, the city near the castle, where he intended to establish his new capital and where he had already stored the royal treasure (in the cellars of the old Abbey). Leaving a strong garrison there the prince finally arrived at Poienari castle located high on the mountain cliffs. He warmly embraced Mihnea his two year old son, and his wife Anastasia Maria who was the niece of the Queen of Poland.

Days later he saw through his long spyglass that Turkish mountaineers had set up camp below and were preparing to attack the castle, which was surrounded by the deep gorges of the Arges River. Their many attempts were easily repelled by the one hundred men garrison, who rolled rocks down onto the intruders. The Turkish cannons that were placed on the hills across from the castle opened fire. To their surprise, the castle cannons were aimed downward at them with deadly precision.

But Dracula realized it was a fight the Turks could not lose. He sent his son to nearby Transylvania, while his wife chose to jump off the cliff to her death. Most of his servants and soldiers vanished as well. The prince managed to escape the besieged castle with a saddlebag filled with crown jewelry. Followed by a dozen bodyguards, he arrived at Campulung. His only hope and savior was King Matthias.

☩

On November 3, the Hungarian king arrived in the city of Brasov, not to help Dracula, but to celebrate the patrons of the Saxon city. This was the best way for him to accept donations from the Transylvanians as he intended to apply the money toward the purchase of the Hungarian crown from Emperor Frederick. But he also heard firsthand of the cruelties inflicted by Dracula on the city, including his setting fire to the Catholic cathedral.

When Dracula heard that Matthias had arrived, he rushed to see the king. Leading a small army of five hundred mercenaries who guarded three wagons loaded with royal treasure, he stopped at the small fortress of Orația which he had built to control the Rucar-Brasov corridor. There he stored the treasure before eagerly leading a squadron of viteaz officers through the mountain passage to Brasov. It is said that upon looking back to Wallachia, he pitied himself for being the ruler of such a small country.

The meeting with the king began surprisingly well. Prince Dracula was fluent in Hungarian, and Matthias was fluent in Romanian, both reminisced about their heroic Wallachain fathers and their anti-Ottoman stands. But when Matthias confessed he had just signed a peace agreement with Sultan Mehmed II, Dracula's blood began to boil; he shouted insults, declaring that the king's actions showed disrespect for his crusade which was now proven worthless. The king bluntly responded that Dracula's one-man war had not been wanted by anyone in the first place, and then he dismissed the outraged ex-voievode of Wallachia.

After their meeting, a secret document signed by Dracula was handed to Matthias. It was a letter that had been intercepted, addressed to the sultan whom the prince called "Emperor of Emperors;" he pledged loyalty to the Ottoman Court, offered to hand over Transylvania, and promised to seize Matthias if Sultan Mehmed II allowed Dracula to continue his reign in Wallachia. The letter was written in poor Latin, which did not make sense because Dracula had mastered Latin; furthermore, if he was writing to the sultan, he would have used Turkish, which they both spoke. Equally unlikely was the submissive tone which was not at all Dracula's style. Obviously, it was a clumsy forgery, most likely done by a rival clan of the Draculesti family.

This forgery did not matter to Matthias who summoned Dracula for another audience and both spoke in their maternally Romanian language. This time the Hungarian King offered the fugitive crusader a bargain that was difficult to resist: in exchange for the royal treasury, Dracula could continue to rule Wallachia. The prince agreed. Followed by a Czech mercenary contingent led by General Jan Jiskra von Brandeis, he returned to the Orația fortress to retrieve the promised gold.

What happened next is an example of how a double-crosser is double-crossed in an unmistakably Balkan way of doing business. Jiskra and his men were told to sleep in the nearby village while Dracula and his entourage went to the fortress.

The next day three heavy wagons were lowered from the fortress to the road below, and Jiskra's mercenaries, who outnumbered the Wallachians five to one, took their pre-planned positions to assassinate Dracula. But first the general inspected the contents of the wagons. They were loaded with smoked meats and sacks of grains, not the royal treasure. The stunned Jiskra drew his sword as did his soldiers, but all froze as Dracula smugly faced them and pointed out that if he were killed, Matthias would never see the treasure. With no other option, the mercenaries took the prince prisoner and brought him back to the king.

Surprisingly, Matthias treated Dracula well, and then asked him again to deliver the treasury. When Dracula refused, he was confronted with the forged letter of betrayl. On the basis of this "evidence," Matthias had the Prince Dracula taken to Hungary.

✣

Dracula was treated royally by King Mathias in the capital of Buda. In fact, the king was very proud of Dracula as a guest, and showed him off to all of the foreign dignitaries as a premier fighter for Christianity, and living proof that the pope's money had been put to good use in the last crusade. In reality, by Christmas Dracula at age 31, was no longer a feared former ruler, but a prisoner in the fortress of Buda. The entire ordeal to help Dracula, kept Matthias so busy that he missed the opportunity to campaign against Emperor Frederick, who had been attacked by the Viennese but escaped to rule again. If Matthias had marched on Vienna only a month before, he could have had the crown of Saint Stephen of Hungary at no cost.[12]

Captivity did not change Dracula's attitude. His appearance produced a frightened murmur among guests; what they saw was a rather short man with broad shoulders, a chiseled pale face with a strong chin, a long nose, a large moustache that overlapped his lips, and bright sharp teeth.

Instead of looking and acting like a monster, Dracula, in his military uniform, proved to be a well groomed knight who spoke six languages and had fine manners; he had unmistakable sex appeal for women and superior charm for men. When asked about his use of impaling, he simply stated that wrongdoers impaled themselves.

His big dark green eyes were said to burn holes into his astounded listeners.

Each time a Turkish embassy came to Buda, Dracula was present as a powerful reminder of Matthias's negotiating power. Dressed in war regalia and sporting the visible Order of the Dragon, wearing his knightly ring over gloved fingers that arrogantly rested on the heavy crusade sword given to his father at Nuremberg, the prince stood firmly next to the Hungarian royal throne. Dracula's status at the Court of Matthias was unclear, but he was allowed to convert to Catholicism. He married the king's cousin, Ilona Szilagyi who bore him two sons, during their ten years of marriage. Their residence was in the Hungarian capital where they lived in luxury in a mansion across the Danube River.

Prince Dracula was invited to Matthias's coronation in 1464 where guests from all over Europe competed for a glimpse of the "Tyranum Tyranus" who sat in the first row inside the imperial cathedral.[13] Moreover, he was offered the rank of captain in the Hungarian army and entrusted, as Hunyadi had been, with the Transylvanian borders.

In 1467 everything changed. Matthias wanted to replace Stefan III of Moldavia with a pro-Hungarian contender. The campaign proved to be a disaster, and after his defeat at the Battle of the Baia Mare, the three times wounded Matthias barely escaped alive on a stretcher, with only a third of his army. It triggered the Transylvanians revolt against the Hungarian crown, while Wallachia was in danger of having Prince Laiota (Bassarab the Old) as a perpetual puppet voievod being ruled by the Ottoman Court.

The entire twisted events it prompted Stefan III to install Vlad III Dracula on the throne. Thus, the important role that exiled Dracula played in restoring order in the future Romanian lands increased with each passing day.

When the Turks conducted a number of raids in southern Hungary and built a stronghold on the Sava River, King Matthias realized the immediate danger he was in because the Turks were so close.

The Hungarian monarch faced a frightening situation, and Dracula was the solution to his political and military crises. As the prince was in Transylvania rallying supporters for another comeback to the throne of Wallachia, Matthias offered him a much more important assignment: to help him recover Bosnia from the Turks. Dracula performed beyond any expectations when, disguised as a Janissary officer, he captured at least four fortified cities. Each of his victories were followed by the impaling and massacring of Turks, the actions that brought his name back into European news.

He inspired Pope Sixtus IV to initiate another crusade for which the Venetians pledged their fleet. Furthermore, the best way for Matthias to demonstrate his dedication to the Christian cause proved to be by patronizing the Turk-hater, Dracula. Because he became the cousin-in-law and the right hand of the Hungarian king, Dracula was allowed to settle in the Transylvanian city of Sibiu.

✝

Finally, the Diet of Hungary had endorsed Dracula's candidacy for the throne of Wallachia, held for the fifth time by Prince Laiota (from the Danesti family) who replaced Radu the Handsome who had died of syphilis. It just happened months before, Stefan III won the battle of Racova on 10 January 1475. It was a glorious victory against the superior Ottoman forces led by Suleiman Pasha, the governor of Rumelia who was killed in the battle. Also killed were 45,000 Turks and hundreds of their standards were captured by the Moldavians.

The surviving Ottomans escaped by crossing the Danube River to find shelter in their strongholds in Bulgaria, while many enrolled as mercenaries in the army of Prince Laiota of Wallachia who was waiting for Dracula's attack.

With his country free of the Ottoman's occupation, Stefan III offered to help his cousin Vlad III the Impeller to defeat Prince Laiota and regain his throne of Wallahia.

Pope Sixtus IV was so impressed with Stefan III military

achievements fighting the Ottomans that he bestowed him with the title of *Athleta Christi (Champion of Christ)*. The pope considered Stefan III as *"versus christianae fidei athleta" (the true defender of the Christian faith* [13] and he was called Stefan the Great of Moldavia.

Finally, Dracula had succeeded in gaining the trust and support of the suspicious Saxons, but only after he had agreed to cancel his previous heavy tariffs on the German merchants. The frightened Laiota pledged his loyalty to the Ottoman Empire, which infuriated Matthias, the Transylvanians, and Prince Stephan the Great of Moldavia.

✣

By November of that year, Dracula and Stephen Bathory, now the voievode of Transylvania, led an army of twenty-five thousand troops into Wallachia. They crushed Prince Laiota's army of eighteen thousand, mostly Turks, and killed at least half of them not far from the Orația fortress where the royal treasure used to be hidden. The victors occupied Targoviste on November 6, and some of them marched towards București to join the army of fifteen thousand Moldavians under Prince Stefan III.

Ten days later, these combined forces defeated another of Laiota's army, and Prince Vlad III became the Wallachian domnitor for the third time, taking residence in the new capital of Bucaresti. With their mission accomplished, all the foreign soldiers, except the mercenaries, left for their homelands, and only a small garrison of two hundred Moldavians remained to safeguard Dracula. King Matthias took credit for the victories and rushed to announce them to Pope Sixtus IV.

But things went from bad to worse when at the end of November the re-installed Prince Dracula signed a letter to the Saxons with: *Io, Vlad, voievod si domn a toata tara Ungrovalahiei* (I, Vlad, Lord and Voievode of the whole country of Hungro-Wallachia). This suggested that part of Transylvania was his as well. Furthermore, he named the Brasovians "the good and sweet friends of my reign,"[14] a message that could not have been more pleasing in that it announced his third rule. It turned out to be the ultimate unpardonable mistake. Dracula had made it clear that he was their despot despite his obvious need for money and soldiers from Transylvania. And he continued to impale his enemies—undeniable proof that little had changed.

When Sultan Mehmed II learned that Dracula had no army to speak of, he ordered an immediate invasion of Wallachia with Bucureşti as the main target. Once again Laiota's forces began expanding by setting up a camp of six thousand men only a stone's throw from the capital. Equestrian patrols from both camps spied on each other and engaged in brief mêlées.

Knowing that Laiota was anxiously waiting for the Turkish army to arrive, Dracula decided to pulverize the enemy camp and kill his rival before he became too strong. Taking advantage of a foggy day before Chrismas, the prince put on a Turkish uniform and set out on a reconnaissance mission.

As Dracula and his small squadron rode through an open field, they encountered local Wallachian peasants trying to retrieve animals that had been stolen by Laiota's soldiers looking for food.

Unwilling to get involved in the distracting melee, the prince climbed onto a heap of dirt so he would be able to spot the location of the adversary camp. Suddenly a spear landed next to him, arrows wounded his horse and struck his mail tunic, which was covered by a large Turkish mantle. Peasants armed with axes and pitch forks charged from all directions, trying to kill the "Turkish officer."

Dracula spurred his horse forward, then backward and sideways in an effort to dodge the blows. He kept swinging his Toledo saber, trying to gain time until his bodyguards could rescue him. Forced to kill the attackers closest to him, he vainly screamed in Romanian about his true identity.

Ironically, a Turkish patrol saw "their" officer in danger and dashed to protect Dracula, who was able to gallop into the fog. What happened next is not known and remains enfolded in the fog of history.

What is known is that after the New Year, Dracula's decapitated body was found by his bodyguards among some four hundred dead warriors from both camps. Only ten Moldavians returned to their country to tell the horror story. King Matthias was unaware of these events and most probably reassured Pope Sixtus and the Doge of Venice that Prince Dracula was continuing his successful crusade, while Dracula's body was buried next to his church on the island in the Snagov Lake.

His head was preserved in ice and presented to Sultan Mehmed II in Constantinople. It was promptly impaled on the tip of a lance and placed in front of the sultan's palace for all to see. The most evil *Ghiaur* (Infidel), Prince Kaziglu, the Impaler, was dead on 10 January 1476, under the sign of Capricorn.

☩

Also born under the sign of Capricorn, Prince Vlad III Dracula was a few days short of forty-five years of age when he died. So ended the life of an unruly prince whose grand visions were equaled by cruel deeds that he justified by claiming they were necessary to achieve his grand goal of freeing the Balkans from the Ottoman occupation. The Italian humanist, Filippo Buonaccorsi-Callimachus, called him *maximum illum Imperatorem et Ducem suum Vladislaus Draculum* (the greatest emperor and lord, his Vlad Dracula).[15]

His epitaph might read, "The Last Crusader," which indeed was the character of this prince who seemed born to fight. No grave or tomb of his would ever be made or found.

Dracula would forever be remembered in history for his impaling, even though this form of justice was merely one example of the savagery of the Middle Ages in the Balkans.

Today, his life and actions serve as evidence that only the primeval fear of violent retribution could convince the people of the Balkans to obey the laws and create any kind of social order. Despite revulsion at the horror of impalement, modern Romanians are immensely proud of their medieval Vlad Tepes (Vlad the Impaler) both because he was so determined to keep his nation independent and because he struggled to build an ideal Christian society in Wallachia.

While his crusade was ignored by the western powers, it managed to inspire many small countries to take up arms against the Ottoman domination of Eastern Europe. Eventually, each of the nations in the Balkan area claimed its own version of Prince Dracula. For certain, he was a balkanization determined hero who tried to do right under adverse conditions in which friends and enemies were instantly interchangeable. Only Prince Vlad III Dracula's inborn ambition posed to be a challenge to the impossible odds to defy balkanization.

# REFERENCE NOTES

1. Impalement was a punishment practiced by the Persians and Turks to inspire terror and fear in rebels, just as the Romans used crucifixion. As a public display designed to discourage disobedience, it was a horrifying symbol of absolute power which had a chilling effect on both the population and enemies. For Dracula it was a way to make known his royal message: "This can happen to anyone" who was not willing to behave accordingly to royal wishes.
2. Mircea Dogaru, *Dracula: mit și realitate istorică* (*Dracula: Myth and Historical Reality*) (Bucharest: Editura Ianus, 1993), 236.
3. Dogaru, *Dracula: mit*, 129.
4. Dogaru, *Dracula: mit*, 236.
5. Radu R. Florescu and Raymond T. McNally, *Dracula: Prince of Many Faces, His Life and His Times* (Boston: Little, Brown, 1989), 134, 137.
6. Florescu and McNally, *Dracula*, 137.
7. N. Stoicescu, *Vlad Tepes* (Bucharest: Editura Academiei, 1978), 122.
8. Stoicescu, *Vlad Tepes*, 127.
9. Florescu and McNully, *Dracula: Prince*, 148.
10. Dogaru, *Dracula: mit*, 213.
11. A village named Vlad Tepesh/Impaler is still on the Romanian map.
12. The German emperor became Dracula's biggest fan, reading to his guests from the *Story of a Bloodthirsty Madman Called Dracula of Wallachia*, as told by Brother Jacob, a monk who had barely escaped impalement as a beggar in the capital of Targoviste. A printer from Vienna turned his story into the second bestselling book after the Bible; artists sketched the horrors and troubadours sang about Dracula. This all benefited Dracula, who in spite of the bloody image, was often invited from Matthias' Solomon

Tower prison to the king's sumptuous parties where he was the main attraction for his guests. To them, Dracula was a living legend from a mysterious land, and this was a unique occasion on which they could meet the man who had impaled more than fifty thousand people.
13. It cost Matthias eighty thousand forint and a few Hungarian counties to buy the crown from King Frederick. Finally, in 1464 he ceremoniously received the Holy Crown of Hungary.
14. Dogaru, *Dracula: mit*, 248.
15. Stoicescu, *Vlad Tepes*, 187.

The author Ion Grumeza lecturing about Prince Vlad III Dracula.

## FROM INVASION TO SETTLEMENT

The largest barbarian invasions of Europe took place after the year 500, largely because of the collapse of the Roman Empire and the vanishing of the Sarmatian and Scythian stopping powers northwest of the Sea of Azov. This was also due possibly to the unfriendly climate changes in Eurasia, beyond the Ural Mountains. A sure reason was that there was no longer a military force to defend the Danube River line that separated the civilized world from the eastern lands to push back the countless barbarian populations of invaders who had never seen a brick building, nor heard of Jesus.

It all began with a relentless flood of Eurasian tribes savagely pursuing each other west of the Volga River and aimed either to Rome or Constantinople as their ultimate invasion goals. They sought commercial routes that led to the prosperous cities and rich provinces with the Latin European names, which they eagerly wanted to pillage and destroy. And, what they could never build. Essentially, the primal incentives of hunger, avarice and greed launched an age of migrations that lasted five hundred years. That put the pagan and Christian worlds on a collision course that would change the demographic map of Eastern Europe and the course of entire European history.

The geographic configuration of the Balkan Peninsula determined the route by which the barbarians made their incursion into the West. Before discovering Roman military roads, they followed mountain valleys, most of which ran parallel, north to south, and also the course of the area's rivers, which facilitated their advance. The invading hordes set up encampments in rich pastures so that the energy of their horses might be sustained and the massive herds of animals they used for food might be fattened.

These migratory caravans were made up of hunters and herdsmen who belonged to tribes that were offshoots of the barbarian mega-tribes. They, in turn, were united by a shared language, religion and common traditions; they also had a single chieftain. There was continual friction among the tribes, often causing their migrations to be re-routed so the tribes could deal with immediate problems; however, they instantly united when they were faced with external threats. Typically those threats came from Byzantine armies, but there were also frequent engagements with native settlers determined to hold onto their native lands and defend their families and possessions.

Often, the reputed savagery and the predatory power of the invasions, were perceived as wild animals riding horses, and this caused many of the native people to move away from the invaded areas and resettle elsewhere for safety. This gave the barbarians immediate access to already prosperous regions. Yet, in the absence of a self-sustaining economy, the settlements claimed by the usurpers were doomed to vanish eventually in flames. The barbarians lacked the stability that went with civilized living: their main source of revenue was booty, and their savage warriors, not productive farmers or laborers to provide for their families and communities. So, the invaders charged ever onward, marking their migratory route by burning dwellings and killing the conquered population.

In the early days of the barbarian invasions, the primitive riders, who were unable to conquer fortified cities, overran the countryside's native settlements. They showed no humanity even in victory, as massacring, looting, and raping wherever they went both for the thrill of it and as proof that their raids were successful. Captives for whom they could not collect ransom were murdered because the intruders did not need extra mouths to feed. They forced ancient nations into bloody submission and occupied the lands they had claimed by the sword and summarily declared them their own.[1]

Treaties might be made by these savages, but they would not be honored. Behaving unpredictably, except for their cunning, sadism, and capacity for deception, they destroyed whatever they could not steal from both friend and foe. The magnitude of their destruction was regarded as heroic. The modern world might call them masters of psychological warfare for they were enormously adept at inducing mortal fear in native populations who had thus far felt safe and secure in Pax Romana.

☩

Even though none of the invading hordes, composed of the clans exceeded six hundred thousand, the level of their savagery made them seem more numerous when the trickle of their infiltrations turned into a flood of invasions. Most of these men were physically larger than Western Europeans. Dressed in furs, they were certainly better horsemen, and their ability to deal with hardship, especially on the battlefield, seemed endless. They were basically primitive hunters with an inborn and cultivated killer instinct; daring and godless warriors and they were greatly feared for their lethal efficiency. They readily adapted to any living conditions and all forms of depravation while they charged forward to conquer their next meal.

They lived in extended, polygamous families and had numerous children, but no property or personal possessions except weapons and horses. Death in battle was considered an honor, and they readily volunteered for that supreme sacrifice. Byzantine troops, on the other hand, were primarily mercenaries who wanted to live a good life and retire in comfort.

As in previous centuries, the barbarians approached the Balkan Peninsula "like tributaries joining a river from all directions" and "streamed towards us [Byzantines] in full force, mostly through Dacia,"[2] as described by historian Anna Comnena (Latinized name,) a Greek princess and a historian, when writing about the mountain passes and river valleys of what is today Romania. Because the Danube River constituted a major natural obstacle to accessing more southerly areas, many barbarian hordes, like the Gepids, settled for a while in Dacia or neighboring Pannonia (today's Hungary). Here they regrouped and then attacked the lands ruled by Byzantium, areas that made up what would later be known as the Byzantine Empire.

This Balkan mega state, which covered a greater geographic area when it was the Roman Eastern Empire, was ruled from Constantinople by so-called Roman emperors from long-standing royal dynasties. It extended over three continents, and its enviable riches attracted fierce predatory nomads from the Don and Volga River lands and beyond.

✣

In the beginning, the Byzantine armies were capable of forcing the savage raiders to retreat. But when the invading warriors were followed by their entire families and caravans with their belongings, the Byzantines faced a huge demographic problem: these barbarians, unlike Attila with his hordes did not run back to their bases after engaging in their acts of plunder; rather, they intended to stay in the areas they claimed.

Moreover, they did not invade from the sea, which would have made defense much easier; they arrived by land from ever new directions and invaded over vast areas. It was impossible for the Byzantine army to be everywhere at the same time in order to crush the randomly barbarian attacks. Their attacks were marked by sheer savagery, combined with speed of pursuit and complicated deceiving withdrawal maneuvers followed by massive charges. Furthermore, even when the barbarian warriors were killed in battle and the rest of population was resettled at a far distance, the high birth rate of the barbarians and their quick military recovery presented an ongoing and increasing danger to the imperial Byzantine command.

An example of the military situation that developed as a result of one of the first devastating barbarian incursions into the Balkan Peninsula was described as follows by the Bishop Procopius of Caesarea:

> ...Sirmium [Mitrovitza] and the country around it is under the Gepids. But everywhere, to be brief, is absolutely deserted. Some perished in the war, others by the disease and famine which come together with war. As for Illyria [Albania] and the whole of Thrace [European Turkey], which would include all from the Ionian gulf as far as the suburbs of Byzantium, having in it Greece and the area of the Chersonese Huns, Sclavenes, and Antæ overran it nearly every year from the beginning of Justinian's reign and did terrible damage to the inhabitants. In each invasion I believe that there were more than two hundred thousand Romans killed or enslaved there, so that the Scythian desert came to extend over the whole area.[3]

✝

The invading hordes into the Byzantine Empire included:

**Gepids.** The tribes named Getipaides (children of Goths) by the Greeks proved to be strong enough to defeat a Roman army as they took over some cities and areas ruled by Constantinople. These threatening events prompted Emperor Justinian (r. 527-565) to play some of the barbarians off against others, and he allowed the powerful Lombards to settle in Noricum and Pannonia. As might have been expected, the Germanic tribes turned against the Gepids (who had once defeated the Huns), but in the year 552 Gepidia, which had previously covered western Dacia (Romania) and eastern Pannonia (Hungary) was drastically reduced in both population and living space. Since they were too busy to resettle around the Sirmium region, the Gepids paid little attention to the arrival of another migratory people, the Avars.

✠

**Avars.** The Tartaric/Turkish Avars/Abars, a branch of the Altaic tribes which had originated in what is today Turkestan, were named "Abaroi" by the Romans and "Huns" by the Franks. They were the same people but with different hairstyles: the first wore two braids down their backs; the second had their heads shaved except for a single lock of hair on top. Formidable fighters, the Avars were skilled at equestrian warfare, and using stirrups, they were also able to use hunting bows to rapidly shoot well aimed arrows. They retained the pagan ritual of burying their dead warriors with their cherished horses, further evidence of their military might.

In 561 they settled in the Dacian provinces of today's Bessarabia and Dobrudja, pushing the Bulgars and Slavs south of the Danube. The Avars destroyed Gepidia east of the Tisza River and occupied Pannonia. It became part of Avaria which then contained tribes of Croats, Serbians, and other Slavs. Avars were quick to subdue most of these docile and dislocated tribes and led them in carrying out devastating raids inside the Byzantine Empire, thus forcing Emperor Justinian I to pay them an annual tribute in exchange for peace. Each time the tribute was cut off, however, the Avars with their Slavs (who received a small share of the plunder) would storm the Greek lands, inducing terror in the Byzantine population.

This was particularly the case in 626 when the Avars, who were allied with the Persians, attacked Constantinople's massive walls, only to be defeated. Because of repeated defeats, the Avar military power was permanently diminished. This taught the Slavs and other barbarians a valuable lesson: blackmailing only weak emperors who were willing to pay a tribute in exchange for peace.

From that point onward, barbarian invasions were motivated by the prospect of easily obtaining tributary payments through intimidation. By the beginning of the eighth century, the Avar Empire had been reduced to an area in the western Carpathian region; in 796, it was destroyed altogether by the combined attacks of the Franks and Bulgars. Some Avars escaped into the Dacian lands of today's Banat, Crisana, and Transylvania, and most of the survivors were absorbed into the oncoming waves of Slavs and Magyars. The Avars never created a lasting state, but they were crucial in dispersing other barbarian groups across the various areas of the Balkans, and in ability to create further chaos and conflict in the Balkans.

☦

**Slavs.** None of the migratory peoples appeared on the scene as suddenly and numerously as did the Slavs, a name that encompassed many ethnically diverse tribes of varied origins. These northern Indo-Europeans, commonly known as Slaveni, provided the basic Pan-Slavic language. However, the majority of their population was under the leadership of the Antes, a powerful and huge tribe that dominated Eastern Europe in the fifth century after the Goths and Huns had evacuated it.

Their main homeland encompassed the vastness of southern Russia between the Bug and Volga rivers. Dislocated by the powerful Khazars, they slowly drifted westward with their women and children in oxen-pulled wagons. Most often these proto-agrarian people occupied lands abandoned by other migrants, mainly Goths. This pattern caused some tribes to shift to areas east of the Carpathian Mountains.

A different case represented the powerful mega tribe of the Antes, which resulted from the breeding of the Slaves with the Alani. The Antes alone or by joining with other Slaves, raided the northern Balkans many times. Suddenly, they became allies of the Byzantines who paid them to settle and guard the main gate to stop the Eurasians from invading the Empire. For more than a century, after occupying the lands of the last leg of the Danube River, the settled Antes did just that. In fact, they were so dutiful, that they made numerous barbarian enemies. In the seventh century, the Avars shattered and dispensed the homogeneity of the Antes Federation. It was believed the Croats immerged from one of the Antes' splinters.

The Slavs spoke a basic *lingua franca* of their own, which evolved into distinctive western, southern, and eastern dialects. Since they had no concept of centralized leadership, each tribe conducted its own independent raids. After establishing some temporary farming settlements in former Dacia (today's Banat and Dobrudja,) they continued to expand their numbers and ultimately spread farther west and south. They were armed with axes and nail-studded clubs, and shot poisoned arrows to increase the fighting power of their many foot soldiers.

Unlike other barbarians, however, they possessed nautical skills. Their warriors could use boats and barges for transportation and so cross any major river and penetrate deep into the Balkan mainland. For this reason they were able to occupy regions like Dacian Moesia (today's Bulgaria) and Illyria. The lack of unity among the Slavic tribes caused them to be easily subdued by the socially superior Avars. When Constantinople ceased paying its annual subsidies, the Avars made use of the Slavs as "bulldozer," sacrificial troops in their various invasions.

With no other place to go, the Slavs followed the Avars and penetrated deeply into the Balkan Peninsula as far as the Sea of Marmara and the Aegean Sea; eventually, they invaded the Peloponnesus. Although they were successful at first, they would be pushed beyond the Danube by General Priscus in the years 592 and 597. In addition to being defeated, the Slavs were scared off by the Black plague. Unlike most other predatory migrants, they became agriculturists and wanted to gain a foothold in any fertile land they could. When the Byzantine armies became ever less capable of repelling barbarian attacks, the Slavs settled in farming areas which were already occupied and either killed the natives or forced them to vacate villages and towns.

Most affected by this were the Vlachs (from Vlachians or Wallachians) offspring of the Romanized Dacians who lived south of the Danube, since they were forced to accept the unwanted Slavs as lazy and rapacious neighbors. Because they were unable to cross over the mountains where the Vlachian shepherds ruled supreme, the Slavs occupied the lower lands around this area. Soon their settlements, named *sclaviniae*, became major strongholds in Moesia, Illyricum, and Thracia. Since they were not under any sort of imperial control, these settlements were the precursors to Slavic statehood.

The Avars and Slavs continued to challenge the military power of the Byzantine emperors and, by taking advantage of their internal and external crises, they almost captured Greece itself. When Avar domination was vanquished and the Byzantine army was in continuous decline, the Slavs became bolder and more aggressive. John of Ephesus, a contemporary who was not from the Balkans, commented thusly on this new set of conditions:

> Three years after the death of Justin II under Tiberius [i.e., 581] the cursed nation of Slavs campaigned, overran all Hellas, the provinces of Thessaly and all of Thrace, taking many towns and castles, laid waste, burned, pillaged, and seized the country. And dwelt there in full liberty and without fear, as if it belonged to them. This went on for four years, and until the present, because the emperor was involved with the Persian war and the armies were in the east.[4]

Their lands took over in the Balkans of almost Biblical proportions, allowed the numerous of Slavic large groups north of the Danube large water who waited for this migration opportunity, to journey across the river and look southward for an area to permanently settle.

✠

**Bulgars.** Also known as Bulgari, Bolgars, Bolgari and Bolghars, were a mixture of Mongols and Turks with a touch of Ugric (Finnish) blood, and historian Procopius referred to the Bulgarians as "Huns."[5] Most likely because the Proto-Bulgarian tribes who spoke a Turkish dialect, were once part of Attila's invasion of Europe and, implicitly, of the Balkans. Moreover, after Attila's death, these tribes rightly identified themselves as Hunic and temporarily settled between what is today the Kuban region and the Caspian Sea. In time, they took advantage of the Avar evacuation of the land north of the Caspian Sea and the banks of the Volga River, where the equestrian nomad Bulgars occupied many of their abandoned settlements.

Part of them kept riding south, and ended up above the Danube Delta. After they swarmed over southern Ukraine, the tribe of the Kuturgur Hun Bolgars finally settled in today Bessarabia from where they headed toward the Danube into the Byzantine- possessed lands.[6]

Majority of the pagan Bulgars remained west of the middle Volga River, who believed in *Tangra, the Sky Father*, and lived according to the Asiatic habits and horse culture. They were a loose union of tribes, but militarily and social organized enough to establish their *Old Great Bulgaria* between years 630-635. But they were displaced by the Iranian Khazars and pushed south towards the Danube Delta. Under the leadership of their Khan, Asparuh, they cross the Danube River and tried to occupy part of the Dacian Moesia.

When the Bulgars tried to cross south of the Danube, Emperor Constantine IV (r. 668-685) campaigned against them, but an attack of gout kept him from optimally leading his capable army to destroy them. When he retreated, the suffering emperor could never have guessed that he might have altered the fate of the entire Balkan Peninsula. If only he had finished off the Bulgars before it was too late to do so, he would prevent an incredible powerful military alliance between Bulgars, Slavs and the native Vlachs, the Daco-Romans of Dacia Aureliana.

Their unexpected victory over Byzantines, drew the Bulgars into the middle of the Vlach population of Moesia, which was had already been settled by Slavic tribes. The Bulgar warlords wasted no time in gaining control over the loosely organized Slavs. By exploiting the Slavic military power, they developed an alliance that proved to be a formidable menace to the Byzantines.

Mixing with already Slavic settlements, the Bulgars made non-negotiable territorial claims among themselves. This, in turn, forced them to adopt the Slavic language in order to maintain their position of dominance. These two radically different groups shared aspirations of expansion and consolidation. In year 681, they proclaimed the foundation of the *First Bulgarian Empire* under Khan Asparuh, partly on the land of the Byzantine Empire.

It was soon to be recognized by the Byzantine emperor who gifted them with additional territories and an annual tribute in exchange for peace. Like previous invaders, the Bulgars enjoyed the fruits of others' labors and brought with them essentially nothing that would improve life in the Balkans. Countless numbers of natives were massacred or taken captive for ransom, and large numbers fled the blind fury of the barbarian invaders.

The only way for the Byzantine emperors to control them, was to baptize them as Christians and make them obedient to the Orthodox Patriarch from Constantinople. He had the divine power to crown the barbarian chieftains to be officially and spiritually legally recognized. Moreover, these actions set a "submission" trend that would be followed by the next migratory tribe, the Serbs.

**Serbs.** Initially the Serbs were a Turkish people of Iranian extraction. Along with the Serboi (identified by Claudius Ptolemy as being in Sarmatia on the Lower Volga) and Sarban tribes, they had migrated from the Caucasus toward Europe. Traveling possibly farther than any other tribes in search of a new homeland, the Serbs ended up settling throughout the Danubian basin until the sixth century.

At that point they were pushed westward by the Avars; by the 600s they had settled in so-called White Serbia on the Elbe River, only to end up at the confluence of the Danube and Sava rivers. From there they made predatory incursions into the Balkan Peninsula where Emperor Heraclius (r. 610-641), who was unwilling to deal with yet another barbarian threat, granted them a region in western Macedonia that was renamed Serblia. In exchange, he wanted peace with the newly arrived immigrants. But that area was too small for the many Serb tribes who had fought their way back into lower Pannonia and Dardania. These areas were still controlled by the Avars.

In fact, the Dacian legacy was so strong there that the Serbs bore the name Tribalii, another Celtic tribe which had been Dacianized a thousand years earlier. The restless Serbs battled the Slavs who had settled on the Drina River and then moved again towards Dalmatia where they finally established a stronghold named Ras, after the region of Raska (north of today's Albania), and became known as Rascians.

As their population and their power expanded, and as still more tribes moved westward in search of a homeland, the Serbs extended their domination to the area that is today Croatia, Hercegovina, and Montenegro, at the expense of the Slavic tribes already there. By the year 630, they had conquered Singidunum (from Latin, *Segedunum*/ strong fort) and renamed it Beligrad (the White City; later Beograd/ Belgrade). This event put them on the map as permanent barbarian settlers named "Skje" by their Vlach neighbors. A second influx of migratory Serbs and Croats divided this land and its population among themselves; they then had to learn the Slavic language. These new powerful tribal symbioses finally brought the Avars' regional supremacy to an end.

☦

**Croats** were believed to be of Iranian origin, but they may have their origins in a group of Sarmatians who were dislocated by the

Huns. They were unfairly considered Slavs because their good deal of Ostrogothic blood. They found themselves in the midst of a sea of Slaveni in the huge Pripet Marsh area. The Hrvat tribe, with its own distinctive language, was one of the first barbarian groups to establish its own White Croatian domain, named Chrobatia, in the Vistula region, while some Belocroats/White Croats settled north of Bavaria. The Czechs forced many Croatian tribes to migrate across the Carpathians where they were pushed in diverse directions by other barbarian tribes until they eventually found refuge on the Dalmatian coast.

There, most likely, they met up with another branch of the Hrvat tribes who had already settled above and around Ragusa (Dubrovnik) at the beginning of the seventh century. They had been granted that land by Emperor Heraclius on the condition that they fight off the Avars and other invading barbarians. They did just that, and by defeating the Avars, who retreated in 626 from their siege of Constantinople, the Croats earned the right to claim part of Illyricum as their homeland.

**Other Western Slavs:** Bohemia and Moravia were inhabited by the Celts and Germans who in the sixth century were displaced by Slavic tribe of the western Slavs.

The west Slavic tribes were so military powerful that in the year 631 they revolted against the Avars, and led by Samo they established the first Slavic Empire above the Adriatic Sea. A Frank by birth, this merchant valued the military potential of the local tribes and helped them regain their freedom and national identity, which was based on higher values and more ethical standards than that of the other tribes. Only the Great Moravia is left as a sure identification of the Samo Empire.

The **Slovenians** branched out from the original Slavini of Vistula. After being forced in all directions by the eastern and western tribes of Europe they raided the Byzantine provinces up to the border of Greece. In 588, Emperor Maurice (r. 582-602) allowed them to settle on the Dalmatian coast at the north end of the Adriatic Sea. This proved to be one of the best locations from which they could maintain their dominance since it was out of the path of the other chaotic barbarian invasions. Eventually, the Slovenians became allies of convenience with Constantinople where their mercenaries were included in the imperial army. Justinian II was even comfortable with having thirty thousand Slovenians serve as his bodyguard unit, and their language was commonly heard in the Byzantine capital.

Up to this point, the Byzantine emperors had been content to watch one group of troublesome barbarians decimate another and thereby prevent other hordes of Asians from attacking the imperial provinces south of the Danube River. In 635 Kubrat, the Bulgarian chieftain, successfully battled the Avars and further reduced their military power and dominance of southern Dacia and lower Pannonia. As a result, the Bulgars became even stronger. When the emperors found they couldn't win at fighting the Bulgars, they bribed them, and so turned them against the other barbarian tribes who sought an equal (or greater) share of Byzantine riches. Describing Justinian's diplomacy and its effect, Procopius wrote:

> He kept lavishing great sums destined for the state on any Huns he came into contact with; as a result it came about that the land of the Romans was exposed to constant attacks. Once these barbarians had tasted Roman gold they would not any longer keep off the road which led to it[7]

Indeed, no payment was sufficient to satisfy the greed and rapaciousness of the barbarians once they had been exposed to the plentitude of life in Europe. Invasions continued from still other tribes.

✠

**Pechenegs,** who were Turkish tribes from the banks of the Ural River, found themselves pushed (in a sort of domino effect) by successive migratory waves until they settled on the Don River within the Khazars' lands. At the end of the tenth century, adverse circumstances brought them into what was formerly Eastern Dacia. They then forced their way into today's Moldavia and settled there, dominating the area until middle of the twelfth century. Pressure from the much stronger Cumans caused many of the Pecheneg tribes to migrate again and offer their military services to the newly established Magyars along the mid-Danube.

Renamed Besenyos (Eagles) by the Magyars, the aimless Pechenegs persisted in raiding the northern Balkans and even tried to gain ground in Thracia during the reign of Alexius in 1086. They were repulsed and tried again to find a place of their own. They were driven out multiple times by the Cumans who pushed them still farther toward the Black Sea. Since they retained confidence in their might, the Pechenegs invaded the Byzantine Empire one more time. Traveling with full caravans loaded with their families and possessions now their intention was to settle on the Maritza River.

But in 1091 at the Battle of Levounion/Lebunium, the combined armies of the Byzantines, Cumans, and Vlachs delivered a mortal blow to the eighty thousand Pecheneg warriors. Instead of finding a new home they were slaughtered en masse and the civilians were included. The survivors escaped by crossing the Danube and moving into Wallachia where they regrouped with other related tribes. In 1122 they invaded Bulgaria again. History repeated itself and a wholesale massacre occurred this time at Beroia. The Pechenegs never recovered and this marked the end of their threat to any other group in the Balkans. Some of the surviving warriors enlisted in the Byzantine army, but the rest melted into the Bulgar, Hungarian, and Vlachian populations.

✞

**Patzinasks** tribes were related to Pechenegs and both were Turkish barbarians. They continued to migrate westward from Eurasia until they reached the Siret and Danube rivers in Moldavia. From there they carried out savage raids into the Balkans. They were often misnamed Scyths or even Sarmatians because they settled for a while on the land once occupied by those ancient people. Patzinasks were merciless raiders of the Byzantine lands especially during the reign of Isaac I (r. 1057-1059). They specialized in attacking across the frozen Danube. In most invasions they followed the Pechenegs, their stronger partners-in-crime, with whom they shared the same tragic end.

✢

**Cumans** were tribal warriors who originated in Turkish lands and came to Eastern Europe in the eleventh century. For a while, they had a foothold on lands near the Volga River. Unlike other Semitic tribes who had dark skin and eyes, the Cumans were fair skinned, blond, and blue-eyed; this set them apart from other groups and was later a source of puzzlement to historians. They looked and acted like the Scythians, and it is thought by some that they might in fact have been a lost tribe of that ancient people, renamed and forced by the Mongols into former Dacia in 1087. Indeed, their intrusion into the Byzantine Empire impressed Eustathius, Bishop of Thessalonica, based on this conjecture. He wrote in a letter to Emperor Isaac II (r. 1185-1195 and 1203-1204):

> This is the people which is not stationary, and does not stay in one place, or know how to settle down, and therefore it has no institutions. It moves all over the earth and rest nowhere, and is constantly wandering. These are flying men, and hard to catch therefore, and have no cities, and know no villages, but bestially follows in their path. Not even the vultures, that carrion-eating and loathed tribe, can be compared to these people.[8]

The bishop compared their habits of those wolves "bold and greedy, the wolf knows well how to flee whenever something terrifying appears." He concluded that the Scyths/Cumans were "wild beasts among mankind" or "men among wild beasts." [9] In reality the Scyths and Cumans were different tribes and people, as Anna Comnena clearly stated that the "emperor's (her father Alexius I) policy was to make use of the Scyths against Cumans, if the later again approach the the Ister (Danube River) and tried to seize territory beyond it." [10]

In her view the Scyths were the Turkish Patzinaks, much like Pechenegs, not the Cumans, whom Bishop Eustathius confused with each other, as he was most probably describing the Turkish invaders. There is no relationship between those whom the Byzantines called "Scyths" and the ancient Scythians who had melted into the Dacian population long before the Roman invasion.

The Cumans were most certainly predatory barbarians. Once inside Dacia they co-existed peacefully with the local population. Their solid partnership with the Vlachs, who were dispersed throughout the Balkan Peninsula, points to the common language of these two people. Moreover, the arrival of additional Cumans defeated by the Kievan Rus increased their presence in what is today Romania and gave them a certain pre-eminence.

Their unusual peaceful co-existence with the Daco-Romans, especially in Moldavia and Wallachia, lends credence to the speculation that the Cumans were related to them. [11] It is possible that, based on the physical description we are given of them, the Cumans were in fact a group leftover from the Scythian tribes who were close to the Dacians in ancient times. This would explain why they settled in the Dacian lands for almost three centuries and kept migrant tribes of Pechenegs, Bulgars, Magyars, and Slavs at bay.

The Cumans fought valiantly against the invading Mongolian Horde, but in 1238 some of their tribes were defeated and left Transylvania for Hungary. More than forty thousand families settled in the buffer zone between the Danube and Tisza rivers, where an equal number of warriors doubled the strength of King Bela's army as it confronted the fast approaching Golden Horde. Accused of spying for the Tartars,[12] the proud Cumans migrated south of the Danube where they remained until King Bela IV asked them to return to Hungary; at that point, Hungary had been devastated by Mongol invasion. Many other foreign tribes also were invited to repopulate that almost empty country, and the Cumans blended with them until they vanished from the pages of history altogether.

✠

They were proto-Slavic tribes of Goplanz, Lendizi, Polans/Polanians, Vistulans and other non-Eastern Slavs. They occupied the large middle section of upper Europe from the Baltic to the Black seas, extending in today's Moldavia which at that time was Eastern Dacia. According to the Russian *Chronicle of Nestor* [13] (850 to 110), their large territories were known as Lechia. Their southern Danube borders were pushed back to the Vistula River by the Volochi, the Russian name for the Vlachs/Wallachians.

✠

**Ukrainians and Russians** were nonexistent in ancient Eurasia; there was no Russian or Ukrainian population—only the super tribes of Scythians and Sarmatians with their uniquely non-Slavic culture and religion. The Ukrainians descended from a combination of Sarmatians, Scandinavians, Scythians, and Antes, a subgroup of the Alani and maybe also of the Venedi super tribes. Each migratory group that arrived from Euroasia flooded their lands, which were located on the last leg of the Danube River and its Delta. Because it was the largest gate to cross into the Balkan Peninsula and the Byzantine Empire, a great deal of the blood of Avars, Goths, Huns, and Magyars must course through the veins of the modern Ukrainians.

However, most important for the earlier Russian and Ukrainian settlements were the Scandinavian traders, known as Wiking or "sea warriors," and the Rus/Russes or "rowers" of long boats, used first as their trade mark recognition.

People of large body frames, blond and blue eyes, natives of the Scandinavian Peninsula, mainly where Sweden is located today, they were wild pagans who believed in Odin and Thor, the Vikings were raised in warrior's culture of heroism, happy to die in battles, for they would go to their heaven in Valhalla.

By the eight century they discovered during their river trading trips that it was more rewarding and they acquired better goods by plundering the rich inland settlements even if they had to murder the resisting owners. Quickly, the Vikings became famous for their cruelty as they began by rowing their flat bottomed boats to trade inland in Northern Europe. Yet, by building bigger boats with a keel and by adding a large sail, they could cruise along the seashores of Western Europe. They savagely raided peaceful but wealthy settlements, towns, and their churches and monasteries along the coast of Britain.

Under Ivar, a self-proclaimed king, the Vikings succeeded to establish two large colonies in southern Britain, where they influenced the local Anglo-Saxon language, while the locals succeeded to Christianize the pagan Vikings. Nevertheless, the mention of the name Viking was enough to scare to death all European people living within the reach of these merciless predators.

However, rowing on the Ladoga Lake, they discovered a large and well to do trading post which was being run by the Eastern Slavs. Their tribes lined the banks of the Volkhov River where they made a living selling quality furs from the animals they hunted. All furs for sale ended up in Staraya Ladoga, which the Vikings took ownership of, and it then became the capital of the region.

By rowing south on the Volkhov River, these Norsemen of Scandinavia discovered another prosperous trading center which was named Novgorod (New City). Because it was the main location for the exports to the Byzantine Empire handled by the Greeks, this area became so prosperous that it attracted many Vikings and their families to populate this river bonanza known as the Varangian route. Those Vikings entered the local history as the Ruse, the original short rowers' name which was easy to pronounce and they claim enough land to have their Rosland which included Kiev and Novgorod.

The same trading development of furs, precious stones, silver and gold took place on the river named Moscovia by the Vikings/Ruse. It was the same name as the river which flowed into the commercial town. Later, both were made to be Russian like as Moskva/Moscow, the capital of Russia which was named from the Ruse name.

Similar patterns were applied by the Ruse navigators to Kiev Ruse located on the Dnieper River. The Viking traders were rowing their flat bottom boats on most of the rivers between the great rivers of Don and Volga. This area was inhabited by those Slavic tribes of the Drevlian, Polesie, Severyans, and the Polian mega-tribes, all were horse-breeding people who spoke a common Slavic language. They settled around what is now Kiev, and despite their vast numbers they relied on the Cuman and Pecheneg as allies. The early Eastern Slavs who did not migrate were the ancient reservoir for the Russians, Belarusians and the Ukrainians.

As for the Vikings moving into the continental Russia in large numbers to dominate its fur, mineral market and slave trades with the Arab world, they became the dominant commercial and military power of it. Those Vikings became so strong that in the year 860 they sailed with 200 large ships into the Black Sea and attacked Constantinople with 10,000 warriors. With no chance to assault the towering walls of the city they accepted defeat. But, they carried out retaliatory pillages, which decimated the suburbs of the Byzantine capital. Their incredible ferocious raids attracted the attention of the Byzantine emperors and for the next one hundred years they hired the Viking-Varangians (living south of the Ladoga Lake) as their storm troopers.

Basil II the Bulgar-slayer used 6,000 Vikings in 988 to win a civil war, and impressed by their heroism in battles, devotion, integrity and loyalty, plus with their imposing good and powerful looks, the emperor decided to recruit them for his personal praetorian guards that he could trust. He disregarded the Greek or European mercenaries were easier to bribe and change loyalty to the best bidder for the throne. Basil's proven example was followed by all Byzantine emperors and they hired the distant Varangians to be their Imperial Guard for the next 300 years.

✠

**Magyar** is the westernized name of the Fino-Ugric/Ugrian speaking tribes of Modjars/Megyeri/Mogeri, a non-Indo-European people, speaking a Uralian language. They were the forefathers of the Hungarians and were referred to as Ogors/Ugrs and Onogurs, (meaning Ten Arrows or Ten tribes). They are known to have slowly migrated from the region of the Oka River and across the Ural Mountains to the steppes east of the Volga River.

There they formed the loosely organized settlement of Levedia at the end of the ninth century. The Pechenegs forced them west of the Dnieper where they formed another temporary settlement under the control of the Khazars and Pechenegs. They were unable to co-exist with any outside authority. The homeless Magyars led by their elected chieftain Arpad entered the Lower Danube looking for easy looting. For a short time in 895 they settled in what today is Bessarabia (Dacian and Romanian land).

When in 796 Charlemagne conquered the Avar Empire in Pannonia he had never heard of Magyars or Hungarians. At that time they were settled in their own Levedia between the Volga and Don rivers and 1,500 miles/2,400 kilometers away from Pannonia. Magyars were constantly being pushed westward by other invading barbarians such as the Bulgars. They were forced to cross above the mountainous area of Dacia.

In 896 the Magyars settled with their families and horses in the hospitable pastures west of the Tisza River, the western border of

Transylvania. By that time, their leader Arpad (r. 895-907) of the Onogur tribes succeeded in uniting most of the Proto-Hungarian hordes into a tribal federation.

Desperate for plunder and more grass land, these excellent pagan horsemen invaded the Danubian Bulgarian Empire, but were thoroughly defeated. The Magyars regrouped in Pannonia to restore their military power. In 906, the Magyars attacked the Moravian princedom where their destructive rampaging put an end to that Christian state.

Next the Magyars who were suffering from famine tried to settle in Slovakia. Arpad then led them back to eastern Pannonia, which at that point was occupied by the Bulgars and Pechenegs. After a violent struggle they reclaimed part of the "liberated" Pannonia as their homeland.

From then on the Latins collectively called them Hungarus. This was clearly a name for the future country of Hungaria/Hungary. Part of this Hungarian coalition was the *Szekely*, an uprooted Scythian tribe who interbred with the Avars and other Mongolian invaders. They eventually joined the Magyars in their journey of killing and pillaging throughout Eastern Europe. The Szekely founded their own settlement along the Tisza River, while the Slavs of Pannonia migrated farther westward and settled in what is today Slovenia.

The Magyars continued their predatory missions and succeeded in forcing the Byzantine Emperor Leo VI the Wise who was more of a scholar (he wrote 60 books) than a soldier. He agreed to pay them tribute after bribing them to attack the Bulgarians. Raiding westward, the Magyars sacked Basel in 917; they also burned Bremen and then invaded Bavaria and Burgundy, cutting an immense swath of destruction wherever they went. Their chain of aggressive actions even extended as far west as the present-day Holland. Ridding south, they tried to advance into Lower Panonia, but the Magyars where suddenly defeated by the Croatian army led by King Tomislav in 925. His army was so strong, that he annexed part of Pannonia and

Dalmatia into the Kingdom of Croatia which was founded in the same year.

Again in 955 the Germans of Otto I pulverized the Magyar hordes in the Battle of Lechfeld and forced them back into their part of Pannonia. However, a large segment of the Magyar population was left behind between the Caspian and Black seas as vassals of the Khazars. When the Russians defeated the Khazars in 965, the Magyars (many of whom had adopted Judaism) migrated west of the Tisza River and settled among other Magyars.

Since they were people of an equestrian culture, the primitively armed Magyars could not battle the armies of the heavily armored knights. Later, they were at last able to put a stop to the savage raids on the West. The Magyars then turned toward Transylvania which was well defended by its Cuman settlers. Thus, the vacant and undisputed Pannonia became the site of the Hungarians' permanent yet chaotic settlement. Their population at that time was about 60,000 of which some 20,000 were predatory horsemen.

Bishop Otto of Freysing spoke of the Hungarians as "ferocious" at the time of the crusades:

> Their eyes are sunken, their stature is short, their behavior wild, their language barbarous, so that one can either accuse fate or marvel at divine patience for having permitted these monsters the possession of an enchanting land.[14]

The Magyar pseudo-settlements required serious enforcement of societal rules. The Hungarian kings of the twelfth century invited the Germans to migrate to the area along the Transylvanian border, one that was too often transgressed by the Cumans and other barbarians. The Szekely tribes, who were trustworthy as frontier guards were not strong enough for the task. The German Saxons joined the Szekely (whom they called Szekler), and for a time fulfilled their military obligation. But, encouraged by the Cumans to abandon their assigned duties the Szekely began to inch their way into the new land of

Siebenbürgen in Transylvania.

During the next century, a second migratory wave of Germans coming from as far away as Bavaria settled on the Carpathian border with Moldavia and Wallachia. There they established large and prosperous settlements that soon grew into strong, fortified communities in the heart of what would later be named the Romanian principalities. The Romanians called the Szekely "Secui" (from the Latin *Seculi*) and the Saxons "Sasi/Sashi." The latter opened a corridor through Hungary to the Holy Roman Empire and the rest of Western Europe. Many Magyars used it to leave the barren Hungarian steppe to settle in the immensely rich Transylvania.

In time, cities came to carry dual names in German and Hungarian, such as Brasov/Kronstadt/Brasso, Cluj/Klausenburg/Kolozsvar, and Sibiu/Hermanmstadt/Nagyszeben. All were built upon the original Dacian foundations as they had been upgraded by the Cumans. These settlements proved to be so sheltered from the stormy military and political events of the rest of Europe that Hungarians who immigrated to the area came to believe Transylvania was their real homeland.

✠

**Turks** were also intensely colonized the Byzantine Empire. After the end of the White Hun Empire (420-552) in the Far East, they approached the Balkans, but unlike other invaders, they arrived from the opposite side of the peninsula. The loosely organized tribes of Turks became part of the Seljuk State and converted to Islam. Doing so gave them a religious identity and united them militarily. The name "Turk" meant "strong" in their earlier language, and the tribes that migrated into Anatolia (ancient Phrygia), proved to be just that.

Named "Turci" by the Byzantines, they inflicted a decisive defeat on the imperial army in 1071 at Mazikert (Malazgirt) and enjoyed a similar victory in 1176 near Denizli. After this point, the Byzantine control of Anatolia was practically eliminated. Despite the fact that the Mongol invasion essentially ended the Seljuk Empire, a capable ruler, Osman I, put the rivalry among Turkish tribes to good use by redirecting their military might. This enabled him to extend the borders of his new state to the Strait of the Bosphorus across from Constantinople.

In the year 1362, an Ottoman army led by sultan Murad I invaded the European Trace and conquered the important city of Adrianople (named after the Roman Emperor Hadrian) and renamed Edirne, soon to become the European capital of the Ottoman Empire. They were located only a few miles from the Bulgarian and Greek borders, and this victory gave the Turks their first official foothold in the Balkans. This achievement had important ramifications for the future of Eastern Europe.

It led to more conquests, and the Turks extended their suzerainty into Bulgaria and thus, permanently settled in the Byzantine Empire. The Turks had no moral or ethical doubts about taking over the Balkan lands since the Ionians of Anatolia and the Hellenes of Greece had expanded across two continents. This, too, was the situation with the Thracian tribes who had lived for two thousand years on both sides of the Bosporus. An interest in migration seems to have been in the Turkish blood; settlement, however, was an Ottoman policy.

✟

**Gypsies and Jews** were two other migratory peoples who also came to Eastern Europe, they did not impose themselves on existing settlements with the sword, but rather by providing help to the host societies with their skills. They became an international people with a marked ability to survive. They never constituted a nation; nor did they have a homeland anywhere else in Europe or in the world.

While the Gypsies were considered barbarians because of their heritage and unique behaviors, the Jews were acknowledged for spreading civilization through trade, for their dedication to scholarly work and gaining respect and prestige as the people of the Old Testament. Nevertheless, both groups of people stood apart from the rest of the population in the Balkans, because of their looks and even their clothing was different from those of the other ethnic groups.

Gypsies (believed they came from Egypt, also known as Tsygani) arrived later in the Balkan Peninsula. They were brought there from the Afghan-Persian Empire by the Ottomans in the fourteenth century as blacksmiths and toolmakers for their armies. These dark-skinned nomads with Indian features spoke a Hindu related language that originated from the Baluchistan region. They became extremely important to the Turkish army when it began to rely on firearms, including the cannon. The Gypsy caravans with their iron workers and portable forges were essential to servicing the new weapons.

After the fall of Constantinople in 1453, the Ottoman expansion into the Balkan Peninsula brought with it the Gypsy camps and the Gypsies were introduced into the occupied territories as part of the garrisoned troops. Vlad Dracula had the distinction of bringing them north of the Danube into his Wallachian Princedom because he wanted to use artillery and other firearms in his campaigns. Because they were skilled as coppersmiths, tinsmiths, and jewelry makers, the Gypsies soon left their military camps and drifted into civilian life where their skills were more in demand. They also became renowned as fortune tellers and performers of witchcraft, but most of all as talented musicians.

Nomadic by nature, they did not assimilate into any mainstream population and tended to adopt the host ethnicities from which they borrowed words for their vocabulary. They were not allowed to own land and so drifted on the fringes of communities and ended up in almost every nation of Eastern Europe, forming their own small land patches of "Tsygania." They were often accused of thievery, creating bad omens, and other illegal practices, and so developed a mixed reputation which still accompanies them now.

✢

The Jewish Diaspora in Europe began with the Roman occupation and destruction of Jerusalem in the year 70. The Jewish presence in Western Europe would increase dramatically as international trade became a vital necessity. The Hebrew language, religion, diet, and practice of circumcision separated the Jews from the Christian population, and they lived in tightly knit communities apart from the goyim/gentile world. As early as the seventh century, Jews played an important role in the trade carried on by the Byzantine Empire. Jewish settlers of the ninth and tenth centuries found there a welcoming land in which to apply their expensive mercantile skills. Their prosperity attracted new waves of Jewish migrants. They were also keen to identify the demands of the local population and became known for lending money to princes and kings who were always in need of it for their wars. These skills allowed the Jews to extend their shtettles/ settlements to every corner of the Balkans, but it was the land closer to the West, such as Dalmatia, Bohemia, Hungary, and Poland, that most attracted them. Later, the crusaders brought more Jews south of the Danube River, and they settled in the major cities of the Byzantine Empire.

The first major Jewish influx into the Balkans followed their expulsion from Western Europe in the thirteenth and fourteenth centuries, the same time as the Ashkenazi Jews migrated to Eastern Europe. Their artisanship in the making of beautiful dresses and jewelry and their craftsmanship in producing utilitarian goods were complimented by their skill at peddling and money lending. This economic and diplomatic proficiency had a strong impact on other less sophisticated settlers. Given that they had virtually no serious competition (except for the Armenians and Greeks), the Jews prospered so greatly in the Balkans that they attracted the envy of the other non-Jewish people.

The result was pogroms and royal decrees to stop "the killers of Christ" from occupying top administrative positions that were sold to the highest bidder. However, Bulgarian and Romanian principalities continually provided safe havens for Jews who would flee social and political threats and prosecution, but would leave when circumstances were favorable.

✣

In conclusion, happy people do not migrate. Hungry and uprooted people with nothing to lose are willing to take risks and look elsewhere for a better place to live even at the expense of others. This is what happened in the space of five hundred years. Each barbarian incursion created a chain of violent incidents in Eastern Europe that transformed farmlands into blood-soaked fields and reduced prosperous cities to ghostly ruins. The bellicose Avars wanted only to participate in the next act of pillage and plunder and return to their camps. The more pastorally inclined Slavs sought land and wanted recognition of their settlements.

In the course of this lengthy and brutal tidal shift in the locations of various peoples, migratory families came to be clans of blood relatives. They in turn belonged to ethnic tribes which had merged into larger tribal formations defined by race. Eventually local tribes came to form super-tribes, and these in turn were united into a tribal coalition.

In summary, these vast and diverse hordes of people evolved into tribal confederations, leagues, states, and eventually nations. All of them were being greatly influenced by the native populations. The latter were most often culturally and religiously advanced, and therefore they civilized the incoming pagan invaders. These numerous and ongoing clashes eventually produced a new genetic fabric of nascent nations. All of them shared a barbarian-Byzantine heritage that transcended the ethnic and state borders of the Balkan Peninsula, and the lands beyond it.

# REFERENCE NOTES

1. Today, archeologists and historians trace these vanished settlements by the cemeteries they left behind. Needless to say it is a confusing task to separate invaders from aboriginals. In the future DNA testing may solve many demographic mysteries. It could potentially affect what we presently take to be the history of this region.
2. Anna Comnena, *The Alexiad of Anna Comnena*, trans. E. R. A. Sewter (London: Penguin Books, 1969), 309.
3. Procopius, *History of the Wars: Secret History and Buildings*, ed. H. R. Trever-Roper (New York: Washington Square Press, 1967), 327.
4. John V. A. Fine, *The Early Medieval Balkans: A Critical Survey from the Sixth to the Late Twelfth Century* (Ann Arbor: University of Michigan Press, 1991), 31.
5. Robert L. Wolf wrote about "the Hunic tribes of the Bulgars" being assimilated by the Slavs. Jonathan Shepard, ed., *The Expansion of Orthodox Europe: Byzantium, the Balkans and Russia* (Burlington, VT: Ashgate Publishing, 2007), 168.
6. It is believed that Bulgars raided Macedonia and Thracia in 517, but this may have been done by the Gepids, Ostrogoths, or even the Huns or other tribes. In any case, the Slavs were in full rampage in the Byzantine lands.
7. Procopius, *History*, 301.
8. Robert L. Wolff, "The Second Bulgarian Empire': Its Origin and History to 1204," in *The Expansion of Latin Europe, 1000-1500*, ed. Jonathan Shepard, (Burlington, VT: Ashgate Publishing, 2007), 267.
9. Wolff, "*The Second Bulgarian Empire*," 267.
10. Comnena, *The Alexiad*, 230.

11. Anna Comnena referred to their main weapon as sickle/scythe also used to reap the harvest (this fact caused them to be confused with the tribes of Scyths). It is a weapon that strikingly resembles the Dacian curved scimitar, a coincidence that puts the Cumans and Dacians together as a common enemy of the Byzantines.
12. The real story is that Hungarians captured an enemy who turned out to be a Cuman warrior. He had previously been captured by the invading Tartars and forced into their ranks. Claiming treason, King Bela ordered his soldiers to massacre the Cuman king and his court who were seeking refuge in Hungary. The outraged and humiliated Cumans moved out of Hungary, leaving a trail of destruction behind them. The departure of its only ally further weakened the Hungarian armed resistance against the Golden Horde which at that time had already reached the city of Pest on the Danube. The Tartars faked a retreat and then ambushed the Hungarian army and utterly destroyed it. King Bela "heroically" escaped the slaughter with a small band of men. The only heroic deed left for the decimated Hungarians was to try to break the ice bridge of the Danube so that the Tartars could not cross into their capital. What saved the Hungarians and their country from being wiped off the face of the map was the death of the Mongol emperor. This prompted Batu Khan to lead his Tartars back to Asia in the hope of seizing the vacant throne. Before leaving, he ordered the execution of all captured Hungarians who would otherwise slow down the speed of the Golden Horde. As for Bela IV, he returned humiliated and penniless to Hungary.
13. Indeed, early Romanian historical records referred to the Polish people as the Leși/Leshi, a name they obviously knew and related to. As for the Sarmatian blood infused into the Polish nation, it later became a major issue for the Poles who tried to copy the Sarmatian look, from wearing similar clothing to sporting the famous drooping moustache. Their aim was to disassociate themselves from the Slavs of Ukraine and Russia.

14. Emil Lengyel, *1,000 Years of Hungary* (New York: John Day, 1958), 21.

## III

## FROM TRIBES TO COUNTRY

Empires colonized barbarian lands until the early Middle Ages when a reversal took place and the barbarians began to colonize empires, specifically the Byzantine Empire. The barbarians had no concept of country or nationality when they first reached Europe. The most they had achieved by way of social organization was to be part of a clan or a tribe with a common language and religion, similar habits, and common enemies. They had no respect for written documents or treaties, including those made among themselves. They fought against each other over anything, including the plunder obtained through victory.

At first, they viewed occupied land as a disposable possession since most of it was the vast, empty, and dusty pusztas of the Eastern European wilderness. However, after they entered the Roman Empire, they quickly realized the value of the alien land they had seized, and their deadly raids of plunder and pillage became a full-time occupation. They had to fight and conquer in order to have access to food and supplies because they had no other source to sustain themselves and their families. Their migration was not aimed at working occupied land or rebuilding ruined settlements; rather, they sought bring back to their encampments as much loot as possible and to extort long-term tributes from the natives.

Since the time of the earlier massive invasion of the Goths and Huns, any barbarian presence in the Balkan Peninsula was regarded as alien to the Byzantine world and therefore equivalent to a human plague. The word "barbarian" was used to describe someone who spoke a "barabara" language, had one single name, wore fur and he was always dirty, savagely violent, and always ready to kill.

Nothing good could be expected from them, so, by definition, they were the enemy. This belief was reinforced when new hordes approached the populated and prosperous Danubian lands, looting them and dragging captives to their encampments in the wilderness. But leaving and returning to home base was exhausting for the warriors and their horses.

The raiders began to bring their families with them, and whole caravans approached the lands they pillaged. Before long, they recognized the expediency of permanently occupying those lands, and, after struggling through famines, they also realized that instead of killing the productive natives, they could make use of them. Slowly but steadily, the primitive barbarians who had never had a homeland became land hungry while at the same time they became aware of a culture they could try to copy in order to improve their lives.

Soon, they understood why settlements had been located on commercial routes and why strategic military posts had become fortified towns. These attracted skilled laborers within their walls and placed farmers outside of them. They observed that villages were built in clusters on large estates anchored by a manor or a castle. Their headmen recognized that this resulted in a functional economy based on a clearly ordered social system. It had a military chain of command to defend it.

Therefore, by the power of example, permanent settlements were established on the assumption that a larger tribe had a better chance of survival. A tribal union offered greater mutual protection and ensured more effective military action. Additionally, the idea of possessing some sort of stronghold led to the idea of chiefdom. The concept of statehood with its tribal borders and an empiric government was in the making.

✢

Any nation needs land it calls its own, and in the Balkans this meant Byzantine soil that was already occupied by ancient natives like the Greeks, Ilyrians, Macedonians, Daco-Vlachs, who never migrated anywhere, because happy people do not move from their lands. Yet, they became the subjects of Constantinople. In contrast, the barbarian nomads kept migrating all the time, looking to find a better life some other place. After they temporarily settled in the Byzantine Empire, with one skill to offer which was to fight and kill regardless of the reason. In fact, that brutal skill was for hiring for the higher bidder who could also be hired to fight off other incoming tribes. They had no concept of sins or of guilt.

With that offer in mind, Emperor Michael II used the Bulgar Khan Omurtag to crush a Slav revolt in 823; in exchange the barbarian leader was allowed to stamp his own coin with the Byzantine seal.

But, as typically happened when benevolent emperors granted favors to the barbarians, the outcome was not the civilized response that was expected. They tried in vain to make the barbarian settlers obey imperial decrees and pay taxes. Simply put, the barbarians had no concept of law and order. The fact that one Slavic tribe agreed to respect a signed treaty meant nothing to the rest of the nomadic tribes who acted independently with disregard to any agreed upon pact. Nor, did the written treaty mean much to the tribe that had signed it.

Still, the Roman legacy and the dynastic Byzantine social order kept the empire militarily strong and economically solid. This imposed the respect of the barbarian leaders who came to seek the same status and prestige among their tribesmen. Above all else, the pagan chieftains, who were also the chief priests, often wanted their people to be baptized because a Christianized mob was easier to control and more likely to establish permanent roots in the Balkans.

The new religion was an enormous stabilizing force in the lives of the convert barbarians. It was necessary in order that they be perceived as legitimate and given a spot on the map in contrast to their merely looming threateningly on the European horizon in dusty and hungry hordes.

A distorted sense of civility and honor developed among those of the new settlers who decided to take over the homeland of others and set down roots. They had many capable leaders, but it was only when the royal throne and crown were handed to them by the Byzantine emperors that they became legal heads of an official state. This fact alone allowed the ungoverned barbarians to finally establish a place for themselves, often on land claimed by more than one tribe or group of people. Stable communities led to a growing power that also fertilized seeds of violence among the greedy owners.

The Gepids and Avars never took this crucial step to permanently settle their differences despite their success in occupying land in Dacia and Pannonia during the sixth century and establishing their own primitive kingdom. Their Gepidia came to an abrupt end with the invasion of the Avars and Lombards in 567. The mighty Avars then extended their holdings from the Volga region to Pannonia. Because they were strong and much feared in the beginning by the Byzantine emperors, who paid them a heavy subsidy to stay away, the Avars proved to be savagely vengeful when their terms were not met.

After their failed attack on Constantinople in 599, they took more than twelve thousand Byzantine captives and butchered them when Emperor Maurice refused to pay a ransom for them. However, infighting among the Avar chieftains and numerous military collisions with the German Franks brought the Avar Empire to an end in 796. To avoid total annihilation they simply fled their heavily fortified capital at Rhing, and the once mighty Avaria vanished forever from the map of Europe.

The Slavs met with a different fate when it came to building a state that would endure over time. Their initial invasions were to reduce Roman landmarks to heaps of ruins. However, because it was in the Slavic character to be beholden to authority, the Slavs were easily exploited by the Avars, who forced them to cooperate on their devastating incursions into new various areas within the Byzantine Empire. The result was that countless tribes of Slavs were abandoned on the pastoral lands of Dacian Moesia, Macedonia, Thracia, and other imperial provinces.

Their societies were tribal democracies with no classes and ranks. Captured prisoners were not enslaved, but sold for ransom and eventually freed to work on and enlarge the Slavic settlements. In time, their chieftains and war heroes emerged as the tribal elite. They retained the habits they had when living on the steppes, but now they aspired to be rulers of lands newly acquired from people who possessed a superior culture and civilization.

Exhausted from their centuries of wandering, the Slavs continued to search for a place of their own. There is relatively little documentation of this, but one source from this period, Isadore of Seville, a bishop and the last historian of the ancient world, states that in the fifth year of Heraclius (i.e., 615) the Slavs took Greece from the Romans…the Slavs occupy all Epirus, most of all of Hellas, the Peloponnesus, and Macedonia…The Chronicle of Monemvasia dates the Slavic settlement of the Peloponnesus from 587…[1]

Because of all these regional takeovers, the Slavs established their own territory about which "Patriarch Nicholas III of Constantinople, writing in the late eleventh century, also states that, for 218 years (from 589 to 807) there were no Byzantine officials in the Peloponnesus."[2] One might wonder if those who occupied these Greek lands were the Vlachs who did indeed populate those areas and still do, but were erroneously named Bulgars and Slavs.[3]

All these demographic shifts happened because the Bulgars/Bulgarians were forced out of Great Bulgaria above the Sea of

Azov by other migrant barbarians and settled for a while in southern Bessarabia (today's Republic of Moldova). Pressed still farther by Avars and Slavs, they ended up south of the Danube, where they formed another tribal league in the year 632. The main area in which these proto-Bulgarian tribes were concentrated covered a huge loosely defined territory between the Volga and the Dniester rivers.

Yet another Bulgar state with its main territory in former Dacian Moesia was created when related tribes were led in battle by Asperuch/Asparuch (r. 680-702) to dominate lands from the Dnieper River to south of the Danube Delta. The Bulgars delivered such devastating attacks on Byzantium that Constantinople was forced to recognize this Slavic state in 681. It was initially, and pompously, called the First Bulgarian Empire (ending in 1018). It was held together militarily by the Slavic language, a tongue that became common to both the Bulgars and the Slavs.

The Bulgars conquered Serdica (Sofia) in 809, but established their capital at Pliska. It was almost destroyed by the Byzantines in 811, but it was subsequently revived and enlarged as a fortified city by Khan/Prince Krum (r. 803-814). This savage ruler, who drank from the skull of Emperor Nicephorus whom he killed in battle, also proved to be also something of a visionary. As he issued strict laws to protect the poor and to punish any form of debauchery among his subjects. His firm grip on Bulgarian society and the Bulgarian military helped him double the size of his empire by extending it north of the coast of the Black Sea to the Adriatic Sea.

Khan Boris I (r. 852-889) however was the real founder of the Bulgarian state. After receiving baptism he changed his title and name to Knyaz/Czar (Caesar) Michael. He then converted his mixed-race nation from paganism to Christianity. With the new Cyrillic alphabet, which could accommodate Slavic sounds, Bulgaria became a permanent reality. These Bulgarians were different from those who lived in the Volga Bulgar emirate with its capital at Bolgar. The latter adopted Islam and were decimated by the Golden Horde in 1238.

The Serbs/Serbians underwent the same process of Slavicization as did the Bulgarians, but their society was more advanced. It was led by zupans/leaders united for the first time in 825 by a warlord named Vlastimir. He acted as their common ruler and founded the Serbian confederation of Rascia (Northern Montenegro), Trebounia (eastern Herzegovina), and Konvali (southeast of Croatia), thus establishing his own dynasty and creating a tribal homeland for his people.

His oldest son, Mutimir, succeeded him and consolidated this imperial Serb state. Its level of culture was elevated when Christianity was adopted there. The absorption of the Bulgar Empire into the Byzantine Empire in 1185 and its subsequent dissolution were followed by the meteoric rise and rule of Stefan Nemanja (r. 1166-1196). He used Orthodox Christianity to extend his empire between what is now southern Serbia and Montenegro/Zeta, eastern Bosnia, and Herzegovina/Pagania, as far as the southern coast of Croatia.

This ruthless and opportunistic Grand Prince Nemanja then declared his state independent of Constantinople and founded his own dynasty, a historic act that kept the Serbian state alive. It was followed by the Serbian Empire of Stefan Dusan (r. 1346-1355), one of the largest states of Europe at that time and one that reflected the giant size of its handsome emperor, literally the tallest man of his era. The legacy of this empire was, however, one of vast ethnic unrest. The nations that once belonged to the Serbian Empire, unhappily situated between Bulgars, Byzantines, and Hungarians, would find themselves at war with each other in the future.

The Croatians were greatly affected by the unstoppable barbarian invasions into their area of the Balkans. In the seventh century, they were located between the south of Poland and Bavaria in their own Chrobatia (White Croatia). The Czech invasion resulted in a parallel Croatian state that covered those areas which today make up the regions of Bosnia, Croatia, Dalmatia, Serbia, and Slovenia. The Croats proved to be constructive occupiers who created a well ordered society and had a clear concept of how to administer their zupe/counties on the beautiful Dalmatian coast. There they established their own state with its capital in Biograd (White City).

Their economic and social laws were enforced upon any and all new arrivals, and the Croats proved disciplined and industrious. They possessed advanced farming techniques, metal working skills, and elaborate systems of commerce. Their military power was impressive: King Tomislav (r. 910-928) succeeded in building an army of 160,000 foot soldiers and cavalrymen along with a fleet of 180 ships.

In 926, he successfully defeated Czar Simeon I who was forced to retreat with his invading Bulgarian army. Even the Venetian ships dutifully paid taxes to the new state when they traveled along the Croatian coast. At this point in time, Croatia ruled Bosnia, costal Montenegro, Pannonian Croatian, and half of the eastern islands of the Adriatic Sea. These were rarely raided by the barbarians. Although they were formally under the authority of Constantinople, the Croatians promptly established better political and religious connections with Western Europe rather than with the Byzantine Empire.

Pope Alexander III honored them with a visit in 1177, and the people of Zadar greeted him with songs in the Croat language. It was described by the Italian chronicler Baronius as *eorum Sclavica lingua*, a form of slang that became very popular in Constantinople.

From 1102 onward, the Croats and Hungarians shared a newly built state under common Hungarian and Croatian Kings. The kings were crowned twice, once with the Hungarian crown and once with the Croatian crown, thereby confirming their independence from the Byzantine Empire. The Hungarian menace threatened Bosnia and Hum/Herzegovina, partially Catholic and partially Orthodox, whose populations of this two-part empire would undergo dramatic changes after the Turkish occupation in 1463.

✝

Other Western Slavs were united by various supreme chieftains and their lands covered what are today Austria, Czechia, Slovakia, and Slovenia. Most of the tribes of Wends after 658 were scattered by the Avars however the Slovenes remained in their safe corner of Carniola, northeast of Venice. The principality of Carantia (Karantanija) eventually emerged from this land, and in 771 it was included in the Frankish Empire. The Czechs and Slovakians were pushed north by the Magyar invasion of Pannonia and formed the principality of Nitrave (Nitra) and, later that of Carniola (Krajina) which sheltered the two major tribes. After 830 all of these incipient states were included in the Great Moravian Empire of Prince Mojmir. The Magyars annihilated the Moravian army in 907, when the empire ceased to exist.

✠

The Cumans persisted by creating their own Terter dynasty (1280-1322) their two czars, who extended the borders of Bulgaria were heavily involved in Byzantine affairs. The resourceful Cumans settled in Wallachia and Moldavia (part of former Dacia), where they founded their second Cumania, a strong military base that was instrumental in creating the Second Bulgarian Empire (1187-1280,) referred to by Pope Gregory IX as Blachorum et Bulgarorum (of the Vlachs and Bulgars).

It was led by the Vlach dynasty of the Asans. When this dynasty collapsed, Bulgaria became subject to the Byzantines, Serbs, and Mongols. However, north of the Danube the main land of Wallachia like its sister province of Moldavia, was a principality that suffered little political interference from the Cumans. Instead, it acted as their protector.

The Cumans also founded the Basarab dynasty (1310 -1529) in Wallachia. It retained its independence after the Wallahians (the future Romanians) defeated the invading Hungarian army of 30,000 at Posada in 1330. Some thirty years later, Moldavia under Bogdan I also regained its freedom from the Crown of Hungary. Transylvania, the cradle of the Daco-Roman civilization, shared the Cuman's protection against the Magyar intrusions into the Carpathians. The legacy of Cumans as state-makers vanished as they were without a state of their own.[4]

The invasion of the Golden Horde in 1241 undid the power of the Cumans. This attack paled in comparison to the apocalyptic onslaught of the Hungarians who were, in fact, in no position to impose their will on Transylvania, the land of the ancient Dacians.

✢

After the Mongolian tsunami, Hungary's new king was Kun Laszlo/Ladislas IV (r. 1272-1290). His name Kun identified him as a Cuman on his mother's side. He lived like a Cuman with his Cuman entourage in the city of Buda, fleeing from there to Transylvania when any threat presented itself. Because of him, the Cumans felt at home in Hungary where they lived in the regions of Greater and Lesser Cumania. Many Hungarians reciprocated the welcome by relocating to Transylvania. As in previous centuries, Transylvania's rich gold and silver mines proved to be an irresistible magnet for migrants from a poor country. The Catholic Church included Hungary in the Diocese of Cumania with its seat at Milcov in Wallachia. Since the fourth century the Vatican eagerly tried to convert the pagan Cumans, and eventually the Eastern Orthodox Romanians.

✢

Almost every migratory wave from Asia passed through the vast steppes of what was the Southern Russia, making it impossible for any state to establish firm borders there. There was therefore no Ukrainian state in the year 882 when Rus Prince Olaf/Oleg came from Novgorod and took control of many of the docile Slavic tribes there. They were to become his tributary vassals. He used their military power to wrest the city of Kiev from his fellow Scandinavians. As prince of Kiev (r. 882-912), he was instrumental in establishing the Kievan Rus state together with his proto-Russian subjects. He used their fighting power to force Constantinople to negotiate with him. By doing so, he coerced Emperor Leo VI (r. 895- 908) to recognize his Slavic kingdom as an equal commercial partner, putting his state on the map of Eastern Europe. Prince Ingvar/Igor (r. 912-945), also a Varangian, continued the work of consolidating the state by allying himself with the Pechenegs. He then conducted further attacks on Constantinople in 941 and 944. He died trying to collect tribute from the Drevlian tribes included in his confederation.

His widow Princess Olha/Helga/Olga (r. 945-962) took over his reign. She became famous for slaughtering or burning five thousand Drevlians alive to avenge her husband's death, as well as for baptizing herself in the Orthodox faith. Olga was the first Rus to be sanctified. Her name became synonymous with "Holy."("H" did not exist in the Russian vocabulary, and it was replaced mostly with the letter "G.")

Christianity was imposed upon the Slavs with the baptism of Vladimir the Great (r. 958-1015), the grandson of Olga, who married Ann of Constantinople. He united them under the sign of the cross and was responsible for extending his princedom to the shores of the Baltic Sea. The next ruler, the south of Russia would elevate his state to a historic highpoint, taking over the thrones of Kiev and Novgorod. He was wise in his marriages and those of his children and was able to ally himself with the powerful Poles and Scandinavians. He even murdered his siblings to retain absolute power. He brought great glory to his state when his army defeated the Pechenegs in 1036. He raided in 1043 the Byzantine Empire as far as the Walls of Constantinople.

The ever opportunistic Yaroslav ensured peace by marrying his son to the daughter Anastasia of Emperor Constantine IX. By bridging his relationship with Western Europe, he felt strong enough to remove the Crimean Chersones from Byzantine control and take over the peninsula. Upon his death the Kievan state became divided once again. Control over many Kievan principalities was loosened so that it gradually disintegrated. Additional barbarian invasions accelerated this process. Today what is now the Ukrainian land and its population in the distant past was placed under the protection of the Golden Horde, Lithuania and later Poland.

Since the Russians were under Oleg of Novgorod in 882 he was able to increase his military power by seizing control of the numerous Slavic chiefdoms which surrounded it. The principality that arose was the precursor of the Russian state. It copied the pattern of the Kievan administration and so was able to rule most of the eastern Slavs, who were later referred to as Russians. Novgorod (meaning "Big New City") was in the ninth century their main economic and political city. In the mid-twelfth century, a new major city, Moscow, was built. Its name was mentioned for the first time in 1147.

After the city's wooden structures were burned to the ground by the Mongol invaders in 1238, it was rebuilt in stone and bricks with the Kremlin as its innermost fortress. This city would become the capital of the Muscovite state whose Orthodox religion made them spiritually able to be accepted by the Byzantine Empire. After its Ottoman occupation of the empire, the center of the Eastern Orthodox Church moved from Constantinople to Kiev. This will make the future Russian Empire a major military power in the Balkans and Eastern Europe.

☦

The Magyar and Hungarian tribes arrived later in Europe and never were part of the Balkan Peninsula. Their pillaging raids into the Balkan lands and later their rulers tight relationship with the Byzantine emperors, automatically includes them in this balkanization study. Being pagan invaders they never settled because they always had to look for food and looting in order to survive.

Their improvised state north of the last leg of the Danube River in Pannonia, was not founded until Prince Arpad (r. 895-907,) their first dynastic ruler who settled them in the Tisza RiverValley. This princedom served mostly as a collection of military tent camps for the Magyar hordes that continually carried out their pillaging forays in and beyond the neighboring countries. The Magyars attacked Constantinople in 934. Many of these missions ended in crushing defeats for the Magyars.

Thus in 995, King Otto I destroyed their devastating power and forced the "modern Huns" to permanently settle in the Pannonia grasslands called Pascua Romanorum. Prince Geza of Hungary (r. 972-997) had the distinction of being baptized by a Benedictine monk. This fact changed the course of history for his people. Even though he continued to worship pagan gods, the Magyars were exposed to Catholicism. The pope conferred the royal crown on Geza's son, Istvan/Stephen I (r. 1001-1038) on Christmas day in 1000. It made him the first Hungarian king with a mission to convert his countrymen to Catholicism using the sword.

He used the sword because of his countless resistant pagan nomads who had already converted to Orthodoxy of the Byzantine Empire. The Orthodox Magyars when in danger could ask for protection from the Eastern Orthodox Christians. This spiritually subordinated them to the ecumenical patriarchs of Constantinople. However, King Stephen needed to be baptized Catholic before marrying Gisela of Bavaria. She was a relative of Otto II, the Catholic Emperor of the Holy Roman Empire. Therefore, Stephen forced his subjects to convert to Catholicism. Yet, out of 47 pillaging raids by the Magyars 38 of them took place in Western Europe, but none of their raids were in the Byzantine Empire after the year 970.

During their early history, many future Hungarian kings were groomed in Constantinople to be helped to obtain the monarchic throne in Budapest. Or, not to take refuge in a European capital, but preferring the Byzantine capital as that may help them in regaining it.

This historical event of Christianization gave the aimless Magyars a state, albeit one that was awkwardly located between the East and West. They declared themselves Hungarians as they continued their ferocious invasions of foreign lands in the Western Europe in search of booty:

> They were the modern Huns and the forerunners of the Tatars and Turks. In the face of this danger the Western world fell on its knees: 'From the Magyars' wrath deliver us, oh God!⁵

In 1241 the violent situation became reversed for the Hungarians when the Golden Horde was approaching their borders from three directions simultaneously. Like Attila's Huns (from whom Hungarians proudly claim to be descended,) the Golden Horde transformed the young country into a wasteland, annihilating its fighting men and taking away its women and children. As one fourth of the population was killed and their settlement being made of wood was reduced to ashes. King Bela IV himself became a fugitive like most of the Hungarians who survived the apocalyptic event.[6]

What saved the Hungarians and their country from being wiped off the face of the earth was the death of the Mongol emperor. This prompted Batu Khan to lead his Tartars back to Asia with the hope of seizing the vacant throne. Before leaving, he ordered the execution of all of the captured Hungarians since their being allowed to remain alive would slow the progress of the Golden Horde moving back to Asia.

As for the deserter king who returned humiliated and penniless to Hungary now he welcomed the Cumans, Kipchaks, Patzinaks, Pechenegs, Slavs, and other barbarians to settle and rebuild his ruined country. Thus a new nation was born of many human types of blood and genetic mixtures. It was an amalgam of many ethnic groups which in turn gave birth to a "Second Hungary." King Bela IV (r. 1235-1270) is fondly remembered by the Hungarians as "the Second Founder of our Country." He is also credited with the creation of the modern Hungarian state.

A common misconception is that young Bela IV, who was sent by his father in 1226 to the Carpathians to convert Cuman chieftains to Christianity, brought about the Hungarian colonization of Transylvania. The mere fact that a few Cuman leaders acknowledged his overlord ship did not mean that he ran a Hungarian government in Transylvania. Even though he later called himself King of Cumania, this was more like an allegory since he never fulfilled that role.

Bela's grandson Ladislas IV was anything but Hungarian. His mother was a Cuman princess, he and his court of Cumans wore Cuman clothes, his mistresses were Cumans, and he alienated the Hungarian nobility who asked the pope to replace him. All the pope could do was to excommunicate the king who did not actually care about Catholicism and had taken refuge in Transylvania. Eventually, he returned to the throne. A civil war followed in Hungary, during which Ladislas looked again for shelter among the Cumans until he was finally assassinated in their camp.

The next Hungarian king Andrew III (r. 1290-1301), was born and educated in Venice. Even though he wore the Holy Crown, the Hungarian nobility (who had previously arrested him) questioned his legitimacy. They declared his father to have been a bastard and called him "the Italian." He retained his throne after being endorsed by the friendly Transylvanians who would do anything to spite the Hungarians. To the end of his reign, Andrew battled the Hungarian aristocracy with greater ferocity than he did his external enemies.

For the remainder of their history, the Hungarians' affairs epitomized the process of Balkanization as they tried to subjugate Eastern nations. At the same time they were being either included or excluded from various empires. These regimes alternately dismembered or gifted Hungary with portions of land, thereby creating a sort of ultimate ethnic and political nightmare. "How to win by losing" seemed to be the Hungarians' national slogan.

They obeyed foreign kings, including King Matthias who was born in Transylvania of a Romanian father. Matthias (r. 1458-1490) brought the Hungarian culture to its Golden Age only to have it tarnished by the Ottoman occupation after his death. Still, even if the domain of the Hungarian Crown extended east of the Tisza River, Transylvania was not part of Hungary. Moreover, it was not Transylvania but most of Hungary that the Turks occupied for more than 170 years. Fortunately for the Hungarians, the Austrian and German domination of the country polished the nation, providing them with a pattern for orderly and modern living.

☩

The presence of the Ottoman Empire in the Balkans was also a late addition to the map of the much barbarian population. Its foundation was the result of a long and twisted chain of historic events. The major portion of the Ottoman Empire lay in Anatolia and Asia, but Turkish military involvement in Byzantine affairs led to the capture of Adrianople in 1361 and Thessaloniki in 1387, followed by the occupation of Bulgaria in 1396. The rapid expansion of the Ottomans into the rest of the Balkans precipitated the inevitable siege and capture of Constantinople in 1453. This marked the end of the Byzantine Empire.

In a matter of days, Hagia Sofia (Church of the Holy Wisdom) became a mosque, an unmistakable sign of a new era and the rise of an Islamic power in Europe. It was the Turks who changed the ancient name of the Haemus Mountains into "Balkan," meaning a chain of wooded mountains. This then came to be adopted as the modern name for the entire peninsula that mostly belonged to them for hundreds of years.

By the end of the fifteen century, Eastern Europe was a land in which tribal confederations had developed into small autonomous states with their own capitals and monarchies. These sovereigns ruled within well-defined borders but wished to extend them into larger territories. Most importantly, the same spoken language and the same religion and cultural values would define the further borders of these nations and states.

However, all the incipient states gained legitimacy only after they adopted Christianity, after a pope or an emperor crowned their princes and kings. The sultans were an obvious exception to this rule. Still, even with the massive and numerous geo-demographic border shifts, ancient nations continued their existence in Eastern Europe. Albania, Greece, and Romania are three of the nations that have the historical distinction of not having been being assimilated by the Slavs. The latter two would also never convert to Islam.

The Albanians inhabited the land of Illyrians, the oldest inhabitants of the Balkan Peninsula who settled in the middle of the Dalmatian coast. They spoke their own language, one that bore no relation to any other branches of world language. This is an indication that their tribes were of a different genetic makeup than the rest of the Europeans. Albania, because of its mountainous terrain suffered fewer traumatic invasions from the barbarian horsemen than did the other nations of the Balkans.

Regardless of who occupied or divided the Albanoi, they persisted in speaking their own language (Lingua Albanesca). Some of them, Arvanites, migrated to Greece where they became a prosperous and powerful ethnicity. Most of the Byzantine province of Illyria was Slavicized, a process that led to the creation of many Slavic states that have lasted until modern times. Control of Albania was disputed mainly between the Byzantine Empire and Serbia until the former collapsed. The Ottomans would have to confront the ferocious military opposition of the Albanians before they were able to occupy that country in 1479.

The Eastern Empire was inhabited by both numerous ancient peoples Dacians, Greeks, Macedonians, Illyrians and Thracians) and also incoming ethnic groups, such as Avars, Bulgars, Magyars, Serbs, other Slavs, etc. The latter group dwarfed the Greeks, now a minority in the Byzantine Empire.

However, the Greeks seemed to be unaffected by the ravages of time and proudly retained their national identity and original territory, becoming neither Romanized nor Slavicized. Foreign settlers, such as the Slavs in the Peloponnesus and later in the Turkish settlements, did not affect the Greek way of life and thinking. There was no effect on the Greek culture from the massive presence of the migrant Jews who settled only in the commercial areas.

The Byzantine basileis (emperors) belonged to different ethnicities, but they bore Greek names and they needed the support of the Greeks.[7] Beginning in the seventh century, Latin was replaced by Greek as the official language of the empire since Greek was the commercial language of Eastern Europe.

To deal with the constant demographic flux in the Balkans, the emperors of Constantinople applied an important lesson learned from the previous emperors of Rome. They would not trust any barbarian group with important matters of state and would not allow German generals to lead the armies of the empire. To ensure its political unity and survival, the empire had, since Constantine the Great, robustly identified itself with one God and the one religion of Orthodoxy. Greek influence was visible in every aspect of life and at all levels of society, dominating all of Eastern Europe. Not surprisingly, when Greek independence ended with the fall of Constantinople in 1453 a significant impact was felt by all of the Balkans and Eastern Europe.

Macedonians could trace their origins back to the thirteenth century B.C., when they were put on the map by Alexander the Great. But following the Roman occupation of 160 B.C., Macedonian national power declined. Subsequent numerous invasions of Bulgars, Slavs, and other barbarians brought in foreign settlers who changed the ethnic mix of the nation. At the end of the tenth century Macedonia became part of the First Bulgarian Empire and later was renamed a thema, or province of Bulgaria under the administration of Constantinople.

In fact, Macedonia was shown on the Byzantine map as being located between Bulgaria on the west, Paristrion (Moesia on the north,) Thracia on the east, and Strymon on the south (above the Aegean Sea). For practical purposes it was re-situated away from its original location. Byzantine Macedonia now with its capital at

Hadrianopolis (Edirne), was formed at the expense of Thracia another defunct ancient state.

Over two centuries (867-1056) the Macedonian emperors led Byzantium to the zenith of its power. During medieval times, it was a Balkan region inhabited by ethnic Albanians, Bulgarians, Greeks, Jews, Serbs, Turks, Vlachs, and others.

The Ottoman conquest caused the name of Macedonia to disappear from the map, but the Macedonians survived even as their land was divided among other nations who imposed different languages on them. To their credit, the proud heirs of Alexander the Great have maintained their ethnic identity to the present day and now have their own free republic.

☦

The Romanians/Vlachs/Wallachians descended from the population of Dacians whose tales of war against the Romans were carved on the magnificent Column of Trajan which stands in the middle of Rome. Not too many other ancient nations had the honor to have their heroic war against legionnaires, sculpted in 155 images on the 38 meters/125 foot tall Carrara marble column. The Dacians have the rare distinction not to ever have migrated from their millennial Carpathian and Danubian lands.

The Roman occupation of a portion of Transylvania, as well as of Dacia south of the Danube in Moesia (the former land of Dacia Aureliana, Dacia Mediterranea, Dacia, and Dacia Ripensis,) produced the Proto-Romanian people speaking a Latin dialect of the Romance language in the sea of the Slavs and Magyars. Yet, too many Eurasian barbaric tribes flooded the Balkan region and changed it since the Roman times.

> The arrival of the Slavs overwhelmingly changed the ethnic and linguistic composition of the peoples of the southern Balkans. But it seems that at least one pre-Slav group, who came to be known most commonly as Vlachs, survived the

onslaught. With the arrival of the Slavs, they took to the uplands or migrated. Their most important distinguishing feature was their language, which was derived from Latin and, as is evident from the small groups that still survive today, is closely related to Romanian.[8]

By the fifteenth century the Vlachs had mastered a distinct language rooted in Latin, which Romanians still speak today. They were referred to by the Byzantines as Vlachoi, Vlachs, and even Blacs, names that came from Greater Wallachia, a Romanian principality that was part of Central Dacia. The other principalities of today Banat, Bessarabia, Moldavia, and Transylvania were temporarily occupied at different times by powerful tribes of Avars, Cumans, and Pechinegs. The Vlachs living since immemorial times in Dardania, Moesia, and Pannonia were less connected to the Byzantine Empire because more Slavs and other barbarians invaded their lands. The ancient Vlachs suddenly were confused with the newly settled migratory barbarians around them, for the simple reason that they were more numerous and visible than the original hosts.

A paragraph written by historian Anna Comnena illustrates the utter confusion that reigned among the Byzantines about who was who in the Carpatho-Danubian lands:

> When the Dacians refused to observe any longer the ancient treaty with the Romans and deliberately broke it, the Sarmatians (who used to be called Mysians in the old days) heard of their action and became restive themselves. They were not satisfied to remain in their own territory (separated from the Empire by the Ister) and when a general uprising took place, they crossed the river to our lands. The reason for the migration was the deadly hostility of the Getae, who were neighbors of the Dacians and plundered Sarmatian settlements.[9]

The translator of her book (originally written in Greek) assumed in a footnote that by Dacians, Comnena meant Hungarians and that "Sarmatians are better known as the Patzinaks." Both assumptions are, however, historically incorrect. Her mistaken identity of the Sarmatians as Mysians is obvious from a geographic point of view. They formerly lived above the Sea of the Azov and eventually trickled into Eastern Dacia. Constantine the Great resettled many Sarmatians in Macedonia and Thracia, but not in Mysia/Moesia. The Mysians she mentions have to have been the Vlachs of Moesia who lived there both before and after Roman and Byzantine occupation.

Those who became restive and crossed the Danube during Isaac I's reign (1057-1059) were not the Caucasian Sarmatians, but most likely the Turkish tribes of Patzinaks and Pechenegs, along with the Magyars of King Andrew I. They could not have been mistaken for Dacians. Comnena was correct, however, in noting "the deadly hostility of the Getae" towards the "Sarmatians." Getae was another name commonly used for the Dacians who obviously did not want Turkish settlements on their land. The revolting Geto-Dacians plundered them, forcing the "Sarmatians" to migrate south of the Danube when the river froze, and "dumped themselves down on [Byzantine] territory.[10]

This misunderstanding illustrates how little she knew about the demographics of the populations who once lived in the former Dacia. That was not the case with the historian Niketas Choniates, who dedicated tens of pages to an accurate description of the Vlachs and their lands. In many cases the identity of Vlachs and Wallachians shone through the fabric of history:

> The Valachs lived not only in the territory of present day Moravia, but also resided throughout the vast regions of the Carpathian mountains. At the closest distance to us, this included the territory of Upper Slovakia, south Tesin and south Poland. History also instructs us that the Valachs, the mountain shepherds, were involved in a special kind of

herdsman ship entirely unique in Central Europe and that they originally came from Balcany in what is now Romania.[11]

The question of the ownership of Transylvania was an even more confusing one and continues to need clarification. Until the end of the thirteenth century, only a small number of Magyars and Hungarians trickled into Transylvania, an area which they later claimed to be their homeland. The Chronology of Transylvanian History states that in year 896,

> ...as the seven Magyar tribes sweep into the Carpathian Basin, the tribe of the gyula (military warlord) and the tribe of the kende (titular ruler) occupy the area that will become Transylvania.[12]

In other words, it asserts that Transylvania would not exist if not for the invasion of the Magyar tribes. But, in fact, in 896 the Magyars advancing toward Transylvania were twice defeated by the Bulgars (in the battle of Southern Buh) and the Pecheneg armies. The Magyar survivors scrambled for shelter anywhere they could, including in the Carpathian forests that were called Silva Vlachorum/Forest of Vlachs.[13]

At that time, the defeated, homeless, and starving, the decimated Magyars were a mere shadow of the previous mighty horde and were in no position to occupy any land. When Prince Almos (father of Arpad) tried to enter Transylvania circa 903, he battled the natives in the area that is today Satu Mare (Romania). During an appalling military defeat there, he lost his own life. There is, therefore, in no way was it possible in the tenth century that the Magyars could have controlled the Mures/Maros Valley and conquered Transylvania. Besides, the defeated invaders from a flat land do not venture into the unknown mountains to fight. In the next three centuries it was militarily impossible for anyone to take Transylvania away from the

Pechinegs and Cumans since they were among the tribes most feared by the Hungarians.

The Hungarians may have conducted invasions into the Romanian principalities and imposed certain terms on some regions there, but they certainly did not occupy the land. From the end of the fifteenth century Transylvania was arbitrarily considered a part of the Hungarian crown, but that Romanian land was never at any time, "the Third Hungary" in the Carpathians.[14]

✠

In conclusion, the uniqueness of this new demography of the Balkans was that in a few centuries all of the conquests and settlements took place at the expense of the indigenous population. They either resettled into the impregnable mountains and forests, as did the Albanians and Vlachs, or they remained where they were, like the Greeks and Macedonians.

By the close of the eleventh century, most of the invaders had been Christianized, and, to maintain peace, Constantinople granted them homelands. The role of the Byzantine Church cannot be emphasized enough in recounting the history of this period. It considerably elevated the level of cultural and spiritual life of the settled barbarians and generally served to ensure greater civility. It was at this point that the "sacred roots" of many dynasties originated savage warlords that became transformed into mythical heroes and saints.

Both new and ancient nations and states would continue to undergo numerous demographic and territorial changes as leaders made volatile alliances and the winning armies shifted borders repeatedly a phenomenon that has continued to the present day. Despite the many violent clashes with Constantinople, the countries that were founded, as described in this chapter, have lasted. Most of them feature the dikefalos/duokephalos Byzantine eagle on their coats of arms and flags. After the fall of Constantinople, in spite of the countless revolts and wars of rebellion against Ottoman occupation, the Balkan nations adopted the deeply rooted political and economic corruption inherited from both empires. The never-ending border disputes between Eastern European nations continue to demonstrate that they are rooted in the historic process of Balkanization.

# REFERENCE NOTES

1. John V. A. Fine, The Early Medieval Balkans: A Critical Survey from the Sixth to the Late Twelfth Century (Ann Arbor: University of Michigan Press, 1991), 62.
2. Fine, Early Medieval Balkans, 62.
3. The historian Niketas seems to have misnamed just about every ethnicity that was not Greek. The names of the "Bulgar" local settlements, even those near Marathon, are Bistritsa, Boucovina, Granitsa, etc. were old Walachian names with Slavic roots, identical names of locations that can today be found in Romania. These settlements can only have been inhabited by the Vlachs, not Bulgars. This fact sheds an entirely different light on the process of Slavic "colonization" of the Balkans. It leads to an account that diverges greatly from the views of modern Bulgarian scholars who play down the roles of the ancient Wlachians and Vlachs living south of the Danube River in today Bulgaria.
4. Their memory is preserved in Romania through the popular use of names like Coman, Comana, Comaneci, Comanescu, and possibly cumatru/godfather. Above all else, the strong presence of the Cumans in the Carpathian Basin preserved the domain of the Romanized Dacians in what is today Romania.
5. Emil Lengyel, 1,000 Years of Hungary (New York: John Day, 1958), 20.
6. The saga of the king's escape from Mongolian captivity reads like a Hollywood script. After exhausting all venues for foreign help, while the Mongols turned cities to ashes and slaughtered their populations, Bela saw the Mongols retreat and felt brave enough to attack them at Mohi where he was lured into a mock victory. While the Hungarians celebrated all night and their king failed to organize a defense of their camp, the Mongols surrounded them and engaged in an onslaught; Bela and his court miraculously

escaped. With a Mongolian squadron on his heels, he fled to Pozsnoy/Bratislava, only to end up in Hainburg where he was sheltered by his friend, Duke Friederick of Austria. The friendship ended when the Duke confiscated the Hungarian treasury Bela had brought with him and also asked for three border counties to be handed over to Austria. Robbed and desperate, the king fled to the safety of Zagreb. But this time he was followed by an entire Mongol army which flattened the city and burned down its new cathedral when it refused to extradite Bela. The king then fled from one city to another until he reached the Adriatic shore. The Tartars, in close pursuit, shot arrows at his boat as it departed to take him to safety in the fortress of Trau/Trogir in Croatia.

7. The English translation of Greek names made their original names irrelevant in modern days. Emperor Constantine was Konstantinos; Justinian I, Petrus Sabbatius; Theodore II, Theodoros Laskaris; and John I, Iōannēs I Tzimiskēs.
8. Tim Judah, The Serbs: History, Myth and the Destruction of Yugoslavia (New Haven, CT: Yale University Press, 1997), 8.
9. Anna Comnena, The Alexiad of Anna Comnena, trans. E. R. A. Sewter (London: Penguin, 1969), 122.
10. Comnena, Alexiad, 122.
11. Zdenek Konecny and Frantisek Mainus, *Stopami Minulosti: Kapitol z Dejin Moravy a Slezka/Traces of the Past: Chapters From the History of Moravia and Silesia/* (Brno: Blok, 1979).
12. http://www.hungarian-history.hu/lib/transy/transy02.htm, and John F. Cadzow, Andrew Ludanyi, and Louis J. Elteto, eds., Transylvania: The Roots of Ethnic Conflict (Kent, OH: Kent State University Press, 1983), 11.
13. The community of Vlaha, near Cluj-Napoca, testifies to the Vlah/Vlachian's presence in the heart of Transylvania, and today's archeological findings also show Gepidic settlements there.
14. The British governance of eighteenth century colonial America proved to be only an imperial illusion of grandeur. At present, the

Crown of England may include Australia and Canada, but that does not mean that these nations belong to England. Likewise, if the later Austro-Hungarian Empire included Transylvania, that was not what the Romanians wanted and they often rose up against it.

# IV

## VOLATILE ALLIANCES IN THE BALKAN PENINSULA

Alliances were never straightforward in the Dark Ages between the sixth and sixteenth century. Traditionally they were almost inevitably destined to fail. Keeping a promise was impractical in the face of endless acts of greed, predation, and revenge. Any oath that was taken to alleviate a desperate situation was readily broken as soon as a better opportunity arose. Often alliances were based on distorted beliefs and suspicions about the other party, until the naked reality of betrayal, quickly turned friend into foe. Other reasons for violating an alliance included the fear of dying, the desire to save lives in unnecessary fights, pure cowardice, and the obvious futility of maintaining an alliance where the benefits were negligible to one or both of the parties.

Whether they were freely entered into or coerced, treaties could be made among barbarian tribes, between barbarians and Byzantines, and sometimes between a Western power and an Eastern European ally. Alliances were forged instantly between barbarians when the parties faced a common enemy, and they were broken just as quickly when it came to sharing the plunder or partitioning the occupied land. Playing enemies off against each other, and dividing and conquering them by entering into unexpected alliances, was the Byzantine way of maintaining territorial dominance. However, this strategy backfired in many unexpected ways.

There were so many invasions into the Byzantine Empire that its ambassadors and negotiators found it necessary to establish a rule for the co-existence among the barbarians who were flooding into the imperial provinces. Their efforts were in vain. Constantinople relied on either military force or bribery to maintain peace with the invaders, and they tried to build alliances with them.

This had little historical impact since the barbarians who had now settled there had no notion of moral integrity, and no respect for written agreements. They had no compunction about committing treason once an alliance had served its purpose, or if they sensed the slightest suspicion of wrongdoing or some sort of personal offense. Their decisions to either join or break an alliance were made in a flash, the critical factor being whether an ally was victorious in a battle or war, or just about to lose in one. In the words of historian Anna Comnena, "The truth is, all barbarians are usually fickle and characteristically unable to keep their pledges."[1]

Royal marriages sealed alliances among countries and nations and thereby created friendly or adversarial relationships. Some pagan leaders became Christianized through the influence of their wives, a fact that gained them the support of Western European powers, but in most cases included them in the Eastern Orthodox nations. The Polish King Mieszko married a German noblewoman. King Geza of Hungary had first a German and then a Byzantine wife, and his son Stephen I became the brother-in-law of Emperor Henry II because of his Bavarian wife. King Bela III's two marriages created a bridge between the Hungarian nation and Western Europe, while Stephen V of Hungary married a Cuman princess. The second marriage of John Asen II of Bulgaria made him the son-in-law of the Hungarian

King Andras II, and by his third marriage he became the son-in-law of Byzantine Emperor Theodore I. His alliance with Byzantium was further ensured when Asen's daughter married the son of Emperor John III. In an effort to keep his throne and establish a Byzantine-Serbian dynastic union, King Milutin married the six year-old daughter of Emperor Andronicus II. One of Murad II's seven wives was Mara/Maria Hatun of Serbia, who proved to be an excellent negotiator between her father, Despot Brankovich, and her sultan husband. Moreover, she was hugely instrumental in convincing her stepson Mehmed II, the Conqueror of Constantinople, to save Greek Orthodoxy, and implicitly the Orthodox Church, in the entire Balkans from Ottoman annihilation. The marriage of Polish Queen Jadwiga to Lithuanian Duke Wladyslaw II cemented the union of these two countries and laid the foundation for the Jagello dynasty that later ruled Poland, Lithuania, and Hungary.

✝

The first major barbarian coalition was between the Avars and various tribes of Slavs. Since the Avars were better organized both militarily and socially, they quickly took control of the aimless Slavs, a loosely connected group of tribes with no concept of alliance. At the end of the sixth century, the Slavs were still trying unsuccessfully tried to settle in the Balkan Peninsula, whereas the Avars had already established themselves in parts of former Dacia and Pannonia. Together they invaded the Byzantine Empire only to plunder or extort ransom or tribute from it, and then they returned to their camps. While the Avars were militarily efficient, they were not numerous and so had to depend on the many Slavic tribes already present in the Byzantine territories to be raided.

Switching sides was a talent for the witty Avars. They continually played the Byzantines off against the Slavs, and joined only the side that proved victorious. Often, the Slavs were merely waiting for someone to direct them so together they could collect a tribute from the Byzantines, and in such cases, Avars never failed to be their ally.

Constantinople didn't always co-operate in this scheme. After the death of Emperor Justinian I (r. 527-565) the following emperors refused to pay a yearly subsidiary to the Avars and Slavs. To avenge this insult, the barbarian coalition plundered the defiant empire, forcing the next emperor, Justin II (r. 565 – 578) to seek alliance with the Turks to keep the Avars and Persians at bay.

The next emperor, Tiberius II (r. 578-582) paid the Avars a tribute of sixty thousand gold coins to keep them peaceful, only to have them attack the empire. They also received the city of Sirmium as an additional pay off. The Slavs also ignored peace agreements and attacked the empire from the opposite direction by invading Illyricum, Thrace, Thessaly and regions of Greece.

When in 599 Emperor Maurice refused to pay off the Persians and refused to be blackmailed by the Avars, they slaughtered twelve thousand Byzantine prisoners. When in 626 the tribute was once again withheld by Maurice, this time the Avars put together a military coalition of eighty thousand Gepids, Bulgars, Slavs, and attacked Constantinople. They staged a seven-mile wide siege that cut off the city from the rest of the peninsula until their primitive fleet was destroyed by the Byzantine navy. The barbarian coalition was supported by the Persian army which attacked Constantinople at the same time from the Asian side.

Maurice's generalship proved to be so successful on all fronts that it made the former allies, the Avars and Slavs, so unhappy that they ended up fighting each other. It was good timing for the Bulgarians to liberate themselves from Avar control, and the Croatians established their own state in Dalmatia.

Unfortunately, the military successes of Maurice stirred the envy of his general Phocas who assassinated the good emperor and his six sons. The next day Phocas became the emperor and faced barbarian attacks from all sides of his Byzantine Empire. Unable to make any alliances he now faced an inside rebellion, and he was executed as well. The Byzantine Empire seemed to be at the will of the barbarians.

Improbable alliances were also made by Justinian II, who was dethroned in 695 and exiled to Crimea, after which he fled to Khazaria and married the khan's sister. When Constantinople demanded his extradition, Justinian took shelter among people who had previously been his sworn enemies, the Bulgarians. He struck up a friendship with their leader, Tervel, who then promptly led an army to attack Constantinople.

During this unsuccessful siege of the city, Justinian sneaked inside the capital and reclaimed his throne. He then bestowed honors on Tervel such as had never before been given to any pagan chief, including the title of caesar/tzar. Ironically, the emperor flattered Tervel into submission but ended up having to pay him a tribute to keep the Bulgarians in place. He subsequently sent an army to the Crimea to push the Khazars out.

As former allies may become mortal enemies, Justinian was assassinated as a result of the Khazars' plot to punish the man who married their princess and denied her the right to rule the Crimea. As for Tervel, he led his army into Thrace, pillaging the Byzantine province when tribute from Constantinople ceased to flow. Still, he offered precious military help to Constantinople when it was besieged by the Arabs in 717, knowing he would benefit from a generous reward. As a rule, the Bulgars executed those of their leaders who lost battles or made peace with an enemy. An exception to this was when a rich reward was attached to such a compromise.

The Khazars and Byzantine rulers also cultivated strong friendships. Leo III (r. 717-741) married his son, the future Emperor Constantine V, to the khan's daughter who was baptized Irene in 733. This marriage provided a strong alliance between the distant states, and for many years to come it prevented barbarian invasions of that area along the coast of the Black Sea.

Emperor Leo VI (r. 886-912) took the epithet "the Wise" because he was a philosopher. He was also recognized for his acuity in employing the Magyars, whom he had transported by ship in 895 to invade Bulgaria, while the Bulgarians were conducting a pillaging campaign in the Byzantine territories. That invasion constituted revenge against Czar Simeon I (r. 893-927) who once had been a humiliated hostage of Constantinople, and now declared himself Emperor of Bulgaria. His army was caught between two massive attacks from opposing sides. In desperation, he appealed to the powerful Pechenegs the former allies of the Byzantines in their fight against the Kievan Rus. In 897 the unlikely allies were victorious against the Byzantine army and forced it to accept peace and to pay a tribute.

The Pechenegs then turned against the Magyars a group who had been a perennial menace to them. They defeated them so severely that they were pushed out of the Balkan Peninsula, and off their land east of the Pruth River, and driven to an area north of the Black Sea. The catastrophic side effect of this was that the Magyars were forced to detour and migrated west above the Pecheneg occupied Dacia. Under their king Arpad they finally settled west of the Tisza River. After they had dislodged the Slavic tribes from most of Pannonia the Magyars ended up in what today is Hungary. Once again, a chain of volatile alliances had led to unpredictable events that proved to have historical importance.

✝

The Bulgars came to pose the greatest threat to the Byzantines as they could do little to stop their leader Simeon from winning nearly every war he fought. Soon, he would create the First Bulgarian Empire one that would extend from the Adriatic and Aegean seas to the Black Sea. In so doing, he alienated many other neighboring barbarian tribes. Predictably, they then put aside their differences in an effort to form a loose anti-Bulgarian coalition.

While the Pechenegs were waiting on the sidelines to see who would pay them the most, Simeon aimed his forces at his strongest enemy the Byzantine army. He annihilated it in August

917 at Acheloos. This was followed by another victory whereupon Constantinople was forced to recognize the Bulgarian Empire with Simeon as its undisputed ruler.

Yet, when Empress Zoe refused to allow her son, the future emperor Constantine VII, to marry Simeon's daughter she had no option but to ally her kingdom with the Magyars, Serbs, and other Slavs who all hated the Bulgars.

In 924, in a state of fury Czar Simeon successfully battled the Serbs and after beheading the captive Serbian nobility annexed their state. While the barbarian allies were busy pushing the Bulgarians away from the area north of the Danube, the Magyars settled in most of Pannonia. That area then became a sort of reservoir of Magyars who were a savage enemy of the Byzantines.

Czar Simeon, who never ceased his plunder of the Byzantine Empire died of a stroke after a failed attack on Constantinople. He had bitterly fought the Byzantines who crowned him tzar and allowed the Bulgarians to settle in Moesia, thereby putting them firmly on the map.

With three major players Bulgaria, Hungary, and Serbia were involved in Byzantine affairs, the military dynamics of the Balkans became a complicated unsolvable situation. Therefore, the future alliances were destined to fall apart.

✟

Factions of barbarians frequently struck up alliances among themselves and attacked the Byzantine Empire. These were acts of aggression for which there were many precedents as well as reasonable expectations of gains. When Kievan Prince Sviatoslav invaded the Bulgarian and the Byzantine Empires, he was attacked in his home state by the Pechenegs who in turn had been manipulated by the Byzantines. He defeated the Pechenegs and after convincing them to join his forces pillaged Bulgaria. They sacked its capital of Preslav, and the city of Philippopolis in Thracia. There they impaled some twenty thousand captives who heroically resisted the siege. Sviatoslav also used the Pechenegs to shatter the Khzar dominance of the Kiev land, only to end up being assassinated by his allies.

With the arrival of the Cumans and Patzinaks north of the Danube River in the former land of Dacia, another formidable barbarian power was available for hire if the payment in gold or money was enough. The Bulgars of Dobrudja quickly employed them to strike against the Byzantine domination because they protested an imperial heavy taxation. A horde of "about 80,000 men,"[2] Slavs, Patzinaks, and Vlachians were "led by one Solomon,"[3] the former king of Hungary. How Solomon became a leader of such an unlikely alliance is explainable only in terms of the other alliances within the Hungarian realm which had been made and then broken.

Solomon was the successor to a sorrowful legacy. He was the son of King Andrew I whose brother Bela I had allied himself with King Boleslaw II. Then, the latter's Polish troops had installed Bela on the Hungarian throne. Solomon left for Austria from whence he returned with German troops. He gained the crown after he married King Henry III's daughter in 1063. However, Bela's three sons took advantage of the Polish alliance and together they entered Hungary. One of his sons Geza I (r. 1074 -1077) dethroned Solomon in 1074. Solomon was once again helped by Henry's army and returned to Hungary.

In the meantime, the country had elected Ladislaw I (Geza's brother) as king. Solomon failed to gain any further foreign support and ended up in prison. When he was finally released he fled to the enemy territory of Dacia where he married the daughter of a Pecheneg chieftain. In 1085 a Pecheneg expedition led by Solomon invaded Hungary but was defeated. However, the ex-Hungarian king continued to lead barbarian raids into the Byzantine Empire where he died in 1087 while fighting near Adrianople.

These barbarian raids were carried out mainly by Patzinaks (then also called Pechenegs and Scyths), who plundered for two years south of the Danube into Thracia. They decimated every Byzantine army they encountered and killed its two capable generals. The Patzinaks sought an alliance with the Byzantines, but "Alexius saw through the Scythian fraud: their embassy was an attempt to evade the imminent peril…and he refused to hear the envoys."[4]

Indeed, the emperor successfully attacked the barbarians who even in the face of defeat pillaged many provinces while they were retreating. Later, the emperor had no choice but to pay a ransom for his people who had been captured. The barbarians returned to Dacia with much needed plunder. On their way back, they met the army of the Cumans to whom they previously had appealed for help in defeating the Byzantines, but now their help was no longer needed. When the Cumans saw the enormous booty and the multitude of prisoners they wanted their share and told the "Scythian" chieftains:

> We have come a great distance to help you, with the purpose of sharing your danger and your victory. Now that we have contributed all that we could, it is not right to send us away empty-handed. It was not from choice that we arrived too late for the war, nor are we to be blamed for that…Either therefore divide up all the booty in equal shares with us, or instead of allies you will find us ready to fight you.[5]

The Scyths refused so the Cumans launched a punishing attack against them. It was a disaster for the Scyths who fled for their lives. At this point, the barbarian coalition broke down. Emperor Alexius I selectively drew on the resources offered by either side with the stronger horde of Cumans who had successfully battled their co-tribes in 1091. This shift created an even more serious problem. The victorious Cumans invaded the Byzantine lands on their own in 1114, only to be forced back by the emperor's better trained troops.

A new wave of Patzinaks, dislocated from above Black Sea, "crossed the Istros (Danube River) and plundered Thrace, destroying everything under foot more absolutely than a host of locusts."[6]

Emperor John II (r. 1118-1143) advanced with his army to meet the invaders and tried to negotiate their withdrawal with an invitation to some of the chieftains whom he won over [and] greeted with every kindness. He set sumptuous feasts before them and charmed them with gifts of silk garments and silver cups and basins.[7]

Without realizing it, the emperor had just intensified the greed of the barbarian leaders who now saw how many more riches were potentially available to them. During the truce, more Byzantine troops had arrived to join the main defensive force that ultimately defeated the barbarians.

In that same year (1123) John made the best of the fact that he had access to these victorious troops and attacked the Serbs (called Tribaloi by Niketas), who also habitually plundered the imperial lands. After winning a decisive victory, his troops looted the Serb settlements and relocated the captives to the fertile province of Nikodemia. Four years later Niketas described another invasion:

> In the summer [1127], the Hungarians crossed the Istros and sacked Braničevo, where they tore down the walls, whose stones they transported to Zevgminon. They also plundered Sardica, again repudiating and tearing into shreds their treaties of friendship.[8]

The reason for this was that Duke Almos, the brother of the Hungarian ruler Stephen II, defected to the Byzantine camp where he was well received. Once again, John and his troops who were in good military condition to intervene in the bloody conflict defeated the Hungarians and recovered the Byzantine land occupied by them. The emperor imposed a truce on all of these barbarians and believing he had achieved a lasting peace turned his attention to the Turkish invaders in Anatolia.

☩

Often an alliance was planned in advance and meticulously orchestrated as was the case with Manuel I (r. 1143-1180) and the Hungarians. The emperor was on his way to restore the glory and power of the Byzantine Empire, and for that reason he needed weaker enemies. When King Geza II died in 1162 his brothers Istvan IV and Laszlo II were already in Constantinople befriending Manuel aiming to make him their ally and protector. Istvan went so far as to marry a niece of the emperor in exchange for the Hungarian throne. Laszlo knew better and refused to marry a non-Catholic since this would cause the Hungarian nobility to reject him as a monarch. They accepted Geza's son Istvan III who had already been named the legitimate heir to the throne by his father, and as predicted denied Istvan's candidacy for fear that Manuel would turn Hungary into a satrapy of Constantinople.

Manuel used military force to intimidate the Hungarians and bribery to convince their nobility to accept Istvan as their ruler. Meanwhile, Bela III who was Geza's son almost married the emperor's daughter and therefore forced the Hungarians to compromise and chose Laszlo as their king. However, Emanuel threatened them with war and Istvan IV gained the throne in 1163. In the meantime, Istvan III found a powerful ally in the person of Frederick I who ruled the Holy Roman Empire.

Frederick I provided troops to dethrone Istvan IV who was later poisoned to death. Istvan III kept his throne for nine years by handing Croatia and Dalmatia over to the Byzantines and sending his brother Bela as a hostage to Constantinople where he took the Christian name of Alexius. After Istvan's sudden death, Bela promised a large sum of money and unconditional loyalty to Manuel I. Thus, the other Istvan became the next Hungarian king (r. 1172-1196).[9]

After Emanuel died in 1180 Bela III considered himself to be relieved of the oath he had taken. He re-conquered all the Byzantine provinces granted to Manuel by each former candidate to the Hungarian throne. After striking an alliance with the new Emperor

Alexius II, Bela further cemented his alliance with the Byzantines by marrying his daughter to the next Emperor Isaac II (r. 1185-1195 and 1203-1204). Both of them fought against Serbian expansionism. After his wife's death Bella married the daughter of Louis VII, thus establishing a lucrative connection to France. This would put Hungary on the path towards sound cultural development.

Greed and vanity were the main attributes of the Emperor Isaac II who married the daughter of King Bela III in order to establish an alliance with the powerful Magyars. But, the excessive taxation he imposed in order to finance his wars against the invading Normans, and pay for his wedding led to a Vlachian uprising in Moesia. When Frederick I Barbarossa advanced through the Byzantine lands with his crusaders, Isaac allied himself with Saladin the sultan of Egypt and Syria. Saladin was the deadly enemy of the German emperor.

The Third Crusade against the Turks was seriously sabotaged when the Byzantines blocked their march through the Balkan Peninsula, and the Germans conquered Philippopolis in August 1189. A Byzantine army which was sent to push the Germans back failed in its mission, and in their effort to retreat the soldiers plundered their own people.

Afraid of losing his throne Isaac finally granted passage to the crusaders and Frederick arrived in Gallipoli from which point his knights were ferried toward Asia Minor. Isaac's failure to defeat the revolting Vlachs and recognize their "empire" created resentment. This led to him being dethroned, blinded, and imprisoned by his brother Alexius III.

☩

The Vlachs constituted a special ethnic block within the Balkans because their livelihood was not restricted by any borders. Emperor Basil II mentioned them in a decree of 1020 as the "Vlachs of all Bulgaria." Shortly after Constantine VIII used Vlachians as mercenaries the author Kekaumenos described their revolt from

Thessaly in 1066. He also described them as descendents of the Dacians, and the Bessoi (the Bessoi were never part of ancient Dacia,) but in the time of Kekaumenos they were living with the Vlachian population in the province of Thracia.

He mentioned that their King Decebalus had been defeated by the Roman Emperor Trajan in Transylvania, north of the Danube. Anna Comnena described how Emperor Alexius tried "to enroll new men for a term of duty from the Bulgars and the nomads (commonly called Vlachs)."[10] These men were shepherds who lived all over the Balkans and were not subject to any geographical borders. Comnena also wrote that "a certain Poudilus, one of the leading Vlachs, came and reported [to Emperor Alexius I] that the Cumans were crossing the Danube."[11] In another instance, she noted that "the Cumans were shown the way through the passes by the Vlachs."[12]

As mentioned in previous chapters, the Vlachs who were the Wallachians living south of the Danubian River, were the inheritors of the Daco-Roman legacy. They were dispersed throughout Eastern Europe. Because of their demographics they could forge reliable alliances among themselves that proved dangerous to other groups.

A case in point is the Asan brothers' revolt in 1186. They asked for military help from their relatives in Greater Wallachia north of the Danube (at this point under the Cuman occupation).

The Vlachian brothers returned to Moesia with the needed help and subsequently benefited from Cuman participation in their anti-Byzantine coalition. By the middle of 1197 Niketas records that Emperor Alexius I (r. 1081-1118) had decided "to bring deliverance to the Thracian cities which were ravaged by the Vlachs and Cumans."[13] However, the motives of each party were considerably different. The Cumans were there to plunder the cities, and the Vlachs had united to enforce their rights and gain national recognition from the Byzantines.

The revolt lasted for more than ten years and led to an independent Vlacho-Bulgarian state under King Ioannitsa (Kaloyan) called in Latin *Blachorum domino/Lord of Wallachians*. In 1189 he believed he had found a reliable ally in Emperor Frederick Barbarossa, who had broken an alliance with the Byzantines. The Vlach king wanted to join the crusaders in order to conquer Constantinople, and eventually destroy the Byzantine Empire. He was turned down because Barbarossa's ultimate mission was to liberate the Holy Land, not to get entangled in Balkan affairs.

The Vlach-based army scored one victory after another against the Byzantines, while Ioannitsa sought recognition of his reign and the title of emperor. Furthermore, Pope Innocent III saw the advantages of having the Vlachs in his camp and initiated a long and complicated correspondence to establish a Catholic foothold in the middle of the Balkans. This was something he had not succeeded in doing in Bulgaria.

While the pope persisted in dragging his feet on a commitment to recognize Ioannitsa as emperor, the Fourth Crusade entered the Vlachian territory. He sought an alliance with the Latin knights and attempted to impress them with his victories against the Byzantines. Ioannitsa's expectation of their success proved correct when the crusaders entered Constantinople in 2004, and pillaged the great city.

Soon, the new emperor Alexius IV needed the powerful Vlachs and Cumans as allies to protect him from the fury of the crusaders who had turned against him. In exchange, he would grant the imperial title to Ioannitsa along with the patriarchal independence of own Orthodox Church. As it turned out the crusaders savagely sacked Constantinople because they had not been paid the sums promised by Alexius. A new Latin Empire then developed, and new governmental rules and borders were established in the Balkans.

Adapting to this new Balkan order, Ioannitsa again extended his friendship to the occupying Western knights, only to be treated in ways that might befit a slave, but certainly not the king of the thoroughly tested brave Vlachs. Instantly, the knights became the object of his fury and Ioannitsa allied with his former Byzantine enemies who had escaped the predacious Latins.

By late 1204 he was in charge of a powerful military coalition. It put the Vlachs in a position to demand of the pope that he order his knights to return all their ancient lands that had been placed under the control of the Latin Empire. If the pope did not agree Ioannitsa would fight the crusaders, which he successfully did for the next three years occupying much of Macedonia and Thracia.

However, Ioannitsa essentially became too powerful for his own good. His trusted allies the Byzantines and Cumans became uncomfortable when the Vlachs became a major power in the Balkans. Suddenly, Ioannitsa the emperor to be was assassinated by a Cuman chieftain in October 1207 while conducting an attack on Thessaloniki (Salonica) in Greece.

☩

The year 1172 was not a good one for Nemanja, the Grand Prince of Serbia. His anti-Byzantine coalition with the Venetians and Hungarians collapsed, and his Serbian army was massacred by the army of Emperor Manuel I. The latter was on his way to recover the imperial lands that he had lost to the barbarian invasions. In order to save his life and his "empire," the proud Nemanja walked barefoot to Manuel, surrendered his sword and obeyed to be taken to Constantinople where he should have a chance to be able to redeem.

In time, he regained Manuel's trust and after pledging never to violate it again was reinstated on the Serbian throne. When Manuel died in 1180 Nemanja considered his sacred vow to have expired. He had given it to a specific emperor, and not to the entire Byzantine Empire. He then decided to attempt to reoccupy what he viewed as Serbian lands.

Three years later Nemanja allied himself with King Bela III of Hungary. Their united armies took over the key cities of Belgrade, Niss, and Serdica (Sofia), as well as several adjoining regions. Changing camps in 1191 Bela united with his son-in-law Emperor Isaac II against Nemanja.

When the Hungarians unexpectedly left the coalition and headed home, the aging Nemanja found himself in a most vulnerable position. He was once again facing the Byzantine might alone. He quickly proposed that Emperor Friedrich Barbarossa discontinue his crusade to the Holy Land, and he offered him twenty thousand Serbian troops to attack Constantinople instead. The Byzantines learned about the secret plan, and Emperor Isaac II blocked the Germans from reaching Bulgaria.

Taking advantage of the fact that these two emperors were locked in conflict in their efforts to impose their wills on each other, Nemanja directed his army to occupy the land from Kosovo to Skopje. He then incorporated it into the Serbian state.

Isaac could not tolerate such losses, and in 1191 he led an expeditionary force that crushed the Serbian forces in Southern Moravia. The octogenarian Nemanja then went into hiding. But, the Serbs were not finished. They continued to harass the Byzantines forcing them to fight an unconventional war they could not win.

In 1186 Nemanja's son Stefan II married Princess Eudocia of Constantinople. The disputed lands were then divided among the in-laws in an effort to make peace. The underlying concern still was that the Serbs might ally themselves with the Bulgarians. Thus Kosovo and Zeta as well as other provinces came under Serbian domination.

In 1196 Nemanja abdicated in favor of Stefan II and became a monk. His sons fought against each other until Vukan won and forced Stefan to leave the country. As Niketas pointed out:
> When fratricide spread as a pattern, model, and general law from the queen of cities to the far corners of the earth, not only Turks, Russians, Serbs, and afterwards Hungarians [1203] but also the remaining rulers of barbarian nations filled their countries with seditions and murders, drawing their swords against their own kinsmen.[14]

The Serbian saga continued when Stefan's oldest brother Vukan, who allied with Pope Innocent III and the Hungarian King Emerich, using their help he dethroned and expelled Stefan I. Serbia now faced both religious reform and Hungarian vassalage. Taking full advantage of the religious and political situation Stefan (now exiled in Bulgaria) pursued the Vlachian king Ioannitsa to militarily endorse an attempt to seize the throne in exchange for eastern Serbian lands. The Bosnians also claimed some Serbian lands, and the opportunistic Stefan found them to be a ready ally and useful in overthrowing his brother. He regained power in 1204.

When Constantinople was sacked by the crusaders, one year later Stefan divorced his Byzantine wife and married Anna. She was the granddaughter of Dandolo the blind Doge of Venice and the leader of the crusaders. Stefan I promptly pledged his alliance to Rome and Pope Honorius III crowned him the first Serbian King in 1217.

Not surprisingly, the Serbians could not accept Catholicism forcing Stefan II to break the alliance with the pope. This was mostly because his other brother Sava established an independent Orthodoxy of Serbia, and he crowned Stefan as the rightful king and head of the Serbian Church. If Serbia had not entered into these volatile alliances it would not have survived to become a powerful empire in the next century.

As for the Komnenos family who ruled the Byzantine Empire at that time, they continued looking for new opportunities to form alliances. Its various members wanted to succeed in keeping control of the throne. They were a far cry from Manuel I who recovered most of the Balkan territories through straight forward wars or diplomacy. The family retained what was conquered by Basil II.

However, after his death the conflicts between the royals (Isaac II was dethroned in 1195, and was blinded by his own brother Alexius III). This forced the emperors to ally with the enemies of the empire in order to secure their crowns. Isaac and his son even defected to the Turks, while Alexius led the Normans in 1185 to raid Greece, and to sack Thessalonica.

The mortal blow for the empire came from Alexius IV (the son of Isaac II) who led the crusaders to conquer Constantinople for his own gain. He became the emperor for a mere six months. Whoever promised a larger bribe to the enemies of the empire had a better chance of ruling it all at the expense of the Byzantine people. The rest of the Balkan Peninsula was in a royal and military turmoil as well.

When Michael Asen III of Bulgaria wanted to invade and dissolve Serbia in 1330, he did what the Asan kings always did during military crises he appealed to his brethren Wallachians from the north side of the Danube River for help. His army was reinforced with Wallachian and Moldavian contingents, but they were defeated in a surprising night attack by Prince Stefan IV Dusan. Tzar Michael Asen III was captured, and he died from battle wounds. He paid the ultimate price for divorcing Stefan Uros II's daughter Anna and marrying the Byzantine princess Theodora to cement an alliance against the Serbians.

After Stefan IV killed his father Uros III by strangling him, he married the sister of the new Bulgarian Czar Ivan Alexander. He was the nephew of the deceased Michael Asen III.

Taking full advantage of the new alliance King Stefan Uros IV invaded the Byzantine Empire. He completely disregarded the fact that he was supposed to be an ally of Constantinople which had sheltered him for six years. His military move could not have been better timed. In Constantinople the imperial command was at its lowest point due to the civil war (1341-1347) that had erupted between the underage Emperor John V Palaiologos and his regent John VI Kantakuzenos. Both of these men were backed by adversarial and self-interested factions.

Neither of them was strong enough to win in the six-year struggle for the power that followed, and they both appealed for, and accepted foreign aid. They relied on mercenary troops of any conceivable origin. Quick to capitalize on the empire's misfortunes Dusan IV extracted enormous favors from it while at the same time allying himself with either candidate. His Serbs occupied Macedonia and extended their domination in the southwest as far as the Peloponnesus.

Dusan aimed to conquer Constantinople and even approached the pope to sanction his grand ambition to create a new Greco-Serbian Empire. Yet, the experienced General John VI found a formidable ally in Sultan Orhan from Anatolia. He sent ten thousand Turks to repulse the Serbs and restore order.

The Turks did just that, but their successful endeavor led to astonishing complications when they occupied Gallipoli in 1345 and refused to leave. This was probably because they were not paid in full for their mercenary services. Once again, Stefan IV Dusan was quick to take advantage of the situation and declared himself "Emperor and autocrat of Serbs and Greeks" (r. 1346-1355). Thereby he established his own Orthodox Serbian patriarchy.

Dusan was now free to pursue his own military ambitions, using his favorable momentum that he had gained when he conquered Epirus and Thessaly. His empire then expanded to its maximal geographic size, almost replacing the Byzantine Empire in the Balkans. By now he wanted to carry out a crusade of his own against the Turks. He urged Pope Urban V to mobilize the rest of the European knights and the Venetians to provide the necessary fleet to eliminate the Muslims from Europe.

However, Stefan Dusan the Mighty went too far in seeking Western allies who would introduce their Catholicism into the Orthodox Balkans. In 1355 the Serbian emperor was poisoned by his own court and died. He was one of the greatest conquerors and he succeeded to make Serbia a glorious empire.

☦

As for the Turks, they extended their military power and domination by declaring Adrianople their European capital in 1366 and renaming it Edirne. This permanently sealed the fate of the Balkan Peninsula and its nations.

In spite of that Ottoman military success, Mircea the Elder (r. 1386-1418) bravely fought the Turks and scored a major victory at Rovine in 1394. He also single handedly repelled two Ottoman invasions of his Wallachia. That entitled him to interfere in the civil war between the sons of Beyazid I. Hence in 1411 he supported Prince Musa for the Ottoman throne against his other brothers. If Musa had won Romanian history would be different, but he lost and thus drew the enmity of the next sultan Mehmed I.

Since the odds were severely stacked against him Prince Mircea agreed to pay tribute to the Ottoman Empire in exchange for ensuring Wallachia's freedom. But, his son Prince Vlad II (r. 1436-1442 and 1443-1447) the son of Mircea sought help to gain the throne by joining the Order of the Dragon in Nuremberg. This made him a pro-Catholic and anti-Ottoman knight.

Soon he realized he could not fulfill any of these obligations, and he was assassinated by his Orthodox boyars. His son Vlad III Dracula (r. 1448, 1456-1462, 1476) tried to renew the alliances his father had created but he switched them too often. He lost and gained the throne just like his father had done before him. Dependence on foreign benevolence had again proved problematic.

Having created similar unstable alliances Princes Dan II and Laiota the Elder ruled Wallachia during five different periods before and after Dracula. They failed to put together a Christian coalition and stubbornly fought the Turks alone. Before he was able to take part in a favorable alliance, Prince Vlad III the Impeller met the same tragic end as his father.

Prince Vlad III Dracula was daring and brave beyond description. He ruled over only 500,000 Wallachians, and he had no militarily powerful allies. He could not fight the Ottoman Empire which could supply an army of 500,000 warriors.

With the Ottoman power growing even stronger and as more land in the Balkans was being occupied a Christian coalition was a vital necessity. The Ottomans had to be stopped from overrunning Central Europe. The Battle at Kosovo Polye in 1389 demonstrated the firm commitment by the anti Ottoman alliance of Prince Lazar of Serbia, King Stephen of Bosnia, Czar Ivan of Bulgaria, and Prince Mircea the Elder of Wallachia, plus small contingents of Bosnians and Croats. All of these militaries fought the Turks under the father and son sultans Murad I and Bayezid I.

The Christian coalition lost the war and Serbia faced the Ottoman occupation. Many Serbian elitists tried to make the best of the situation by marrying their daughters to the sultan and his nobility. In 1396 this new alliance had a disastrous impact and another sad story is attached to it. In the Battle of Nicopolis, the last and strongest Christian coalition of Bohemian, Bulgarian, Burgundian, Dutch, English, French, German, Italian, Polish, Scotch, Swiss, and Wallachian troops, all supported by the Genovese and Venetian fleets were defeated by a coalition of the Ottomans and Serbs. The reason for the Christian defeat was not a lack of bravery, but a lack of unity in combat. That military fault was deeply rooted in the nationalistic and social order of the various crusaders:

> The sense of unity and universality that had been the foundation of Empire and Papacy in the early Middle Ages was passing away, and in its place the separatism of independent kingdoms was arising. This new separatist tendency demonstrated itself amidst the crusading medley before Nicopolis. There was no unity of purpose, no unity of arms and companies, and no common tactics in the camp of the Christians. The Turkish army was, on the other hand, a perfect example of the most stringent discipline, of a rigorous and even fanatic unity of purpose, of the concentration of supreme tactical power in the sole person of the Sultan.[15]

Two other notable elements marked the crusaders' defeat. One was the refusal to fight from both the Wallachians and the Transylvanian cavalry corps under Prince Mircea the Elder to engage in the already doomed fight. Second was the lack of a crucial charge from the Serbian Despot Stephen Lazarovich whose five thousand horsemen helped the almost defeated Ottomans win the battle. This did not stop the Turks from later occupying Serbia.

In the meantime, given that their borders were directly threatened, the Hungarians signed a pact with the Ottoman Empire on July12, 1444,

> ...written both in the Hungarian and Turkish languages; King Ladislaus Jagelo swore upon the Gospels, and the sultan swore upon the Koran, that it should be truly and religiously observed.[16]

The solemn pact was soon breached by the young Jagelo when he joined a military coalition of Bohemians, Bosnians, Croatians, Germans, Moldavians, Poles, and Wallachians. They were all supported by the Genoese, Papal, and Venetian fleets. All of these groups had decided to push the Turks out the Balkans forever. The former adversarial armies met in the same year on a battlefield near the fortress of Varna where they duplicated the disaster of Nicopolis.

Another Christian coalition came together four years later, this time with the reduced participation of Hungary, Moldavia, and Wallachia, but along with a late arrival, the Albanians. During the second Battle at Kosovo in 1448 firearms proved their superiority to other weapons and the Ottomans dominated once again.

The Turkish army had annihilated the military coalitions involved in three consecutive Balkan crusades, and the future looked gloomy for the Eastern European nations. The Ottomans were nevertheless defeated in the middle of Moldavia in 1475 at Vaslui. Yet the Turks claimed ownership of the Dacian land of Bessarabia (renamed Budjak) east of the Pruth River.

The conflict produced the unlikely coalition of this area's rightful owners, the Moldavians, and the aspiring owners, the Poles and Hungarians. The latter participating with only a symbolic few thousand soldiers and both were eager to occupy the land. The Turks were supported by the Bulgarians and Wallachians who also hoped for a slice of the disputed area.

A special solidarity always existed between the Romanian principalities of Moldavia and Wallachia (Muntenia) which was based on their common Dacian ancestry, language, and religion which later would be known as Romanians. They often used war to gain independence from the Ottoman occupation.

The Wallachian and Moldavian rulers often acted as suzerains without paying the customary tribute to any of the super powers to whom they formally "submitted."

They simply became the allies of convenience of Poland and the Ottoman Empire who were the fierce rivals of Hungary. They played them off against each other each while maintaining the independence of the future Romanian people. The typical situation presented itself before the Crusade of Nicopolis,

> ...when Mircea [the Wallachian ruler], who had been hesitating between the Turks and the Hungarians, had eventually fled to Sigismund's court, where he was well received and was granted the duchy of Fogaras [Fagaras] and the county of Severin. Mircea's flight was not actuated by love towards his Christian neighbour and hatred to an infidel sultan; nor was Sigismund's bequest a Christian act of charity to a dethroned, but noble ally. The Wallachian prince meant simply to play off one deadly enemy against another, while the Hungarian monarch intended to seize a golden opportunity for the subjugation of a restless neighbor, whom he hoped to employ against the Turks. Whatever their secret aims may have been, their interests coincided for a time in presence of a common foe.[17]

The two Romanian principalities found their most powerful ally in John Hunyadi voivode of Transylvania (1441-1444) captain general (1444-1446) and regent of Hungary (1446-1453) who due to his Wallachian origin[18] was willing to help the future Romanians. When a Turkish army tried to pillage Wallachia in 1442 Hunyadi defeated them, and ensured the independence of the future Romanian principalities. The fact that his first language was Romanian helped him become the voievode of Transylvania where the majority of the population was Vlachian.[19] He successfully supported Wladislaw III (r. 1434-1444) who became the king of Poland and Hungary, an act that secured him a strong position among the Hungarians.

John Hunyadi was catapulted to military stardom by his many crushing victories against the invading Ottoman armies in Albania, Bosnia, Bulgaria, Herzegovina, Hungary, Serbia, and Wallachia. He was a main defender of Christendom. He was called the "White Knight of Wallachia," and he was given the title of Atleta Cristi by the pope when he undertook the defense of Belgrade on his own.

No Hungarian noblemen wanted to join this battle against the Ottomans. Hunyadi died of the plague in 1456 in Belgrade. He was buried at Alba Julia in Transylvania, a fact that attests to his non-Hungarian origin.[20]

During his illustrious military career Hunyadi succeeded in maintaining most of the borders of the Danubian basin, and he prevented the Ottomans from invading Hungary and the future Romanian lands. The inevitable happened when the allied Christian nations could not replace their lost soldiers for another crusade against the Turks.

During his long reign Stefan the Great (r. 1475-1504) won 34 out of 36 battles, but getting older he pledged Moldova vassalage to the kings of Hungary and Poland. Next was to the Ottoman Empire which had an inexhaustible amount of supplies that were necessary to keep on fighting. It was also capable to easily replace its fallen soldiers along with any other military needs. Again, the numbers of superiority in men and supplies decided the outcome of winning the wars, as it always has happened in the course of history.

✝

With the fall of Constantinople in 1453 the Byzantine Empire came to an end. At that point the power of the Muslim Crescent dominated the entirety of the Balkans. It was only a matter of years until the Ottoman Empire would take over the whole Peninsula and the lands beyond it.

The history of this Byzantine era shows that kings and monarchs trusted mercenaries for protection more than they did their own people. The foreigners had none of the impediments of inherited feelings of revenge nor were they nationalistic or susceptible to religious pathos. Furthermore, they were in no way attached to any disputed land. When they allied themselves with foreign powers these rulers increased their national military potential because they were counting on support that was usually more reliable than that which they would have received from their domestic sources.

Most of the time alliances kept a nation from defecting to the enemy. The next best way to maintain an alliance was to exchange hostages mainly the close relatives of the rulers involved. Broken trust and misplaced faith made for a bad legacy.

Typically, an alliance was defined by who won a war. A victor attracted submissive partners, and the groups that were in need of defense. Often the losers also united to crush the victor and to retrieve lost lands and its people to restore their national pride.

In all of this there seems to have been one rule that never changed, the one in need bit the hand that fed it. Hence, an ally in need was an ally no one needed. This was the reason why after the failed Crusade of Nicopolis the Western powers had lost their best knights battling the Turks. Also, they had spent a huge amount of money (two hundred thousand florins in gold) to ransom their survivors. The Westerners again did not mobilize to help Eastern Europe in a doomed fight as they also had not done in Varna in 1444 and in Constantinople in 1453.

Consequently, at the end of the fifteenth century a pro-Turkish policy was adopted by many Balkan states in order to avoid self-destruction. Still, if there was even the slightest hope of winning a battle or war they would revolt against the Ottoman domination. This ongoing struggle created unexpected alliances, and governed the unfolding of historical events for centuries to come.

# REFERENCE NOTES

1. Anna Comnena, The Alexiad of Anna Comnena, trans. E. R. A. Sewter (London: Penguin Books, 1969), 230.
2. Comnena, The Alexiad, 217. Comnena mistakenly described them as "Sarmatians Scyths and a large contingent of Dacians."
3. Comnena, The Alexiad, 217.
4. Comnena, The Alexiad, 221.
5. Comnena, The Alexiad, 228-229.
6. Niketas Choniatēs, O City of Byzantium: Annals of Niketas Choniatēs, trans. Harry J. Magoulias (Detroit: Wayne State University Press, 1984), 10.
7. Choniatēs, O City, 10.
8. Choniatēs, O City, 11.
9. Bela was so spoiled by Emanuel that he hoped to inherit the Byzantine crown along with the Hungarian throne. But, the emperor was surprised with a son and Bela lost his affection, and was also dropped from the list of his daughter's prospects for a husband. Worse yet, Bela the Constantinopolitan became a Hungarian king (supported by a Byzantine contingent) whom no one wanted, including his mother. After sending her into exile and imprisoning his other brother, he convinced the Hungarian Church of his Catholic faith, all the while remaining obedient to his Orthodox benefactor Emanuel. He even put the Byzantine double cross on his coat-of-arms and Hungarian coins. Bela was highly sophisticated by the standards in his semi-barbarian nation, and so introduced reforms that entitled him to be called the Hungarian Empire Builder.
10. Comnena, The Alexiad, 252.
11. Comnena, The Alexiad, 298.
12. Comnena, The Alexiad, 299.
13. Choniatēs, O City, 267.

14. Choniatēs, O City, 292.
15. Aziz Suryal Atiya, The Crusade of Nicopolis (London: Methuen, 1934), 71.
16. Edward S. Creasy, History of the Ottoman Turks (Beirut: Khayats, 1961), 66.
17. Atiya, Crusade of Nicopolis, 7.
18. Historian Matthew Spinka described him as a "man who became the most famous Turkokiller, the Romanian general John Hunyadi" in A History of Christianity in the Balkans: A Study in the Spread of Byzantine Culture Among the Slavs (Hamden, CT: Archon Books, 1968), 153. In many documents Hunyadi is simply named Janos Olah (Olah being the Hungarian word for Vlach/Wallachian). The counter-argument is that today in Hungary many family names are Olah (meaning Wallach,) an obviously "important name," the Romanians might add.
19. Born in the Wallachian village of Corbi/Ravens, to a Vlach father and a Transylvanian mother, at baptism his first name was Ioan or Iancu and last name Voicu. When his father later moved to his wife's estate in Hunedoara in Banat, he adopted the last name of Hunyadi in 1409 to honor the Hunyadi Castle which he had received as a present from King Sigismund. His son John/Ioan/Iancu/Joannes/Janos, who was known by the full name Ioan Corvin de Hunedoara (abbreviated in English as John Hunyadi; Edward Gibbon spelled his last name Huniades) proved to be born a military leader, in spite of the fact that he was not able to read or write. This was an indication that he did not come from Hungarian nobility, especially since his mother tongue was Romanian. In numerous battles Hunyadi commanded the Romanian contingents, and in the Battle at Varna the Wallachian troops saved his life while he was making a desperate retreat.
20. The Corvinus House was named after Hunyadi's Romanian birthplace Corbi. His son Matthias was born at Napoca/Cluj, an ancient Dacian city in Transylvania (where his equestrian statue

now stands). Most likely he spoke Romanian before he learned Hungarian. Probably his birth name was Matei Corvin or Mateiaş Corvin. After his father's death he had to be rescued from the Hungarian nobility who had taken the young Matthias to be a Wallachian (Romanian) foreigner and condemned him to death. He was rescued by the governor of Bohemia and given shelter in Prague. He took the throne of Hungary with the help of his Transylvanian uncle Mihai/Mihaly Szilagy, who led an army and forced the Hungarian Diet to elect Matthias as king while he was still in Prague. In defiance to the Hungarian nobility, the young monarch proudly displayed the raven on his coat of arms. It was later given a mythical interpretation by the Hungarian biographers, some of whom still deny Hunyadi's lineage. King Matthias (also known in Europe as the Raven King, Mateja Korvina, and Matej Corvine) was by far the greatest ruler of Hungary. He made it into an empire at that time of its greatest geographical extent. After his death his son Janos Corvinus was rejected as heir to the throne by the Hungarians. The "raven dynasty" came to an end. After the fall of Communism in 1990, the free Hungarian Parliament voted to restore the traditional crowned coat of arms, now without the once iconic Corvinus bird, yet retaining the Byzantine double cross.

# THE AREA'S SHIFTING BORDERS

Ancient borders traditionally followed the lines of rivers, like the Danube River and its tributaries, or deep valleys or mountain ridges like the Balkan and Carpathian Mountains. This often offered resistance to the hungry and homeless nomads of the Early Middle Ages. The border of the Byzantine Empire consisted of the basic *vallum* of elevated earthworks with fortified towers and garrisons left from the Roman border fortifications, all the defense system inherited from Roman times. It was however inadequate for thwarting the massive barbarian invasions coming from Eurasia. Within the empire there were provincial borders, regional lines of demarcation, city limits, and other topographic partitions, each of which had its own distinctive ethnicity, administration, economy, cultural, and religious characteristics.

In the beginning borders meant nothing to the barbarian raiders unless there were high border walls to deter them. Over time they found themselves drawing their own lines of military takeovers. Soon enough establishing a border was a way to gain the status of land ownership for each barbarian tribe. It identified how forceful and strong was the leader who had consolidated enough power to defend his own people's living space and how much land he was able to conquer. The simplest means of acquiring new land was marriage between leading families. The most effective way to impose new borders and enlarge old ones was always achieved by large scale invasions and military conquests.

While in the beginning the Byzantine armies appeared to be keeping the brazen Gepids and Avars in check, because they seemed to be willing to negotiate. The Slavic tribes who arrived at the fringes of the empire presented a more difficult challenge. When the emperors in Constantinople were militarily strong, they were able to keep the invaders in a position of semi-vassalage.

When they were weak the barbarians rampaged throughout the Byzantine provinces attempting to extend the borders of their chiefdoms. Rudimentarily armed with farm tools but also with poisoned arrows, the Slavs compensated for their lack of advanced weaponry with a large supply of foot soldiers. In addition their cavalry used stirrups which freed there hands to fight. They mastered new weapons, the lasso and the net which they used to incapacitate and capture their hunted animals and enemies. However, their lack of stone throwing machinery and siege tactics made the Slavs hesitant to attack fortresses or fortified cities.

Like many other barbarians they preferred to fight in swamps, thick forests or in and along the narrow river valleys that were ideal for ambushes where they could make quick escapes. They also conducted their raids during the winter using the frozen rivers to help and increase their speedy attacks.

Emperor Justinian I, because he was aware of the barbarians' weak points, paid a great deal of attention to the natural defensive line provided by the Danube River. He enforced it with fifty-two fortresses. At the same time he guarded his native Dacia Mediterranean with sixty-nine fortresses. As a precaution he built defensive lines with twenty-seven fortresses in the middle of Dacian Moesia along with forty-six fortresses in Macedonia, and thirty-seven in Epirus,

Thessaly, Thracia, and Southern Greece.

Justinian tried to confine the Slavs to Pannonia where he granted them land to settle and offered an annual subsidiary to keep them peaceful, and uninterested in crossing south the natural border of the Danube River. All of these military and political measures secured the safety and prosperity of the Byzantine Empire while it was enjoying a golden age that would never again be duplicated.

In fact, it was the enviable gold that attracted the barbarian invasions south of the Danube River into the Byzantine Empire, when Justin II refused to buy peace from his savage invaders. Unfortunately, when the Persian border was threatened in Anatolia by other barbarians the Byzantine armies were transferred to Asia Minor to keep the empire's borders from being destroyed.

This left the Balkan frontiers with less military protection a fact that did not go unnoticed by the Avars. They took advantage of the situation and invaded across the Danube in 574. They achieved two major victories over General Tiberius (the future Byzantine emperor), who was forced to renew the customary tribute payments. The general's defeat meant the imperial border was from now on vulnerable and it proved to be easily penetrable by the cascades of the Eurasian pagan mega tribes.

In the year 582 the Avars conquered Sirmium (Mitrovitza) and two years later Singidunum (Belgrade) the most outstanding of the Roman bastions on the northern Balkan line. This deprived the Byzantines control of the Pannonian border, and broke the military dam that had held back the barbarians. Their outpouring was now irreversible.

Fighting to regain whatever control he could of the empires borders General Priscus led the Byzantine armies in three victories against the Avar-Slav coalition and re-took Viminacium (Kostolac). In the year 600 he forced the Avars to recognize the Danubian line as the inviolable border of the empire.

Maurice was the first emperor of Constantinople to understand how vulnerable the Byzantine frontiers really were. They were now ceaselessly under attack by the barbarian hordes riding horses. His first priority was to re-establish the old northern borders adjacent to the Danube as the natural line of defense. He manned them with highly mobile cavalry troops that could quickly respond to distant emergencies. But, lack of money followed by his assassination at the hands of his own military, left the Byzantine frontiers wide open to the barbarian invasions.

Suddenly the unpaid Byzantine armies that were stationed to secure those lines mutinied. This led to the election of their commander Phocas as emperor (r. 602-610). However, instead of fighting at the border his priority was to destroy his personal internal enemies. The Avars and Slavs took advantage of this imperial crisis by invading Illyria and Dalmatia where they created their own borders.

The arrival of the Cumans and Patzinaks in Dacia triggered new barbarian invasions as far south as Macedonia. These new invaders had total contempt for any borders, and so they returned to the northern Danube where they had earlier established family-based camps. "Living alongside the territories of the Byzantine Empire, they treated them as their own and plundered them at will and with complete license."[1]

Bulgars used the Slavic tribes to violate the Byzantine borders and headed toward Constantinople in 710. Together they raided southward, deep into Macedonia and Greece, exhausting the imperial military power and draining the treasury of Constantinople. Their rapacious persistence paid off, and soon the borders of Bulgaria under Khan Krum (r. 803-814) extended from Adrianople south of Serdica (Sofia), Naissus (Niss), and from the Iron Gates of the Danube River to the northeast beyond the Bug River.

When Boris I who Christianized his subjects and took the name Michael I, he built the first "barbarian" borders around his newly created kingdom. His son Vladimir tried to extend them into the Serbian lands but failed. He also failed to return the Bulgars back to paganism. Boris blinded his son who died imprisoned in a dungeon.

However, his third son Simeon I the Great proved to be militarily successful when he defeated the Magyars, the Serbs and even the Byzantines. He extended the Bulgarian borders to its largest lines ever into the end of the Balkan Peninsula. He became the tzar of the most powerful country in the entire Eastern and Southeastern Europe. Thus the Byzantine borders were again dramatically redrawn and reduced.

Czar Simeon I carried out relentless campaigns of conquest in Epirus, Macedonia, and Thracia, and so the First Bulgarian Empire covered many of the Byzantine lands on the Balkan map, reaching its zenith.

☦

The rise of the distant Kievan Rus was felt when its military extended their territory against the Bulgars who subsequently moved their capital from Pliska to Preslav. The Kievan occupation of eastern Bulgaria and Dobrudja in 968 forced the Bulagarians to establish their new capital at Pereyaslavets/little Pereslav (near today's Isaccea Romania). This was a clear case of dismemberment and capture of Byzantine lands.

After a Russian fleet unsuccessfully attacked Constantinople in 941 the Kievan Prince Sviatoslav used the Pechenegs in his pillaging mission and captured Philippopolis where he impaled 20,000 captives. This prompted a retaliatory campaign led by the Emperor John Tzimiskes I (r. 969-976) a former capable Armenian general. He succeeded to keeping intact the borders of his native province of Armenia, which was dangerously located between the Arabs and Russians. After he drove the Russian invaders out of Bulgaria he enthroned Prince Boris II (a former hostage of Constantinople) as tzar of his kingdom. However, the royal title he wanted, came with an unwanted price, when the Emperor John I Tzimiskes captured Preslav the capital of Bulgaria. He took Boris II and his family prisoners, and the czar lost all of his titles and privileges along with his entire royal treasury. With the entire Bulgaria incorporated into the Byzantine Empire in 971 the First Bulgarian Empire symbolically ended.

With a bigger and stronger army Emperor John I inflicted such a defeat on the attacking Russians that all of the lands they occupied were lost and recaptured as well. The borders of those Byzantine lands shifted to an enlarged extent to match the wars victorious results.

After Emperor John I was poisoned by his own people he left behind a solid restored Byzantine Empire whose borders included most of the Balkans and Asia Minor. The imperial border into Palestine stopped above Jerusalem. His nephew Basil II (r. 976-1025) succeeded him as the emperor of a very strong empire.

Basil's military activity consisted of recapturing the Byzantine regions in the south of the Balkan Peninsula. By 1006 his army had crushed the rebellious Bulgars near Thessaloniki and advanced north into the Bulgarian heartland towards the Danube River. They inflicted gruesome punishments on the populace along the way.

Finally, in 1014 the Byzantines resoundingly defeated the Bulgars in the Battle of Kleidion where countless were massacred, and their Tzar Samuil barely escaped due to his very fast horse. Only fifteen thousand were spared but they were blinded and allowed to return to their lands led by a few of their comrades who had been blinded in one eye only.

When he saw the mutilated soldiers Samuil suffered a heart attack and died. Basil came to be referred to as the "Bulgar-Slayer" and continued to subdue any residual Bulgar resistance until 1018 when the defunct Bulgarian Empire became a Byzantine *theme*/province.

Thus five decades of military conflicts between the Bulgars and the Byzantine Empire ended and borders shifted again. Basil continued to extend his imperial borders into his conquered part of the Crimean Peninsula. This emperor was a true Byzantine hero despised only by the Bulgarians.

Yet, the pagan and rapacious barbarians kept crossing the Byzantine borders. There was too much fighting for the imperial army being in constant warfare which exhausted the financial resources of Constantinople. It was almost bankrupted after the flourishing empire left by Basil II.

Eventually, through the diplomacy of Alexios Comnenus I (r. 1081-1118) who was able to make use of Cuman military might was able to almost destroy the Pecheneg invaders who by 1091 had reached Constantinople. Defeated, they then ravaged Thracia and many other southern Byzyantine provinces.

Once both of those barbarian tribes left Bulgaria, Alexios restored the Danubian frontier of the Byzantine Empire. This was a rare accomplishment in itself.

✝

Nevertheless, the empire's borders in Asia Minor were violently trespassed by a new breed of barbarians the Seljugs Turks. They occupied so much territory inside the Byzantine Empire that it alarmed the Western military powers. Pope Urban II preached in favor of the First Crusade (1096-1099) with the mission to free the Holy Land from the Muslim occupation of the Seljugs.

It turned out that the first crusaders of the "People's Crusade" were mostly hungry destitute European peasants including women and children who once crossed the Byzantine border, they began to loot almost equally as much as the barbarians. To stop the devastation Alexios had to feed and care for some 100,000 crusaders at the empires expense. In October these "crusaders" were decimated by the Seljuks Turks in the Battle of Civetot. The next real crusaders of the Knights' armies pushed the Turks back. They restored the Eastern Byzantine frontier and by liberating Jerusalem in 1099, the Holy Land was returned to the Christians.

Since this Christian victory in Palestine little has changed in the Balkan Peninsula and within the Byzantine Empire. An exception to this is that all the crusaders who crossed into Anatolia placed a tremendous financial and manpower burden on Constantinople in order to accommodate the European warriors.

At first, the idea of a sacred war generated Christian enthusiasm but over the years it degenerated into rivalries and conflicts at all levels among Crusaders and the Byzantines. It almost duplicated a barbarian invasion except that the Crusaders were in transit to the Holly Land. It meant that a huge column of hundreds of thousands warriors with their horses and luggage, tents, artillery pieces, repair shops, mobile kitchens, medical supplies along with all of the other vital needs for an army to slowly move on the Byzantine territories.

✟

Back to the Balkan Peninsula, Vlastimir I (r. 825-850) who founded the first Serbian homeland had three sons who defended their borders against Bulgarian invasions. The older son took over the domains of the younger brothers whom he handed over to the Bulgarian Khan Boris as a pledge for keeping peace and retaining the new Serbian borders. A tug of war between the Bulgars and the Byzantines over the numerous ethnic problems generated by the Serbian ruler resulted in the Byzantine hegemony over the entire Slavic area. However, the restless Serbians kept fighting the Byzantines, and other foreign groups who sought to dominate them. They gradually expanded their borders at the expense of the Byzantine Empire.

While the Byzantine emperors were busy with the Crusades and shouldering the religious wars in the Holy Land, the older barbarian settlers took advantage of this to protect their many national interests. Especially to extend their borders inside the empire as the Byzantine armies were busy assisting the Crusaders or fighting other new barbarians.

Duke Stefan Nemanja took full advantage of Emperor Manuel I's wars against the Hungarians, while the Serbian leader extended its borders into the Morava Valley, raided Singidunum (Belgrade), Niss, and Serdica, conquered Zeta (Montenegro) and Kosovo, and entered western Bulgaria.

In spite of his humble surrender to kneel in front of Emanuel in 1172, the emperor reinstated his title of "Grand Zoupan" to Nemanja who unified the Serbs. Military strong again, he extended the borders of Serbia outward from Lesser Rascia, between Dalmatia and upper Moesia. Thus, by force of arms, Nemanja shaped the identity of the Serbian nation and initiated the Serbian Empire. His chain of conquests was halted in 1191 when he was defeated in Southern Moravia by a Byzantine army led by the next Byzantine Emperor Isaac II.

The occupying imperial troops ravaged the Serbian holdings, but could not win in a Serbian guerilla war. A peace accord was reached on the basis of a compromise over land between Isaac and Nemanja. However, the treaty was sealed by the marriage of Stefan's son also named Stefan to the emperor's niece Eudokia Angelina. Nemanja agreed not to ally himself with the Bulgars and kept Arbanas (Albania), Kosovo, and Zeta.

Nemanja after repelling a Hungarian invasion in 1193 retained the northern territories, and Rascia (today's Raska, on the rivers Raska and Ibar bordering with Bulgaria). Three years later he abdicated and retired as a monk. His two sons divided the nation until the third son Sava reunited it.

However, by then the Byzantine Empire was providing a much needed wedge between Bulgaria and Serbia. In essence this wedge prevented their alliance and another war against the Byzantine Empire

✝

The most egregious violators of the European borders in the Middle Age were the Magyars, later named the Hungarians. Defeated by the Bulgars in 889 and forced by the Pechenegs to settle in the Pannonian flatlands this pagan migratory tribe could not be confined within any definite boundaries. Their predatory instinct led them to cross one European border after another. They invaded the Moravians in 902 and five years later defeated the Bavarians thus entering the gateway to Central Europe.

These ferocious raiders defeated the armies of Alemmanni, Burgundians, Franks, Lombards, and Saxons. They even attempted to storm Venice and in frustration sacked or reduced to ashes many Italian cities such as Pavia and Verona. They also plundered villages and towns in the vicinity of Naples and Rome. Their movements westward brought them to the English Channel and to Denmark.

By 924 they had ravaged what is today France and had almost reached Spain. For nine years they collected a tribute from Henry I of Germany who was buying time to build his army. He ultimately pulverized one Magyar horde. Another Magyar horde attacked Constantinople in 934 and in frustration of their failure devastated Macedonia and Thessaly.

For the next thirty-five years these barbarian hordes terrorized the Byzantine Empire and the rest of Europe with their repeated military assaults. In 955 at Lechfeld, Otto I (r. 936-973) inflicted a military disaster, and the defeated Magyars stopped further incursions into the West. Another defeat came while joining the Rus army at Arcadiopolis in 970, when forced the Magyars back within the Pannonian borders which was flat lands of pasture for their horses.

Thirty years later, the ferocious Magyars became Christians under Stephen I. He was crowned as the first king of the Kingdom of Hungary. Finally, Bavaria and Austria were able to continue their existence without the fear of an invasion by the rapacious Asiatic neighbors.

However, in spite of their successful raids all across Europe the Magyars had difficulty extending their western border even for a few miles into their neighborly rich Transylvania. There were three reasons for this: first, if they invaded the area they would be moving eastward toward Asia, and away from the readily available rich plunder of civilized Europe.

Second, by traversing the Carpathian Mountains it would require them to work, and even though it would mean access to gold and silver to extract from the mines it was not what the nomads on their horses wanted to do.

Third, at that time Transylvania was divided into powerful Daco-Roman *voivodates*/dukedoms. These would have been extremely challenging to conquer because of their mountainous locations and because of their military enforcements provided by the hosted mega tribes of Avars, Cumans, and Pechenegs. All of these tribes were present in Transylvania and were feared by the Hungarians.[2]

✢

According to *Gesta Hungarorum*,[3] when the Magyars (Mogerii) settled on the Tisza (Tyscia) River they found Slavs (Sclavi), Bulgarians (Bulgarii), Vlachs (Blachii), and the shepherds of the Romans (*pastores Romanorum*). The last two of these people were the unmistakable Vlachian inhabitants of the Pannonian and Transylvanian lands. They were a society that possessed a solid Daco-Roman historical background. Also, they were the only ethnic group that spoke a Latin dialect in the Balkans.

The first expedition of Magyars into Transylvania encountered the Wallachians led by the voivodates of Glad in the Banat region, the Menumorut north of Banat in the Bihor/Crisana basin, and, to the east, the central land of Gelu, *dux Blacorum* (leader of the Vlachs) as it is referred to in *Gesta Ungarorum*. The same Hungarian document reported that when chieftan Arpad used force to settle his Magyars in Transylvania, he was confronted at the line of the Temes/Timis River by Voievode Glad, who was leading a powerful army of Bulgarians, Cumans, and Vlachs.

Another historical source, *The Chronicle of Nestor*, written in Kiev before the twelfth century clearly stated that the Voloh/Vlach army of Transylvania had no Hungarian soldiers when it fought the Bulgars in 1210.[4] Prior to that, King Geza II (r. 1141 – 1162) encouraged Western Europeans known as Saxons and Szeklers to settle in Transylvania. Thus, they indirectly colonized it with Catholics who would depend on his benevolence which he was not officially or legally entitled to exercise. These new settlers were wandering people and penniless misfits who did not belong to any German state. They preferred to take refuge in the rich Transylvania believing the Hungarian kings will endow them with lands which in reality never belonged to Hungary.

When the Teutonic Knights returned defeated from the Holy Wars in Palestine, again the Hungarian King Andras II (r. 1205 – 1235) with no legal entitlement allowed them to settle in Transylvania. They founded the city of Brasov and in 1212 built the Bran Castle with wood from the Fagaras Mountains. At that time, Transylvania was known as the "land of the Vlachs."

In fact, "Transylvania" was named by the Romans, which in Latin "Trans Silva" meant "Beyond the Forest." That vast forest was the natural border that the Romans were afraid to cross. Located South of Transylvania it was mythically very dense and mysterious known as the "Vlasia Forest./Forest of Vlahs". This forest began from the vast grain fields of Vlasca (Vlachian region) which belonged to the Western Wallachia/Muntenia.

This rich land was populated since ancient times by the Dacians, renamed Wallachians, in short Vlachs, and their Vlasia Forest extended north to the wet marshes of Bucuresti/Buchareat, Prince Dracula's capital. It was located on the well known commercial route connecting the Vlasca grain basket with the grain markets of the city of Lvov in Poland, a route known as Via Wallachiensis.

More than one million Wallachians populated Transylvania and Wallachia before the arrival of the Hungarians. The Hungarians managed to control seven counties in Transylvania, two of which were ruled independently by the Saxons and Sekelys.

In 1222 the annoyed Hungarian nobility forced the powerless Andras II to award those counties the Golden Bull which limited their king to grant lands and favors to foreign nobles and knights. Obviously, the seven "Hungarian" counties from Transylvania were an abuse which was corrected by the new royal document. This prohibited the king from giving land away even if it was not inside the

Hungarian borders. Therefore, the prior "Hungarian authority" and the ownership of any land in Transylvania came to be merely symbolic and not legal. The western Hungarian border with Transylvania was marked by the Tisa River.

Transylvania's demographics were further changed more than 800 years later as to motivate why Transylvania belongs to the Hungarians with the invented arguments that:

> ...the presence of a [fourth people, the *Wlachs* (Walla-chians)]. The earliest written records of their existence in Erdély date from 1210 and 1222. The Wlachs came from the Balkan Peninsula as semi-nomadic shepherd folk. In the ensuing centuries, their leisurely and voluntary immigration was transformed into wholesale flight from Tartar attacks, Turkish invasions and the oppression of their own Phanariote rulers. Incidentally, these Tartar and Turkish wars, while increasing the number of Wallachians (later called Rumanians) in Transylvania, decimated the indigenous Hungarian population of the country.[5]

This highly contestable and historically inaccurate explanation is typical of how today the Hungarians dismiss any Romanian claim to ownership in Transylvania. Despite their theories, the truth about Transylvania is clearly carved in marble on the Trajan Column. It shows that it was inhabited by the Dacians whom the Romans fought from 101-106 A.D. to defeat them in order to occupy Transylvania. The reason was to loot 165 tons of gold and 364 tons of silver from the Dacian mines of Transylvania which belonged to the future Romanians. The Roman legions fought the Dacians, not the Magyars or the Hungarians!

Somehow, in the capital of Buda between the years 904 and 1500 more than ninety voievodes were formally approved by the Hungarian kings to govern Transylvania. In fact, they were local warlords and clan leaders (maiores terrae) who originated from different parts of

Transylvania. They had accepted Hungarian suzerainty in the hope of gaining protection from barbarian and Ottoman invasions. Most of them were independent rulers and some were involved in the internal affairs of Hungary, such as Mihaly Szilagyi.[6]

Furthermore, although Hungarians take credit for bringing Christianity to Transylvania this religion was in fact present in the Carpathian Mountains since the Roman legionnaires were stationed their in occupied Transylvania until 275.

More than six centuries later, the Magyars arrived at the Danube River. Prior to the tenth century Christian Orthodox monastic establishments were located in Dacia on the Mures River at Morisena (near today's Cenad) and Salaj in the Crisana region. At that time, the Hungarians had never herd of Christianity.

Each time the Magyars tried to extend their borders into Transylvania they were met with the overwhelming military force of the Cumans who were settled in the former Dacian land. Ironically, seven Cuman tribes settled in Hungary, and not a single Magyar tribe settled in Transylvania.

However, the geopolitical consequences had been shuffled for the Hungarians just as bad as it had been in Transylvania. Separate states now shared a common king who was recognized by the local independent rulers. They in turn were approved by the Hungarian monarch who demanded their loyalty.

Because of territorial matters that involved, Pope Urban II it led to the countries concerned to enter the Pacta Conventa in 1102 and formed a union of independent states. A new kind of Hungarian Empire was formed in which each country will be an associate of Hungary but remain an independent state. This was done just to add more ruling titles to the king's name.

The king was represented by a ban in Croatia and a voievode in Transylvania. The only Hungarian administrator elected from the rank of barons who were in charge of some estates. He was formally the chief judge and military commander. This was part of the Hungarian strategy applied all over Eastern Europe to claim lands and imaginary borders by assuming hegemony backed by military strikes.

Hungarian King Andras II was coerced by the Saxons of Transylvania to grant them financial and judicial autonomy, and this nearly ended Hungarian control of Transylvania.[7] Yet, the Hungarians persistently crossed other borders assuming ownership of other lands. The same way they infringed on the borders of independent Croatia which in the mid 1060s included Bosnia, Slavonia, and a strip of the Damatian coast.

After King Laszlo I occupied Croatia in 1091 and declared himself as Croatian king he extended the Hungarian borders over that country. The next Hungarian king Coloman (r. 1097-116) also invaded Croatia. Biograd became a vital sea port for the continental Hungary where he crowned himself ruler. He considered Dalmatia and Slavonia part of his Hungarian kingdom as well.

As with the Transylvanian occupation, most of the Hungarian ownership of land in the former Dacia, was a result of marriages and dowries. The main reason for Hungarians to include additional Dacian land was to extract the gold and silver from the Transylvanian mines. This was the same reason why these regions were incorporated centuries later into the borders of the Austro-Hungarian Empire.

✠

When the last Comnenus emperors strangled each other fighting over the Byzantine throne, King Bela III (r. 1172-1196) who had taken an oath in Constantinople never to attack the Byzantine Empire (he helped Emperor Manuel I to campaign against Hungary), now saw an opportunity to extend the Hungarian borders south of the Danube. He invaded Moesia and allied with the Serbs to destroy Niss and Serdica. Eventually, he reasoned with his son-in-law Emperor Isaac II and re-focused his aggression on the Bulgarians, without any territorial gains.

Despite a roller coaster of incidents and wars between Byzantines, Hungarians and Venetians, all of whom badly wanted possession of the Dalmatian coast, Southern Croatia-Dalmatia, and Bosnia, these lands remained relatively free. For the most part they were "royal cities", and they continued to be self-governing with their borders remaining relatively unchanged.

A large "Serbian" population within Bosnia was actually composed of Vlachs from northern Albania and Montenegro who always maintained their independent status. Traditionally the Vlach shepherds of the Balkans were strong militarily, and were exemplified by their killing Prince David (brother of Tzar Samuil) who for a short time ruled the regions of Macedonia and Thessaly. When the Bulgars, Serbs, and the Hungarians became too possessive as far as land was concerned they all asked the Byzantine Empire for protection. The Golden Hordes invaded in 1240 any European borders erasing any notion of a country or state they savagely invaded and pillage.

Nevertheless, the Hungarians made a spectacular comeback. Their Louis the Great (r. 1342-1382) considered himself the king of Hungary, Poland, Dalmatia, Croatia, Rama, Serbia, and Galicia. He also ruled part of Bulgaria, Moldavia and Wallachia which were his fictional vassal princedoms, and also were his enemies. The noble pretext for the Hungarian kings' determination to occupy the neighboring countries was to convert them to Catholicism, and establish a common front against the Ottoman expansion into Eastern Europe.

☩

In the eastern lands towards the area of the Volga River the well-established Khazars desperately defended their borders against the restless Bulgars, nomadic Slavs, and countless other wandering barbarian tribes from Eurasia. Their leaders used titles that sounded good to them, but had little real meaning, such as beg, khan, qugan, and czar. They conducted plundering raids which caused vast population migrations. Their ignorance of geographical boundaries made them roam over the vast land of what is today Ukraine which at that time translated as the "borderland" to Europe. In this land with only a few unmapped commercial roads and trade posts the Grand Prince of Kiev Vladimir I (r. 970-1015) took the matter of borders very seriously.

He was aware that unless these tribes were subdued there would be no kingdom to rule. He spared no military or diplomatic efforts, and even kidnapped his future pagan wife Rogneta (after killing her father because he had rejected his marriage proposal). He also married many others in order to create the state of the Kievan Rus. Since the Pechenegs continued to invade his territory, Vladimir had fortifications constructed which duplicated the Roman defense system. They encircled Kiev with a radius of more than 100 miles of border. From this base of operation he conducted successful campaigns in Galicia, occupied land between Poland and Lithuania, and extended his borders into Volga Bulgaria.

✝

At this point in the history of the Balkan Peninsula and the Byzantine Empire a historical parenthesis must be opened to introduce a huge military event which affected all of the inhabitants of these two lands. It was the beginning of the Crusades to liberate the Holy Land from the Seljukes' occupation. Their Holy War greatly affected all of the borders involved in these giant religious wars. These wars were between 1096 and 1270 when western European Christians engaged in eight main Crusades. The Byzantine Empire was greatly impacted by the Crusaders who crossed it to arrive in Palestine, which later was called the Levant, to finally reach Jerusalem.

In their crossing to the Levant, they stayed long enough to affect the emperor's authority and control over the Byzantine Empire affecting its stability, welfare and national interests. For once the Byzantine emperors wanted the Crusaders to extend and consolidate the imperial borders, since they did not want to be part of the war effort. Some leaders of the Latin West claimed border changes and even autonomy and leadership in certain regions of the empire.

The military strategies and war tactics of the Byzantines versus the Crusaders were the most disputed. These were so different that they affected even who would pay for their food supply, how it was transported and distributed, and other logistics which needed to be coordinated for maximum efficiency. It reached the highest conflict during the Fourth Crusade in 1204 when the European Crusaders sacked Constantinople instead of fighting the Ottomans in Palestine.

In the meantime, south of the Danube the Byzantine armies subordinated an array of nations and ethnic groups. Perhaps, the most poignant examples of this were the Macedonians and Vlachs. The Macedonian Empire which had its zenith under Alexander the Great (356B.C. to 323B.C.) who conquered Persia, and he later extended its borders from Greece to Himalaya and the Indus River, continuing South to Egypt and Libya. The Macedonian Empire became a Roman province in 146 B.C.. Under the Byzantine Empire Macedonia was a thema belonging to Tracia and for two centuries until 1018 it was part of the First Bulgarian Empire.

A rare twist of history took place when the emperors of the Macedonian dynasty began to rule the Byzantine Empire from 867 until 1056. They extended the borders of the Orthodox Empire to its largest known surface. Due to geopolitical shifts in the Balkan Peninsula, Macedonia's initial borders were moved to an area south to the shores of the Aegean Sea.

The crusaders of the Latin Empire divided Macedonia and it was again divided by the Serbs and Bulgars. Its borders and its name were then erased under the Ottoman occupation. As portions of their land were assimilated by their greedy neighbors, Macedonians came to be mistakenly known as Albanians, Bulgarians, Greeks, Serbs, and Thracians.

The geopolitical and economic situation was different with the Vlachs[8], a numerous and distinctive society of people of Daco-Roman origin who recognized no borders and lived all over the Balkan Peninsula. They were often mistaken for other ethnicities until in 1186 a very important incident took place. It had unforeseeable major historical implications which effects put them solidly on the Balkan Peninsula map. It began when two Vlachian brothers had an audience with Emperor Isaac II and

> request[ed] that they be recruited in the Roman army and be awarded by imperial prescript a certain estate situated in the vicinity of Mount Haimos (Balkans), which would provide them with a little revenue.[9]

They asked the emperor for official recognition of their Vlachian land with its own borders and government. In exchange they were willing to enroll the Vlachs in the Byzantine army. When their request was denied the Vlachian brothers

> spat out heated words, hinting at rebellion," and "Asan, the more insolent and savage of two, was struck across the face and rebuked for his impudence[10] by a high imperial dignitary. The humiliated brothers kept their word and a successful rebellion followed in which they counted heavily on military help from the Cumans and Vallachians living north of the Danube.[11]

Their contemporary historian Niketas hardly mentioned the names of the Bulgars when he described these events. But, he clearly stated that "the Vlachs were afflicted with the disease of open rebellion" and "the emperor marched out against them"[12] in the spring of 1186 and not against the Bulgarians. He also referred to the Cumans as "auxiliaries," not the main fighters in this conflict.

✢

But Niketas clearly wrote that the two brothers Asan and Peter were Vlachs by "race" and the leaders of the Vlachian uprising. In

1192, they ambushed and annihilated a Byzantin army in a narrow mountain pass, and almost capturing the emperor. Afterwards they sacked Anchialos, captured Varna and partially destroyed Serdica (today's Sofia).

When a civil war erupted between the Vlachs and their Asiatic Bulgar allies, Asen and Peter were assassinated and emperor Alexius named their younger brother Ioannitsa Kaloyan (Handsome) to be in charge of the Balkan frontiers. Thus he became an unchallenged king of the Vlachians and Bulgarians.

☩

Moreover, four years later General Constantine Aspietes who "was strongly exhorted to pursue the war against the Vlachs," instead thought it better "to pay them their annual wages."[13]

Indeed, their leader and future King Ioannitsa marched out with a large and mighty force," aiming to destroy many Byzantine cities, including Adrianople (Edirne) and Didymoteichon (Dimetoka); intending to "cause the Romans [Byzantines] to withdraw from Thrace, he could leave the land fit to be inhabited only by wild beasts.[14]

What Ioannitsa the youngest and most accomplished brother of the Asans wanted was to establish a Greater Wallachia in Moesia and Thessaly, both of which were already densely populated by Vlachs. When the crusaders created a Latin Empire around his kingdom Ioannitsa urged Pope Innocent to

> write to the Latins, to keep away from my empire, and, if they do, my empire will not harm them; but let them not set it at little worth. If they make an attempt against my empire and set it at little worth, and some of them get killed, do not your Holiness suspect my empire because it will not be my fault.[15]

By planting the seeds of terror he hoped to keep the Romans (Byzantines) and the Latins (Crusaders) from interfering with his plans. Ioannitsa's assassination in 1207 ended those plans.

However thirty years later Pope Gregory IX remembered Ioannitsa as Dominus Blachorum et Bulgarorum/Lord of the Vlachs and Bulgars a true challenger of borders. If there was ever a need to draw a border in the Balkans it was to separate the Bulgars from the Vlachs who were the last to be the masters of the Danubian lands. Regardless of any boundaries the Vlach shepherds traveled with their herds of animals between distant lands (like Dobroudja and Pannonia) that they had owned since the Dacian Empire. But, landmarks began to rapidly change due to another invasion that no borders could stop.

✢

The arrival of the Golden Horde made the European borders meaningless, and certainly, the people of the Balkans were unable to confront and stop their military power. Determined to rebuild Attila's empire and to re-conquer European lands, the Tartar hordes dismembered Volga Bulgaria in 1236 and destroyed the Kievan and Russian states. In 1240-1241 they descended on Poland, Hungary, and Bulgaria. The Mongolians defeated every army that was sent to repel them and inflicted one calamity after another upon the conquered nations.

They reduced cities to ruins and displayed every known form of human cruelty. As they erased the borders of the Eastern European countries all the way from Russia to Austria and the Balkan Peninsula, the Mongolian invasion coined the term "world war," perversely illustrating a kind of barbarian magnificence by the sheer terror and death that they caused.

Ironically, the Hungarians who were always proud to claim their heritage from Attila were hardest hit by the Tartars. They later blamed their apocalyptical defeat on the Cuman desertion from the Hungarian army. In fact, this circumstance of a minor incident also had enormous consequences. It began when the Hungarians captured an enemy who turned out to be a Cuman warrior. He had previously been captured by the invading Tartars who forced him into the ranks of the hordes.

Denouncing the act as a case of treason King Bela IV (r. 1235-1270) ordered his soldiers to massacre the Cuman king and his court all of whom were his guests. This outraged and humiliated the rest of the Cumans who left Hungary leaving a trail of destruction behind them.

The departure of their single ally further weakened the Hungarian border to barbarian attacks, and the Golden Horde quickly reached the city of Pest on the Danube. The Tartars simulated a retreat only to ambush the Hungarian army and utterly destroy it. King Bela "heroically" escaped the slaughter with a small band of members of his court.

The only heroic deed left for the decimated Hungarians was to try to break the ice on the Danube River so the Tartars could not cross into their capital. Those who escaped the slaughter at the hands of the Golden Horde took refuge east of the Tisza River or crossed the convenient Mures River valley to take shelter in Transylvania.

What saved the remaining Hungarians and their country from being wiped out entirely was yet another accident of history, the death of the Mongol emperor. It prompted Batu Khan to lead his Tartars back to Asia in the hope of seizing the vacant throne of his uncle. This saved Vienna from siege, but before retreating from Europe the Mongolians slaughtered all the captured Hungarians so that the prisoners would not slow down the speedy retreat of the Golden Horde.

King Bela IV, now cast out of his homeland, looked abroad for shelter. The royal treasury he carried with him was confiscated by Duke Frederick of Austria. He also forced the Hungarian king to hand over three of his border areas. Subsequent to this bad luck, Bela fled to Dalmatia.

When the humiliated and penniless king returned to his devastated and thoroughly depopulated Hungary, he begged any and all of the barbarians, especially the numerous and powerful Cumans, to return and help him re-build the country with its amputated borders.

These events were most likely the reason that Bela who conducted a prolonged struggle for power (mostly against his father and his son Stephen V) in his own country, called himself rex Cumaniae (King of Cumania).[16] Perhaps, his adoption of this highly impressive Cumanian title can be rationalized because he once governed Transylvania and could justify the extension of the Hungarian border into the Wallachian land that soon was to be evacuated by the Cumans.

Therefore, the Cumans were not the natives of the land to be able to give Transylvania to the Hungarians. If the Dacians would give Transylvania away, then the Hungarian borders would be extended and include Transylvania in their kingdom.

Indeed, the ravaged European continent had not witnessed destruction on such an apocalyptical scale since Attila the Hun's invasion five centuries earlier. There was only one good thing about the incursion of the Golden Horde into Europe: it eliminated the military power of the Magyars and caused them to stop violating nations' borders in the Western Europe.

✝

Certainly, every barbarian invasion created chaos among the nations of the Balkans and renew to change the borders between them. The Hungarian military might revived due to the fact that it had incorporated a multitude of barbarian tribes and wanted to establish a kind of hegemony in the Romanian kingdom of Wallachia. On the other hand, its prince Basarab I (r. 310-1352) felt it was his right to extend his border into the Severin-Banat area and other former Dacian lands which were now under the rule of King Charles I of Hungary.

The angry king rejected Basarab's offer of money to buy the province and instead, in 1330, he led a punitive expedition into Wallachia only to be ambushed at the gorges of Posada and forced to retreat with big looses of soldiers.

His son King Louis I continued to extend the eastern border of the nation and spread Catholicism into the Maramures area. This was another former Dacian land before the powerful Lithuanian and

Ottoman Empires occupied it. He invaded the Romanian principalities and in 1344 established a system of vassalage in Moldavia and Wallachia. He trusted Duke Dragos I to rule Moldavia on behalf of the Hungarian crown provided that he would fight against the Tartars. Taking the title *domnitor* (from the Latin *dominus* for lord or despot) Dragos united the Moldavians into a centralized nation with approximate boundaries.

His successor Bogdan I founded the state of Moldovia in 1363, and in 1365 the Hungarian king Louis I the Great, accepted Moldavia as an independent state with clear borders. Petru I (r. 1375-1391) extended the Moldavian borders from the Carpathians to the Dniester River and to the shore of the Black Sea. Mircea the Elder (r.1386-1418) shifted the Wallachian border still farther towards the shore of the Black Sea, thereby incorporating Dobrudja and achieving the most significant land extension in the history of his country.

The free principalities of Moldavia and Wallachia having a population of one million spoke then the same basic language that Romanians speak today. This illustrates the principle that a common language and national borders define the international acceptance of a country.

✣

South of the Danubian line Stefan IV Dusan who reigned as king from 1331-1346 and was emperor from 1346-1355 learned one thing from his seven years of living in Constantinople. It was better to rule an empire than a kingdom. He successfully fought the Hungarians who were forced to surrender Macva and Belgrade in exchange for peace.

He had the Bulgarians safely on his side (he married the sister of the Bulgarian emperor). He also took advantage of the civil war (1341-1347) between emperors John V and John VI when the Serbians crossed deep into the Byzantine lands and occupied most of the western Balkans and northern Greece.

In doing this Dusan relied heavily on the German mercenaries (also his personal guard) to keep the Serbian adversaries at bay. The timing of the plague epidemic also proved to be fortuitous as far as his efforts at border expansion were concerned.

In 1346 Dusan was crowned emperor in Skopje, Macedonia. He then bluntly declared himself "Emperor of the Serbs, Greeks, Bulgars, and Albanians." His daring and successful campaigns built the Serbian Empire (1346-1371) with its borders on the shores of the Adriatic Sea, the Gulf of Corinth, and the banks of the Danube, Drina, Nestos, and Sava rivers.

However, the establishment of that empire had a significant side effect. The Turks who had been commissioned to defend the Byzantines from the Serbians now had free access to the Balkans. In other words, the land hungry Serbs had opened the doors to even hungrier predators, the Turks who were now the allies of Constantinople.

Realizing the enormity of this error Emperor Dusan was determined to evict the Mohammedans from the Balkan Peninsula. However, the need to deal with repeated Hungarian invasions and his premature death in 1355 from an act of poisoning proved how quickly one can turn from victor into victim.

His incompetent son Stefan Uros V (r. 1355-1371) lost Dubrovnik to the Turks in 1358 and it formally became a part of the Croat-Hungarian Kingdom. This prosperous maritime city, a sort of state within in a state, was called Republica Ragusina. A civil war between members of the Uros family and the state's co-ruler Prince Vukasin dismembered the former Serbian Empire and the "Emperor" Uros died childless in 1371.

That same year the Ottomans defeated a Serbian army (which included Bulgar units) of seventy thousand in the Maritsa Valley and put an end to the short-lived Serbian Empire. The latter had lost most of its aristocracy (including Prince Vukasin) in that same battle.

It was the first and last time that Balkan Christians were in a position to eliminate the Turkish peril from the Balkans. But, instead of the Eastern Macedonia became subordinate to the Turks. The Islamic Empire continued to expand so as to encompass Bulgaria, and to extend as far as the main borders of Bosnia and Serbia.

The Battle of Kosovo (1389) decided the fate of the Serbians. Despot Lazar led a coalition of Serbs, Albanians, Bosnians, Bulgarians, Magyars, and Croatian contingents against the numerically superior Ottoman army. The odds in this horrific fight swung back and forth until Lazar's son-in-law Vuk Brankovich of Serbia who had twelve thousand men including Magyars gave up the fight and fled. Rumors had it that Vuk believed Sultan Murat I would reward him for his treachery with the crown of Serbia.

When the battle was over the tragic results were apparent in the blood-soaked fields of Kosovo. Lazar and Sultan Murad I had been killed and the remaining Serbian nobility was wiped out. Serbian military power would never rise again and the Bulgarians lost all hope of regaining independence, given that their capital of Turnovo was now occupied by the Turks. The results of a few hours on the battlefield had changed the Balkan borders forever.

✝

Still, the Turks were not invincible. They could not cross any border at will without paying a price in blood. The Battle of Rovine in May 1395 proved this when an invading army of forty thousand allied Turks and Serbs led by Sultan Bayezid I was defeated in Wallachia by Prince Mircea the Elder, who commanded only ten thousand future Romanians.

As adversarial cavalry squadrons prepared for another strike and packs of foot warriors pursued and hacked at each other the fierce battle ended with heavy casualties on both sides. Prince Marko who had been the first Serbian knight to fight the Turks but was now their ally was killed in the battle. He later was greatly idolized by the Bulgarians, Macedonians, and Serbians for his enormous physical strength and his labors as the protector of Christians.

The Serbian Despot Dragas (also a former anti-Ottoman fighter) likewise died fighting against the Wallachians. By aiding the Turks, the Serbs had hoped to keep the borders of Serbia free, but their heroic deaths had the opposite effect, the Wallachians won and their country remained independent with untouched borders.

Encouraged by the obscure Wallachia military success, the western rulers who saw the Ottomans encroaching upon their borders decided to organize the first Balkan crusade and force the Muslims out of the almost Byzantine Peninsula. A grand military plan was put in motion with an anti-Muslim coalition that included the French, Hungarians, knights Hospitaller, and the Wallachians. Smaller numbers of soldiers were provided by Bohemian, Bulgarian, Burgundian, Dutch, Italian, Polish, Scotch, Spanish, and Swiss detachments.

As many as fifty thousand Christian troops were supported by the Genovese and Venetian fleets. They confronted some sixty thousand Turks and their Serbian allies. Encouraged by the Turkish surrender at the fortress of Oryahovo (Rahova) where French knights massacred their captives, the crusaders marched on to meet the armies of Sultan Bayezid I and his ally the Serbian Prince Lazarevich.

Officially under the command of the Hungarian King Sigismund each ethnic corps of the anti-Ottoman coalition obeyed the command of its own leader. Deluded by a false sense of security the Crusader army celebrated the Oryahovo "victory" for two weeks, thus giving the sultan enough time to assemble his marching troops. It was an error that would later prove immensely regrettable, and it was paid for with much bloodshed.

The epic crusade took place near the fortress of Nicopolis on the Danube in September 1396. Ignoring valuable advice from Prince Mircea who had recently defeated the Turks and was aware of their devious tactics, the haughty western knights were focused on being the first to attack so they wouldn't have to share the spoils of their victory with others. With their horses galloping at full speed, colorful standards flying high and swords glittering in the sun the chivalrous

French charged uphill straight into a military disaster. The outlook was so bleak that Sigismund's half-hearted unsuccessfully attempted to rescue them, convinced Prince Mircea to withdraw his Wallachians. The Transylvanians who like the Wallachians were reluctant vassals of the Hungarians followed them.

In the fog of battle, with no leader firmly in command, the heavily armored knights having their horses killed under them were now fighting on foot. They performed individual heroics to no avail in their repeated and deadly charges. The Ottoman cavalry of thousands hacked them to bits. Some three hundred crusaders died plunging off the steep hill. Many others met a heroic death on the battlefields, and those who managed to escape drowned in the Danube River under the weight of their shiny armor.

From the top of the hill Sultan Bayezid the Thunderbolt observed it all, drinking wine. His battle plan was being successfully carried out by Janissaries and his troops were going for the final kill. Since another assault would have been pointless King Sigismund and the Grand Master of the Hospitallers fled and managed to escape the hellish battle by using a fisherman's boat to reach a Venetian ship.[17]

The Hungarian army deserted by its king ran away or surrendered while twenty thousand crusaders died fighting. When the battle was over, at least three thousand prisoners had been butchered, in retaliation for the Rachowa massacre of the Turkish captives. The most notable of the Hungarian captives were spared so they might be offered in exchange for a substantial ransom.

In a matter of hours Hungary's borders were accessible and defenseless, without a king or an army. What saved the country was the fact that Bayezid suffered an attack of gout that forced him to cease his aggressive campaign and seek medical care.

At Nicopolis he finally settled the long dispute with Sigismund concerning hegemony over the Danubian line and also over Serbia and Wallachia. In the end, that natural border of large water would go to the Turks, and not to the Hungarians.

The costly crusade amounted to nothing except that it precipitated the collapse of the Bulgarian and Serbian states. It also gave up some southern border provinces to be annexed, and it forced the rest to accept the ruling of the Ottoman Empire.

The crushing victory of the Turks was so devastating for the Western knights that it discouraged any European alliance against their Islamic enemies, who were now in control of the Balkans nations, except for what was left from the Byzantine Empire. The most militarily opportunity to throw the Ottomans out of the Balkan Peninsula, and release the Turkish blockade around Constantinople was lost forever. Suddenly, the Hungarian border separated the Christian Europeans from the Islamic mighty empire.

☩

The Turks rolled the momentum of their victory to cross the rivers of Morava and Drina and occupied part of Bosnia extending the borders of the Ottoman Empire into the Orthodox lands. Their easiest effort at expansion was in Epirus and Thessaly. The Greek bishop of Phocis who behaved with servility so as to ensure Bayezid's benevolence, invited him to hunt in those provinces. This cunning bishop hoped to use the sultan's presence to enhance his authority and eliminate Latin and Greek rivals for his ecumenical post. But, this "cordial" invitation backfired:

> Bayezid responded to the invitation, and by the simple fact of his presence at the head of a Turkish army, the ancient districts of Doris, Locris and Phocis went, not to the Bishop, but to the sultan. Bayezid now returned to set siege on Constantinople, leaving the easy task of overrunning Livadia and the Morea to the care of two of his generals Everenos and Yakoub. With the exception of Athens and Modon which continued for a while to belong to the Latins, both districts passed into the hands of the Ottomans in 1397 thousands of Greeks were carried into slavery to Asia. Turkish settlements were planted everywhere to make up for the depopulation of the land.[18]

From then on, the Turkish process of annexation of the Balkan borders seemed unstoppable. However, the astonishing military campaigns of John Hunyadi between 1441 and 1443 saved the Serbian borders and then those of Wallachia from Ottoman invasion.

Hunyadi also succeeded in regaining the freedom of Niss, Pirot, and Sofia, and put an end to the Ottoman domination of Albania, Bosnia, Bulgaria, and Herzegovina. Sultan Murad II was willing to grant the independence of Serbia and Wallachia in exchange for certain occupied Ottoman lands.

However, the Polish King Wladislaw III ignored a treaty that had already been signed, and eagerly decided instead to fight it out. Clearly, the chain of Hunyadi's victories inspired confidence in the eager 20 year old King and those Balkan nations that now sought to free themselves from the yoke of Turkish oppression. This trend coincided with Pope Eugene IV's intention of extending Catholicism into the Balkan Peninsula.

Along with the large number of Hungarian, Polish, Transylvanian, and Wallachian troops at his disposal King Wladislaw succeeded in recruiting units of Bohemians, Bosnians, Croats, Czechs, Lithuanians, Moldavians, Ruthenians, and Bulgars. They all joined the march of thirty thousand crusaders eager to battle the Turks. Sultan Murad moved an army of forty thousand from Anatolia meeting up with another twenty thousand from Rumelia at the fortress of Varna in November 1444.

Hunyadi and his Wallachian cavalry corps (which also included Moldavians) achieved an initial victory. They reached the Turkish camp and then retreated to unload their booty and regroup.

The inexperienced young King Wladislaw already entrusted with playing a starring role considered it his turn to celebrate a victory and valiantly charged with five hundred Polish knights against the now well positioned ten thousand Janissaries. The latter surrounded their attackers and the situation took its own unpredictable turn, when in the true spirit of knighthood Wladislaw decided to challenge Murad to a duel. Instead he was hacked to bits by the sultan's guard and then beheaded. His body and heavy armor was never found but his head was displayed on a spear tip to be shown to his troops.

A predictable panic spread among the Christian troops and the Ottomans which outnumbered them took full advantage of it, pursuing and butchering at least ten thousand of them.

Vainly Hunyadi returned with his army corps and tried to wrest victory from the jaws of defeat but the battle was already lost. He "fled in despair with the wreck of the troops that he had personally commanded, and with the Wallachians who collected round him."[19] Hunyadi himself gave up the fight, because:

> …the Hungarian rear-guard, abandoned by their commanders, was attacked by the Turks the next morning and massacred almost to a man. Besides the Hungarian King, Cardinal Julian, the author of the breach of the treaty and the cause of this calamitous campaign, perished at Varna beneath the Turkish scimitar, together with Stephen Bathory, and the Bishops of Eilau and Grosswardein.[20]

Swords, lances, mace, and bows and arrows were still the main weapons used in this battle. Now, for the first time field cannons were employed by both sides as well. This was a revolutionary shift in the fighting technique that would from this point forward change the course of warfare.

✠

The Christian defeat at Varna sealed the doom of Bosnia and Serbia and played a huge role in the future history of the Balkans. While Ottoman armies were busy fighting in the Danubian countries in the southern Balkan Peninsula, the moribund Byzantine Empire was reducing its borders to become a city state on a patch of land immediately surrounding Constantinople ruled by John VIII (r. 1425-1448).

It also included the distant Morea (Peloponnesus Peninsula) which was divided between the emperor's three brothers. One of them Despot Constantine (the next and last Byzantine emperor) repossessed Athens, Boeotia, Patras, and Thebes. In 1444, he urged the Vlachs from the Pindos Mountains to liberate Thessaly.

This amounted to the revival of a territorial conflict that after Constantine's ascent to the throne degenerated into a fratricidal fight over land and a power struggle between the two brothers. They called on the Turks to help support their selfish cause an action that ended any further question about ownership of the border areas of their principalities. The dual but contradictory alliances led to a fateful and dangerous journey for the Byzantines from that point on.

Disaster followed upon disaster and another defeat of the Christian armies took place during the Second Battle at Kosovo in 1448. The two day struggle began with progress for the Hungarians and Wallachians who led by Hunyadi reached the main camp of Murat II. But, the delay on the part of the Albanian army which was intercepted by the Serbian Despot Brankovich, now a Turkish vassal, altered the outcome of the gruesome battle. Outnumbered two to one the Christian coalition held together until the Hungarian knights either were killed or deserted. When Hunyadi could no longer ignore the obvious aftermath of surrendering, the victory of Sultan Mehmed II, and his Serbian ally was already sealed.

The two battles of Kosovo became a symbol of Serbian independence. Over the centuries a myth developed around this conflict. It was and is today taken to be an event of great national significance[21] as the Serbian border was opened to the Ottoman control and a new ethnicity and religion were imposed on this land of Orthodoxy. This produced a troublesome legacy of destruction along with the intensity of confusing balkanization which only increased with the passage of time.[22]

☩

As for the Turks, they found a new leader in the person of Sultan Mehmed II (r. 1444-1446 and 1451-1481). He was a diligent student of the new weapon, the cannon. Willing to pay and equip his army with artillery units the young sultan in 1453 positioned them around the walls of Constantinople. In its twenty five hundred year history the stubborn Byzantine metropolis had proven impenetrable to sieges from Avars, Bulgars, Goths, Huns, Persians, Turks, and Slavs. It had also survived the Crusaders' pillaging in 1204. As long as its walls held there was a clear border around the heart of the Byzantine Empire and its Orthodox Church, from which religious hope flowed into the Eastern lands.

By 1453 that border had been reduced to its narrowest limits. It was defended by fewer than ten thousand men under Emperor Constantine XI (r. 1449-1453) who died fighting the Turks on the walls. At the end of May that year they were overwhelmed by relentless cannonades that made breaches in the massive walls and by the frontal assault of tens of thousands of Turkish soldiers eager to plunder the Queen City.

The rest of the Christian world provided the once great Byzantine capital without any military assistance. The Black Plague, the military exhaustion of the West, and the Ottoman occupation of the greater part of the Balkans discouraged any rescue initiatives. The hapless 50,000 Constantinopolitans grew desperate as they became aware of the impending catastrophe.

The fall of Nova Roma was an event of Biblical proportions for the Christians and an unmatched triumph for the Muslims who believed Allah had rewarded them for their undying faith. For the next forty years the Ottomans would occupy Bosnia, Serbia, Albania, Croatia, Herzegovina, and Montenegro. All those country borders meant nothing for the Ottomans.

After the fall of Constantinople Mehmed II confidently moved a massive army of at least sixty thousand men, three hundred cannons and a fleet of two hundred warships to attack Beograd (Belgrade) in July 1456. If this important border city was captured, the Turkish army planned to conquer Hungary and use it as a corridor to invade Central Europe. The immediate and better reason was to extend the borders of the Ottoman Empire into Transylvania to be able to exploit its rich mines of gold and silver, just like the Hungarians for so many centuries had wished to do.

However, the Ottoman campaign was counter attacked by Hunyadi's relief forces which smashed the enemy blockade around the city. A Janissary assault caused their annihilation inside the fortress and severely injured the sultan who fainted and was carried away. This created a mass panic in the Turkish army which now was fighting a chaotic retreat.

However, the victory of the Christians was accompanied by a tragic surprise, the plague broke out inside the city and took thousands of lives, including that of John Hunyadi, the ultimate savior of the Hungarian and western borders.

The defeat delayed the Ottoman expansion north of the Danube. It also put Hunyadi's teenage son Matthias on the throne of Hungary and Prince Dracula on the throne of Wallachia. It provided hope for Albania and the semi-vassals of Moldavia and Wallachia to fight and push the Turks away from their borders, to win their independence.

✣

In 1461 Prince Dracula refused to pay the traditional tribute to Constantinople and conducted devastating raids into Turkish Bulgaria south of the frozen Danube. He believed that the rest of Europe, whose borders were facing imminent peril from the Ottomans, would follow his example. The next summer he fought an armada that Mehmed II led into Wallachia.

By 1465 a tug of war had developed over the Wallachian fortress of Chilia between Hungary, Moldavia, the Otttoman Empire, and Poland. King Matthias led his Hungarian army into Moldavia with the intention of incorporating it into his kingdom, only to be wounded three times. He barely managed to escape after a crushing defeat at the hands of Stefan.

The Turks and their allies of convenience, the Bulgars and Wallachians, rushed to invade Moldavia. They were defeated in a four-day battle at Vaslui in 1475 when the Wallachians reversed their loyalties and chased the retreating Turks out of their country.

Since Matthias did not want to see Wallachia occupied by the Ottomans, the Hungarian king released Prince Dracula who helped by his cousin Stefan, he took back the Wallachian throne for the third time in 1476. That same year Vlad II Dracula died fighting a Turkish-sponsored Wallachian prince, his brother Radu the Handsome.

In the meantime, Pope Sixtus IV paid forty thousand gold coins to King Matthias to host the western European armies for a new Crusade, and asked the Polish king and other kings to join the anti-Ottoman fight. Instead, King Matthias stayed with the policy of Laszlo IV, namely to befriend Transylvania and make it a buffer zone between the volatile Moldavia and Wallachia through which the Ottomans could easily proceed and reach the Hungarian border.

✣

No doubt claiming a border or to extend an existing border was a goal for any chieftain tribe or the ambition of a nations leader. To make sure that history would properly record their role in preserving the borders of their Christian domains.

The princes, kings, monarchs and nation rulers signed their names on important texts with: "By the Grace of God." The word "grace" was taken from the apostolic letters of Saint Paul as approval and blessing from God, in this case to the king.

Actually, King Matthias stated that "by the Grace of God, king of Hungary, Bohemia, Dalmatia, Croatia, Rama, Serbia, Galicia, Lodomeria, Cumania, and Bulgaria, Duke of Silesia and Luxemburg and Margrave of Moravia and Lusatia, for the everlasting memory of the matter." Indeed he was partially worthy of those titles as he extended the borders of Hungary by the power of the sword and by the means of diplomacy into Bohemia, Dalmatia, half of Austria, southeastern Germany, southwestern Poland, and his native Transylvania. Also, in 1469 he was crowned king of Bohemia, Moravia, Silesia, and Lusatia/ Lausitz (a German district north of Moravia).

Yet, regardless of what title the Hungarian kings or any other king bestowed on themselves, they didn't intimidate the Ottomans who persisted in raiding one Christian country after another.

When an expeditionary Ottoman army raided Croatia on their return, a large Croatian Army which counted on their country union with Hungary, intercepted the retreating Turks. In September 1493 a violent battle took place in the Krbava field and ended in defeat for the Croatians who hoped their King Matthias would provide military help.

☦

In order to limit the number of existing borders between their multiethnic Balkan possessions the Turks named the middle of the Balkan Peninsula, the province of "Rumelia," meaning the Land of the Romans. It included mainly those territories of the Vlach population which were spread over the former Bulgaria, central Greece, Macedonia, and Thracia.

The Vlachs were part of the Walachian people who spoke the same Latin-based language, but as they were living in the Balkan Peninsula, they spoke with a loaded Greek and Slavic vocabulary. In 1521 a merchant named Neacsu from Campulung, a city in Wallachia, wrote a letter in Cyrilic using the Romanian language similar to that of the modern day. The Italian humanist Tranquillo Andronico wrote in 1534 that Valachi "call themselves Romans" from which the name Romanians came from.

However, the Turks had difficulty crossing the border of Lesser Albania where Giorgi Kastrioti Skandenberg (r. 1443-1468) continued to fight off invaders, and succeeded in maintaining the independence of his country. During John Hunyadi's campaign at Niss in 1443,

Skandenberg and a few hundred Albanians defected from the Turkish ranks. For the next twenty-five years he scored remarkable victories against the Ottomans. He adopted the Byzantine double-headed eagle flag, and his spectacular victories brought him the papal title of *Athleta Christi*.

Like Prince Vlad Dracula of Wallachia, Skandenberg bravely fought alone against massive Turkish armies, and unsuccessfully tried to involve Pope Pius II and the western monarchs to join in a crusade against the Ottomans.[23] Nothing lasting came out of his efforts and after his death Albania was absorbed into the Ottoman Empire. Still, its people continued to try to regain their freedom. Hungary was next in line to succumb to the Turkish occupation in 1526.

Clearly, creating chaos and terror was the core strength of the barbarian invaders. It was the main reason for the destabilization and eventual demise of the Byzantine Empire. At work in all of this was a relatively simple calculus, the tribe that killed the most people confiscated the greatest amount of land from its victims.

✛

Nevertheless, the border of each state was only as strong as its ruler. When petty squabbles and civil wars erupted the rulers asked for foreign help and established desperate alliances. These Turkish contingents often controlled parts of countries even before the Ottoman expansion began.

Later, apocalyptic battles lasting a few days or sometimes only a few hours determined the destiny of an entire nation. Victory in war allowed one nation to take over previous orders and designate new ones. Each conquest came with a one way territorial gain. This was followed by geopolitical movements that were constantly subject to turbulence and further theft. There were few times of peace in which the borders could be preserved. There were unending events of border redistribution.

Yet, in spite of all this, the borders of these countries continued to roughly follow the lines of rivers and mountains. Bosnia and Herzegovina were separated from Serbia by the Drina River. The Drava River ran between Croatia and Hungary. Slovenia was enclosed by the Drava and Sava rivers. The Moravian line stood between Austria and Slovakia.

The Maritza River divided the Bulgarians from the Greeks and Turks, while the Struma River separated the Macedonians from everyone. The Romanian and Hungarian border was marked by the Tisza River. In the south the Danube River separated Wallachia from Bulgaria. Albanians and Montenegrins were safely nestled in the Balkan ranges, while the vast Pannonian pustza was the homeland for the Hungarians. Most of these natural borders are still on the map having survived endless cycles of imperial domination and socio-political shifts over the last five centuries.

# REFERENCE NOTES

1. Anna Comnena, *The Alexiad of Anna Comnena*, trans. E. R. A. Sewter (London: Penguin Books, 1969), 218.
2. Modern archeology in Transylvania has discovered burial objects from the Arpadian era along the Bega and Mures rivers in the Banat and Bihor regions. These streams provided easy access for the Magyars who wandered into Transylvania. Still, a few Hungarian graves from the eleventh and twelfth centuries does not constitute proof of a conquest era cemetery. Finding one earring and a copper coin minted by Bela III does not imply that the Magyars occupied Transylvania. It is a known fact that Magyar mercenaries were hired by Transylvanian fortified cities and many died there. Pagan and semi-Christianized Hungarians roamed all across Europe and travelers often died or were robbed and killed on their journeys. Greek coins in Poland do not prove that Greece occupied that area. Furthermore, most Hungarian warriors were heavily engaged in pillaging Western Europe, while their Pannonian homeland, (called Tourkia by the Byzantines), was practically defenseless. This left the Magyars in no position to carry out an invasion of Transylvania in the middle of the Carpathian Mountains.
3. *The Deeds of the Hungarians* was written in Latin around the year 1200 by an anonymous French author hired at the court of Bela III. This important document is often selectively read by Hungarian and Romanian historians in an effort to provide support for their historic claims and theories.
4. Although it is not based on any reliable historical evidence, one Hungarian theory states that a Romanian population entered the Carpathian Basin during the thirteenth century before the Mongolian invasion, but their settlements were destroyed by the Tartars. It also claims that as a result of this the Magyar occupation of a virtually empty Transylvania was a normal migratory move.

As for the Romanians today they could have migrated into Transylvania later from south of the Danube. This is the area to which the surviving Vlach population was forced to flee after the barbarian invasions of Moesia. The Hungarians believe the Romance language spoken by the Romanians to be related to Albanian, and they see no connection to the Roman occupation of Transylvania. In 1277 when Voievode Litovoi was killed in battle and his brother Barbat was taken prisoner by the invading Hungarians in the Hateg region. This marked the beginning of the expansion of the Hungarian border into the Romanian principality, and happened after Barbat accepted the suzerainty of King Laszlo IV.

5. Stephen Sisa, *The Spirit of Hungary: A Panorama of Hungarian History and Culture* (Morristown, NJ: Vista Books, 1990), 85.
6. The Transylvanian nobleman Mihaly Szilagyi was the brother-in-law of John Hunyadi. In 1458, he led an army of fifteen thousand and placed his nephew Matthias as King on the Hungarian throne. This was done despite popular Hungarian opposition not to be ruled by three Romanian born men. Just like his father Hunyadi and his uncle Szilagy, Matthias spoke Romanian. Szilagy served as the guardian of the teenage king and acted as regent of Hungary, after which he was governor of Transylvania and an ally of Prince Vlad Dracula. Dracula married a Szylagy countess. One little known fact is that Mihaly Szilagyi was born Mihai Cirin (a Romanian name) but adopted the name of his county (Szilagy/ Salaj) as his surname. It was a popular custom for rich people to be named after their estate. Similar examples demonstrate that before 1500 what occurred was more of a Transylvanization of Hungary than vice-versa.
7. In no way was Transylvania ever the "citadel of the Hungarian spirit," nor was it the case that either the Romanians or Vlachs migrated to Transylvania in the thirteenth century from Albania (Sisa, *Spirit of Hungary*, 85; map, 187). Among the arguments

claiming that Transylvania belongs to them and that it was originally a province of the Hungarian Kingdom there are some that contend that "the name 'Romania or Romanians' never existed prior to 1861." Also "there is no trace of Daco-Roman civilization in Transylvania," and "the Romanians cannot bring proof of their existence for almost a thousand year period between C.E. 275 when the Romans departed and 1200 when their appearance in Hungary (Transylvania) is first mentioned" (Sisa, *Spirit of Hungary*, 186). Basically, what Hungarians presume is that Transylvania was empty before they arrived there from Eurasia. Life in Transylvania began with their occupation of it, and the Romanians later appeared out of nowhere. The Hungarians claim of the ownership of Transylvania would be like the British asserting that India is their ancestral land because they occupied it.

8. In the words of the historian Niketas: "barbarians who lived in vicinity of Mount Haimos [Balkans], formerly called Mysians and now named Vlachs." Niketas Choniatēs, *O City of Byzantium: Annals of Niketas Choniatēs*, trans. Harry J. Magoulias (Detroit: Wayne State University Press, 1984), 204.
9. Choniatēs, *City of Byzantium*, 204.
10. Choniatēs, *City of Byzantium*, 204.
11. Later speculation points to the fact that the Asan brothers were of Cuman origin, but their reputable Vlachian family lived in Moesia before the Cuman invasion of Europe. Modern Bulgarians claim the Asan brothers as their own and have erected impressive statues in their honor. Once again, it is important to note that the Asan family also preceded the Bulgar invasion of Europe.
12. Choniatēs, *City of Byzantium*, 205.
13. Choniatēs, *City of Byzantium*, 235.
14. Choniatēs, *City of Byzantium*, 346.
15. Jonathan Shepard, ed., *The Expansion of Orthodox Europe: Byzantium, the Balkans and Russia* (Burlington, VT: Ashgate,

2007), 298.

16. The heart of Cumania at that time was Transylvania, where the Hungarian kings made a habit of approving governors and local leaders. Before becoming the king of Hungary, Bela governed Transylvania and succeeded in 1226 to convince only two Cuman chieftains to accept his authority. However, a Hungarian administration or a military occupation of Transylvania is not equivalent to ownership.

17. From Nicopolis, King Sigismund traveled to Constantinople where he spent a few weeks. On his way to Rhodes he sailed through the Dardanelles where he witnessed how the Turks lined up the Hungarians and other captives on the Gallipoli shore, and asked the defeated king to come and rescue them. From Rhodes the king continued his voyage across the Adriatic Sea, spent the winter in Ragusa and returned to Buda in the spring of 1397. This highly unpopular monarch was considered a Bohemian by the Magyars and vice versa. He made it possible for German dynasties to rule Hungary until the First World War.

18. Azia Suryal Atiya, *The Crusade of Nicopolis* (London: Methuen, 1934), 118.

19. Edward S. Creasy, *History of the Ottoman Turks* (Beirut: Khayats, 1961), 70.

20. Creasy, *Ottoman Turks*, 70.

21. After the fall of Communist Yugoslavia the province of Kosovo witnessed violent ethnic clashes between the minority Serbian population and the majority of Kosovo Albanians who wanted independence. This part of the Balkan civil wars involved Bosnia, Croatia, Herzegovina, and Kosovo and left 110,000 civilians and soldiers dead along with 1.8 million people displaced. This was In spite of the fact that the United Nations and NATO intervened to end the "ethnic cleansing" there. The fact that Kosovo was placed under international administration did not change the Serbians will to own Kosovo because Serbians still regard Kosovo as its

sacred ground. This is an area where much Serbian blood has been spilled fighting the Turks.

22. The independence of the Republika Srpska/the Serb Republic was declared on August 12, 1992, only to trigger the Bosnian war that produced the largest instance of genocide since WWII. Peace negotiations were held in Paris on December 14, 1995 and an accord was signed: Bosnia and Herzegovina recognized the Republika Srpska with its capital at Sarajevo with its own constitution. By 2008 that constitution has since been amended 121 times.

23. Like Prince Vlad Dracula and his brother Radu, Skandenberg and his brothers spent their childhoods as hostages in the Ottoman Court. Skandenberg converted to Islam, served in the Janissary Corp, and proved a capable officer on the battlefield. His Turkish name Iskender Bey/Lord Alexander implys that his military abilities could be likened to those of Alexander the Great. However, his birth name was Gjergj Castrioti/George Castriota the last name taken from the family Castrioti estate in Debar, then in Albania, now in Macedonia, at that time heavily inhabited by Vlachs. His mother Voisivia Tribalda was from Serbia, but her last name indicates she was from the Tribalia region, which was also heavily populated by Vlachs, the descendents of the Dacianized Tribalii tribe. His brother's name was Stanisha/Staniscia which could be Stannitsa, a Vlahian name. Before defecting from the Turkish army, Skandenberg put a dagger to the throat of the personal secretary of the sultan. Thus forcing him to write to the strong Turkish garrison of Croia ordering it to accept his command because he was named the viceroy of the Ottoman Empire. After he murdered the secretary, he went to Albania with a contingent of followers and according to the document he carried took command of the fortress of Croia. His men disarmed the Turks who were then massacred by the vengeful Albanian population. After Scandenberg solemnly renounced Islam, he was hailed as

a hero and national liberator. For the next twenty-seven years he proved to be just that for the Albanians. Today the Aromanians, Albanians, and Serbians dispute his origin.

## Map 1.

Map 1. Migration of the Eurasian Tribes in Eastern Europe and Years of Their first Settlements, C.E. 500-900. Source: Map created by author, I. Grumeza

# Map 2.

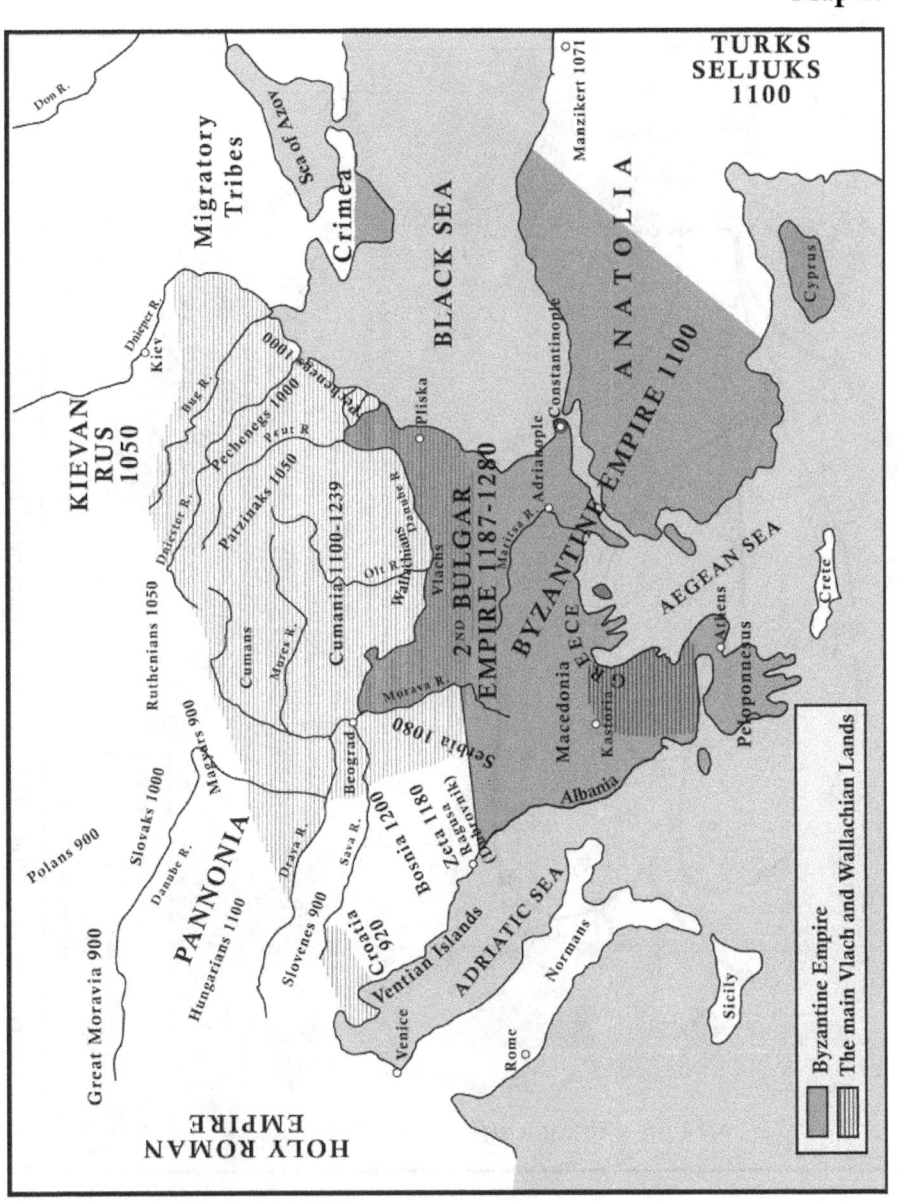

Map 2. Eastern Europe: 900-1200. Source: Map created by author, I. Grumeza

Ion Grumeza

**Map 3.**

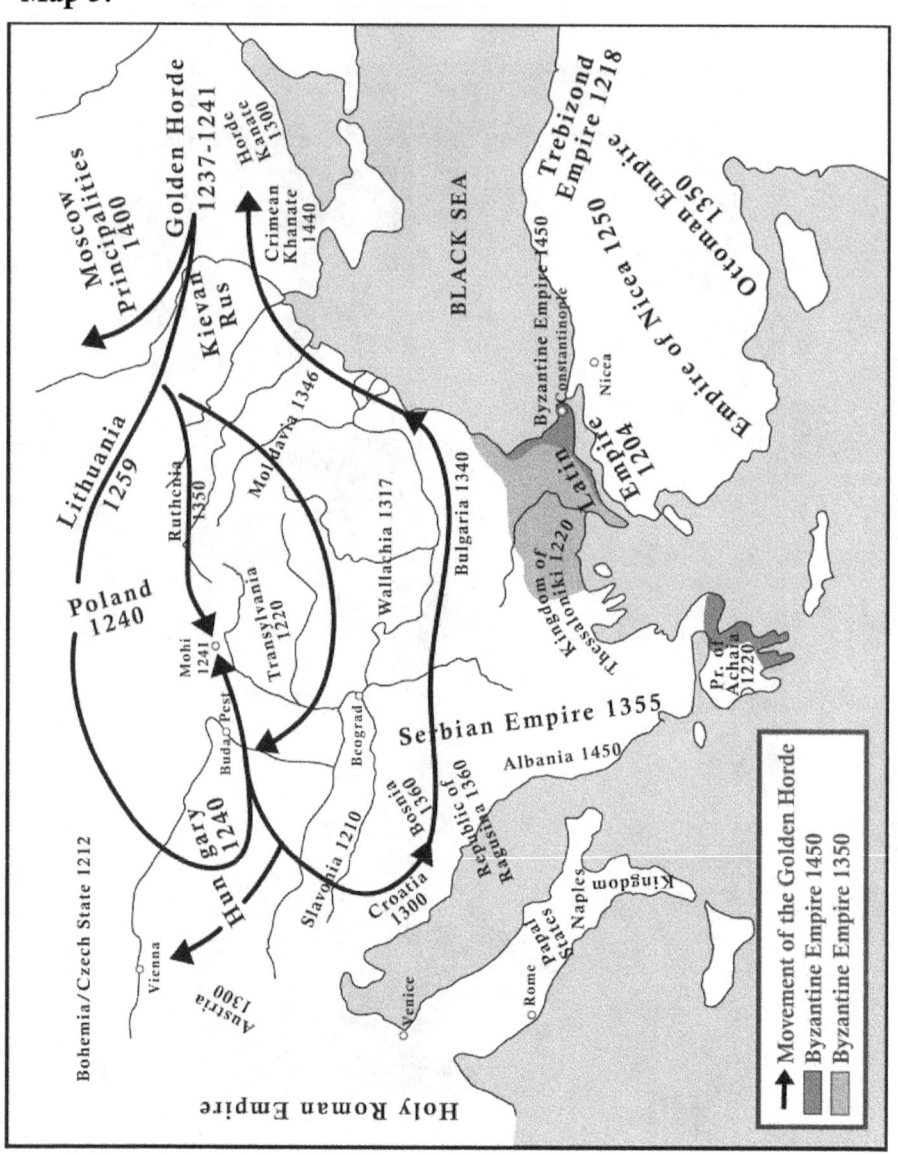

Map 3. Eastern Europe: 1204-1450. Source: Map created by author, I. Grumeza.

BALKANIZATION

**Map 4.**

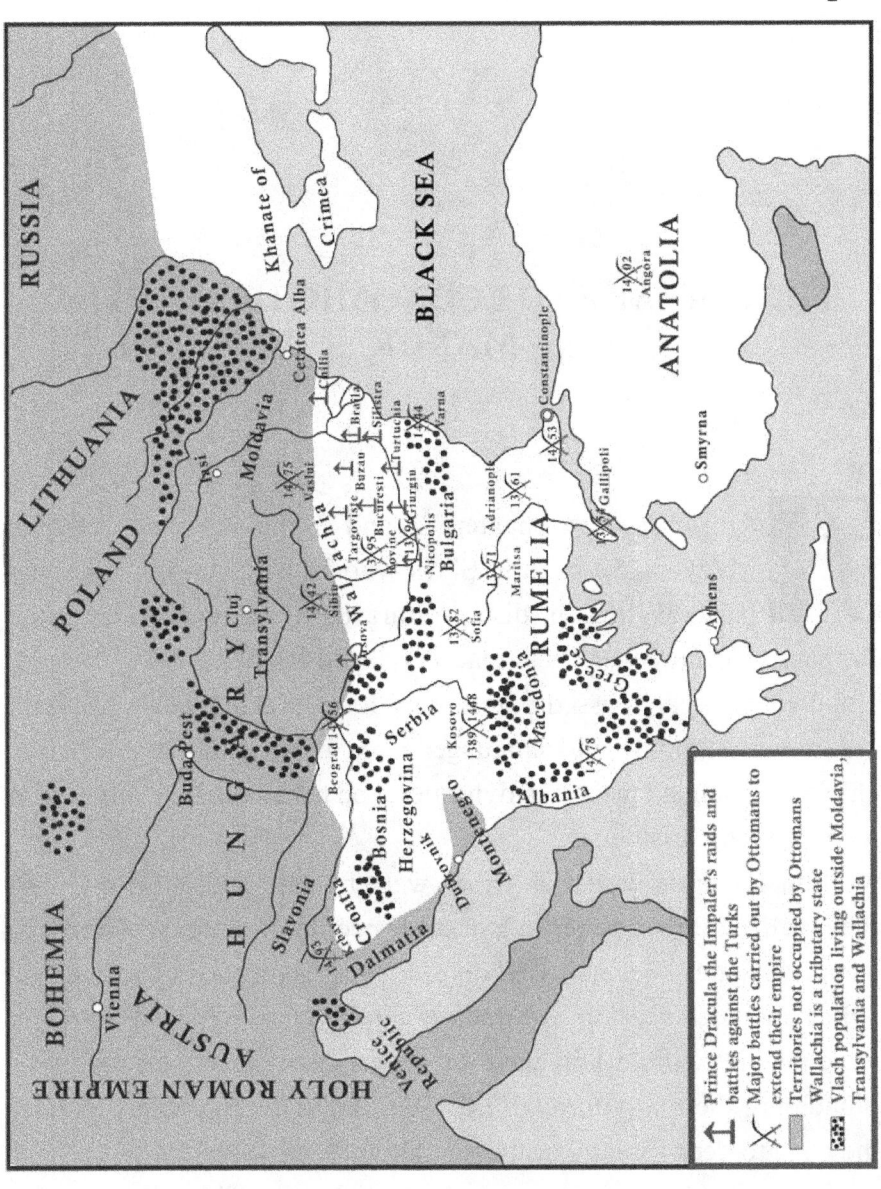

Map 4. The Balkan Peninsula: 1453-1500. Source: Map created by author, I. Grumeza

# THE SOCIAL AND ECONOMIC LIFE OF THE MANOR

As discussed in chapters 2 and 3 the invading Bulgars, Magyars, Serbs, and Slavs who had lived a nomadic and pastoral life in distant Eurasia never encountered the Romans or even never knew that a civilized Roman Empire existed. Hundreds of years passed before they formed clans and tribes with a common ethnicity and language. Even more time passed before chieftains founded their own dynasties, and tribal elitism evolved into a rudimentary aristocracy.

Initially these barbarian tribes were hunters and gatherers until they realized it was easier to loot other people. In time their forest or steppe societies became based on military organization. Their family values included sharing and trading only amongst themselves. They were people with no homeland or government always on the move plundering their way through life. With no self-sustaining economy they had to keep moving or they would face starvation.

Typically, their predatory incursions left trails of blood and swaths of destruction wherever they went, and their savage behavior induced terror in settled societies. Consider the following:

When the black swarm of Hungarians first hung over Europe, above (*sic*) nine hundred years after the Christian era, they were mistaken by fear and superstition for the Gog and Magog of the Scriptures, the signs and forerunners of the end of the world.[1]

This aptly applied to all the barbarian invaders of Europe as being destroyers not builders. After the fall of the Roman Empire countless barbarian tribes massed north of the Danube River pushing each other aimlessly in all directions. Constantinople either looked down on them or ignored them all. Even the good natured and obedient Slavs were considered to be worthless pagans because they were non-Europeans.

✟

The edict of Emperor Caracalla (212) granted Roman citizenship to all free people living in the empire and thereby enabled Rome to collect taxes from them, and enrich its royal treasury. Instead, the newly granted citizens didn't pay any taxes because they were unemployable, or they just didn't want to work because they would receive the welfare benefits and free gladiatorial games, anyway. It turned out that by being citizens, they gained the right to vote. They then elected the Roman officials who kept paying them to do nothing, just to have their votes. That proved to change the Roman government and the last emperors into a barbarian institution, and soon it began to destroy the Roman Empire.

Regarding the Byzantine Empire's demographic situation, the illegal immigrants who lived within the empire did not want to pay taxes to Constantinople. They wanted to have their own country, but continue to be subsidized by Constantinople. This was a development that was intolerable to the Greeks in the Byzantine Empire. This turned out to be a major problem for the imperial treasury which was mostly empty too many times.

Although the barbarians were willing to be a part of the empire and to fight for it in exchange for land, they had no intention of paying taxes. Born to die in the saddle they kept moving about within the empire's borders in order to evade the force of fiscal laws while at the same time they looted the citizens and milked the empire's wealth. By doing this they resisted integration and undermined the economic power of the Byzantine Empire.

✛

The feudal economic system of the empire was as the name suggests. It was based on a fief or a fee that a vassal, usually a peasant, or a laborer paid to his lord for the right to use his land or property. It was close to a barter system. It had begun in the late Roman times when emperors granted lands and other possessions in perpetuity as payments or retirement benefits to their military men.

The former *coloni* (farming slaves) became serfs (semi-dependent farmers) and the rural economy evolved into a manorial system overseen by a landlord. This was not why the barbarians rode thousands of miles to immigrate, were expecting to do: to slave for the rich people.

The massive floods of unwanted savage riders were held at bay until their numbers grew so large that they were able to push past the feeble border troops, and they spilled into the young empire. The emperors then tried to bribe them with money and the allocation of land, but this desperate measure brought more barbarians and a new set of dangerous complications that were impossible to accept or correct by the emperors.

What did the barbarians find after crossing south of the Danube River into the Byzantine Empire? They galloped from the Stone Age into a medieval feudal society that was well ruled by the emperors from Constantinople. Also, they found themselves confronted with Christianity, and its dogma of a Greek-style morality they did not want to understand.

✛

The Byzantine Empire was marked by four distinct social classes: the nobility, the peasants, the soldiers, and the small producers. Another smaller category namely the church servants were more like a religious caste. The nobility included the hereditary princely families, land owners, and knights or warlords. The prince or king owned vast lands and gifted estates to individuals who were loyal or rendered vital services.

They became vassal landlords with their own right to rule inhabitants tied to a specific piece of land. Such landowners also referred to as boyars were important to the monarch because they provided revenues and warriors for the crown. Some of them were knights from the warrior class of nobility and therefore privileged to wear weapons and armor as a status symbol.

Or, they were military officers in uniform who bore different titles in different nations. Their job was glamorous to fight in the name of honor, be it for oneself, someone else, or a noble cause. The knight was for hire as an expensive mercenary during times of war. During peace time he indulged in a life of leisure at his estate combined with hunting and intense military training.

Peasants or serfs farmed the land and they were called *jobbágy* in Hungary, *szolga* in Poland, *krepostnoi krestyanin* in Russia, *şerbi* in the Romanian principalities, and other names elsewhere. Hereditarily, they belonged to the landlords' manor. Since they could not be bought or sold they were not slaves, but they also could not leave their landlord. They farmed the owner's land they lived on and in turn received a small part of the harvest.

They also worked as handymen, in the mines, quarries, forests and as road builders. During times of war they were conscripted as peasant soldiers who fought under the banner of their master who was either a boyar or a knight. The serfs had hard lives working the land non-stop. Their families lived in one room which often was an extension of the animal barn. The members of their families were their only possession. Couples had numerous children since they represented both a labor force and insurance against poverty in old age. The worse type of serfdom was in Eastern Europe and the Balkans. No serfdom existed in Scandinavia the land of the Vikings.

Two types of soldiers fought in the wars and maintained order in peace time and they were the conscripts and the mercenaries. The first were peasant warriors armed with farm tools that served as weapons such as axes, long knives, pitch forks, etc. They lacked military training and therefore tended to be unruly and inefficient. By contrast, mercenaries were professional soldiers usually foreigners, mostly Germans whose individual or group services were purchased by a warlord.

It was common practice to hire a commander who came with a contingent of soldiers well equipped with trained horses, uniforms, body armor, shields, along with the traditional weapons such as swords, lances, bows and arrows, and later with firearms and cannons.

Unlike the peasants who fought to defend their families and the manor, the mercenaries went to war to honor a contract and to acquire booty. In cases of defeat if they were offered a better opportunity they readily switched their loyalty and served the former enemy.

Byzantine armies were made up primarily of mercenaries since there was no law requiring general conscription or making it a citizen's duty to fight for the empire. This system was inherited from ancient Greece where slaves were excluded from military service and allowed to die of old age.

The small producer was a blacksmith, cobbler, carpenter, mason, potter, tailor, shop owner, ambulant salesman, or a professional of another sort. They provided indispensable services to the rest of the population. They were named *trgovci* in Serbian, *targovetsi* in Romanian, and *metrics* in Greek and the Jewish merchants were called *handlarz* in Polish. These producers and peddlers were the most vulnerable members of the society because they carried inventory to market on roads where brigandage was epidemic.

Yet, in time the toolmakers and traders achieved wealth, and with it respect as they formed powerful guilds that acquired influential members. Eventually, their diversified shops led to the creation of commercial streets. Their trading activities led to the production of tall merchant ships that could be easily converted into warships.

✠

In Western Europe a castle was an unmistakable symbol of knightly power. Constructed as a military bastion surrounded by high fortified walls with crenels and watch towers[2] it clearly announced to outsiders "Don't even think about attacking me!" This ensured the safety of those residing within its walls. Built to last forever it was self-sustaining and well manned with people who provided services, supplies, food and its own water source all inside the castle walls.

Within its fortified walls power was centralized at all levels. Vassals came to pay homage to their master and reaffirm their loyalty to him. Pilgrims and travelers from other lands stopped there to rest, spend money and spread the outside news.

In Eastern Europe there were only a handful of castles. These were primarily the legacy of a western power's temporary takeover of various lands such as done by the Germans in Austria (which had some fifteen hundred castles), the Baltic States, Czechia, and Poland.

Barbarians with their primitive weapons were in no position to attack and occupy a large fortification. Their long columns could easily advance some twenty miles a day on the Balkan country roads. Thousands of horsemen were always ready to attack and besiege any smaller fortified settlement or city. Only Constantinople with its many intimidating walls, towers and magnificent edifices was the exception. It was the sole "barbarian-proof" city, which was the reason it became the capital of the Byzantine Empire.

The equivalent of a castle in Western Europe in the Balkans was the manor house. It was a large fortified residence that met all the needs of the landlord, his family, servants, and bodyguards. It had barns for animals, carriages, ploughs and other tools. Fortified monasteries which were themselves large landlords also protected the sanctuaries, clergy, servants, goods and visiting faithful. The manor house (*conac* in Romanian) was constructed with no windows on the first and second floors, and the entrance was built to withstand brutal assaults. Like a castle, a large manor house had an interior courtyard with living rooms, storage areas, and other facilities around it with a well in the center.

It was a place for the landlord who was also the taxman, judge, and warlord which was a kind of local knight. He likely had been a *kavallarious* a horse-mounted soldier from a well to do family whose bravery on the battlefield had been rewarded with land and serfs. Despite the fact that he held only the title of landlord, he had unlimited control over his submissive serfs who would kneel before him and kiss his gloved hand and even his feet.

This kind of blind and servile obedience pervaded all levels of Eastern European societies. Any class conflict was instantly condemned by the Church, the monarch, the landlord, or whoever was in power, who was believed to represent God's will and thus shared His authority. The monarch (*basileus* in Greek) was thought to be protected by God.

☩

From 529 onward the people of the Byzantine Empire were officially ruled by royal and civic laws as well as the twelve books of the Justinian I Code, based on Roman law. It prescribed fair exchanges between people and to legislate certain rights that were to be enjoyed by everyone. However, in practice the oral laws and traditions passed down through generations and the law of the land. Yet, the Biblical concept of justice an eye for an eye and a tooth for a tooth was the way of life in the Balkans. People readily took the law into their own hands to avenge a crime, respond to an insult, or solve a dispute. A man who sought vengeance was showing pride in his family's reputation, and his status was commensurate with the amount of force he used. Public and private violence were so common that the number of male villagers dwindled over time.

Since this unnecessary bloodshed affected revenues, landholders stepped in to terminate it. Any outsider was regarded with suspicion and assumed to be an enemy. If he didn't leave quickly, he was attacked before doing something damaging. Foreign occupation was considered unavoidable and was only reluctantly tolerated. To get even with the hard life, people avoided paying taxes. In fact, dodging the return of any borrowed or promised money became a skill in itself. In short, mocking the authority was viewed as a collective virtue, and stealing from the rich, a heroic deed.

Ironically, the temporary barbarian occupation of the decentralized Byzantine lands freed the peasants from their regulated life and labor in the manorial hamlets and villages. A set of laws was promulgated as "Farmer's Law" which decreed the nonpayment of taxes to be a crime. It condoned the punishment of thieves, or anyone who negatively affected the collection of revenue for the empire's treasury.

If a free peasant did not pay taxes or left his land for more than thirty years, his family had to forfeit ownership of it. The law did allow farmers to exchange parcels of land among themselves.

Subsequently, the rulers of the newly formed barbarian states quickly discovered that laws had to be introduced if a civilized life was need. Before written documents were available in the Slavic societies, royal decrees were orally implemented in each manorial territory. Still, local traditions and customs superseded any new laws.

Family feuds, avenging one's honor and other types of disputes were most often settled by resorting to a duel. In other cases, the judgment of God prevailed. An accused who wanted to prove his innocence had to carry a hot iron in his palms from the church entrance to the altar. Or, one who did not drown when forcibly submerged and held under water was declared "innocent."

☦

Barbarian immigrants needed a long time and had to suffer a great deal of social turbulence before they were willing to move from nomadic tents and mud huts into dwellings that resembled houses. It took them even longer to learn how to handle a shovel instead of a sword and to create their own society modeled on the Byzantine Empire. This was a galaxy of different nations and social structures. During the reign of Czar Boris I (852-889) the Christianized Bulgars adopted a version of the Justinian Code. They omitted punishments for giving a false oath and minting counterfeit coins, but added them for adultery, worshiping pagan gods, and not sharing war booty. Vladimir the Great and his son Yaroslav the Wise issued the written Russkaya Pravda/the Russian True Law which provided the norms of the Kievan society in the eleventh century.

The Magyars made a huge legal leap when they segued from honoring the judgment of a shaman to interpreting Byzantine laws. After year 1000, King Stephen I of Hungary held an open court one day per year during which he listened to, and made decisions concerning the grievances of his subjects, regardless of their economic and social status.

The Golden Bull of 1222, issued by King Andrew I of Hungary established the principles of equality for all of the nation's nobility, and ensured their freedom to disobey the king and not to pay taxes to him. They were not required to pay for his wars. It further stipulated that the aristocracy could hold the king accountable for not respecting the law and could restrict his power. There could be no more arbitrary arrests and punishments without a judicial investigation. In case of war outside the Hungarian border, the king would have to pay for the troops and their knights.

Stricter laws were introduced in 1468 by King Matthias, including some that limited the power of landlords and the aristocracy who had not previously been subject to royal control. His love for justice and his willingness to side with commoners led to the flattery epithet, "Matthias the Just."

The most advanced set of laws was Serbia's *Dušanov Zakonik* (Dusan's Code) of 1349, which came close to being a constitution with its two hundred edicts regulating all aspects of life. It included laws that dealt with the sponsorship of monks, and the fate of escaped prisoners. A death sentence was the prescribed punishment for highway robbery and the murder of church servants, while repeat offenders were to have their hands, noses, or ears cut off, or were to be blinded as an example to others.

The Dusan Code allowed Vlach herdsmen[3] to have their own jurisdiction and electoral system. This edict also applied to the Saxon mining colonies. In Wallachia and Moldavia, versions of the Slavic and Byzantine laws were adopted in the mid- fifteenth century. All these laws were subject to manorial court interpretation and appeals were rarely granted.

☩

The Justinian Code and *lèse majesté* (from Latin *laesa maiestas/* injured majesty) had virtually no impact at the royal level in the Byzantine Empire. However, a case in point was what happened to Emperor Maurice (r. 582-602) and his successors. His decision to reduce military payments by 25 percent led to a mutiny, and to the enthronement of General Phocas in 602.

To make sure that Maurice (who became a monk) and his family could never become a political threat, Phocas executed the former emperor and his six sons. He placed their heads on public display and tossed their bodies into the sea. Maurice's wife and three daughters were exiled to a monastery, and thousands of those who were loyal to the former rulers were murdered.

Eight years later, Phocas himself was overthrown. Upon taking him prisoner, Heraclius (r. 610-641) reportedly asked, "Is this how you have ruled, wretch?" Phocas haughtily responded, "And will you rule better?" but his last word was cut short as his head was chopped off. His mutilated body was paraded throughout Constantinople and finally burned.

The House of Heraclius ended with Justinian II whose nose was cut off by the revolting General Leontius who became emperor was also executed by his generals, as Emperor Tiberius also faced a military revolt and summary execution. In 797 Queen Irene dethroned her son Constantine VI blinded him and then she became the empress of the empire.

In spite of all the humane and civil laws, killing for power became a way of life at the Byzantine court, and it continued for the next four hundred years. Even historian Anna Comnena a woman of character, intellect and a sharp critic of her time, was involved with her mother in assassinating her brother Emperor John II.

When she was exiled to a convent she dedicated her energy to writing about the tumultuous history of her father. Thus she documented the horrors that took place in the Balkans during the reign of Alexius I. Three decades after her death, the child emperor Alexius II, grandson of her father was strangled together with his protective mother. The perpetrator Andronicus assumed the royal title in 1183.

To ensure the stability of his throne the fifty-six year-old Andronicus married the thirteen year-old widow of Alexius II. Isaac II succeeded to the Byzantine crown after his cousin Andronicus I was murdered by a revolting mob in 1185. Ten years later, Isaac II was blinded and imprisoned by his brother Alexius III, only to be placed back on the throne again together with his son Alexius IV in 1203. Both of them were executed six months later by rebels.

In 1261 Emperor John IV was blinded by his second cousin Michael VIII, who wanted to ensure that the eleven year-old would never recapture the throne. The Byzantine society was ruled by its emperors and the subjects learned a lot from them!

The rest of the Balkan rulers followed the inspiring examples of the mighty emperors and sultans, considering murder a legitimate way to preserve their crown and ensure their dominance. Czar Boris

I after ruling Bulgaria for thirty-seven years piously retreated to his beloved monastery and named his son Vladimir as his successor. It turned out that Vladimir hated the newly founded Bulgarian Orthodox Church. He persecuted its leaders and even put its archbishop to death. He sought an alliance with the German King Arnulf and not with Constantinople.

His father who years earlier had murdered fifty-two anti-Christian noblemen and their entire families, came out of retirement in 893. He exercised his authority by blinding, deafening, and imprisoning his rebellious son. He installed his other son, Simeon to the throne warning him that he would suffer from the same fate if he repeated his brother's mistake.

In 1314 across the border in Serbia, King Milutin blinded his son Stefan III Dečanski who had rebelled against his father, and then exiled him to Constantinople. In 1441 the Serbian despot Brankovich blinded his son Stefan when he suspected him of disloyalty, in order to solidify his autocratic position. The Hungarian king Coloman blinded his younger brother and his son Bela II. However, the latter became king in 1131.

Prince Vlad Dracula's father Vlad II Dracul was murdered in 1447 by a rival clan who also used hot irons to blind his other son Mircea and then buried him alive. When he became the ruler of Wallachia Prince Dracula impaled those responsible for the murder of his father and brother. He forced one of them to conduct his own funeral in front of his grave before he beheaded him. Cruelty was the main tool for wreaking revenge, gaining victory, and holding the power of the throne.

At times, clever and deceitful modes of diplomacy were commingled with force. The result was unanticipated social and international tensions. When Bulgarian Czar turned monk Peter suddenly died in 969, his son Boris II was being held as an honored hostage by Emperor Nicephorus II in Constantinople. As was often the case, the vacant throne was challenged by four brothers of another noble family who staged an uprising in unstable and weak Bulgaria. Nicephorus rushed Boris home with a Byzantine military escort who installed him on the throne. At the end of 969, Prince Sviatoslav invaded Bulgaria again and captured Boris and his brother Roman and forced them both into submission.

The Russians and their Pecheneg allies raided south of the Balkan Mountains and produced so much alarm in Constantinople that Nicephorus was murdered by his wife's lover General John Tzimisces. Aiming to take over the throne the general arrested and exiled the empress. Thus, the Emperor John II saved Constantinople after defeating the Russians and forcing them out of Bulgaria. He liberated Boris who was conveniently used to incorporate Bulgaria into the Byzantine Empire. Boris II returned to the throne only to be killed by one of his anti-Byzantine soldiers. His brother Roman became the next czar. Emperor John was also murdered by his own court and Prince Sviatoslav was killed by his former allies the Pechenegs.

It took the powerful Emperor Basil II (r. 976-1025) to re-establish Byzantine supremacy in the Balkans. To do this, he defeated the Bulgars and blinded fifteen thousand of their prisoners as a lesson in obedience. When seeing his mutilated warriors, Czar Samuil died of a heart attack an incident that marked the end of the First Bulgarian Empire.

Paradoxically, throughout the Balkans it was considered an unpardonable offense to intend to harm or to insult a monarch or any authority at the manorial or military level. Such thoughts or behavior were considered to be the equivalent of heresy and treason yet retribution did not require a judge to legislate punishment.

Vlad Dracula was renowned in his own time for inflicting instant "justice." Called "the Impeller" because of his signature punishment, he was determined to eliminate domestic and foreign enemies and create a crime-free society. The fierce Prince of Wallachia seldom gave a wrongdoer a second chance. A dead criminal or adversary could do no more harm, and his impalement served as a lesson for others. Dracula was the ultimate enforcer of *lèse majesté*.

✢

Medieval society was focused on dynastic power rather than on nationalistic or political ideals. Dynasties took over lands through alliances, wars, and marriages thus deciding the fate of millions. Royal weddings were second only to war in being the most important and expensive events of the time. They were credited with both creating and solving most of the problems associated with societies and nations in conflict.

To prevent the destruction and occupation of Bulgaria by the Tartars and the Turks, Czar Terter married his daughter to the son of Khan Nogai in 1285. Terter married the sister of John Asen III, thus securing his throne. In the subsequent century, the sister of Czar Ivan Shishman joined the harem of Sultan Murad I which did not stop his son Bayezid from beheading the czar in 1395. Stephen Milutin II (r. 1282-1321) expertly secured his throne by marrying the daughter of Bulgarian Czar George I, the daughter of King Stephen V of Hungary, and the daughter of Emperor Andronikus II. His multiple marriages on the other hand did not produce harmony in his kingdom. This was evidenced by the fact that he was forced to blind one of his sons to restore order.

Not surprisingly dramatic events often occurred when marriages went awry. When Bulgarian Czar Gavril/Gabriel fell in love with another woman he sent his pregnant wife back to her angered father, the proud King Geza I of Hungary. Meanwhile, Gavril's sister Theodora fell in love with the enemy of her family the Serbian Prince Vladimir. He was released from prison and reinstated with all his rights by her father Czar Samuil. Gavril who reigned for only a few months was murdered together with his wife and child by his cousin Ivan Vlasislav (whose father was murdered by Gavril's father while he himself was saved by Gavril). In 1015 Ivan became the next Bulgarian czar. He also beheaded Vladimir[4] to eliminate any dynastic competition. Ivan was assassinated by his bodyguards three years later.

When the Latin Emperor Baldwin I (r. 1204-1205) was defeated and captured by the Vlachian king Ioannitsa at the Battle of Adrianople he was first treated as a royal guest. But, when he tried to seduce the king's wife his hands and feet were cut off by the jealous Ioannitsa, who threw the emperor in a dungeon where he was left to die. After the king's assassination his only daughter Princess Maria wed the Latin Emperor Henry in 1214. She traveled to Constantinople with a caravan of sixty horses draped in red velvet carrying her dowry. The costly wedding celebration was a national event. Two years later Henry was poisoned and Maria was the first suspect.

After the Bulgarian Czar Michael III divorced Serbian Princess Anna he made a deadly enemy of her brother King Stefan III. In 1330 Michael was captured on the battlefield and subsequently died of his wounds. Czar John Alexander caused public outrage in 1349 when he divorced his Wallachian wife and married a converted Jewess. She changed her name from Sara to Theodora and became the first Jewish queen in Europe.

Legally, a groom had to be fifteen years of age and his bride thirteen, and all royal marriages were arranged between the families for the purpose of forming or ensuring alliances. Ample preparations and negotiations for the exchange of titles and dowries of land, money, and other gifts were trumpeted rituals. A royal couple was expected to produce children especially a son who would succeed his father on the throne. Periodically, unusual marriages took place in order to ensure government stability.

For example, in 1299 at the age of forty-six Prince Milutin married Simonis the five-year-old daughter of Andronicus II. He raped her when she was eight-years old and the wounds left her sterile. Milutin proved a good ally to her father and sent two thousand horsemen to help Andronicus fight the Turks in Anatolia. After his death Simonis returned to Constantinople. Another example is that of King Matthias of Hungary (r. 1458-1490) who married Elizabeth of Celie. She died before the marriage was consummated leaving the Hungarian king a widower at the age of fifteen. At eighteen in order to be crowned king he married nine year-old Catherine of Podebra who at fourteen gave birth and died along with her infant. In 1464 Matthias then married Beatrice of Naples who failed to bear him any children. So the only heir to the Hungarian throne was his illegitimate son Janos Corvinus whose mother was Matthias's mistress.

After Matthias died the boy was ignored by the Hungarian aristocracy probably because he also spoke Romanian. They elected Vladislaus II of Poland and Lithuania known to Hungarians as Ulaszlo II to rule and Beatrice immediately married him in 1491. When this marriage also proved to be childless it was dissolved. Beatrice was sent back home to Italy where she died at the age of fifty.

The absence of male descendants always created dynastic problems most often national crises of succession. All in all monogamy was not a virtue of the czars and emperors. Most of them had extramarital affairs, married many times, and most of their ex-wives ended up in convents. Their illegitimate children often killed each other in attempts to claim the throne.

Dukes and manorial lords tried to keep up with the royal weddings but such marriages were the most glorious and important social events in the life of the commoners.

✢

At the level of the ordinary people, the marriages were planned by the parents who engaged in long and elaborate negotiations over the dowry. It usually consisted of domestic animals, furniture, clothing, money or gold, and other goods that would be exchanged between the families, and bargaining was the norm.

In most cases the bride and groom were from the same village so clannish ties were maintained and family wealth was kept close to home. An outsider needed an entire lifetime to be accepted by villagers, and even his children had to prove to be worthy to be residents. The feudal landlord had to approve any marriage and settlement of a new member in the village.

The honor of a woman and preservation of her purity was one of the few cardinal and unwritten rules that was actually obeyed throughout the Balkans. In the morning after the wedding the groom would show the partying guests the white bed sheet spotted with blood to prove the virginity of his bride. From then on the children born by his wife were recognized without any suspicion regarding the fatherhood. No pregnant woman or a woman holding a child could be harmed in any way.

A wife had to be entirely submissive to her husband but after a crisis she could take over the family affairs. A married woman had to have her head covered with a scarf or a similar garment to indicate that she was married. To touch a woman especially someone's wife was sufficient cause for bloody retaliation. This applied even to dancing. In the patriarchal society of the Balkans men danced with men and women with women in rows that did not touch.

In spite of their lesser social status women were excluded from the code of revenge and violence. In Albania for instance no man walking with a woman could be attacked or harmed. Yet if a wife showed disrespect for her husband she could be subject to corporal punishment and adultery could bring instant death. Divorce was rare and condemned by the Church and the community. The family was indeed the vital cell which held the Balkan society alive.

✠

The Byzantine society was in endless civil turmoil from its inception to its collapse, and all of this was greatly aggravated by the ongoing influx of barbarian migrants. Its traditional Greek civilization was continually tested by daily events. Civility was often maintained by the police as described by Thomas Magister a Byzantine scholar and

confidant of Andronicus II (r. 1282-1328) in his native Thessalonica:
> Their weapon is cruelty. They live the way that wild beasts live; everyday sees them starting or pursing some new quarrel. They steal the property of the rich, as in Athens at the time of the Thirty Tyrants. You can see men pledging their sworn oath and simultaneously breaking it. You can see them in the marketplace, using their fists on people's faces, knocking them down, raining blows upon their backs, dragging others along by the beard—yes, old men too—shouting insults and obscene threats. This is part of the regular way of life here. Such things happen all the time: public brawls that make the night streets hideous, honest citizens set upon by bullies, drunken and dissolute mobs roaming the alleyways, walls broken through, property stolen, houses ransacked, and all that sort of thing—no, worse than that: arson, stone-throwing, vicious assaults, a whole string of murders committed every day, knife and scimitar kept ready for instant action. They do not even take their weapons off to go to bed. You might well think they could not live without them.[5]

This scenario of fast talking and temperamental Greeks always ready to insult and fight any enemy about something quickly found popularity among other ethnicities. It was typical throughout the Balkans. Indeed, if it took place in the city of Thessalonica a metropolis of super-rich commercial establishments that rightly boasted of its artistic and cultural life, its university, splendid churches, and thriving economy, then it could (and did) happen anywhere. In fact, Thessalonica was the second best city to live in within the empire. It is therefore no wonder that such an unruly society was destined to be easily crushed by the equally violent Turks in 1430.

Where the leadership was concerned to be most important in the Byzantine social order in each of the new countries they depended on its ruler and his tile. Serbia for instance retained its traditional *zupan* and *despot* titles. These were borrowed by many Balkan nations. The Hungarian equivalents were *gyula* and *karkha*. The titles of *ban, duke,* and *herzeg/herzog* were prevalent in Banat (Transylvania), Croatia, and Dalmatia. The word for sovereign was *wojewoda* in Poland and *voievode* or *domnitor* in the Romanian principalities.

Nepotism was widespread and was often a sort of double edged sword. Relatives could either aid or destroy a ruler. One's title and social position followed one to the grave and the best burial grounds (very often inside churches) had impressive monuments indicating the military, social and political importance of the deceased.

What complicated the social order of each country were the numerous barbarian or ethnic invasions. These always resulted in social unrest. With Hungary under attack from all directions by powerful enemies and threatened with inevitable Ottoman occupation, more Hungarians poured into the safety of Transylvania. However, their growing settlements and the spread of their language led to unsolvable ethnic conflicts with the ancient local Vlachian population.

Three distinctive societies had parallel and separate lives within Transylvania: the Hungarians, the Germans, and the Vlachians, and each was determined to preserve its own autonomy. Soon the ancient and original Vlachians who were mostly shepherds and farmers came to be considered second class inhabitants and lost their old ownership privileges.

In the meantime, the gold and silver mining areas of Transylvania attracted Hungarian and other ethnic laborers. The *Diploma Andreanum* issued by King Andras/Andrew II in 1224 gave autonomy and special economic privileges to the Saxons and Germans living there. This measure increased the powerful commercial and economic impact of the "guest workers" of Saxons and Szekelys. The latter considered themselves the real Magyar nobility. It led to the establishment of states within the state, independent local colonies, such as Universitas Saxorum and Szekelyland with their own distinctive societies. However, they did not pay taxes to the Hungarian king but to their communities. A similar set of political conditions developed with the Germans in Poland.

✟

The Byzantine emperors ran their *theme (*provinces) with the help of the *strategoi/catepani* or governors. These were most often generals who had a strong army detachment that could keep order, collect taxes, and enforce laws. When taxes were increased too much or the corrupt tax collectors abused their power, populations revolted against Constantinople, as did the Vlachs of Thessaly (named Vlachia Mare/Great Wallachia) in 1066.

Later, the Asan brothers who spoke "the language of the Vlachs," lived independently throughout the Balkans and demanded recognition of their ethnic status. The Bulgars joined their protest and won both national and fiscal independence. For the next twenty years the Vlachs defeated each Byzantine and Latin army that was sent to subdue them, and they created their own economic empire named *Regnum Vlachorum et Bulgarorum*.

✟

The meteoric rise of the Ottoman Empire was based on sheer cruelty, regardless if it applied to the outside or the inside enemies of the sultans.

The ultimate victor Sultan Mehmed II (r. 1444-1446 and 1451-1481) who was glorified as the Conqueror was a luminary of the arts and sciences. The first thing he did when he was aspiring to be named sultan was to eliminate any inherited competition.

When his father, Murad II died his Serbian wife had just given birth to a baby son. Mehmed ordered the baby to be drowned in a bath while his mother was congratulating the new sultan. To prove his innocence and keep his esteem high at his Sublime Porte (Ottoman Government) Mehmed ordered the execution of the assassin. However, when he later issued a criminal and constitutional law he advocated for royal fratricide, claiming that it was necessary for the sake of the empire. This justification was widely used both before and after the rule of Mehmed II.

Before the Ottoman occupation the Balkan nations, kings were named by the powerful landlords who could either establish them onto or topple them from the throne. That changed immediately after the Turkish occupation, when the sultan appointed the rulers of the tributary nations. They were the highest bidders in the royal market of the Phanar in Constantinople. This pro-Ottoman ruler collected taxes from his subjects, and was directly responsible to pay back what he owed for the bid, plus the *camata* or interest he promised when bidding to the Greek royal dealers in Phanar.

Different was the ruler of a vassal country like Moldovia and Wallachia, who paid taxes directly to the sultan, and recognized suzerainty of the Sublime Court. The sultan can name or depose a vassal ruler who had to deliver the annual tribute to the Porte including 500 ten year old boys to be raised to become Janissaries.

Any such puppet ruler was himself riddled with official debt due to the open bid for the throne, and the untold amount of bribery needed if one was even to be allowed to bid. Once he took charge of a tributary or a vassal nation it reached absurd proportions imposing his financial exploitation.

He asked villagers to pay taxes on the basis of the numbers of rooms and chimneys they had, the size of their cellars, the number of horses, oxen, and other domestic animals, etc., all this mounting up to fifty different taxes. To avoid bankruptcy the peasants and the merchants were forced to bribe the taxman. Thus, the word *bakshish* (tip) was added to the daily vocabulary in each language spoken in the Balkans.

Bribery was accepted as a normal way of life and it was impossible to enforce any law in favor of the briber without it. The corruption of officials became one of the rules of the future balkanization. Brigandage became a glorified profession as highway robbers crossed the borders into and out of the empire's countries to sell their loot or to collect ransom.

The Ottoman occupation of the Balkan countries followed the Phanariot system as far as economic measures and taxation was concerned. Thus, it perpetuated the Byzantine administration and the complicated bureaucracy of ruling a land foreign to the Turks after they occupied Constantinople. It was enforced by Turkish and mostly Greek representatives both of whom were fiscally corrupt beyond description.

The Ottoman occupation and the vassalage brought little changes on the hierarchy with respect to old titles among various ethnicities. Of all the occupiers the Turks were interested only in economic and military objectives, primarily fortresses where garrisoned troops were backed up by administrative personnel who supervised the application of the Ottoman demands.

A *pasha* was in charge of the military matters of a *pashalac* (region) a *beg/bey* was the governor of a province, and a *vizier* was entrusted with certain sub-territories. None of them bothered to intervene at the level of the manor or the village where the lifestyle and culture remained largely unchanged throughout the centuries, except for paying taxes to the Ottoman Empire.

Typically, that was the situation with a *rayah*. Mainly, it was made up of the villagers and being a group of people of the same profession, such as the farmers, shepherds, laborers and other members of society. They were the tax payers and the lower class, but paid to the local Ottoman tax collector.

A different tax was paid in a conquered province or a large fortified city including on the land surrounding it. This happened when the Sublime Court sold the high positions to the local leaders or to a pro-Ottoman prince. As long as the prince paid the required tribute to the Porte he could do anything he pleased in his country. Moreover, in the event of a crisis he could rely on a Turkish army to back up his will regardless of whether the problem was with his own nobility, or that of a neighboring country.

This Phanariot procedure was adopted by all the great powers of Eastern Europe. It reached its epitome in Russia where each ruler's despotic ideas amplified the Balkanization system.

✣

Even when Ottoman control of a nation was militarily enforced, Islam was never imposed on Christians. Some people, especially the aristocracy, volunteered to adopt it for obvious economic and political gains. The Ottoman occupation introduced into the Balkans the specialized *kadis* (judges) who were routinely influenced by false witnesses, fake evidence and most of all by the customary bribery.

Any Christian witness who accused a Turk was dismissed as unreliable. A Turk could not be judged or sentenced by a Christian court. This created nightmarish situations when unhappy victims took the law in their own hands. In brief, the Turkish public bath, the mosque, and the Crescent flag were the trademarks of the lost independence of a nation.

In distant Russia, the dominant power of the Golden Horde duplicated the Ottoman methods of imposing authority and collecting taxes. The Tartars dealt only with rulers of the land who were in no position to object to any of the Mongols' requirements.

> With no army and only a flimsy wooden stockade for defense, the early princes of Moscow relied on their wits for survival. They developed a keen political sense, and they knew how to be humble when necessary. Whenever a Tatar emissary or tax collector arrived outside the city, the prince went out to welcome the visitor, kiss his stirrups, and lead his horse through the city gate. Moscow paid whatever the Tatars asked and always filled the quota of young men demanded for the khan's army. (Richard B. Little, *Land Beyond the River: Europe in the Age of Migration* (New York: Atheneum, 1986).

This became such an expected routine duty that "even when the Tatars began to lose their grip over subjugated lands Moscow continued to rule in the Tatar manner. Although the Moskovy princes stopped paying Tatar tribute they continued to collect taxes." The Russian boyars followed the tax system and proved to be so greedy and cruel with the poor peasants, that the serfs became accustomed to being submissive. It remained so for centuries, blessed only by the rich Orthodox priests.

The tribal economies were still strong and visible in local markets or large fairs, and later in the bazaars where grains, wine, smoked meat, honey, spices, furs, artisan's products and other goods were sold or traded. The Vlachs, who owned herd animals all across Eastern Europe were known as *pastores Romanorum* in Pannonia. They were the primary movers of goods by oxen and mule carts, and also the protectors of the commercial caravans crossing the Balkans. It is likely that they had a network of inns with relay stations for changing traction animals (every fifteen miles or so) and providing services for the commercial caravans.

The Vlachs were specialized in selling milk and wool-related items, animal skins and above all salt, that precious food commodity from Transylvania. Since they had free access to land from one end of the Balkans to the other they were perhaps the only traders to carry valuable blocks of ice wrapped in straw from the mountain peaks to the ice cream makers on the scorching Aegean shores.

It is certain that only they supplied dairy products to the monks of Mount Athos. In the complex economics of the Byzantine Empire large revenues also came from making tools, weapons, household utensils, and art and luxury objects all of which required iron, steel, and other metals.

The Byzantines possessed a splendid tradition of manufacturing. From the 550s onward when Christian missionaries smuggled silk worms out of China they held the silk monopoly in Europe. Their commerce was now greatly affected by the invasions that destroyed markets and trade.

Eurasian tribes tumbled into the Byzantine Empire for centuries bringing with them their "barbarian industry." It was based on theft and coercion and continued building the future balkanization habits. Their concept of revenue was similar to that of the Khazars (who lived between the Black and Caspian Seas) in which a chieftain could make a fortune by selling entire families, confiscating their properties, or killing those who could not pay their debts as a lesson in economics for others. Moreover,

> Eastern sources recording the conditions about the middle of the ninth century also report that the Hungarians imposed burdensome taxes in kind on the Slavs, assaulted them, plundered them, carried the Slav prisoners to Byzantine towns where they sold them as slaves. (J.J. Norwich, *Byzantium: The Apogee* (New York, Knopf, 1992), 196-197.)

Eventually, barbarian tribes that had settled in the Balkan Peninsula began to learn the value of hard work from the civilized people there. In time, they also adopted Christianity and the feudal system of the Byzantines. While the center of political power in the empire was Constantinople the heart of commerce was its rich borough of Phanar.

This well known Greek section of the city also became the Orthodox Church center. It was politically stronger, and commercially immensely richer with each passing century. Regardless of any changes elsewhere in the city or the empire this district which was run by the Greeks maintained and even increased its economic power and political influence over every aspect of life in the Balkans. It could make or break important commercial transactions as well as major decisions of military and political leaders.

There was a different economic dynamic in the major cities especially those bordering the main roads and large navigable waterways where strong markets ensured the regular exchange of goods between merchants.

Established city states like Constantinople, Dubrovnik, Thessalonica, and new ones like Novi Pazar (New Market) built by the

Serbians became commercial magnets for both wealth and predators. When the Aegean Sea became a Byzantine gulf, the merchants of Constantinople had the upper hand in all of the commercial activity that took place both north and south of it.

☦

The feudal system in the countryside was based on serfdom (the perpetual servitude of peasants) a vital necessity when it came to settling migrants or relocating homeless people on large estates belonging to landholders. The landowners could be members of royalty, monasteries, or landlords named *boyarin/boljarin* in Russian, *bolyar* in Bulgarian, *boyar* in Romanian, and *grof* in Hungarian. Each of these terms referred to a country nobleman who possessed varying amounts of wealth and power.

In Eastern Europe they established boyar hoods which like any other manor economy resulted in a system of commercial agriculture. Landowners provided the peasants who worked for them with housing, farming tools, traction animals, seeds, mills, and military protection. The villagers who lived on the manor estates were *serfs* (renters) who paid their landlord in labor and taxes.

This system is referred to as a tithe system (a 10 percent donation was required). However, it did not apply to the use of the forests, pastures, and rivers which were shared by each community. It was common for a peasant to have a small lot on which to grow food for himself and his family.

In some cases the family of a serf could receive up to thirty acres to manage and pay for the farming privileges. In such a work setting a cottage industry of making dairy products, spinning wool and looming textiles or making rugs became increasingly specialized. The exchange of goods and services became profitable.

Making wine was also lucrative. High levels of competition developed between small producers (who paid taxes) and the monasteries (which were tax exempt). When a country was absorbed into the empire the serfs were subjected to double taxation. Multiple payments had to be made to both their local and foreign masters. Wars added an extra tax burden, and looting raids reduced the villagers to a total poverty.

Regardless of changes in rulers, dynasties, or foreign occupations, the serfs and villages remained the property of the same landlords who maintained their autonomy and jurisdiction over their manor estate. Earning money by trading products was vital to sustaining the manorial system. The problem was that the governor who had probably acquired his administrative position for a substantial bribe now was always trusted by a monarch to collect taxes from a province.

Typically, the governor did not leave Constantinople to go to his assigned post. Instead, he empowered local tax collectors to do his work. They routinely collected taxes in triplicate. One was required by the state, another for the governor to pay his salary and debt, and another for themselves. Their small armies enforced the collection and while doing so demanded their share of the money as well. This became the standard procedure. Complaints to the emperor by the manor lords did nothing to punish the abusers since they were invariably protégés of a highly ranked courtier.

☩

With regard to import and export taxes between the countries things went from bad to worse and brought about major unrest throughout the Balkans and Eastern Europe. This had many historical consequences. Wars have always had an economic motto that the spoils belong to the victor. However, the first "trade war" happened during the reign of Czar Symeon I (r. 893–927) when the market for Bulgarian goods was moved from Constantinople to Thessalonica which was the commercial capital of the Balkans.

For the Bulgarian merchants the city was difficult to reach by road, and the taxes there were enormous. The Bulgarian czar asked Emperor Leo VI the Wise to reconsider the decision to tax his merchants so excessively. Since much of the profit went to his mistress, the emperor ignored the complaint. Czar Simeon knew how to get the response he wanted. Utilizing a "trade or raid" policy in 894 he invaded the empire and defeated Leo's army in Macedonia.

This economic victory proved to have unexpected consequences because it opened up the path for other trade wars. Having lost the battle Leo pressed the Magyars to attack Bulgaria from the north. Simeon's army caught between two fronts was forced to retreat and defend his pillaged country. He allied himself with the Pechenegs and defeated the Magyars and pushed them back to Pannonia once and for all. Then, in 896 Simeon once again invaded the imperial lands and defeated another Byzantine army and besieged Constantinople.

Leo could not fight back and ended up paying an annual tribute to the Bulgarians as well as handing over some regions by the Black Sea in exchange for peace. Simeon, who wanted more land could not keep his side of the bargain and again invaded southward. This time Leo allowed the Bulgarian border to extend fifteen miles north of Thessalonica. The conflict finally ended with the official recognition of Simeon's right to bear the title of Emperor of the Bulgarians. Subsequently, the Bulgarian market was moved back to Constantinople.

This entire protracted struggle over taxes dearly cost the Byzantine Empire. At the same time it elevated Bulgaria to the status of a major Balkan economic and military power. However, after the death of Symeon his son Peter I proved to be ineffectual. He lost all of the economic privileges that his father had gained.

In 965 Emperor Nicephorus II refused to pay the traditional annual tribute to a Bulgarian embassy which he despised.

> He turned on the ambassadors with a stream of invective, abusing them and their countrymen as a race of hideous and filthy beggars, triple slaves and sons of dogs, ruled by a prince dressed only in the skins of animals. Then he had them scourged before sending them back empty-handed to Preslav.
> *(Annals of Niketas Choniates, 257)*

Wisely, the emperor used the gold to bribe the Kievans to attack and dismember the Bulgarian kingdom. Under Emperor Basil II the Byzantine Empire once again reached a golden age mainly because of the re-integration of territories and the taxes collected from them. Basil II also used his successful military campaigns to occupy Bulgaria and extend the commercial borders of his Byzantine Empire into Armenia, Georgia and Mesopotamia, using his coinage to dominate all markets.

The Hungarians were equally unhappy with the way their merchants were treated by the Byzantines and repeatedly protested to Constantinople. Their pleas were ignored. Like the Bulgarians they were exasperated with this and so took advantage of the Serbian uprising and invaded the empire. They plundered it from Branicevo (near Beograd) to Serdica (Sofia).

Constantine VIII (r. 1025-1028) was renowned for being co-emperor of his father, step-father, his uncle, his brother Basil II and emperor Phokas. He was so spoiled with his lavish lifestyle that he used over taxation to maintain it. He ruled on cruelty, both torturing and blinding his enemies.

In less than three years of his reign, he mercilessly put down any revolt and forced the Serbs to recognize his suzerainty. Somehow, he won all the wars, and succeeded to push back the Hungarians. He deported the prisoners of war to Anatolia where they either became soldiers or settled as farmers to pay taxes. At his death, Constantine VIII succeeded to empty the treasure of the Byzantine Empire.

☩

Since Emperor Anastasius I (r. 491-518) reformed the monetary system and used Greek numerals instead of the Roman ones, the Byzantine Empire had a monopoly over the minting of coins in the Balkan Peninsula.

Its *nomismata* and *hyperpyra* (seventy-two hyperpyra was one pound of gold before the year 1200) and it carried a lot of buying power. However, the Italian *florin* produced in 1252-1253 from 3.5 grams of gold, became the international currency. It was rivaled by the 3.5 grams Venetian *ducat* of 98.6% gold which was internationally adopted since 1284. It was also the basic currency of the Balkans and duplicated in Serbia using a poor alloy.

In the 1370s the House of Basarab minted silver coins with the Latin inscription *TRANSALPINA* (Wallachia) with a shield, cross, and a raven engraved on them. The sister country of Moldavia minted its coins engraved with *MONETA MOLDAVIE*. They featured a shield, cross (sometimes a double cross), and a bison head. The Romanian coin was known as *ban* and Prince Dracula had the distinction of putting a comet on the reverse side of his currency. This was because the comet was considered a divine sign of good luck. He commemorated a comet that burned in the skies when he became *domnitor*/ruler of Wallachia.[6] Later the Turkish silver coins called *akca* (from asper) became widespread in Eastern Europe. However, nothing replaced gold nuggets, silver bars, and gold coins regardless of their denomination.

☩

Typically, the Jewish economic power in Europe was based on trading and financing the monarchies. Indeed, each prince seemed to have his own Jewish backer who loaned him the money that he needed for his public projects and wars. When the ruler could not pay the debt, the Jews were deported or a pogrom forced them to move to another domain.

In 1257 King Bela IV in his desperation to rebuild Hungary granted legal economic status to the Jews. He allowed them to have a say in the management of the royal finances. The result of this was the development of a thriving international commerce for Hungary. The prosperity of Obuda/Buda enticed King Andrew III to move his court to the city of Pest, across the Danube, where it became a flourishing suburb.

Even though they were accepted for their financial prowess, the old prejudices amplified and drastically affected the Jews making them responsible for many unwanted events. When the Black Plague (1347-1352) killed more than twenty-five million people in Europe the Jewish traders were blamed for spreading it. Some two hundred Jewish communities vanished from Central Europe. Those Jews who avoided these punitive massacres took refuge in the hospitable Eastern Europe.

After numerous expulsions from England, Portugal, Spain, and other countries a mass Jewish migration again entered Eastern Europe, especially Poland. The latter was not affected by the plague because of its lack of good commercial roads. It proved to be a haven for this exodus of the Jewish migrants.

Other Jewish traders and money lenders settled in the Byzantine Empire where they established an increasingly rich community in Thessaloniki. Apostle Luke mentions their synagogue in the city (Acts 17:1), and Saint Paul confirmed it in his epistle the presence of a Jewish community and their synagogue. (1 Thessalonians 2:14)

Because of the Black Death terror, a temporary Jewish expulsion from Hungary after 1349 sent them to Bulgaria and Macedonia, the crossroads of the main Byzantine commercial routes. Many returned four years later, but the rest settled in large numbers in Kastoria. The Jewish community again prospered in Hungry until King Louis the Great tried to convert them to Catholicism. When he failed after 1360 he expelled them. Then, they moved to friendly the Moldovia and Wallachia of Dan I.

The Jews of Constantinople, who were still managed by the Greeks, faced the traditional low tolerance for their competitive trade practices. However, they were not forced into ghettoes as they had been in the West as was done in Rome, Italy.

In addition, the Jews and Armenians (Orthodox believers), the Genovese and Venetians wanted to break into the Balkan markets. Their tall ships ventured along the coastal areas of the Black and Azov seas looking for trade centers. They used their large and powerful fleet to help the Byzantine emperors fight the barbarians, and thus Latin merchants and money lenders gained a foothold in Constantinople. They became so rich and independent that they created their own colony of ten thousand and settled in the district of Galata, only to face the loss of all their possessions in 1171 in an economic clash between the East and West. It was the result of the imprisonment of the Venetians and their massacre in 1182. Still, more than sixty thousand Italian merchants continued to do business in Constantinople.

☩

After 1204 the Latin Empire almost eliminated the obstinate rivalry of their Greek counterparts, but in spite of numerous setbacks, the Byzantines got the upper hand in any commercial competition against the Western intruders. When the Ottomans took over Constantinople and the Balkans it made no difference to the Phanar. It remained the heartland of the resourceful Greek entrepreneurs who were ever ready to switch their allegiances and serve any new master to enrich themselves.

As always bribery and corruption were their main secrets of success. The innate sense of how to arrange things, and control situations from commerce to religion made the Greeks the brokers of the Balkans. This continued to increase their power as they represented the interests of the Sublime Porte in occupied Eastern Europe. In brief the Phanariots emerged to dominate the Balkans politically and economically, as well as to control much of Eastern Europe for the next five centuries.

It is difficult to draw a general conclusion, but when it comes to judging the actions of monarchs who captured thrones by means of treachery and violence, it is clear that they proved to be above the law. Their behavior is what is behind the Balkan saying "a fish rots from the head down," aptly corroborated by the fact that the emperors' bad example set the tone for the rest of society. Their disregard for the law gave people tacit permission to behave in the same way. The laws that applied to the common people were hardly enforced.

Since they were kept on their knees by the Orthodox Church, and forced to bow to any authority, the submissive people of the Balkan nations nursed their instinct for revenge. They allowed it to flare up whenever something triggered their innate sense of justice and pride. Just like the Jews, the Byzantine Greeks remained a distinctive group of people in the Byzantine Empire, competing with each other in the international trade. The Jews were totally overpowered by the massive Greek presence in the leadership of the Eastern Orthodox Church which was submissive to the Ecumenical Patriarch from Constantinople.

✢

A different social order was reflected in the life and economy of the Jews of Europe. By the twelfth century they numbered more than one million. Most of them lived in the west where the continent's main expensive commercial activity took place. Like the Greeks they had an enormous cultural advantage over the rest of the Balkan nations since they were literate. They were able to communicate in international business through letters and contracts making them tremendously successful in commerce and in the lending industry. They faced increased attacks and massacres and many Jews migrated to Eastern Europe which was free of anti-Semitism.

Since the Jews were a nomadic people of a different race and religion. They were never integrated into the feudal system nor did they ever belong to the serfdom or aristocracy of any country. In fact, they were not allowed to own land. They lived in hermetic communities away from the *goyim* (impure Gentiles who ate pigs) population, and no Jew could be seen eating or socializing with a Christian in public.

In the Byzantine Empire the Jewish society was ruled by their rabbis and powerful guilds of different trades. They did not belong to one nation but to their own very distinctive international community. They all dressed in black and the men wore round yarmulkes. They never shaved their sideburns a custom that was called a "Payot." It was also a commandment from their God, just like their being circumcised.

The Theodosian Code had 33 laws regarding the Jews including their own Court of Law, and restrictions being only symbolically enforced. Because of it, there was a great tolerance and no persecution of the Jewish communities, which totaled almost 6,000 Hebrews that were living in the early Byzantine Empire.

✞

Ironically, it was Islam not Christianity which made use of their Old Testament, who most thoroughly emancipated the Jews. The reason was that Orthodoxy was a state religion and found the Jews guilty of making Jesus suffer and killing him. They were not regarded above the pagans and heretics because they went to their moral fabric of the Balkan and Byzantine societies. Yet, the increasing wealth of the opportunistic Jews increasingly became the envy of the Gentile population who resented them, which ended in pogroms or their expulsion.

After the collapse of the Byzantine Empire, the shrewd sultans now residing in Constantinople used the Jews and their inborn skills to increase the Ottoman economy. The sultans made the best use of these Jewish communities, by using them as the Turks could not possibly be present in the Western European trading markets.

Also the Jews were assigned to the highest administrative and financial positions, since the Ottoman domination of Eastern Europe did have a positive impact on international commerce. There were no wars between the occupied countries, and therefore there was no interruption in the Jewish flow of their goods and services along the trade routes. Along with allowing this universal economy to flourish (one in which ethnicity meant little) the Ottomans recruited the best possible military commanders and functionaries from among the Christians toward whom they proved extremely tolerant. Once again, the Jews proved their adaptation to serve in key positions in the Sublime Court.

The Ottoman promotional system fully applied to the Jews who took full advantage of it. They filled many profitable economic roles that were greatly in demand. Their international trade connections also generated a full diplomatic corps for the isolated sultans who needed to inch their way into their acceptance of the Western Europeans. That went hand and hand with the Ottoman's access to the best markets in Europe.

The Jewish opportunity to share the prosperity of the Ottoman Empire attracted so many Jews that by the end of the 16th century the Islamic society hosted the largest Jewish community in the world numbering 150,000 of the Hebrew descendants. This was more than any other country in the world, including Palestine, where once the Great Davidian Kingdom of Israel dominated the Levant.

The overlap of the Byzantine and Ottoman administrations combined with the unfailing barbarian instincts for trickery created societies with generational entrenched bad habits. Later, all of this came to be expressed later by the term "Balkanization." These behaviors of economic, political and social conditions that perpetuated from one century to another began to become the normal way of life throughout Eastern Europe.

# REFERENCE NOTES

1. Edward Gibbon, *The Decline and Fall of the Roman Empire*, ed., Hans-Friedrich Mueller (New York: Modern Library, 2003), 1013.
2. Eventually, the use of cannons caused castles to be built in a circular shape so as to better deflect the destructive projectiles.
3. The Vlachs are often perceived by historians as nomads because they roamed over large territories with their flocks, but that was the nature of their livelihood. In summer, they allowed their huge herds to graze in the mountains, and in the winter they traveled to the Danubian fields or the warm southern area of the Balkans. For this reason their population extended to most areas of the Balkans. Like the Native Americans of the United States the Vlachs retained their distinct ethnic identity.
4. This was a bizarre assassination. Ivan trapped Vladimir by sending him a cross to show his harmless intentions. Vladimir traveled to meet his rival Ivan and went to a church to pray before the meeting. When he stepped out of the church Vladimir was murdered on the steps. His grave became a site of miracles and pilgrimages.
5. Peter Arnott, *The Byzantines and Their World* (New York: St. Martin's Press, 1973), 225.
6. There were three main Wallachias/Vlachias: Wallachia Transalpina (Muntenia with Dobrudja and Oltenia), Moldovallachia/Black Wallachia (Moldavia between the eastern Carpathians and the Dniester/Nistru River), and Transylvania or Ardeal (Hungarian Wallachia (sic), including Maramures and Vlasca in Banat). In addition to these Romanian principalities which lie north of the Danube, other Wallachian entities are: White Wallachia in Moesia/Bulgaria; Great Wallachia in the Thessalian Mountains; Upper Walahia in Epirus; Little Wallachia in Aetolia and Acarnania;

Valachia of southern Macedonia between the rivers Struma and Vardar; Mavrolachia/Morlachia on the coast of southern Dalmatia and Albania, which may have included Maior-Vlachia in southwestern Croatia and Sirmium Wallachia on the Sava River; Minor Valachia (Mala Vlasca) in western Slavonia; Old Valachia located in the valleys separating the mountains of Herzegovina and Montenegro; and Istro-Vlachia in the Istrian Peninsula. On the map of modern Czech Republic, in eastern Moravia there is a large area of Wallachia/Valassko, former Valassky/Moravian Wallachia, and pockets of Vlachs live in Hungary, Ukraine, Poland, Serbia, and many other locations of Eastern Europe. In the eleventh century, the Byzantine author Kekaumenos described in his Strategikon manual that Vlachs were present in Thessaly and identified them with the Dacians living south of the Danube in the former Aurelian Dacia, evidently Moesia now occupied by the Bulgars. In the fifteenth century, historian L. Chalcocondyles mentioned in his Historiarum Demonstrationes that Vlachs from Northern Greece in the Pindus Mountains spoke the same Dacian language and were like the Dacians on the Ister/Danube River; evidently they were similar Vlachs who lived in Wallachia, Bulgaria and Serbia. But, in addition to the fact that some groups were separated (Aromanians, Megleno-Romanians) from the main community during the Age of Migration, many other Vlachs could be found all over the Balkans, as far north as Poland and as far west as the regions of Moravia (part of the modern Czech Republic), and the present-day Croatia. It was from there that the Morlachs gradually disappeared; also the Catholic and Orthodox Vlachs took Croat and Serb national identities. They reached these regions in search of better pastures, and were called Wallachians (Vlasi/Valaši) by the Slavic peoples. Actually, the Germans and the Poles named the Vlachs as "*Wlochi,*" meaning in lose translation "foreigners of the Latin ethnicity. The Greeks called them Vlachos, to describe them as "shepherds" or "wild mountain men," a close sound of the word "Vlakos" which meant to describe an "idiot." Despite of this low opinion, the Vlachs would produce many of Greek writers, politicians and other important personalities.

# SPIRITUAL and CULTURAL LIFE

The spiritual life in the Byzantine Empire was rooted in Eastern Orthodox rites. The Byzantine Church was regarded as the body of Christ and Orthodoxy claimed to possess a true understanding of Divinity. Spirituality meant following Jesus' example by living a saintly life, one in which a person endured pain and injustice. Indeed a life of misery and suffer, was considered a virtuous life.

To ensure that one would be saved it was important to fear God's punishment, obey the Decalogue (the Ten Commandments), and observe the rules articulated by the Church. God's punishment for disobeying the church ranged from personal sickness and misfortunes to earthquakes, the Bubonic plague, Mongol invasions and other misfortunes. Anathema hung over believers and the priests made sure to remind them of it. Through a deep devotion to prayer, fasting, and meditation, the body and soul could be healed. A better human would then emerge, one that was prepared to face the Last Judgment.

The Orthodox Church teachings were as austere as its two dimensional icons. They promoted blind obedience to the priest who led the church goers, and to the ruler who governed the land. Both of them were taken to be appointed by God. To be a good Orthodox Christian required that one acquiesce to any authority and kiss its punishing hand. Thus the meek believed to live as God demanded, and the resentful felt humiliated and angry. This submissiveness on the part of the population led to a double standard in ethics and morality, one that came to be a way of life.

The ancient nations of the Dacians, Greeks, Illyrians, Macedonians, and Thracians were already Christianized by the time of the barbarian invasions when the Slavs brought paganism and *volkhv or* shamans with them. They believed in sacred animals, mountains, trees, etc., and in gods named Dabog, Mokos, and Perun among others.

Their Stone Age religion suited the barbarians whose belief system was simple, to have faith in something, pray to stay healthy, make sure you have enough to eat, and avoid being killed. For them there was no clear distinction between right and wrong and no such thing as guilt. This worked well for people who had little respect for human life. So for several centuries the Slav invaders retained their religion. The very distant and invisible Christian God could not replace the worship of beautiful and "real" deities provided by Mother Nature.

Nevertheless, Orthodoxy was an inescapable fact of life in Eastern Europe and monks were active missionaries. The Slavs (excepting the heavy traders, the Khazars, who converted to Judaism as early as 730) found themselves ever more attracted to the Byzantine religion. In their societies looting and trading were interchangeable, and brigands asking for ransom were at the same level as political negotiators. Even though this was a way of life for the barbarians they looked around and began to think there might be a different and better world, one in which their survival was not constantly being threatened.

Since they were curious and superstitious the barbarians were attracted to the visual symbols of Christianity. The cross made an appealing talisman that could be worn as a necklace or painted on a shield. Its message and the Jesus saga were easily understood and moving to the barbarian mind. The pageantry of Orthodoxy with its intricate religious service was fascinating enough to entice the Slavic communities to listen to the Mass even though it was preached in Greek or Latin.

They saw the Church as offering a secure afterlife in heaven in exchange for following certain simple rules that were beneficial for familial and social relationships. Furthermore, it was comforting to know that in the eyes of the new God everyone was equal.

Most appealing to them were the rites of communion, bread and wine were luxury foods for the poverty stricken barbarians. They also enjoyed the festive Christian holiday celebrations with having freel meals and alcoholic drinks on days where no one worked.

Recognizing the importance of this pleasure aspect of Orthodoxy Vladimir I (who was baptized after he married Princess Ana of Constantinople in 988) rejected Islam because it prohibited the consumption of alcohol. "The Rus' liked wine whether it was drunk at parties and meals or consumed as part of the communion service."[1]

Prince Vladimir was a pagan prince with seven wives and eight hundred concubines. He continued to carry out ritual human sacrifices even though his grandmother Princess Olga was a Christian (baptized in Constantinople in 957). When a Byzantine monk showed him a painting of sinners burning in hell the prince experienced an awakening and was baptized in 988.

He used the sword to Christianize his subjects and with their "donations" he built the magnificent Church of the Tithes. For their spiritual deeds and roles in the history of the Kievan Rus the royal Olga and Vladimir were sanctified. He routinely inaugurated Orthodox churches with lavish feasts, and since he believed that drinking was the joy of the Rus, he designated eight days of unending feasting to celebrate his new church of the Feast of the Transfiguration.

The event transformed Russian pagans into Christians and Vladimir was called the New Constantine. Old Church Slavonic which copied the Greek liturgy was adopted under his rule as well. Kiev became a renowned center of Orthodoxy for the Russians. Its thriving Greek community supplied olive oil for the votive lamps, wine for communion, candles, icons, attire for priests, and other church related accoutrements.

☦

The conversion of the barbarians from the Byzantine Empire, came about not because they feared eternal damnation, or believed that Jesus would save them from hell, or because they understood the meaning of the preached gospel. They were only eager to adopt a new faith and they wanted to be baptized.

Rather, their leaders were aware of the political advantages to be had from it, and so they imposed it upon their subjects. First, the tribes would be united and fortified under the same religion. Second, the Christian blessing would allow them to hold on to their thrones. Third, they and their people would be socially elevated to the level of the Byzantines.

Those rulers who shared this crucial wisdom were Prince Viseslav of Croatia, who became a Christian in 800 even though his nation is reputed to have begun converting to Orthodoxy in 751. Prince Mojmir in 822 and then Prince Ratislav of Moravia in 846 converted to Christianity. Khan Boris in 864, who changed his name to Mihail/Michael and baptized the Bulgarians, Knez Mutimir christianized the Serbs around 870. Mieszko I of Poland was baptized in 966. Istvan/Stephen was crowned by the pope as the Christian King of Hungary in 1000 (and would later be canonized, even though he executed all of his subjects who did not want to be Catholic Christians).

All of these leaders became merciless protagonists of the new religion. Furthermore, Boris the opportunist declared the Bulgarian Church to be independent of Rome and Constantinople. The old gods died hard in the pagan population, and he simply massacred his own people who refused baptism. Christianity had come a long way since the era when some outraged pagan Magyars forced a Venetian missionary into a barrel lined with spikes and rolled him into the

Danube River to quiet his preaching.

The Duke of Bohemia, Wenceslaus I was responsible for turning the Czechs into a Christian nation. He became a martyr after his younger brother conspired with pagan nobility and in 935 murdered him on his way to church. Wenceslaus was canonized and became the patron saint of the Czech nation.

Divine revelations changed the spiritual lives of many rulers and their sacred missions were later glorified. The Hungarian legend about divine intervention in the creation of the Arpad dynasty (896-1301) begins with Almos's mother. She dreamed that she had been impregnated by a mythical falcon and that her son, grandchildren, and great grandchildren would become masters of distant lands. Giving credence to this revelation her grandson Arpad united with and led the Magyar tribes to Pannonia. There the Hungarians maintained their base as they persisted in their efforts to occupy other nations.

According to another legend when Prince Jovan Vladimir was imprisoned after a battle he had a dream that predicted his future. An angel appeared and told him he would be freed, but that he would die a martyr. Indeed, he was beheaded in 1016 on the church steps in Prespa by an adversary and shortly thereafter he was sanctified. He was the first Serbian saint to be depicted holding his head in one hand and the cross with a palm leaf in the other. A monastery was built in his name in Albania.

When Prince Stefan Nemanja was imprisoned in a cave by his brothers it was said that Saint George freed him. He commemorated this miracle in 1171 when he built the Church of Durdevi Stupovi/ Pillars of St. George, the Monastery of Saint Nicholas in Kuršumlija, the Monastery of the Holy Mother of Christ near Kosanica-Toplica, and others. In 1190 he completed construction of the Temple of the Immaculate Holy Virgin the Benefactor. From that time on the Nemanja dynasty was considered to have been blessed by God.

He died at the age of 86 in front of the magic icon of Virgin Hodegetria (The Three-Handed Virgin). According to legend, holy oil seeped out of his tomb, and because of this and other miracles that occurred over his dead body, he was canonized in 1200 only one year following his death.

King Milutin (r. 1282–1321) achieved sainthood in a very different manner. He was married several times including at one time to a five year-old Byzantine princess, and his entire life was full of sinful events. Yet, he made restitution for this by making Serbia a great power, and by building some forty churches and monasteries.

Among these are Bogorodica Ljeviska Church (1309), King's Church of Studenica (1315), St. Nicholas Church in the Hilandar Monastery on Mount Altos. All of these feature portraits of him on their walls. He redefined Serbian architecture with the building of the Gracanica Monastery in Kosovo in 1321 which displays the last image made of him.

Stefan Uros IV military invasions into the heart of the Byzantine Empire brought Serbia its largest borders. He was canonized by the Serbian Orthodox Church despite the fact that this mighty ruler dethroned his father by strangulation, and killed his half brother in battle. His father is buried in the Visoki Decani Monastery in Kosovo (which they both built).

Uros was laid to rest inside the Monastery of the Holy Archangels (which he built) near Prizren. It was later destroyed by the Turks. His son King Stefan Uros V nicknamed "the Weak" was a gentle ruler who suffered numerous betrayals, including at the hands of his mother, uncle, and other members of the nobility. He finally lost his father's great Serbian Empire. He died in 1371 but his good nature and noble soul triumphed in the end. He was canonized two centuries after his death.

☦

For Balkan rulers it seemed that building new churches meant more than just providing a place of worship for their obedient subjects. It was also a way of salving their guilty consciences, and diminishing the guilt they had incurred because of the suffering they had wrought upon so many people. "Build a church and save your soul" seemed to be the royal mantra. Orthodox churches were simple structures unadorned except for wall paintings that illustrated the Bible for illiterate worshippers.

✝

A regular Orthodox church consisted of one to three towers and one to three large bells. They all rested on round simple cupolas or domes of different sizes and shapes. They were supported by round arches between the walls with slit windows proper for a safe defense. The windows were high and hardly let any daylight inside the square interiors. This caused a darkness which created a mysterious spiritual mood of a religious enigma.

The Orthodox wooden altar is at the far end of the rectangular "nave" extending from wall to wall. There were two lateral doors reaching some two-thirds high without reaching the ceiling. The colorful and beautiful encrusted altar is adorned with glittering icons, and the most important and most kissed being was that of the Virgin Mary holding the half naked baby Jesus. They were lit from above by the hanging votive candles, and from lit candles stuck in the sand of round wooden urns, they added moving shadows on the walls along with a pleasant scent to the pious parishioners.

In front of the altar there is a large table where parishioners bring food offerings, mainly koliva of boiled coarse bulgur wheat, decorated with crosses made of colorful candies, powdered sugar and small candles, to commemorate their dead relatives.

The priest keeps half of the gifts and the other half is evenly divided with the rest of the congregation, especially the poor members and gypsies waiting outside the front door of the church.

The priest chants most of the time from behind the mysterious altar. A deacon reads the psalms from his outside pulpit situated on the right side of the altar, with a widow behind him. Because only a few pews are lined up along the walls, the church attendees stand or kneel while praying and hitting the stone floor with their foreheads as self punishment. Once in a while, they are doing genuflections and crossing their hearts to show their devotion and submission.

In small village churches, only the tall altar is crowded with icons framed in fake silver and gold. The priest's robe is embroidered with silver and gold threads with colorful precious stones sown around the embroidered cross on the front and on the back. These are the only two luxury objects.

Even the robe's precious colorful hem deserved obedience, and was to be kissed by the kneeling believers as the bearded priest passed through their rows. He was swinging the smoking thurible with aromatic incense burning inside. It was suspended from fine chains with jungle bells attached to it. At the end of the service all would take communion of wine and bread. The people lined up to partake of communion, and to kiss the hand of the priest.

From above the entire congregation, from the round cupola, a large triangle with God's eye inside it, watches the entire ritual below. On the side of the cupola there could be Jesus blessing with his three fingers, and the Virgin Mary.

Inside of each church built by a ruler, there was his image that was painted with a crown on his head and a mace or scepter in his hand. Being a prince implied that an individual had a "royal bone," meaning one of his parents descended from a king, *cnez*/czar, or emperor. The emperors inherited the title, were named (sometimes by themselves) or chosen by God to wear a crown, and sit on the royal throne.

Pious princes and kings were painted holding a miniature of the church they built as a testimony of their sacred charity. They endowed the churches with large estates with many villages and serfs. They felt blessed to belong to a church, in spite of the fact that they were slaves to an unscrupulous priest or abbot.

The rich churches of the cities or monasteries had spectacular gold mosaics displaying the saints, kings and biblical scenes. Above the main roof were one or more towers with large bells to call and remind the faithful to come to, or to leave the church. The Orthodox Church was to inspire fear to sin, repentance, obedience and to enforce deeply felt religious beliefs.

Tyrants viewed it as a sort of mission to pay for their sins by giving gifts to the Church. Often in their correspondence they appended to their names such phrases as "by the grace of God," thus demonstrating the approval of the Almighty of their status as His understudy on earth.

When they approached old age many of them became very spiritual. They would retire to and often were buried in the churches and monasteries they had built. These burials marked and led to the construction of new shrines for the next generations. They would then be worshipping sanctified rulers who had once been more feared than the devil.

From the earlier Roman basilica of the austere Catholic Church shaped like a huge rectangular barn or a monolithic castle having a tower and a bell, they quickly evolved into higher constructions of different sizes and architecture.

By the 13th century, very high cathedrals with many angular pointed towers now with arches inside resting on the rib vaults and domes seemed to reach to the sky. They were all supported by flying buttresses. They looked so different that the pope named that style "Gothic" recalling the wild invading Goths.

Inside, elaborate decorations in stone or marble including statues and magnificent colorful stained glass and rose windows were meant to induce meditation and prayer. Above all everything was enhanced by a choir and complex organ music. The Catholic Cathedrals became architectural religious monuments.

Yet, nothing could match the massive Hagia Sofia with a height of 55 meters/180 feet completed in the year 537. This was the Cathedral of Constantinople during the Byzantine Empire which inspired the models at a smaller scale for the Orthodox Churches. Each of the churches had a cemetery placed behind it marked with a beautiful ornate cross for each grave. After the church service the parishioners would go to light candles at the graves of their loved ones. Food and even drinks would be brought to share and celebrate life and the afterlife. The entire gathering was a memorable event that was repeated weekly. It was a good opportunity for the people to socialize.

✣

North of the Danube River the Wallachians had been Christianized since Roman times and their faith was kept alive by their voievodes (princes) who rendered homage to God by building churches and monasteries. This anchored the spirituality of the future Romanians. It transformed the landscape of the country and defined its social order. A monastery was built in the year 1315 which was named after *Voivod*/Prince Radu the Black who was buried there. He was the founder of the *voivodat* Wallachia/Muntenia the first national capital at Campulung-Muscel. (The author of this book is a native of this place).

By building the Church of Saint Nicholas and a palace (both in a true Byzantine style) at the distant Curtea de Arges Prince Basarab I (r. 1310-1352) maybe a son of Radu the Black established the second capital of Wallachia there. At the same time, many small wooden churches were built by the Wallachian shepherds deep in the mountains where they had their settlements.

Later, in 1461 Prince Dracula completed construction of the Snagov Monastery, and he moved his capital to the location of Bucharest/Bucuresti because of his devotion to his church. In Moldovia, his cousin Stefan III the Great was famous for building a church after each of his thirty-four victories (out of 36 battles), to praise God for defeating his enemies.

His successful commitment to fight the invading Turks led Pope Sixtus IV to name him *Athleta Christi*/Champion of Christ. Among his living legacies are the Putna Monastery, where he was buried in

1504, and the Voronet Monastery, which marked his victory against the Turks at Vaslui in 1475.

The monastery church features masterful outside mural paintings that he dedicated to Saint George, the patron saint of the Wallachian farmers and shepherds, and the mounted hero who slays the dragon with a spear. Communities whose names are rooted in monasticism, such as Calugareni (of the monks), Chilia (monk cell), Manastirea (monastery), Schitu (hermitage), and many others, are still to be found in Romania today.

This same Saint George was also the patron saint of the Vlach shepherds living south of the Danube River. They used a Romanian dialect to celebrate their mass. All across the Balkan Peninsula they were the strongest ethnicity within the Orthodox faith during the barbarian invasions.

Their spirituality was anchored in the holy site of Mount Athos which is off the peninsular east coast of Greece. It was inhabited by hundreds of monks who needed supplies from the Vlachian men, while the women were forbidden to visit the saintly Place.

The Asan brothers claimed divine inspiration for their anti-Byzantine revolt from St. Dimitri/Demetrius and only after they built a church in his name were the Vlachs convinced to follow them in war. They subsequently built the Second Vlach-Bulgarian Empire (1185-1396).

This Vlachian-Greek spiritual connection was maintained indefinitely. Most likely Grigore Palamas/Grigorie Palama (1296-1359) Archbishop of Thessaloniki was of Vlach origin. His strong attachment to the Vlachian born Nicodemus/Nicodim (1320-1406) the spiritual adviser of Prince Mircea the Elder indicates that they were of the same ethnic origin. With a generous grant from the Wallachian prince, Nicodemus was involved in the construction of many churches. He was sanctified as Nicodemus of Tismana after the famous monastery.

Another famous monastery was the Voditsa Monastery which he founded in Wallachia. His ties with the Patriarch Eftimie of Tarnovo (Bulgaria) led to the exclusive calligraphic production of Slavonic versions of the Tetraevanghel (Four Gospels). Eftimie was also sanctified and the spiritual work of the two united the Vlachs from the North and South of the Danube River. They also shared the same traditional Orthodox rites.

One of these rites took place on January 6th each year in conjunction with a celebration of the Epiphany. A synod of priests tossed a cross into an icy cold river, and young men competed to find the holy object. Giotto di Bondone in 1306 painted *The Nativity*. It depicts the baby Jesus attended by his mother the Virgin Mary, angels flying above, with sheep and cattle around them, even the magi and his stepfather Joseph were in attendance.

It was the first artistic celebration of Christmas and today we celebrate the nativity. It took many centuries for the Christmas holiday with all its trappings to come to being.

☦

The northern Wallachians diligently included the Daco-Roman traditions in their celebrations of the Christian holidays. Among them were the *plugusorul/* (the plowing carol) sung on New Year's Day to cheer for a good harvest in the year to come. This involved cracking whips, jingling bells (to keep evil spirits away), and cutting a furrow in the snow all the while being accompanied by songs.

Shouts of encouragement ended each verse invoking Emperor Trajan (r. 98-117) the former occupier of Transylvania[2] as their leading farmer. Other caroling consisted of well wishing chants accompanied with the gentle touches of a *sorcova*, which were branches decorated with colorful flowers and ribbons (like a long wreath with a handle). They were held by the young children.

A traditional Wallachian ritual practiced north and south of the Danube was the Holy Saturday midnight celebration. It involved a walk around the church during which everyone sang about Christ having risen from death. Afterwards, they cracked colored eggs all the while reciting the same celebratory verses, and later eating lamb as part of a feast.

As far as daily life was concerned, each Orthodox family would pray in their own house kneeling in front of an icon of the Virgin Mary holding the baby Jesus. This icon is still the most popular and it is usually adorned with a draped embroidered scarf, hung above to frame it, along with a lit votive lamp beneath it. It is always placed on an east wall.

☦

Spirituality was not only connected to traditions like those described so far, but was also reflected in the ways people ate and socialized. Many joyful feasts celebrated the church patrons and the Othodox holidays. At funeral feasts a special porridge of boiled bulgur with honey and nuts mixed in was served in memory of the dead. All of these celebrations were carried out in keeping with the Church traditions. A thanksgiving prayer was recited by a priest who also sprinkled *ayazma* (holy water, from the Greek word *hagiasme*) to bless any food offerings.

There were no weddings or other festivities during Lent, Christmas, Easter, or other periods of abstinence when basically only non-animal products could be eaten. The exception was fish which was allowed on a few days in order to re-supply needed protein. Since Orthodoxy had strict dietary rules almost half of the year was designated as meat-free meals. On Wednesdays and Fridays dairy and eggs were also forbidden. The church prohibited alcohol consumption on all of the days preceding its holidays.

Christianity could not eliminate age-old superstitions. An itchy left hand meant money would be received, and if the right hand itched money would be given away. Ringing in the right ear meant good news would be heard, and in the left ear bad news. Breaking a dish was a sign of good luck, while socks or other clothing worn inside out brought bad luck. A black cat crossing the road was an omen, while a rooster singing in front of the door forecast unexpected guests.

A cross as a necklace was considered the ultimate good luck talisman, and even the Turks would not touch women who wore one. For the Turks sneezing calls for a blessing, "may Allah have mercy upon you!" It was not only the commoners who were superstitious.

Czar Simeon of Bulgaria visited the Emperor Romanus I in 924 to discuss tax issues between the two states. While they were looking out on the waters of the Golden Horn they saw two eagles flying overhead. One was flying northward and the other was flying towards Constantinople. This clearly indicated to both of them that their negotiations were futile. In fact, only Simeon's sudden death saved Constantinople from another Bulgarian siege that was based on economic quarrel.

Murad II laid siege to Constantinople in 1421. The Byzantine defenders credited their successful resistance to the vision of the Virgin Mary who saved the city by leading the sultan and his army off to a more important campaign in Asia Minor.

Religion typically shapes the functioning of both individuals and societies, and this certainly was the case in the Balkans. The Orthodox Church was a vast and complicated institution with a hierarchy based on nepotism and patronage. The church was the first schooling for all of the children. Its leaders were politically involved at all levels of government.

Unlike Catholicism where the pope appointed the heads of state in Eastern Europe, the autocratic Ecumenical Patriarch from Constantinople named the Church leaders of Orthodox nations. They were subsequently totally submissive to their emperors or kings. The servants of Orthodoxy were first of all servants to whoever held the throne, and wielded the political power.

This system encouraged corruption among clerics who sought to advance themselves. It also inspired the common people to follow their example. The ordinary priests were the foot soldiers of the church. They officiated at all religious rites from praying the liturgy and hearing confessions to performing baptisms and conducting funerals. The faithful invested unlimited respect and trust in them.

While they promoted the values taught in the gospel many lived lives that were contrary to their preaching that urged love and equality among all men and espoused poverty as a virtue. Although they belonged to the most privileged echelon of society they fought bitterly amongst each other.

They competed for the wealthiest parishes and there was no limit as to how rich and arrogant they could be. Unlike in the West where priests could not marry and had to leave all of their accumulated wealth to the church, the Orthodox priest passed his possessions on to his children. At least one of his sons was expected to continue the family tradition and ideally increase the family's wealth.

This kind of behavior produced the saying "do what the priest says, not what he does". It also gave new meaning to the word "demagogue" its original ancient meaning having been downgraded from that of a real leader of the people to someone who is dishonest and tyrannical, but he pretends to be people's savior.

Certainly this applied to life under Czar Peter I (r. 927-969) when Bulgarian monks and priests were known to be continually drunk and fornicating. Those who were entrepreneurial left their monasteries and churches and became tyrannical landlords on the estates donated to the church by Peter. Corruption was rampant in the church, and it triggered the *Bogomil* (Dear to God) movement considered heretical by the Byzantines.

In the West its followers were named Bulgari. They believed that God had a good son (Jesus) and an evil one (Satan), each of whom had his own eternal domain. Generally, the Bulgari refused to pay taxes to their landlord or to do free work for anyone. They also dodged military duty since all of these types of obligations were manmade and not divine. In spite of all this Peter was sanctified while most of the Bogomil adepts converted to Mohammedanism which was the new religion of the invading Turks.

☩

The Ottoman invasion of Anatolia and the Balkans introduced the religion of Islam that proclaimed "there is no God but Allah, and Mohammed (Highly Praised) is his prophet." With it came *jihad (*holy war) against the Christians who were regarded as Infidels. This new religious movement was initiated by Mohammed (570-632) a prophet who like Jesus was illiterate, but he knew how to speak to people who had fallen away from other religions.

Islam proved most successful in uniting the Turks and other tribes under the crescent flag and the battle cry, *Allahu Akbar*/Allah is Great! A series of capable chieftains used the Muslim bible, the Koran, to discipline their warriors. They were told that fighting and dying for the cause of Allah brought them an immediate entry into his paradise. That promise led them to be a militarily great power. This was an extraordinary achievement for these desert nomads who believed that the first human was created after Allah breathed his spirit into Adam (causing him to sneeze), and that their sultan was the shadow of God on earth.

To them there was only one God in the universe. They rejected Christianity with its concept of the Trinity as being a polytheistic religion not much different from paganism. This kept the two kinds of religions apart. Islam did not concern the Greek prelates whose only aim was for Constantinople to be more powerful than Rome. They sought ever more political and religious control in an effort to fight the Catholics. They concluded that it was better to accept the Turkish fez rather than the pope's tiara. The Greeks received the symbolic fez after the fall of Constantinople, after they had scarcely defended the city.

Under the Turks the initial Phanariots, the wealthy Greek families from Constantinople who lived in Phanar district, continued to dominate Eastern Orthodoxy. In the case of the Romanian principalities where they owned large church estates they mercilessly exploited the serfs, and pocketed most of the profits intended for Mount Athos the sacred ground of Orthodoxy:

> Thus Athos was a major source for the spread of manuscripts, texts, and theological ideas, as texts were copied and translated on the mountain and then carried back to the different Orthodox lands. Athos was also the source from which the Slavs drew ideas about Church law and Church organization. For example…Byzantine Canon Law was to reach Serbia via Athos. Athos was also a center from which various political ideas and Byzantine secular legal texts spread to the Orthodox world.[3]

In the Byzantine Empire and Eastern Europe, the Orthodox Church ruled supreme and went largely unchallenged by its intimidated believers. By contrast, in Bohemia the Catholic Church was confronted by Jan Hus. In 1404 he began a movement against its secular power and wealth. The protest rallied followers from every social strata of the Czech population. They revolted against the Church, and its main supporters the ethnic Germans who subsequently moved their university from Prague to Leipzig.

In 1415 Hus was burned at the stake. His close associate Jerome of Prague suffered the same fate. Eventually in 1436 Emperor Sigismund negotiated with them and the Hussite rebels elected their own king.and the movement achieved a significant spiritual and economic victory against Catholicism. However, the Croatians, Hungarians, and Poles cherished Catholicism and they used it to advance their societies and bring them closer to the spiritual and cultural life of Western Europe.

No such religious uprising was possible in the context of the Orthodox Church which was ruled with an iron fist. Occasionally, some Orthodox monarchs and nations sought to depend less on Constantinople's domination out of a sense of pride. The "national churches" of Bulgaria, Romania and Serbia severed their connections to the Greek Church. As in the Byzantine Empire religious prestige was second only to military might as both of them enforced a hierarchal society. This remained so unsurpassed by any changes over time for every Orthodox nation.

Christian and Islam are monotheistic and Abrahamic religions founded by one single spiritual visionary: Jesus and Mohamed. Billions of people entrusted their faith and life in their doctrine with different rituals to celebrate religious events.

Each Christian worshipper entrusted his or her destiny in the Holy Trinity of God the Father, God the Son and God of the Holy Spirit. Each Muslim does the same worshipping Allah. They pray in different ways and seek compassion and help from one of the two different gods.

So, it is normal and logic for the thousands of soldiers from different opposite armies, asking their gods to end the battle while still alive and victorious. The problem arose when two different armies who believed in the same god, and prayed to the same God to destroy each other. How would the wise and beloved God decide what army to endorse to win?

✝

The culture of Eastern Europe was vastly different from that of the rest of Europe even though the great Hellenic traditions had established the standards of the Western culture. At this point, they combined Homeric literature and classical philosophy with a Roman influenced Latin enlightenment. The Greeks proved to be a people who had the strength to endure. As the Roman occupation did very little to change the Greek character. To the contrary, the Greek art and civilization always dominated Rome and its Byzantine Empire.

The Eastern Roman Empire was now referred to by the Greeks as *Basileia ton Rhōmaiōn*/The Empire of the Romans. To keep up with that title the people of Byzantium, now referred to as Constantinople

(Nova Roma -the New Rome) called themselves Romaioi or Romans. In spite of the fact that Latin initially was the official language of the Empire, the Greeks continued to speak their mother tongue the language of Plato and Aristotle. Art and culture were distinctively Greek achievements.

During the Dark Ages, the Byzantine Empire was superior to any other European civilization and was better administrated and ruled than the Anglo-Saxon, French, German, and Italian lands. However, in Europe civilization was interchangeable with Christianity.

Unfortunately, the Greek lands were continually plagued by barbarian invasions. When the Eurasians arrived in the Balkans their plundering directly affected the Byzantine culture, and modified its established patterns in negative ways.

Basically, for the Byzantines, like the Romans before them, any person who did not wear sandals and togas, could not make olive oil and did not cover their houses with red tiles were barbarians. The farther away they lived from Greece, the less civilized they were thought to be. The kings of many ethnic nations within the empire were considered to be as simple as the steppes from whence they came. The more primitive their beliefs were the more tenaciously they seemed to cling to them and their primitive gods.

Little is known about the culture of the distant eastern Slavs, but when the Russians attacked Constantinople Patriarch Photius characterized them as:

> A nation dwelling somewhere far from our country, barbarous, nomadic, armed with arrogance, unwatched, unchallenged, leaderless, has so suddenly, in the twinkling of an eye, like a wave of the sea, poured over our frontiers, and as a wild boar has devoured the inhabitants of the land like grass, or straw, or a crop…sparing nothing form man to beast…but boldly thrusting their sword through persons of every age and sex.[4]

A much milder image was presented by the chronicler Nestor

who was a monk from twelfth century Kiev. He described them as farmers and herders sporting bowl shaped haircuts. The Kievan Rus men shaved their heads leaving a lock of hair on top, and they used a basinet to wash their hands before dinner. They were raiders who lived off what they pillaged from others, and they shared their loot with the Jewish Khazars. Most Slavs arrived in the Balkans having already experienced slavery and abuse at the hands of still more powerful barbarians. Therefore, they had little problem adjusting to the manorial system, and became obedient serfs.

However, the Bulgars were a different lot. Khan Krum (r. 803-814) led them against the Byzantines. He was so victorious that he caused three emperors to be dethroned, and two of them were assassinated. Emperor Nikephoros was killed in a battle. In July 813 Bulgarian armies besieged Constantinople in order to force Emperor Leo V to sign a pact with Krum. He was busy astonishing the defenders of the city with animal and human sacrifices, parading his concubines, and sprinkling his soldiers with sea water he had personally sanctified.

Since he was fully aware that he could not conquer the city, Krum agreed to a compromise. He asked the emperor to allow him to stick his lance in the Golden Gate as a sign of a barbarian triumph. When his request was refused he led his troops in a devastating pillage around Constantinople. After a few days, he returned with another proposal: he would stop the carnage if he were handed a huge amount of gold and the most attractive young women in the city. Leo again refused but countered with a proposed truce.

A meeting with Krum took place in a no-man's land. At a critical point Krum sensed danger and darted away on his horse while his companions were hacked to death by Leo's concealed bodyguards. The revenge of the khan was proportionate to this insult: the Bulgars decimated the villages and lands outside of Constantinople's walls. They looted even the churches and monasteries, and also one of the imperial palaces. After this, they set fires that reduced everything to ruins.

Nearly everyone living in these areas was slaughtered. All the marble columns, magnificent doors, furniture, art objects, and the craftsmen who could make them were taken to Krum's capital at Pliska where he built a dazzling palace of his own. The whole event from proposals for peace to vengeful retribution was typical of the sort of "cultural exchange" which routinely took place between barbarians and Byzantines.

Over time, a process of cultural osmosis took place between the newly formed nations who admired the imperial glamour of Constantinople. They envied it so much that they tried to destroy it. Byzantine culture affected all who came into contact with it. The undisciplined barbarians could absorb only so much.

Basically, it was easier to follow bad examples than to try to understand and relate to the sophisticated thinking behind Hellenic ideals. By the end of the twelfth century the Byzantine culture had advanced beyond that of the rest of Europe. In addition to creating private schools, Constantine IX founded public academies of law and philosophy, and Alexius I advanced theological studies.

When rabbi Benjamin of Tudela (Spain) visited Constantinople around 1170 he wrote with amazement:

> The Greeks who inhabit the country are extremely rich and possess great wealth of gold and precious stones. They dress in garments of silk, ornamented by gold and other valuable materials; they ride upon horses, and in their appearance they are like princes. The country is rich, producing all sorts of delicacies, as well as abundance of bread, meat and wine, and nothing on earth equals their wealth. They are well skilled in the Greek sciences and live comfortably, 'every man under his vine and his fig tree[5]

Constantinople was still the city of lights with paved streets, and its one million inhabitants enjoyed a rich cultural life. The other side of the coin was less glittery as the Byzantines continued to be beset by problems with the barbarians who did not fit into this cultural climate.

The Serbians are a case in point. William Aarchbishop of Tyre and chronicler of the Crusades of 1179 described the "rebellious Serbs" under Prince Stefan Nemanja as "an uneducated people, lacking discipline, living in mountains and forests, unskilled in agriculture. They are rich in herds and flocks and unusually well supplied with milk, cheese, butter, meat, honey and wax."[6] Nemanja himself lived a rustic life and preferred to sleep on the floor.

The only rapid transformation that occurred in the barbarian culture was with respect to language, and this either separated or united groups of people. Upon their arrival in the Balkans the Bulgars and Serbs spoke their own languages. However, the overwhelming number of Antes and Slaveni made theirs dominant and it became known as the Slavic language. This dynamic led to the Bulgars and Serbs also being called Slavs.

Once again, superiority in numbers and the force of weapons dictated membership in a culture. Still, the Byzantines had a significant cultural impact on local cultures especially where Orthodoxy was concerned.

Parallel to the Slavicization of the Balkans the language of the Byzantine Church changed when in 630 Emperor Heraclius halted the use of Latin. The result was that refined Hellenistic Greek came to be used in imperial documents. At the same time its vulgar dialect spread throughout the empire and competed with the Slavic language.

The latter was a disadvantage because there was no way of writing Slavic sounds. There was no Slavic alphabet to convey its unique phonetics which did not exist in Greek or Latin.

✠

However, such an alphabet became a reality in the 860s. Two monks who were brothers Cyril Constantine (c. 827-869) and Methodius (c. 825-884) of Thessaloniki not only spoke the Slavic language, but had also mastered Greek and Latin. Constantine was additionally competent in Arabic, Hebrew, and other languages. They used Greek letters and added signs to them to accommodate the written needs of spoken Slavic, thus inventing the Galgolitic alphabet. This became the foundation for the Cyrillic alphabet and the church retained the language.

The process of Slavicization was vehemently condemned by the popes of the time who declared that only Latin, Greek, and Hebrew were fit for the liturgy. But Constantine and Methodius translated the Bible into Slavonic using this new alphabet. This act brought lasting legitimacy to the Slavic language, and it began to be used in churches.

This meant that the liturgy could be conducted in a language that the common people understood. Subsequently, it became the official spoken and written language of most of the Balkans and was approved by Constantinople as the fourth language of the church. Ironically, the Slavic languages outlasted Latin.

Perhaps equally important was this first step in spreading the Byzantine culture into the Slav world as it was adopted by the non-Slavic Macedonians. It also migrated into the Catholic Balkans and the Latin speaking Romanian principalities.[7] Constantine, who was now called Cyril and Methodius became apostles in their own right. A generation of disciples continued their work both with the alphabet and with evangelization. For their legacy of enlightenment and their role in strengthening Christianity in the Slavic world the two holy brothers were sanctified and are still honored in the Balkans.[8]

In 893 the Slavic language became the official language of the Bulgarians. The Galgolithic and Cyrillic alphabets made it possible for the Slavs to write their own literature which initially focused on religious subjects. In 1189 Prince Miroslav of the Hum (modern Bosnia) put Slavic literature on the cultural map with *Miroslav's Gospel,* a book that contained masterful calligraphic illustrations.[9]

Many Balkan ethnicities adopted the Slavic language focusing on Old Church Slavonic. Therefore, they established a certain cultural pattern which the Vlachs did not. They had a longer history in the Balkans and their Daco-Latin language reinforced and helped maintain their ethnic/national identity. As mountain people with the skills necessary to survive never had to migrate from their lands. The barbarians of the steppes did not venture into areas which were either densely forested or located at high altitudes.

Even though they were now split into large pockets by the invaders they remained strongly united by their language based on the Vulgar Latin (like Hebrew for the Jews in the Diaspora). It caused them to be identified somewhat differently in various parts of the Balkans in which they lived:

> The Romance-speaking people who are called Vlachs south of the Danube River came to be called Romanians north of the Danube, though all are closely related to each other.[10]

The Albanians referred to the Vlachs as *rămăńi*, *rumăńi*, and *romăńi*; Greeks called them *rumân*, *arumâni*, and *armâni*. They formed an independent Great Wallachia in parts of Macedonia and the Pindus Mountains in Albania and Greece (in Thessaly). Lesser Wallachia was located in Aetolia and Acarnania in west central Greece, and Upper Wallachia was in Epirus. Hungarians named them *cincár*. The Turks acknowledged them as *ciobani*, which in Romanian means shepherds. This was their main occupation and source of their trade.[11]

The Vlachian language was in fact spoken across the Balkans. Historian Niketas provided invaluable documentation on the Vlachian population inside the Byzantine Empire when he described their King Asan who spoke "the language of the Vlachs."[12] It was an offshoot of the Vulgar Latin and Dacian language.[13]

Further evidence of this is provided by Pope Innocent III who in 1199 talked about the "Roman descent" of King Asan which implied that his language was related to Latin. The pope did not want to name Ioannitsa emperor because his title was in conflict with the Latin emperor from Constantinople. His new state was known as the Bulgarian Empire because the Bulgars, who lived alongside the

Vlachs, were the most despised enemies of the Byzantines. What drew Romanians into the Slavic camp was the replacement of their Latin liturgy with the Old Church Slavonic. Thereafter, it was assumed that they shared the same culture with the Slavs.

It took many centuries for the barbarian invaders with their primitive culture and pagan religion to relate to the Byzantine world of arts and its sophisticated civilization. That happened through different venues mostly via tradesmen. They brought from Constantinople and other imperial cities art objects made of porcelain and refined metals, jewelry, utilitarian objects, and most importantly, silk clothing, intricately and ornately engraved weapons, and illustrated manuscripts.

In many instances Byzantinism was introduced by visiting students and the freed hostages from the ethnic nations. Most of the students were the offspring of wealthy or princely families. They were sent by their parents to Constantinople to be educated or initiated into the secrets of leadership. They came into contact with the great scholars of the empire, learned manners from their tutors, and closely observed the royal pomp and circumstance which seems to have been what impressed them the most. When they got back to their barbarian lands they transplanted their newly acquired knowledge with the force of the sword.

The would-be Czar Simeon I lived for ten years in Constantinople and returned to Hungary in the year 888 as a changed person and his people called him "Half-Greek." He understood the need for a higher culture in Bulgaria and so whole heartedly promoted Byzantinism there. Even though most Bulgars were illiterate he was the patron of the disciples of Cyril and Methodius. Using the Cyrillic alphabet they translated the Bible and many literary works from Greek into Bulgarian.

In an attempt to duplicate the brilliance of Constantinople on a smaller scale Simeon beautified his new capital at Preslav with some twenty churches and a glorious cathedral. He created his own aristocracy and military nobility also modeled on the pomp and circumstance of the Byzantine elite. However, commoners in his land still lived in their steppe society.

Two would be Serbian kings also lived in Constantinople for a period of time. Their influential contacts there launched them to the thrones of their own country. Stefan Nemanja used his year in "prison" in Constantinople (1172-1173) to educate himself by befriending Emperor Manuel. The latter became his mentor.

The second was a young man Stefan Dusan (who would make and enforce a universal system of laws inspired by the Byzantines) and who spent six years in Constantinople (1314-1320) where his father and mother had been exiled. While they were there, both Nemanja and Dusan learned to appreciate the arts and royal life, elements of which both later tried to introduce into their own culture.

Similarly, the would be King Bela III lived in Constantinople prior to 1172 and assimilated so much of life there that he assumed he would succeed Emperor Manuel I on the throne. Instead, he was sent by the emperor back to Hungary, There he became so estranged from his own people (he changed his name to Alexius, became the emperor's brother-in-law, and fought alongside the Byzantine army against his countrymen). Even his mother did not want him as an Orthodox king. It was to be expected that rulers such as these, who had absorbed so much of the Byzantine culture, would enforce cultural and social changes in their realms, including the manners at their courts.

All of these embellishments were overlaid on the pre-literate Balkan culture of the earlier young Middle Age nations. An oral literature was in place which had been inspired by a rich variety of epics about past national heroes, fairytales for adults and children, and jokes and witty stories containing moral lessons. Usually the greatest folk heroes of each nation were mythologized (many of them were glorified) and later sanctified for their memorable military and religious deeds.

The Serbians' Tzar Lazar in 1389 died while heroically fighting the Turks at Kosovo. His knight Miloš Obilić who assassinated Sultan Murad I also produced epic folklore, as well as the Albanian Skandenberg who was undefeated by the Ottomans. Since heroes and idols live beyond their place and time, their stories were versified and became folk songs. Many were sung by minstrels to entertain the royal courts in the west.

In Wallachia it was said that Prince Radu Negru (Black Radu) dismounted his horse and his foot prints remained in stone. To commemorate the establishment of his country he chose his capital to be in Campulung in 1290. Almost two centuries later the orally transmitted legends of Prince Vlad the Impaler, and the stories of the cruel punishments he inflicted on his enemies, crossed the borders of Wallachia and were later immortalized in German, Russian, and Turkish writings.

☩

The most enduring cultural institution of the Balkans was the monastery where monks lived in seclusion from the rest of the world. In the Catholic world, churches were seldom fortified but in the lands of Orthodoxy they were often enclosed by walls built to make a fortified compound around a church. The area surrounding the monastery contained living quarters for monks along with self-sustaining facilities. Overall, the establishment was an oasis of spirituality and a place of refuge when danger arose. The people living outside the compound could rush in for shelter.

To ensure inaccessibility many monasteries were built on top of cliffs and mountain spurs having vertical walls at heights that prohibited the ingress of potential attackers. These were most often equestrian barbarians from the flatlands. The mountainous and rocky landscape of the Balkans, especially Greece abounded with "eagle's nest" monastic establishments that garnered respect in the past, and they continue to dazzle modern visitors. They seem to be located closer to heaven, and their dramatic architecture blends with the environment.

Because monks were well schooled the monastery proved to be the fertile ground for the development of culture. It included a *scriptorium* or room for scribes who prepared calligraphic manuscripts on pergament (parchment - animal skin) and later on paper. They did translating, painted icons, and in the later years handled the printing presses. Such monastic activities caused the arts to spread throughout the Balkans and Eastern Europe.

Byzantine monks were skilled at penmanship and book binding. They artistically decorated the covers with carved silver, gold, and ivory. Before the invention of the printing press they used colorful hand drawings to illustrate texts that depicted the lives of the saints, emphasized the difference between good and evil, and heaven and hell. Gold leaf and gold inlays embellished the intricate floral designs and miniature illustrations. Their artistic endeavors served as examples throughout Eastern Europe.

Laic manuscripts also abounded as emperors wanted to leave written proof of their legacy. Writers close to them such as Niketas Choniatēs and Anna Comnena excelled in documenting the Byzantine history of the twelfth century, and they produced informative works about the cultural and spiritual life of their times. Like many other manuscripts theirs were written in Greek the pre-eminent language in the Byzantine Empire.

Some forty thousand handwritten manuscripts survived primarily because they were stored safely in monasteries. Over time, the Slavic monks especially those who were Bulgars and Serbs proved themselves equal in talent if not more so than the Byzantines. They greatly influenced their northern cousins in the more rustic Russian culture.

☦

The ways in which people feed themselves is also a part of the Balkan culture. The barbarians gobbled their simple and frugal diets mostly based on eating horse meat and drinking the mare's milk. The mounted riders carried chunks of raw meat under their horses' saddles to be marinated by the horse perspiration. Later, this was known as the "Tartar steak," in fact it was ground meat marinated with spices. Basically, the barbarians ate what they could pick from the trees and fields, fishing and hunted, and they grilled the meat on an open fire. The ethnic dishes of the settled barbarians consisted entirely of a different cooking style from the ancient natives of the Balkan Peninsula.

The Byzantines inherited much of their culinary sophistication from the Greeks cuisine knowing that they "invented the cooked food." The Greeks were the most versatile to cook dishes served with *avgolemono* a soup made with chicken, rice and colorful vegetables in a lemon flavored broth. It went well with *moussaka* which consists of layers of eggplant and minced meat all baked in a tomato sauce. A very popular was *souvlaki* with pieces of lamb or mutton seasoned with salt and pepper and skewered along with cut vegetables. All were brushed with olive oil before being broiled.

A popular beverage was *braga* made of fermented grains such as wheat, bran, or rye with added sprout. The result was a thick beige liquid having a sweet and sour taste with very little alcohol content.

Albanians honored special guests with a baked sheep's head. Macedonians loved *tavche-gravche*, a bean casserole enriched with smoked meats and sausages.

The Vlachs, most of them shepherds included all varieties of cheese in their cooking especially *telemea* (the Greek *feta*). They shared yogurt with the Greeks. Most popular was *ciorba*, a chicken (or other chopped meat) soup with almost any chopped vegetables boiled in water and enriched with sauerkraut. They cooked *ghivetch*, which was mixed vegetables gently fried in lard and then left to simmer in a covered pot. Pieces of previously browned meat could be added.

Holidays and special occasions such as wedding celebrations brought a community together around grilled and roasted meat, and pies sweetened with honey. All of them were served on ceramic dishes accompanied by jugs of wine and mead (honey wine). An equally popular beverage still in demand today in the Balkans was *slivovitz* also known as *palinca, raki* or *tzuica*. It was fermented and distilled brandy made of varieties of plums, apricots, peaches and pears. It was considered the drink of the strong men of the Balkans. Also, the strong smelling prune brandy was sometimes distilled two or three times, and it was considered as a medicinal to kill any microbes.

In time the settled barbarians updated their meals with available sources they could scavenge from farms. As nothing could be wasted the Bulgarians made tripe soup. The Serbs specialized in bean soups enriched with smoked ribs. The Slavs ate the basic *kasha* (stew) of boiled triangular seed like whole grains from various cereals, and salted fish and mushrooms. Also, anything else they could find to improve the taste of this filling and easily prepared dish. It went well with *kvass*; a drink brewed from bread crumbs, and was later upgraded to *vodka* made from grain.

Other nationalities had specific dishes often named after them such as *Szekely Gulyas* (Hungarian goulash) which combined whatever greens and herbs the nomads found on the land where they traveled together with horse meat. It was all mixed together and stewed in a cauldron above the campfire. Later, the dish was so much improved that it became an international specialty.

The most versatile and new cuisine was that of the Turkish invaders who introduced *pilaf*. This was a dish that blended the oriental spices and rice and was simmered alongside lamb or beef that was often cut into pieces called kebabs (Muslim laws prohibited the consumption of pork). Their *piyaz* salad was based on cooked buttered beans, and *sasuka* with many vegetables including tomatoes and zucchini cut into cubes and flavored with olive oil, garlic and dill. They are the winning dishes. *Inegol kofee* is grilled meatballs of different shapes, made of mixed ground lamb and beef, onions and breadcrumbs then served on pita.

*Sarmale* was stuffed cabbage with ground meat and spices then boiled or baked with sauerkraut and tomato sauce. The signature serving was (and still is) *kag kebab,* a cylindered chunk of marinated lamb roasted on a horizontal spit and cooked over an open wood fire. Any meal was complimented by a drink called "the wine of the Muslims" coffee, since the Islam religion prohibits consumption of alcohol.

Cooked food was so important even in the Ottoman army they used large cauldrons for each company. If a cauldron would be lost in a battle that unit would be disbanded and erased from the military records.

✟

In all the Balkan cultures when people go to church to celebrate important events or even when attending social meals came dressed in their best "Sunday" clothing. Weapons were left at the door, and the people offered prayers of thanks before and after a meal. There would be a rigorously observed seating order at the table which marked the importance of each person in attendance. Entertainment was as important as the food that was being served. Musicians, acrobats, dancing bears, and magicians would perform, and the guests themselves would sing and dance. In the Balkan Peninsula the most popular dance of all of the nations was and still is the *hora*. It is a rythmic Greek dance done with linked arms and it moves in a counter clockwise circle. It is a dance where each of the above mentioned nations claims to have originated it. In Greek, *hora* means an hour of 60 minutes. The long arm of a clock has to go around once to complete a circle. To say that *hora* means to go in a circle entitled the Greeks to have the copyright as the originators of the *hora* dance.

As time passed the assortment of china dishes, silverware, pots and pans, furniture, table coverings, and table manners also became more refined. However, some things didn't change as the taste of the food. It was expected that guests would get drunk. Often insults were exchanged, and some were so vitriolic that they created family feuds that lasted for generations. All in all, food reflected and continues to reflect the Métis cultures of the Balkans. It is often described as *talmesh-balmesh,* a dish whose ingredients cannot be identified.

There was a certain wisdom in Kievan Prince Vladimir's saying that the best way to change people's thinking was through their stomachs. To be added it was said that what people eat and the way they dress is how they look and what they think.

✞

The Vlachs and the Wallachians were herdsmen and their lonely occupation stimulated them to create a myth about *mitul mioritic* (the universe of shepherds). Basically, it was a ballad about a young shepherd betrayed by his fellow herdsmen who envied his excellent sheep. Facing death he was at peace feeling he was going to a better place. He accepted the tragic destiny with dignity and wisdom that combined the Dacian beliefs in the after life with the example of Jesus.

Nothing could take away from the lonely shepherd's love of his herd and dogs. Since he was unmarried, he trusted they would attend his burial. It would be like his wedding ceremony being witnessed by the forested mountains, the sun, the moon, and the stars. More than a thousand versions of this ballad demonstrate the extent of the Wallachian lands, and the common philosophical folklore of the Vlachs.

✞

As for the culture of Orthodoxy what most clearly defined it was the church architecture. Emperor Justinian I achieved many commendable things in his illustrious reign but perhaps the greatest of them was the construction of the Hagia Sophia (Church of Holy Wisdom) in Constantinople. For one thousand years it remained the largest cathedral in the empire, and in the entire world.

With its magnificent dome and breathtaking colorful mosaics it dazzled visitors then and it continues to do so now. Its immense and elaborate structure inspired the Byzantine style of church building that was imitated by the Albanians, Bulgarians, Macedonians, Romanians, Serbians and other Orthodox groups. Russia drew inspiration from the Byzantine church architecture and then added its own onion domed ornate style to it. Monasteries were built around the same time. They were fortified structures that became cradles for the spread of culture. Numerous manuscripts (among them litopysets /chronicles) were masterfully written, and most colorfully designed by the diligent monks.

Between 1045 and 1050 Vladimir of Novgorod built an astonishing stone cathedral that was thirty eight meters high and had five domes. He named it Saint Sophia. In 1330 Ivan I hired an Italian architect and workers to complete the Assumption Cathedral in Moscow.

King Matthias of Hungary benevolently lent his master builders and artists to Czar Ivan III who also engaged in large scale personal and public constructions. Matthias was so popular that after he visited the Slovakian city of Levoca in 1474 an entire altar was dedicated to him inside St. James Gothic cathedral. In fact, the face of Saint John resembles the features of the king.

In contrast to the Orthodox world where the monks basically lived and died in the same monastery which was built by a rich patron the Benedictine monks canvassed Eastern Europe. In the eleventh century they built their own Brevnov Monastery in Western architectural style near Prague. Prince Trpimir of Croatia also welcomed them, and as a result of their spiritual work more than forty monasteries dotted the Adriatic coast.

These religious structures demonstrated the striking difference between Byzantine and Catholic architecture, something which was also reflected in the arts and cultural life. The Catholic area of the Balkans used the Latin alphabet. In the twelfth century Croatian Archbishop Grgur of Bar wrote *Ljetopis popa Dukljanina* and *The Croatian Chronicle,* a historiography of his nation.

King Bela III of Hungary immersed in Catholicism and western culture and ordered one of his Latin scribes (recorded as *Anonymus*

*Bele Regis Notarius*) to write *Gesta Hungarorum: The Deeds of the Hungarians*. It was written before 1200 and it glorifies the Arpad dynasty and its invasion of Transylvania. Unlike the humble and anonymous artwork done by the Balkan monks in Hungary, the kings like Charles Robert Anjou employed Italian masters to work for them and produce artistic pieces. Furthermore, because the Hungarians were in close contact with central Europe they progressed in the field of arts, architecture, fashion, and many other areas especially during the reign of King Matthias.

His *Biblioteca Corviniana* contained up to five thousand volumes, and it was the second largest library in Europe after the Vatican Library. He spent thirty three thousand gold coins a year to acquire books. His palace contained vast splendors, and the entertainment at his court was known to be sumptuous. King Matthias' taste was ahead of the Renaissance era of reviving the Greek and Roman arts adding the touch of the nudity and sumptuous furnishings.

☩

Music has always been a part of human life and culture as well. It has generally played a role in self expression. It has also been used in entertaining, military drills, religion, courtship, dancing and many other artistic and spiritual endeavors. In the Balkan cultures folk tunes were often combined with lyrics to underline the feelings of happiness, grief, love and celebration. Each nation or ethnicity had a rich tradition of vocal and instrumental music that was orally transmitted. Every generation seemed to polish the musical pieces before passing them down to their children.

Religious music became highly refined in the Catholic Church, and an array of musical instruments among them the organ attracted virtuoso composers, players, and singers. In time these compositions evolved into laic music of great artistry and sophistication.

In contrast to this, in the Orthodox Church most of the music was provided by the chanting of the priest along with his all male altar assistants. It rarely included a choir or allowed for any attendance participation. Ecclesiastical music was regulated by the Byzantine Church with various and unique types of staff notations and instructions. All of these were shared by the subordinate churches throughout Eastern Europe.

The same musical notation had been in use in Western Europe since the 520s. The music of Orthodoxy was subject to such a high level of control that even hired funeral mourners had to follow a particular musical pattern. Most monks learned the church music phonetically. Certainly, none of the folk singers or instrumentalists knew how to read the musical notes of the church. These notes would be practically impossible to be applied to a tzambal, a soundboard dulcimer played with little soft hammers.

To what extent in the Dark Ages was cultural life experienced by the ordinary people, like the serfs who lived in half dug huts with no windows that were lit only by wood stoves? Certainly, there was dancing and singing. Incidentally, Gypsy music did not arrive in the Balkan Peninsula before the Turkish invasion.[14]

✛

People were judged by the kind of clothes they wore, and the dictum "clothes define a person" was applicable in the Balkans and the rest of the world. Civility was important in the Byzantine Empire as was indicated by the elaborate portrayals of clothing in the artwork of the time. One of the early and great influences on Byzantine fashion was the daughter of the leader of the Khazars who took the baptismal name of Irene when she married Emperor Constantine V. With her dowry she brought to Constantinople her beautiful national dress the *tzitzakion*. She proudly wore the garment and it drew admiration and respect in both the royal circle and from ordinary subjects. Seeking to flatter her and win her approval the court ladies copied it. Soon there was a style of court dress for women and ceremonial robes for men. Distinctive court clothing became fashionable for all important leaders and functionaries, and it spread throughout the entirety of the Byzantine Empire and Eastern Europe. This trend lasted for hundreds of years.

Ironically, it was perceived as Greek fashion. Similarly, wearing barbarian trousers was more practical than the Roman toga. Later influenced by the Turkish military uniform the boyars adopted the turban, *shalvars* (balloon-like pants), a wide belt made of silk and colorful shoes with the tip curled upward to which many small jingle bells were added.

One of the most unique traditional costumes was that of the Vlachians/Wallachians who inherited the ancient dress of the Dacians. Very little has changed over the centuries as can be seen in the chiseled figures on Trajan's Column in Rome depicting the war events in the early 100s. Vlach and Wallachian men wore tight white pants made of felt, and white shirts with long large sleeves that were colorfully embroidered. They hung over the trousers which were held up by a wide studded leather belt with many pockets. Leather moccasins, a conic lamb fur hat with the top rolled down, a well-tailored waistcoat, and a sleeveless sheepskin coat carried on the shoulders as a cape, all completed the shepherds' outfit. Men proudly carried long clubs with the handle carved in the shape of the Dacian flying dragon.

Women wore overlapping woolen skirts (in some regions only two aprons, front and back) covering an ankle-length white underskirt with an embroidered hem. The skirt was loomed with colorful motifs, and the blouse/chemise was equally embellished and artfully laced. Also, decorated the same way was the white scarf that generously covered the head, neck, and shoulders. A narrow belt woven with geometric designs, knitted woolen socks, moccasins that were similar to those worn by the men, along with a well tailored hip sized sheepskin completed their wardrobe. A necklace made of large beads or gold coins strung on a gold chain showed the wealth and social status of the woman. Married women always wore scarves.

The Vlachs steadfastly preserved their cultural heritage without trying to impose it on others. They were spread across different countries where their immensely profitable shepherding was highly respected by other ethnicities. Versions of their costumes (described above) were adopted by migratory people, who came wearing furs and could not possibly have come from Eurasia wearing this same attire. A simple look at the Bulgarian, Hungarian, and Serbian national folklore costumes are a version of the millennial Vlachian traditional dress. It is easy to see that the barbarian invaders copied the Vlachian style once they settled in the Balkan Peninsula.

✟

Combining the beautiful designs of the Roman jewelry with the intricacies of the Middle Eastern craftsmanship of their jewelry, the Byzantine style added the colorful precious gemstones and long drop earrings, usually ending in a pearl. It was common for every Byzantine to wear a gold ring of a different weight and design. In addition, they wore chains, necklaces, brooches and tiaras of heavy gold embellished with colorful expensive stones. The richer society became the more sophisticated and bold jewelry became fashionable and was used to show the social status of a person. Their long expensive gowns were sown with gem quality beads, and were often decorated with gold medallions the larger, the better. Almost all of them were the same style and imitated the roman togas. They covered the body from the neck to the toes. Men and women differed mainly because of their size and colors.

A mosaic picture of Emperor Justinian I reveals many of the mentioned jewels, including his exquisite tiara of rows of colorful gemstones and a round clasp featuring an oversized red ruby encircled by 10 large white pearls, along with three extra large drop pearls (see first round picture on the right on the front cover.)

Not to be outdone Vlad the Impeller's portrait (see first round pictures on the left on the front cover) was painted wearing a conical red velvet hat with a headband consisting of nine rows of white pearls.

In the front center of the band there is an eight sided gold star with a large rectangular ruby surrounded by 8 smaller pearls in the middle of it, and above there is a gold shape containing 5 giant sized pearls and a white tuft. All of these expensive adornments such as the colorful gems and pearls were abundantly supplied from India and China, and then transported to Constantinople on the silk and spice routes from Asia.

✠

Speaking and dressing like a Greek aristocrat was a hallmark of the Balkan nobility. The boyar was the local knight but unlike the western knight who had to excel in hunting, appreciate epic poems, and be able to decapitate a victim with a single blow of the sword, the indolent boyar paid someone else to do these things in his name. He was less interested in charming women with his wit and musical skill, or in dominating men with an iron fist. He preferred to patiently wait to take over a throne or inherit a manor from a deceased parent.

Unlike his western counterpart, the Balkan knight scarcely touched any shining armor with the exception of his straight sword. It was to be handled with both hands. He preferred to wear heavily ornate Byzantine robes sewn with gold and silver threads, and headgear that reached preposterous shapes and sizes. Eventually, and ironically the cross that was traditionally sewn onto his robes was adopted by many armies to look knightly.

✠

Middle Ages were the age of chivalry in the western world. Western knights traveled widely and when they reached their destination, they relaxed and partied accordingly to well establish etiquette that was likely held in the castle of another knight. One of the most prized forms of entertainment was to display their military skills to their potential allies during friendly games of expertise and valor. All of their displays of bravery were dedicated to conquer the hearts of the ladies in the audience.

In Eastern Europe knightly activities took on a different cast. The Balkan knight was basically sedentary. His fighting skill was measured by how adept he was at elaborate games of intrigue, since the acts of backstabbing and deception were applauded. Arrogant and drunk with power he made certain that every event was pre-arranged and every goal achieved with a minimum of risk to himself.

His main partner and protector was the Church, and this gave him the right to dominate others. He was the tyrant of his manor flogging and even arbitrarily killing his subjects. Needless to say his chameleon like behavior greatly influenced the moral values of his serfs.

Guilt and repentance was a cultural asset and it was preached by the Orthodox Church at Mass to people on their knees with their foreheads piously touching the cold stone floor. Outside of the church the people blamed each other for any problem. They bickered and falsely accused one another, and had an unquenchable thirst for vengeance for a real, or a perceived reason.

One sign of intelligence was to posses more by doing less, and to steal without being caught. It was inconceivable to ask for a favor from someone without offering a bribe. It was common to hate anyone who did better than oneself, and then to scheme to destroy him. Biting the hand that fed one was considered the right way to avenge economic injustices. To be cruel was to show courage, and assassination was the best way to eliminate an enemy.

Certainly, revenge was a sign of honor. Someone who had a chip on his shoulder was viewed as just excessively proud and superior. At the same time, people perfected the role of the victim, and learned how to cleverly ask for pity. Invoking God's mercy was the best hope to avoid any harm.

Everyone bent over for someone including the emperor, even though he bowed only to an icon. Everyone knew all too well that a bowed head made it possible to avoid the blow of the sword. Nevertheless, the king or emperor's scepter and crown represented the supreme power bestowed on him by God himself, and it was a power that was not to be challenged.

Reasoning was an act of convenience. Correctness and discipline were broadly negotiable since the Balkan people changed their definitions according to what was beneficial to them. To dodge authority was the way to ensure survival. The mob went with the master who promised the most regardless of the number of lies involved.

Broken trust and misplaced faith were so common that Balkanians accepted that as part of life. They also believed that "God gave it you, and God will take it away from you."

Since they were traditionally servile to any foreign power the people rejected any change since it caused an adjustment that required an effort to adapt. What they had achieved was in their view good enough, also this was to justify their false modesty.

Their rulers surrounded themselves with foreign mercenaries and acted preemptively to weed out any potential enemies by mercilessly killing them. This included their brothers, fathers, siblings and friends. No mercy was ever shown to a defeated enemy. Somehow all these hallmarks of the Balkan characteristics came to be overlooked when they were all rolled together with a blind love for their motherland and the Church.

All these inherited attributes created mythical heroes with inflated legends that found their place in the history books of each nation. No doubt people wanted to look up to someone besides God. If there was no such ideal person to command respect, a legend and a hero had to be invented and cherished. Later, a big heroic statue would be dedicated to him. These acts brought a much needed sense of national pride for their identity and stability in an otherwise unstable world around them. The legend proved to be greater than reality every time.

☨

To summarize, spirituality dealt with the meaning of human life. Since it led the individual to think beyond the limits of the material world it involved the search for the ultimate divinity. Religion interpreted those beliefs and Christianity used the prophetic teachings and mysterious miracles of Jesus to install faith in the frightened but obedient believers. The Orthodox Church did more than that. It converted multitudes of barbarians by trying to change their primitive minds and savage instincts to be polite and dutiful. However, to mold them into orderly societies was to culturally change them into a harmonious force of acting civilized to each other, and to enjoy a peaceful, and beautiful life style.

This process of assimilation came at a heavy price. Even though the Greeks were initially culturally more advanced than the rest of Western Europe, barbarian invaders kept intruding into the old Balkan societies. By sowing the seeds of certain bad social habits, they soon dragged the Orthodox Byzantines down to a level below that of the English, French, Germans, and Italians who also happened to be Catholics.

While the Catholics were building universities and rapidly advancing toward the Renaissance and while evolving a superior culture of many arts. At the same time the Orthodox believers went to visit their sacred Mount Athos, along with a collection of churches and monasteries. They believed this was enough to inspire their highest spiritual and cultural needs. The Orthodox Church was more concerned with ensuring the stability of its nations than it was with encouraging cultural and scientific progress.

No change as to how to live was a good thing. It was the way God wanted it, and people should be thankful and happy with what they had, because looking for something better would lead to sin. In brief, a good life was to be thankful for what one has. Oblivious to the passage of time and to new discoveries the Orthodoxy remained dogmatically rigid and no religious anarchists or heretics dared to try to change it.

Many religious changes took place in the West yet nothing happened in Eastern Europe, especially in the Balkan Peninsula which stagnated at a fourteenth century level of arts, science and ethnical culture. Its strict religion that was endorsed by tyrannical rulers who claimed to be "crowned by God," made sure they enjoyed unchallenged control over their "boot licking nations."

After the fall of the Byzantine Empire the Turks took pains to ensure that change did not happen, and they also added their Islamic oppression. Therefore, they continued fertilizing the roots of a cultural bazaar. The combination of the two religions and cultures was enough to increase the phenomenon of Balkanization.

# REFERENCE NOTES

1. Thomas S. Noonan and K. Kovalev Roman, "Prayer, Illumination, and Good Times," in *The Expansion of Orthodox Europe: Byzantium, the Balkans and Russia*, ed. Jonathan Shepard (Burlington, VT: Ashgate, 2007), 175.
2. It is likely that Serbian folklore concerning "Czar Trojan" refers to Emperor Trajan, whom the later migrant Serbians could not possibly have known; they borrowed the legends from the Vlachs of Moesia who like the southern Dacians, lived under Roman occupation during his reign.
3. John V.A. Fine, *The Late Medieval Balkans: A Critical Study from the Late Twelfth Century to the Ottoman Conquest* (Ann Arbor: University of Michigan Press, 1994), 39. Francis Dvornik, *Byzantine Missions Among the Slavs: SS. Constantine-Cyril and Methodius* (New Brunswick, NJ: Rutgers University Press, 1970), 49-50.
4. Peter Arnott, *The Byzantines and Their World* (New York: St. Martin's Press, 1973), 246.
5. William of Tyre, *Historia Transmarina* 20.4; see also Roger of Howden, *Chronicle*, Madrid: MS Esc. Gr. 265 [Y.II.10]: 1180, fols. 368-372, as described in G. de Andrés, *Catálogo de los códices griegos de la Real Biblioteca de El Escorial* Vol. 2 (Madrid, 1965).
6. As noted, Latin was the official language of the Croatians although the Cyrillic alphabet was used in the church until the nineteenth century. Even today the Glagolitic liturgy is still performed in some churches in Croatia. Romanians used Old Church Slavonic in official documents until the end of the sixteenth century; for liturgical purposes, and they continued to use it still longer even though it was understood only by a handful of elite.
7. The cultural and spiritual legacy of the two saintly brothers is

reflected in modern institutions, such as Cyril and Methodius National Library of Sofia, St. Cyril and St. Methodius University of Veliko Turnovo (Bulgaria), Sts. Cyril and Methodius University of Skopje (Macedonia), University of SS Cyril and Methodius, Trnava (Slovakia), and Ss. Cyril and Methodius Cathedral in Prague (Czech Republic). Numerous churches and monasteries throughout Eastern Europe bear their names.

8. A map of Europe (approximately 6 x10 feet), drawn in 1154 by an Arabian geographer hired by the Norman King Roger II, did not show most of the newly formed Balkan countries. However, he identified the locations of many cities of Garuasia (Croatia) which he had visited. More than one hundred years later, *The Travels of Marco Polo* (*Il Milione*) described the adventurous trip of this tradesman of Dalmatian origin to the Far Orient between the years 1271 and 1298.

9. Warren Treadgold, *A History of the Byzantine State and Society* (Stanford, CA.: Stanford University Press, 1997), 967n3.

10. Large communities of Daco-Moesian Vlachs spoke a Latin dialect that is still spoken today by Aromanians in Albania, Istro-Romanians in Croatia, Kutsovlachs in Macedonia, and Tsintsars living in Bulgaria and Serbia, as well as in areas of Czechia, Slovakia, Hungary and the Ukraine. This proves how extensive the Dacian lands were in Eastern Europe before, during, and after the Roman Empire.

11. Niketas Choniatēs, *O City of Byzantium: Annals of Niketas Choniatēs*, trans. Harry J. Magoulias (Detroit: Wayne State University Press, 1984), 257.

12. Based on some tendentious linguistic arguments (as presented in Stephen Sisa's *The Spirit of Hungary*, Washington, DC: Dumbarton Oaks Library and Collection, 1984, 187), it has been said that there is little in common between the lexicon of the Romanians and the Vlachs of the Balkans. The Romanian language consists of more than 75 percent Latin words, and the

rest is heavily imbued with words of Slavic origin. But according to the "findings," the Vlachs south of the Danube River adopted more than 50 percent of their language from the Greeks; and only some 20 percent of it is rooted in the Romanian language. If that is the case, it surely demonstrates how little the Vlachs interacted with the Bulgarians or Serbs, even though they shared the same land. It should be noted that a different linguistic paradigm was in place a thousand years ago when Daco-Roman Vlachs from the north and south of the Danube spoke the same language. What is certain is that today a Romanian can read an Italian newspaper, as can a Macedo-Romanian, an Istro-Romanian (called Ciribiri) these people speak an old Vlaski language, which is still another Romanian dialect. Despite opinions to the contrary, Romanian grammar is closer to Latin than Italian even though the two nations are hundreds of miles apart. In addition to the twenty million people inside Romania who speak Romanian, another five million outside of its borders also speak that language, or dialects of it. The contention that Romanian (even the Dacian) language comes from the Albanian language is absurd since the latter is not related to any other language in the world. If there are some one hundred words shared by both languages it is because the Vlachs introduced them in parts of Albania where they lived for centuries.

13. One of these was a document written by Nestor in 1113 that referred to the Vlachs, whom he called "Volochi," and their efforts at fighting back the Hungarians.
14. In modern times the Gypsy presence and their music is a common denominator in all Eastern European countries.

# VIII

## IN THE NAME OF GOD

Constantine the Great (r. 306-337) imposed the dogma of a single church in the Roman Empire and declared Sunday to be the official day of rest for Christians, unlike Saturday for the Jews. He used the Council of Nicea in 325 to protect Christianity against schisms and disputes over the authenticity of the gospels and manuscripts about the time and teachings of Jesus, including the Gnostic texts and other controversial documents of the earlier church. Some of these texts have been either destroyed or discarded.

Christianity claimed to be a monotheistic religion, but God had a son who was in the company of saints who possessed different kinds of protective powers. This was a new spiritual pantheon that was not too different from that of Greek and Roman mythology. With the Creed of Nicea, Christianity was set on a solid foundation as far as its beliefs, canons, and decrees were concerned. It fixed the church calendar and its celebrations and feast days, and thus united the Church under a single doctrine.

At the close of the year 500, when the Roman Empire split into the East and West with capitals in Rome and Constantinople, Christianity also became divided into the Orthodox and the Catholic churches. Orthodoxy was led by a Byzantine emperor who was taken to be God's entrusted representative on earth, and whose throne was thought to be divinely protected. The Catholic Church was headed by a pope in Rome, and was considered to be the Vicar of Christ. There was an important difference between the governance of the two institutions: the emperor could name the bishops who were in full charge of their church, while the pope considered the bishops to be his lieutenants and granted them no autonomy.

The two churches differed on many doctrinal and practical matters from the interpretation of the Lord's Prayer, faith, the role of icons, baptism, confession, holy matrimony and priestly ordinations. Each was in charge of the spiritual life of many nations and was the foundational institution of a large state. Most of all it offered divine blessings to Christian warriors.

When the barbarian invasions from Eurasia brought in millions of pagans who settled in the Balkan Peninsula, the Catholic and Orthodox churches aggressively competed with each other over the vast numbers of potential converts. Consequently, both the papacy and patriarchy began a race to convert the barbarians, crown their kings, and vest their bishops, so as to attract them into either the Western or Eastern Church denominations. This race reached its peak during the ninth century after most of the barbarian invaders had moved south of the Danube River and settled in the Balkan Peninsula. There, inside the Byzantine Empire they continued to carry out their predatory incursions.

While the migratory exodus was from east to west, the religious movement extended in the opposite direction. In the eastern lands, there was chaos at all levels while in the west people lived in more orderly societies. It was at this time that Charlemagne became Emperor of the Holy Roman Empire. Its borders constituted a clear line of demarcation between Eastern and Western Europe.

Catholicism had an active interest in expanding eastward and so helped Prince Mojmir to create Greater Moravia in 833. There fourteen warlords were baptized and pledged their unconditional allegiance to the new religion, one that covered the areas of what now is Austria, the Czech Republic, Slovakia, Hungary and Poland.

The huge Slavic military power was thereby defused and unable to unleash its force against the Catholic world. This new state provided Central Europe with a military buffer against the barbarian perils of the Avars and Bulgars, who together with the eastern Slavs raided deep into the Balkan Peninsula and repeatedly laid siege to Adrianople, Constantinople, Thessaloniki and other wealthy Byzantine cities.

Eventually, the Byzantine Emperor Michael III established an Orthodox presence in the eastern lands through the missionaries he sent to the barbarians. He was thereby able to repel any lingering German influence. However, his most important religious conquest was the Bulgars who were courted by both the German and the Latin powers. When Boris I became czar of the Bulgars in 852 he masterfully played the religious card against the Byzantines, the Germans, and the Moravians. He did not have a preference for either Catholicism or Orthodoxy, but was keen to choose the one that would give him more land and greater religious independence.

A surprisingly powerful attack by the Croatians, and an intensified threat from the Byzantines in 855 prompted Boris to choose Orthodoxy. He wanted his own church and so he approached Pope Nicholas I. His actions initiated a crisis that led to the schism between the Eastern and Western churches.

Aware that Bulgarian Catholicism might advance into the main Byzantine lands Constantinople agreed to the autocephalous status of the Church of Bulgaria in 870. If Boris had joined the Franks instead of the Byzantines Catholicism would have spread throughout the Balkans and most likely different languages would be spoken in the peninsula today. For the time being the Bulgars represented a defense between the East and the West.

Khan Simeon also challenged Constantinople when in 926 he received a crown and a scepter from Pope John X making him the official Catholic emperor of the Orthodox Bulgars. He was the head of the Church and recognized papal primacy, but he was also determined to prove his independence from Rome. He made his point by invading Thracia and defeating the Byzantines four times. Later, his son Peter I re-established ties with Constantinople by marrying the daughter of Romanus I (r. 920-944) who recognized both his royal title and the Bulgarian Patriarchate. With this shift the pope and Catholicism were no longer needed in Bulgaria.

However, Croatia accepted Frankish suzerainty and therefore aligned itself with Istria and Venetia. It is noteworthy that in this period arbitrary claims of Catholicism and Orthodoxy were made over lands and nations. Their missionaries which were (usually attached to diplomatic missions) had to do the real conversion and plant the definitive flag of either Constantinople or Rome. In short, the main dilemma that a barbarian ruler faced was to choose between obeying an emperor from Constantinople, or a pope from Rome.

To the dismay of the Orthodox Church which was dominated by Greeks, two monk brothers Constantine and Methodius from Thessaloniki engaged in a mission to provide the Slavic speaking people with an alphabet that would give them a written language. This led to the elimination of liturgical Greek in the Slavic churches, and it was a major blow for the prelates of Constantinople. The brothers continued their missionary work north of the Danube River when in 861 they failed to compete against Judaism and Islam in converting the Khazars to Orthodoxy. Constantine and his brother would be remembered for building the first bridge of understanding between Catholicism and Orthodoxy. Thus, ironically the two brothers from a distinguished Greek family became Apostles to the Slavs whom they drew away from the West by developing a new alphabet for the Slavic people.

A serious problem came from inside the Orthodox Church when in 726 Leo III prohibited the veneration of icons (even a crucifix). Pope Gregory II was appalled and condemned the sacrilegious emperor.

Meanwhile, one year later Leo III decided to attack Italy and unite the two religions under his dominion. Unfortunately, his fleet was destroyed by a storm, and this natural disaster was perceived as a bad omen, or as an act of God to protect the pope.

In 732 a Muslim army of seventy thousand advanced toward the heart of Europe and occupied Bordeaux where they butchered its residents and burned their churches. The invaders continued on their path of destruction through the Frankish lands until they faced Charles who led Frankish troops between Tours and Poitiers. After a week of skirmishes, the Turks were defeated on the first day of Ramadan, another bad omen for them. Not properly dressed for the cold weather they simply left the battlefield and never returned to their camp or attempted a similar campaign.

For his important victory, Charles the Frankish leader took the name Martel (the "Hammer) and is considered by many to be the knight who saved Christianity. One of his successors was Charlemagne (r. 768-814) his grandson who was crowned Holy Roman Emperor in Rome for his efforts to achieve Pax Romana in Europe. Like the other Charles, he extended his territory with a cross in one hand and a sword in the other, as he advanced into Slovenia and along the Dalmatian coast.

Empress Irene (r. 797-802) foresaw a Catholic intrusion into her Byzantine Empire especially after Croatia sought protection from Charlemagne. She restored image worship and prevented a war initiated by the Byzantines against the West when most of the Slav territories that had been incorporated into the Carolingian Empire were returned to Constantinople. These territories remained Catholic but Orthodoxy was stronger than ever in the Byzantine Empire.

Bulgars and the Serbs were initially inclined to choose between the Catholic and Orthodox Church. In 1077 Duke Mihajlo Vojislav established the Kingdom of Zeta (Montenegro) and received a crown from the pope becoming a vassal of Rome. Now that he was a king he declared that his land was no longer part of the Byzantine Empire.

The Serbs were set to become Catholic when Prince Miroslav (who was responsible for the *Miroslav Gospels*) was excommunicated in 1181 by the pope because he had murdered a bishop. The prince joined his brother Stefan Nemanja who had been baptized Catholic but remained in the Orthodox camp due to his friendship with Emperor Manuel I.

This did not stop Nemanja from entering into an alliance with the Venetian Republic which encouraged the Slavs on the Adriatic coast to attack the Byzantine Empire. Nemanja had a change of heart when he realized that by accepting Catholic domination he would lose exactly what he wanted in the first place his independence. So he began a campaign to eliminate every trace of Latinity from his realm including any Catholic influence on his Serbs.

The ambitious Nemanja aimed to replace the Byzantine Empire with his own. He once again looked to Rome asking the pope to put together a coalition of western kings to help him build an Orthodox Greco-Serbian Empire in the Balkans. This grand idea was perceived by his Orthodoxy leaders as an act of submission to the Catholic Church. His son succeeded him in 1217 after having been given the title of king by Pope Honorius III.

Two years later Stefan II also received a crown sent by the patriarch of Nicea, and became the first true king of Serbia (r. 1198-1228). His trust in Orthodoxy was thereby fully restored. This served as a final confirmation of the fact that the Balkans would never be incorporated into Catholicism. However, this did not stop the Bulgars and Serbs from acting on their bellicose intentions to occupy and plunder Constantinople which was well renowned for its wealth and glamorous life.

Meanwhile, to the northeast above the Sea of Azov neither Catholicism nor Orthodoxy could prevent the powerful Khazars who controlled the vast steppes of today's Ukraine from converting to Judaism as early as the eighth century. Most likely this was done despite the Byzantine Empire's encroachment from one side, and an Islamic incursion from the other.

Theirs was a spiritual decision intended to preserve the Khazars' ethnic neutrality and independence. When the Pechenegs invaded their empire many Khazars who were related to the Magyars were forced to migrate to the Pannonian fields, and still more of them followed after the Kievans confiscated their lands. Suddenly, Judaism was present in the middle of Europe.

The majority of Hungarians converted to Catholicism in 1000 under King Stephen/Istvan who had received his crown from Rome.[1] Hungarian kings tried hard to satisfy the Catholic Church, except for King Ladislaus/Laszlo IV (r. 1272-1290) who

> led a merry life with his Cuman companions and left the cares of the government to others. During this period the royal court was more pagan than Christian. Thus, the Catholic Church in Bosnia was left without its natural defender. It was with the purpose of stimulating the king to a resumption of a pro-Catholic policy that the pope sent a legate to Ladislav's court (1279). The king promised to exterminate the heresy and actually gave orders for a renewal of the persecution of the non Catholics, but as a matter of fact nothing was done.[2]

Ladislav whose Cumanian roots were in Transylvania preferred to align himself with the East. The pope reacted by ordering a crusade against the heretical king forcing him to pretend he was loyal to the West.

The Hungarian crown passed from King Wenceslaus III in Buda to his father the king of Bohemia in Prague, then to Otto the Duke of Lower Bavaria (who abdicated the throne). Finally, in 1301 to Charles Robert of Anjou who at the age of thirteen came from Naples to rule the Hungarians. This shows how close the Catholic connection was between Hungary and the western nations. After the end of the

Arpad dynasty the Hungarians were essentially ruled by foreign kings and monarchs who never admitted to being part of the Balkans or of Eastern Europe.

Yet, the nation was treated by the West like a poor relative with an embarrassing past. This fact became evident when the Golden Horde invaded Hungary and King Bela IV ran for his life, and asked in vain for help from his powerful Catholic neighbors. They had promised to protect his people but never actually did so.

In spite of their multiple and deadly raids on the West including the destruction of the Moravian empire the Hungarians were forcibly integrated into the culture and spirituality of the West. They continued to expand outward toward the Balkans as they swallowed up Croatia, Dalmatia and Slavonia. Also, they considered themselves westernized and not part of the Byzantine Empire, nor did they belong to the family of the Balkan nations. The reality was a little different since the Hungarians did not fit into the Holy Roman Empire as a German or Latin nation, regardless which of God's religious denominations they choose.

The saga of Stephen III who remained a devoted Catholic asked for help from Frederick I who sent German troops to help him occupy the Hungarian throne. However, Emperor Manuel proved more successful in grooming the future King Bela III (the brother of Stephen III). He was educated in Constantinople then changed his name to Alexius and became brother-in-law to the emperor. In 1166 they co-presided over the synod of the Byzantine Church all of which were viewed as unpardonable deeds by the Hungarians. Consequently, Bela could not occupy the throne of his deceased brother and was forced to submit himself to the Catholic patronage (Pope Alexander III). He was crowned in 1173. The shrewd King Bela played it safe with Orthodox power and in 1185 he married his daughter to the Emperor Isaac II.

During this twenty-year long religious royal event, there was a spectacular revival of Orthodoxy, and Manuel almost forced the pope to crown him the sole emperor of the East and the West. For obvious religious and political reasons this did not happen. Subsequently, no reconciliation was possible between the two major Churches of Europe. However, they negotiated in sharing the Christian territories located between Eastern and Western Europe.

✝

The Catholic Church relentlessly disputed the rites and administration of Orthodoxy. The turning point came on Saturday July 16, 1054 when papal representatives disrupted the liturgy in the Hagia Sophia and placed a bull of excommunication on its altar. This marked the beginning of the Great Schism. It was based on the refusal on the part of Orthodoxy to accept the doctrine of *filioque* (in Latin, "and from the Son") that proclaimed Jesus to be equal with God his father. Many rituals were contested as well i.e., Orthodox believers held the thumb, index, and middle finger together to represent the Trinity when they crossed their hearts, while Catholics used an open palm. The Orthodox served pasca at communion while the Catholics used bread and each had its own way of performing baptisms and other rites. The irrevocable split between the two Christian churches had colossal geopolitical effects on both of them.

Their differences caused the Byzantines to fear western invaders and their Catholicism. Anna Comnena named them *Kelts* and this included the Franks, Latins, and crusaders "brazen-faced, violent men, money-grabbers and where their personal desires are concerned quite immoderate."[3] When their counts came to see Emperor Alexius I they proved to know little about royal etiquette. They showed lack of respect for him talked endlessly and behaved rudely.

Things were different in Bohemia where with the blessing of the Catholic Church, Charles IV (r.1346-1378) built the new city of Prague with its turreted stone bridge and statues over the Vltava River, as well as the University of Prague, Cathedral of St. Vitus, and the fortified Castle of Karlstejan. These magnificent architectural structures made it an imperial city, and the cultural center of Central and Eastern Europe. King Charles raised the Bohemian state to an unsurpassed level of power and led its people into an unprecedented golden age for which he was named *Pater Patriae*/Father of the Country.

Like the Czechs, Croats, and Hungarians, the Poles adopted Catholic rites not because of their religious beliefs but in order to enter into convenient alliances with the western nations. Mieszko I a Slavic King understood the liturgy of Cyril and Methodius but accepted Catholicism in order to protect his nation and keep it prosperous. Becoming a Catholic almost guaranteed better security and a richer life.

In contrast, in the ever troubled land of Orthodoxy terror could strike at any time and in any place, and there was no way to prevent or control it because of the barbarian invasions. When King Casimir III the Great died in 1370 and his throne was occupied by his nephew Hungarian Louis of Anjou the religious fate of the Poles was sealed. They would forever be associated with European Catholicism.

In spite of their repeated attacks on Constantinople the Russians were the only Slavs who never entertained the idea of switching from Orthodoxy to Catholicism. Nevertheless, after Constantinople fell the capital of Orthodoxy was transferred to Kiev and Moscow was its new bastion of Orthodoxy. Czar Ivan III (r. 1462-1505) used it to take over the entirety of the Russian lands, and due to his influential wife Sophia Paleologue created a Byzantine-like court in order to enforce his tyrannical rule.

Pope Paul II's hopes of including Russia in the Holy See quickly evaporated when Ivan eliminated his brothers and behaved like an emperor. He was one who certainly did not want to share his power with any pope. To make his commitments perfectly clear he adopted the double-headed eagle emblem of the Byzantine Empire. He basically used the Orthodox Church to enslave the Russians and prevent them from getting beyond the Dark Ages.[4]

The Russians bitterly and successfully fought the Teutonic knights and later the Swedes and thus eliminated any Catholic interference in their lands. On the other hand they had a way of re-inventing things so as to make them fit with what they wanted to believe. They created their own version of Orthodoxy and Kiev was proclaimed the New Jerusalem, Moscow and the Third Rome. The Russians affectionately called the city "Holy Mother Moscow."

☩

Eastern and Western European knights met very rarely and only because certain alliances brought them together. This happened during the crusades against the Ottoman armies when they shared a series of battles that lasted for a while. Many eastern rulers tried to make the best of both worlds and among them was Vlad II. In 1431 he participated in the Nuremberg tournament where the Wallachian prince was declared the winner. The prizes were an imperial ring presented by Emperor Sigismund, a Toledo sword from the knights, and a gold buckle from an admiring lady in the audience.

Most importantly, the victory brought him induction into the Order of the Dragon which was certified by a gold collar with a dragon insignia engraved on it. As a member of the elite *Drachenorder* whose membership consisted of only a few European nobles he came to be named Dracul by his countrymen. They also named his son Dracula. Dracul converted to Catholicism in Nuremberg and his son was baptized Catholic. Both invited Franciscan missionaries to come to their land since they wanted to bring Catholicism to Wallachia.

Dracul and Dracula were dedicated to the fight against the Ottomans and wished to have the pope on their side, but they could not overcome the now well-established Orthodoxy in Wallachia. A struggle followed, and both met violent deaths at the hands of their own people. A note of interest, the historic images of Mircea the Elder, his son Vlad II, and his grandson Vlad the Impaler all show them dressed in knightly regalia, and not in heavy Byzantine robes.

They were dressed in the western fashion, a fact that demonstrates their western orientation.

In 1211 on the western side of the Carpathians the Teutonic Order came to Transylvania. There they founded the city of Brasov and a cluster of fortresses. A year later they established Bran Castle (later known as Dracula's Castle). While they were there they protected Hungary against the invading Cumans. The Hungarians resented the fact that this powerful order pledged their loyalty to the pope instead of the Hungarian king. Since they were concerned that the Teutons would take over the rich Daco-Roman lands the Hungarians expelled them in 1225. If they had stayed longer they probably would have built the city of Malborg and the largest brick castle in the world Marienburg (Castle of Mary) in Transylvania instead of in Poland.

The Magyar, Saxon, and Szekely colonists brought a different culture to Wallachia even though they introduced the architecture of the Catholic Church and changed the Transylvanian landscape. In the meantime, the Romanians of Transylvania had no political representatives in their own land, and their church was not included in the ruling of it. Elsewhere, throughout most of Eastern Europe the Orthodox Church remained unchallenged until Islam entered the Balkans, and duplicated the bitter experience of occupation by the Turks, in the Biblical land of Palestine.

✠

The hostilities and the bad blood in Jerusalem also called the City of Peace began in 614 when the Persians conquered it. They were aided by some twenty six thousand Jewish residents to whom the city was handed over to by the occupiers. According to a monk named Theophanes (who chronicled this event two hundred years later) ninety thousand Christians perished. The Holy Sepulcher was set afire, Christian shrines were desecrated, and the True Cross, the Holy Lance that pierced Jesus on the cross, the sponge that wiped his blood and other relics were stolen.

When the Byzantines later conquered the city in 629 they took the anticipated revenge on its Jewish and Arab inhabitants. Emperor Heraclius (r. 610–641) became famous for recovering from the defeated Persians the *True Cross* on which Jesus was crucified. After he conquered Jerusalem while parading the Holy Cross he massacred the Jewish population including the Jews from Galilee to avenge the crucifixion of the son of God.

He restored the True Cross to the Church of the Holy Sepulcher, and was subsequently glorified as God's champion and the first holy Crusader.

The Muslims occupied the city in 638 as they returned blood for blood and laid claim to the city from whence Mohammed had journeyed to heaven. By this time all three Abrahamic religions were represented in the city. A series of spectacular conquests in 1071 by the Seljuk Turks gave them control of Palestine, and the most sacred shrine of Christianity the city of Jerusalem. They closed all the Christian sites, stopped pilgrims from visiting their holy shrines, and robbed or murdered anyone who subsequently attempted the journey. The Muslims just eliminated God and his son Jesus from Jerusalem and the Holy Land.

What happened in Palestine with the Christian holy sites was an unimaginable humiliation for Europeans. From their perspective Jerusalem had fallen on evil times. In November 1095 Pope Urban II addressed a huge crowd in Clermont, France with the message, "Christ Himself will be your leader," as he held a large cross above the delirious audience. He assembled the First Crusade of the Western knights to liberate the Holy Land of Palestine.

To motivate them the pope decreed that anyone who went and fought in the Holy Land would have their sins forgiven. The first crusaders (the name derives from the Portuguese *cruzado*/cross), or "God's soldiers of the Cross," proved their faith when in 1097 they crushed the Turks and conquered Nicea. The following year they occupied Antioch. They were exhausted, militarily fragmented, and ready to quit their mission when they were revived by a miracle.

Legend has it that the apostle Andrew appeared in a dream to a crusader who was otherwise a drunken and immoral individual. As a result of his vision he pressed Count Raymond to excavate the area under the patio of St. Peter's Church saying that there he would find the holy lance that had pierced Jesus on the cross. Indeed, after much digging a rusty spear was found. Convinced that faith and fate were on their side the exhausted and dispirited troops arose ready to battle and defeat the Turks, which happened shortly thereafter. In 1099 the crusaders reclaimed Jerusalem as an act of God.

The city's frightened Muslims rushed to find shelter. This was viewed by the crusaders as the ultimate insult. They were vengeful in victory and believed it was time to teach the pagans a religious lesson. The knights indulged in indiscriminate butchery of the Muslims as they sought refuge in the Dome of the Rock Mosque. Ten thousand Muslims were massacred and the heaps of corpses and streams of blood resulting from the atrocities were intended to please the Christian God. Many Jewish men (who like Muslims were circumcised) were killed as well.

Contrary to their hope of having Palestine returned to them or at least being allowed to pray in their sanctuaries the Jews were treated as Christ-killers. At this time the Christians celebrated their freedom and flaunted their position of dominance in the Jerusalem. The knights pretended to discover the relics of the True Cross which they carried into the next victorious Battle of Ascalon. They then founded the Latin Kingdom of Jerusalem (1099-1291). A Latin patriarch replaced the Greek orthodox one thus making it perfectly clear that Catholicism and not Orthodoxy was in charge of religious matters in the Holy Land.

The news of the victory reached Europe and unleashed a wave of such jubilation that Pope Urban died of what seemed to be extreme happiness. This religious enthusiasm led to a parallel military campaign in which some seventy thousand westerners lured by the riches of

Palestine, put themselves under the command of Peter the Hermit and Walter the Penniless. This so called Pauper's Crusade took place in 1096. This poor and unruly mob crossed Hungary and Bulgaria leaving in its wake a wide path of destruction, rape, and pillage. They headed to Constantinople where they killed Greeks, mistaking them for Turks. Emperor Alexius I conveniently ferried them across to Anatolia. There the Seljuk Turks competed in massacring the ragged "crusaders" whose misplaced faith had motivated these incidents tolerated by the Christian god.

At this historic juncture events had taken a pathetic turn for the Christians and a Second Crusade (1147-1149) was carried out by a combination of French and German warriors. They were defeated by the Seljuk Turks and the group's survivors ended up in Jerusalem from whence they unsuccessfully attacked Damascus. Their defeat allowed the Muslims under Saladin to attack and re-take the city which surrendered in 1187. The Third Crusade began in 1189. It aimed to expel the Turks from Jerusalem and the Holy Land, but its leader the Holy Roman Emperor Frederick I Barbarossa ingloriously drowned in a river in Anatolia.

The campaign concluded with a compromise and the knights allowed the Muslims to occupy Jerusalem in exchange for free passage for pilgrims who wished to visit Christian shrines. The only winner of this crusade was the Serbian ruler Stefan Nemanja. He tried to manipulate Barbarossa into a coalition against the Byzantines by taking advantage of the fact that the crusaders were advancing toward Constantinople and he occupied lands from Niss to Kosovo and Skopje. At least God helped one Christian king.

The Fourth Crusade which lasted only two years produced an unexpected twist. The Bible was dropped from being held in one hand so that both hands could grab the hilt of the sword, not to kill Muslims but to massacre their fellow Christians. It all began with repeated shaky regimes in Constantinople. Imperial power was collapsing there as the city struggled to fulfill its commitments to pay back a huge debt to the European knights.

Alexius V whom they had supported as the final candidate for the throne failed to pay them off, and the knights decided not to conquer Jerusalem but the Byzantine capital instead. They stormed Constantinople in 1204. In their fury they demonstrated unlimited cruelty in killing and torturing their fellow Christians regardless of their age or sex. Their behavior well surpassed a barbarian savagery. They plundered the Hagia Sophia where they placed a prostitute on the throne of the patriarch and sacked the rest of the city's churches and palaces as well. In spite of all this, the western chronicler of these act Villehardouin had only words of praise for the crusaders' achievement:

> They all rejoiced and gave thanks to our Lord for the honor and the victory he had granted them, so that those who had been poor now lived in wealth and luxury. Thus they celebrated Palm Sunday [the Sunday before Easter] and the Easter Day following with hearts full of joy for the benefits our Lord and Savior had bestowed on them.[5]

A massive amount of war booty was carried back to the west mainly Venice, along with other pillage was the magnificent statue of four horses from the hippodrome. This would be placed above the porch on Saint Mark's Basilica. This sealed the Great Schism between Catholicism and Orthodoxy and both were under the same God. It was also proof to the Turks that Constantinople's years were numbered.

Meanwhile, an *Imperium Romaniae*/Empire of Romania and many Latin kingdoms replaced parts of the Byzantine Empire. These lands were then ruled according to western laws introduced along with Catholicism. This did not succeed as the Balkan people had an entirely different mindset than westerners had when it came to matters of governance.[6]

The Albanians were temporarily occupied by the Venetians, while the Vlachs under their King Ioannitsa fought against the Latin occupiers, and by defeating them captured and executed Emperor Baldwin. In spite of this, in 1205 a papal emissary crowned Ioannitsa king, and he and his Vlachs never compromised their religion after that point. Nor, did the Greeks compromise and re-occupied Constantinople in 1261. It was at this point that most of the Latins, along with their Catholicism, were forced to leave the Byzantine lands.

The Children's Crusade of 1212 was not driven by the force of weapons and chivalrous knights, but by religious fantasy. Some fifty thousand children who were believed to be pure souls headed toward the Holy Land. Most of them ended up in the hands of pirates and were sold into slavery. Some returned home sick and in rags, and the rest died of unknown illnesses in unknown locations.

The fifth and sixth crusades achieved very little except for the fact that Frederick II crowned himself "King of Jerusalem" in February 1229. When he departed from the city he left so much quarreling and confusion among residents that the Turks occupied it in 1244. The arrival of the pagan Mongols in the Holy Land sealed the fate of the next three crusades as the knights tried in vain to use them against the Turks.

After two hundred years of pursuing the noble dream of keeping the Holy Land and Jerusalem Christian, the crusaders found little reward from their God. In contrast, the Ottomans seemed to have been fully supported by their Allah.

✛

Certainly, the gods of the Mongols favored them to build an empire under the invincible sword of Genghis Khan who ruled one fifth of the planet's land area, from the Sea of Japan to the Caspian Sea. After his death in 1227, his son Ogadai continued the conquest legacy, and his grandson Batu led the Golden Horde to extend their empire into Eastern Europe. In 1236 he destroyed Volga Bulgaria numerous Russian principalities became his vassals. His divided horde invaded Poland, the Danubian lands and Central Europe. They subdued Moldavia, Transylvania, and the Second Bulgarian Empire almost wiping Hungary off the map and totally devastating Moravia.

The Christian god spared the rest of Europe when in 1242 Batu Khan had to return to Mongolia with his troops because of his uncle's death and new elections for the throne were taking place.

There were a number of reasons why the European crusades failed in spite of the religious motivation and military zeal of their soldiers. The vast distances the knights had to travel meant that the scorching climate in Palestine melted their metal body armor. The sandy soil of the area made for insufficient pastures and water for their horses. And, because they consistently followed the same Roman roads their stops could be predicted and they could be easily ambushed. What affected the outcome more than anything else were the adverse issues that arose amongst the knights themselves.

An old and a new group of crusaders fought endlessly amongst themselves. They killed each other over acquired lands which then often ended up in their wives' hands. With eleven Christian kings ruling the Holy Land in one century many rival parties also killed each other for control of that area. This considerably reduced the military strength of the Crusaders. Simply put, they were in no position to continue fighting the monolithic Turkish army that prayed five times a day to Allah, and was single mindedly committed to *jihad*. Still, the Crusaders succeeded in building some fifty castles several of them were literally on the sand, and they left a lasting legacy of their faith in the land where Jesus had walked and preached.

As a historical parenthesis, the Knights Templar was a new order born out of the necessity to protect the pilgrims who traveled back and forth from Europe to Jerusalem. Initially, the poor and charitable monks who took on this task were totally dedicated to their cause and established their headquarters in the Temple of Solomon (hence their name). Soon they became warriors and then knights of a secret society, and they found many relics left by Jesus and his disciples. Their white mantles with a large red cross on the front distinguished them as elite fighters who ended up controlling the trade between Europe and the Middle East. Merchants competed to bring goods to both worlds and became richer with each transport that was taxed by the Templars.

This produced so much money for the knights that they became successful bankers and builders in the Holy Land and in Europe. Over two centuries, they attained such a power as to be able to threaten both the suzerainty of the Catholic Church, and the kings of Western Europe. This eventually proved to be their downfall. The Church wanted to possess the sacred objects and secret documents connected with the life of Jesus that the Templars had accumulated, and the ever-bankrupt kings wanted their wealth.

Specifically, Pope Clement V wanted their secret possessions and in 1307 King Philip IV of France who was hopelessly in debt to the Templars ordered their arrest and confiscated their possessions. The Knights of Christ were then judged by the Inquisition to be "knights of anti-Christ." In 1312 after they had been tortured and butchered, and some of them being burned at the stake the famous order that had once numbered twenty thousand rigorously screened members was officially dissolved.

☩

As for the Medieval Inquisition set up by Pope Gregory IX in 1233 it was an institution of the Catholic Church whose police force hunted down heretics, and defended the purity and sanctity of God. Under torture they were forced to admit to any religious guilty charges and condemned themselves to public execution. Those targeted included many Jews who had converted to Christianity for economic and political reasons, but persisted in practicing their ancient religion in secrecy. In Spain they were named New Christians but more often called *converses*/converts and *marranos*/pigs. There they were subject to the punishment of the Inquisition and expelled in 1478 and 1492.

The Catholic fugitives and the expelled Jews found refuge in the Byzantine Empire. There they once again had the option of becoming Christians in exchange for tax relief and other obligations. Not many took up the offer choosing instead to enjoy the freedom that existed there like nowhere else. At the end of the ninth century the Jews became so financially powerful in Thessaloniki that Methodius spoke against them in virulent language:

> They had extended their trade all over Eastern Europe and formed their own communities where they lived without the harassment they routinely experienced in the West. An exception to this was the Jews of Prague, who lived in a walled ghetto and were identified by yellow patches on their clothing, as they were in Rome.

The situation was different in the Balkans. In fact, Czar Alexander (r. 1331-1365) of Bulgaria divorced his Christian wife Theodora and married a Jewess. She was then baptized with the same name. This matrimonial event elevated the Jews to unexpected heights. In the Byzantine lands they were named *servi camerae regis*/ servants of the royal court obviously a title of great privilege for them.

The Polish city of Krakow (which became the capital) was the credit of their enterprise, and nearby Kazimierz had its own Jewish town hall, synagogue, cemetery, and marketplace since the fourteenth century. Yet, they never assimilated with the Polish population. Moreover:

> The hermetic solitude of the Jewish communities, coupled with the intellectual superiority of the Jews, who digested huge volumes of abstract commentaries on Scripture, aroused fantasies in the minds of Christians confronted by these autonomous, anonymous, but fiercely unified groups, these

roving traders who made homes in one place but seemed to have roots elsewhere—in Spain, Egypt, Italy, and the like"[7]

They had no intention of trying to pass as Christian Gentiles whom they named *goyim* (those who are ignorant of Judaism and who eat pigs).

The Jews benefited most from the Ottoman conquests. They were welcomed by the sultans who made the best of what they could offer the young empire in the fields of commerce, finance, and the administration. Since the East or West, Catholic or Orthodox, meant very little to them the Jews attended to their businesses in a profitable manner, and their patrons also benefited from them. Most of all, they attended their synagogues to thank their god, Jehovah Shalom (The Lord is Peace).

In the meantime, the former giant Byzantine Empire was gradually being sapped by destructive forces, both internally and externally and only its religious power kept the moribund state alive. It could not match the power of the Ottomans who occupied most of Anatolia and looked across the Bosporus in search of the ideal beach upon which they might land their troops to attack Constantinople. As it turned out there was no need for that. They were brought to the Balkans by the Byzantine civil war of 1341-1347 when the supporters of the adversaries John V and John VI battled each other to gain the throne and sought Turkish military help.

The Turks arrived by invitation and put an end to the political butchery, but they overstayed their welcome and occupied the Gallipoli Peninsula, and they never left it. By now it had become their bridgehead into Eastern Europe. Some speculate that Greece and the Balkans would now be different if the Venetians had continued to occupy Thessaloniki after its capture in 1387 at the hands of the Turks. The Ottoman armies soon proved unstoppable in their efforts to occupy Macedonia, Bulgaria and the entire Balkan Peninsula.[8]

✛

At this point, both the Byzantine and the Western leaders realized that the Turks had to be stopped at any cost. Within two years armies of longstanding enmity met on the killing fields of Kosovo where a battle raged on all fronts. This test of wills was remarkable for the sheer cruelty that was perpetrated in the name of the participants' respective deities of two different gods. The defeat of the Christian coalition put an end to Serbian power, and Turkish flags marked the Danubian line showing the borders of the Ottoman Empire reached the eastern edge of the Balkan Peninsula.

The future of Eastern Europe and for that matter of the entirety of Christendom was now at stake. This was a predicament that triggered a series of so-called Balkan crusades. The most important of them was aimed at Nicopolis where in 1396 the united armies of Eastern and Western Europe attempted to stop the Turks from advancing any farther north of the Danube River. Both sides geared up for a major battle but the Christian coalition had a bad start. The Hungarian King Sigismund who was entrusted with the campaign had lost control over the conflict a long time before the first clash of arms. According to a contemporary commentary:

> Without delving into the various controversial aspects of Sigismund's character, we may conclude two main points contributed immensely to the failure of the Crusade: his weakness and his immorality. He failed to persuade the leaders of the foreign auxiliaries to believe in the wisdom of his defensive plans both at Buda and at Nicopolis, and he was, from the beginning of the campaign, more of a follower than a leader. His royal license helped to demoralize an already demoralized army. Women of infamous character were gathered on the way to Nicopolis wherever the Holy Warriors halted; and the siege became remarkable for immorality and gambling rather than for organized military enterprise.[9]

In spite of this, the heavily armored French knights valiantly engaged in a pitched battle heading uphill under the scorching sun against well-prepared Janissaries who stood their ground. When their horses were killed the knights fought on foot ramming the sultan's formidable elite guard. The latter was ready with a counter attack that proved murderous for the exhausted assailants who were already crushed under their metal body armor.

In no time at all an entire army of the best knights of Europe was cut down by the Ottoman's swords, almost to the last man. The captives were executed in the name of Allah under the crescent flag. Sadly, the arrogance and lack of discipline of the various Christian factions the troops who were fighting for ultimately selfish purposes resulted in an error that was to be repeated over and over in numerous crushing defeats. It turned out to have major destructive historical consequences for the Christians.

While the rest of Christianity kept losing ground Manuel II (r. 1391-1425) whose Byzantine Empire consisted of a mere three patches of land around Constantinople, Thessaloniki, and the tip of Peloponnesus remained neutral. He found himself in the humiliating position of having to pay tribute to the Ottomans, and aid them in their destructive raids against the Greek cities. Some of these would eventually be erased from the map.

Emperor Manuel clearly saw that the Christian defeats would lead mainly to the fall of the Byzantine Empire. He secretly tried hard to unite the East with the West in a common fight. "Our last resource [against the Turks]," said Manuel, "is their fear of our union with the Latins, of the warlike nations of the West, who may arm for our relief and for their destruction."[10] They recognized that the partisans of Orthodoxy were crushingly superior in numbers and power. Manuel II and his successor John VIII, both vainly tried to unite the Eastern and Western churches to save the Byzantine Empire from a tragic end.

By this time Islam was already the second religion of the Balkans. Catholic "hegemony" extended only into parts of Bosnia, the Republic of Ragusa (Dubrovnik), the Adriatic and Aegean islands and parts of Transylvania. Orthodoxy was still untouched and still the religion of the Byzantine Empire, Serbia, and the future Romanian principalities. It seemed that the Ottomans were unstoppable in their push toward Central Europe. As was expected they brought with them the unwanted winds of change.

Hunyadi the White Knight proved that the Turks could still be put down. One further mini-crusade united the Hungarian, Polish, and Wallachian armies under the same flag with a cross to confront the Islamic armies at Varna in 1444. The cavalry skirmishes that took place there turned into a war when five hundred knights once again suffered the murderous fate that others had at Nicopolis.

Their leader the young Polish King Wladislaw III was eager to prove himself and attempted to duel with and kill Sultan Murad II, only to meet a violent death by the Janissary guardsmen. His head was displayed in the capital of the Turkish Empire. The Muslim population there praised Allah with songs and dances when they saw it. The defeat of the Christian crusaders by the Ottomans was perceived as the triumph of Islam over the religious infidels.

The Turks had superior military discipline that was strictly regulated by Muslim laws. They won at Varna but at a price in human lives that made Sultan Murad lament, "May God never grant me another such victory." In view of this it is possible to speculate that if one more crusade had followed shortly after this the Ottomans might have met their ultimate defeat and the history of the Balkans would be different.

It is important to note that Byzantine troops were absent from all of these mini-crusades, and this was further evidence that the emperors from Constantinople did not want to provoke the fury of the Ottomans. It was better to maintain almost submissive neutrality.

However, their complacency would cost them their empire nine years later, when during the final siege of Constantinople neither Hunyadi nor any other European leader was willing to help the

Greeks against the Turks. Despite the many failures and disasters that followed the crusades temporally uniting Eastern and Western Europe behind a common cause but they were still unable to defeat the Ottomans. The end of the crusades also brought an end to the era of knighthood, and set in motion the era of the Renaissance.

✣

In the meantime, the Byzantine Empire was reduced to a mere patch of land around its capital. It survived mostly because it harbored the headquarters of Orthodoxy which by then was also at its lowest point compared to the Catholic Church. This was most evident when in 1453 Sultan Mehmed II assaulted the walls of Constantinople. Not a single military contingent or warship from the West came to the aid of the helpless besieged citizens. The city possessed an army of less than eight thousand (mostly mercenaries). These men faced the impossible task of fighting back almost one hundred thousand Turks who were armed with some one hundred heavy cannons.

The Constantinopolitans rushed into their churches to pray for salvation. Inside the huge cathedral of Hagia Sophia people believed that:
> an angel would descend from Heaven with a sword in his hand and would deliver the empire, with that celestial weapon, to a poor man seated at the foot of the column "Take this sword" would he say, and avenge the people of the Lord.[11]

But, the victorious swords were wielded by another lord and they swung outside Constantinople's defensive walls.

Their prayers were no substitute for the military force needed to stop the Ottomans from capturing the city of Constantine where Christianity had become an official state religion eleven centuries earlier. This apocalyptic event was taken to be God's punishment for the sins of the Constantinopolitans.

Secretly, many Greeks preferred Ottoman rule. It imposed much lower taxes than the greedy and corrupt Byzantines had. Their wish was soon to be granted. The Turks used their heavy cannons to demolish a segment of the wall and Emperor Constantine XI heroically died fighting the invaders. They broke into the magnificent cathedral of Hagia Sophia taking the trapped worshippers captive as they clung to their crosses. This marked the end of the Byzantine Empire. Hagia Sophia was turned into a mosque three days later. Constantinople was no longer "the shrine city" for Orthodoxy. From then on its Orthodoxy was subject to the benevolence of the occupying Mohammedans.[12]

As a rule, the Turks wanted to replace the Byzantine Empire with an Ottoman one and they cared little for any other commitment. The Serbs experienced this after helping the Turks conquer Constantinople (by providing sappers to dig under the walls). The Serbs believed themselves to be privileged allies yet their aid brought nothing in return except Turkish raids in the territory of Zeta. Later, the Ottoman occupation took over of the entire Serbia.

A similar situation developed after 1479 when Mehmed II and the Venetians exchanged islands and lands in a peace treaty that put Albania, Morea, and Dalmatia under Venetian control. Croia, Lemnos, and Scutari went to the Turks, but almost before the ink had dried on the treaty the sultan's fleet and army invaded the heel of the Italian Peninsula.

Still, the Turks collaborated with the Orthodox Church, and by doing this they felt it would keep the Balkan population in cultural numbness and in a state of social calm. The Turkish manipulation of the political system of the former empire had lasting effects on the Balkan way of thinking. Even though the people's religion remained Orthodox and their spirituality never diminished, it manifested itself in convoluted forms that were difficult for the Western world to understand or accept.

Ottoman domination of the Balkans was considered a negative, but it eliminated the inherited wars between the Bulgars, Croats, Greeks, Serbs, and other nationalities that were "pacified" by Islam.

Certainly, no armies of crusaders would again traverse the Balkan Peninsula and leave in their wake more disasters than any Turkish army had. Moreover, any Christian who converted to Islam was given substantial tax breaks, and this was a powerful incentive to now believe in Allah. This wise policy was attributed to Sultan Mehmed II.

> As a conqueror he finally sealed the foundations of a great Islamic empire; as a statesman he had created within it the structure of a new and enduring Islamic state, worthy in its institutions, traditions, and policies to succeed the imperial civilizations of classical Rome and Christian Greece, and indeed serving as a zealous protector of Orthodox Christendom.[13]

Mehmed II was anything but a devoted Muslim, and he had little concern about Allah. He drank in excess and alcohol quickly sapped his health and made him prematurely obese. He died of syphilis during an afternoon prayer on May 4, 1481 at the age of forty-nine. Nevertheless, he put in place the foundation of a mammoth inter-religious and multi-racial Ottoman Empire that creatively accommodated people to worship their own god. As a rule the sultans never interfered with the religious beliefs of the nations they conquered and occupied in order to avoid the religious wars. The result of the falling of the Byzantine Empire and the Ottoman domination in the Balkan Pennisula created a *talmesh-balmesh* (hodgepodge) that later was named *balkanization,* a term very little understood by outsiders.

☦

North of the Danube River, the Walachians (the future Romanians) kept the flag of Orthodoxy raised high, and between 1462 and 1483 they scored some major victories against the invading Turkish armies. Ultimately, Moldavia and Wallachia came to pay tribute to the Sublime Porte. But, their Orthodoxy remained intact. Islam and Catholicism never took roots among the Wallachians and Vlachs who lived North and South of the Danube River. King Matthias tried in vain to impose his Catholicism on the Serbs who preferred to accept Turkish occupation, since it gave them the religious freedom to remain Orthodox.

As for Mount Athos the peninsular fortress 130 sq. miles/336 sq. kilometers of Orthodoxy having 20 monasteries built by the Greeks, Russians, Romanians, Bulgars and others remained untouched by the Ottoman occupation of the Balkans. It was a sacred place for Orthodox believers and pilgrims. Regrettably, the crusaders and Christian pirates destroyed most of the Orthodox religious sites. Some have survived the vicissitudes of time and some are still intact like Mount Athos is today.

An overview of these events reveals that when the barbarian rulers were enthroned by *Dei Gratia Regina*/By the Grace of God and given unlimited power Christianity became the foundation for new states. It was not that the barbarian mob chose Christianity, but rather that their chieftains imposed it on them. Likewise, it was not the priests who influenced the barbarian world, but the rulers whose military power defined a certain historical path for their nations.

The rivalry between Catholicism and Orthodoxy was the cause of most of the manmade disasters that occurred in the Balkan area. From the Iconoclasm to the Great Schism there was perpetual conflict between the East and the West. It was aggravated by barbarian invasions, the Crusades to Palestine, and the wars against Islam.

The Great Schism did more than divide the European Christian church: culturally and socially, it divided the East from the West. In the end it produced people in each region of Europe who had different mentalities and ways of life. The Christian Church had ready answers for everything including plagues, floods, famines, earthquakes, wars, and other disasters. They were all considered to be God's punishment for sinners who did not sufficiently obey the Church. It was the spiritual voice of the state. Its bureaucratic edicts also reflected the voice of God, and thus ensured that no one could oppose them. The

Church remained the strongest institution of the Middle Ages.

After the fall of Constantinople Mehmed II and many sultans after him, did not try to weaken Orthodoxy. Instead, they chose to use it as a symbol of power and as a spiritual tool against the Catholic Church.

Islam initiated its own Renaissance in the ninth century with extraordinary developments in the arts, architecture, literature, astronomy, chemistry, mathematics, medicine, and philosophy. It was immensely progressive for a short time after which like Orthodoxy it withdrew from the rest of the world. The Islamic society became ensconced in a sort of time capsule.

As the Catholics and later the Protestants marched forward to improve their earthly lives, the Orthodox Christians accepted their modest destiny and thanked God for what they had. They prayed that things would not worsen. Tradition was good and change might not be. If change would come it tended to result from earthshaking events in distant locations. The world's great powers were at work on deciding a global present and future, while the people of the Balkans lived in a glorified past that justified their religious and ongoing ethnic conflicts. Even today, their cherished traditions continue to accompany the Balkan people wherever they live.[14] They are still under the influence of the Orthodox doctrine which is well rooted in *balkanization*.

# REFERENCE NOTES

1. When the Magyars resisted Christianity or Catholicism, Stephan/Istvan proved merciless with his pagans. He punished them and confiscated their settlements and gave the land to the Church. This prompted an anti-Christian revolt in 1046 under a tribal chief named Vatha. He refused to comply with the religious regime imposed upon him by the Hungarian king. His tribesmen were forcefully dispersed throughout Pannonia by King Andras I as part of an effort to defuse their power.
2. Matthew Spinka, *A History of Christianity in the Balkans: A Study in the Spread of Byzantine Culture Among the Slavs* (Hamden, CT: Archon Books, 1968), 168.
3. Anna Comnena, *The Alexiad of Anna Comnena*, trans. E. R. A. Sewter (London: Penguin Books, 1969), 450.
4. Russia remained a primitive country until Peter the Great (r. 1682-1725) opened a window to the west by building Petrograd. He westernized his nation by force.
5. Timothy Levi Biel, *The Crusades* (San Diego, CA: Lucent Books, 1996), 111.
6. To this day the Greeks and other Orthodox nations will never forgive or forget their humiliation at the hands of the Catholic occupiers. Few of them can visit Venice without pointing out pillaged objects from Constantinople.
7. Philippe Aries, Georges Duby, Paul Veyne, eds., *A History of Private Life: From Pagan Rome to Byzantium*, trans. Arthur Goldhammer (Cambridge, MA: Harvard University Press, 1997), 433.
8. Eight hundred years later Pope Benedict XVI delivered a speech on September 12, 2006 in which he quoted Emanuel in his book *Twenty-six Dialogues with a Persian* (Dialogue 7). There, the Emperor stated: "Show me just what Muhammad brought that was

new and there you will find things only evil and inhuman, such as his command to spread by the sword the faith he preached." His comment was merely intended to point to medieval prejudice, but it generated outrage in the Muslim world. The pope subsequently apologized, and visited Turkey where he prayed at the Blue Mosque.

9. Aziz Suryal Atiya, *The Crusade of Nicopolis* (London: Methuen & Co., 1934), 77.
10. Edward Gibbon, *The Decline and Fall of the Roman Empire* (New York: Modern Library, 2003), 1176.
11. Gibbon, *Decline and Fall*, 1212.
12. Again the modern Greeks cannot forget or forgive that their beloved Constantinople renamed Istanbul is still under Turkish occupation.
13. Lord Kinross, *The Ottoman Centuries: The Rise and Fall of the Turkish Empire* (New York: Morrow Quill, 1977), 158.
14. The entire phenomenon may go deeper if one considers the intermixing of the native population with the Asiatic occupiers. It created a genetic type that possesses certain instincts and habits of thought and behavior not found in Western Europe, or elsewhere in the Anglo-Saxon world. The influence of genetics on human behavior is now being debated.

# IX

# THE END OF AN EMPIRE

The former Roman Empire after the year 500 was mainly ruled by the papacy from Rome and by emperors from the city of Constantinople. During the reign of Justinian I (r. 527-565) who wanted to restore the glorious empire of the emperors Trajan and Hadrian recovered most of the lost territories of the Western Roman Empire to incorporate them into his Byzantine Empire. The ambitious Justinian (born Petrus Sabbatius in Dardania) the "emperor who never sleeps," succeeded through his capable generals to encompass the regions around the Adriatic, Aegean, Black, and Mediterranean seas. This included Italy, southern Spain, northern Africa, Egypt, Syria, Palestine, the entirety of Asia Minor, and the area south of the Crimean Peninsula. At the time of Justinian's death it covered 2.07 million square kilometers and had a population of 19.5 million. Justinian also had a regular army consisting of 379,000 permanent troops.[1]

The rich farm lands and prosperous cities of the Italic Peninsula attracted countless barbarian tribes mainly the German Lombards who plundered and pillaged the northern region. Muslim tribes made bold conquests throughout North Africa and Spain all of which in time reduced the size and power of the tri-continental empire.

Despite its Latin sounding name, *Imperium Romanum*, the Byzantine Empire of the East was centered in the Balkan Peninsula and unified by the Greek language. Latin was used primarily for affairs of state and scholarly studies. Non-Greek speaking people were referred to as "barbarians" and according to the history written by Niketas Choniatēs (1155-1216) they all wanted to destroy the Byzantine civilization. Niketas also makes it clear that Justinian viewed the Greeks in the same way he did the Romans destined to match the glorious legacy of Rome. An important factor contributing to the Byzantine unification was the Eastern Orthodox Church with its religious center in the Phanar district of Constantinople.

The city's colossal Theodosian Walls were built in the fifth century during the reign of Theodosius II as additions to other pre-existing ones. They could thwart any attack from land. The city's immense basilica of Hagia Sofia (Sacred Wisdom) was built by Justinian in 562. It was the largest manmade structure in medieval Europe, and both the wall and the basilica were symbols of Constantinople's invincibility. The magnificent metropolis was known not only by the name Constantinople, but also as *Nova Roma* (New Rome) and by its ancient name of Byzantium/Byzantion which was once a modest commercial settlement named Lygos.

The magnificent metropolis was the capital of the Byzantine Empire with a population of 375,000. It was strategically located on a mini-peninsula that almost reached to Asia Minor across the Strait of the Bosporus. It offered religious and royal glamour and a level of sophistication that initially mesmerized the barbarian chieftains who wanted to be connected to it. They hoped to duplicate it in order to demonstrate their power and impress their subjects.

This prosperous city was effectively able to control all maritime traffic between the Black and Mediterranean seas. Its strategic commercial location and its prosperity named it the "city of lights" because of its famous monumental landmark lighthouse in the Phanar district. It was a citadel that seemed to defy conquest in spite of being the target of countless attacks. Goths, Persians, multitudes of Slavs, and other hungry barbarian hordes would renew their efforts to besiege the unconquered Constantinople.

What made Byzantium such a powerful state was its adoption of the Roman tradition of integrating conquered peoples into the empire. In the Roman Empire as long as people obeyed the law and paid taxes all ethnicities could retain their language, culture, and religion as well as travel freely throughout the provinces without borders.

Democratic institutions or doctrines of equal rights might not have existed at that time, but any brave soldier, skillful artisan, or competent trader could be respected and live well in Constantinople. Artists, intellectuals, and foreigners with special talents were welcomed and often became famous citizens. The Roman systems of census, taxation, and budgeting were still in place in Eastern Empire (anachronistically referred to as the Land of the Romans) as was a monetary economy and a centralized government that were made even stronger under the laws of Justinian I.

Most of the Byzantine emperors had some Armenian, Greek, Macedonian, and Roman blood and they came to power either as a result of heredity or military acclaim. Their dynasties proved able to withstand many court intrigues and fratricidal wars. These conflicts would ultimately be extinguished by the Orthodox theocracy.

The downfall of the Byzantine Empire actually started at the time of its birth when Eurasian migratory tribes swept like incoming tides across Eastern Europe and the Balkan Mountains. They continued to do so for five centuries. Since they were hell bent on gaining ever more booty they left behind one ghost city after another and showed no mercy toward their captives. These invading hordes used terror as a means of psychological warfare in their effort to ease their next conquest. Their raw barbarian power consisted with having massive and highly mobile mounted warriors, who with their saddles and stirrups outnumbered those of the Byzantine armies which were generally on foot.

They repeatedly inflicted genocide on most of the Byzantine provinces they destroyed productive manpower, set farms on fire, and ruined their economies and trade. For centuries, the incoming Asiatic attackers were successfully repelled. It appeared that Constantinople which had survived the ravages of time would remain invincible. However, history proved otherwise.

The unavoidable tragedy came from three consecutive bubonic plagues (in the years 542, 558, and 588) which ravaged the city of Constantinople. It cut in half the number of its citizens, and shrunk the population including the armies of the entire Byzantine Empire. On top of that, the same overstretched and reduced armed forces (often in a state of mutiny) struggled to fight off savage barbarians and other unwelcome intruders on all fronts. Ostrogoths and Vandals were pouring into the West while the Avars besieged Singidunum (Belgrade) and Thessaloniki (Salonika).

During the reign of Maurice (r. 582-602) the Slavs conquered Sirmium (Stremska Mitrovica) and raided the Peloponnesus/Morea. They also sacked Dalmatia, Greece, Macedonia, Moesia, Pannonia, and Thracia. They destroyed many prosperous Balkan cities before they reached the Long Wall some 60 kilometers west of Constantinople. This forced the Byzantines to accept the Roman dictum "After God, we should place our hopes of safety in our weapons, not in our fortifications alone."[2]

General Priscus's numerous retaliatory campaigns produced mixed results as cities and territories repeatedly changed hands. He forced the invaders to re-direct their paths of destruction and commanded the imperial army to divide and fight. Thus, its units were streched from the Mediterranean island of Crete to the Tisza River of Pannonia and the city of Tomis (Constantsa) below the Danube Delta.

More problematic was the fact that each time a war was being waged against the Arab expansion into Asia Minor the empire was always short of troops in the Balkans. Byzantine military victories and signed accords with the defeated barbarians guaranteed nothing when it came to actually containing and ruling the illiterate invaders. When the empire was forced to buy peace it found itself short of money. The result was mutiny amongst its troops. Not surprisingly the Slavs fully exploited this, and any other opportunity to inflict new blows on the weakened empire.

During his long reign, Emperor Heraclius (r.610-641) had to contend with many types of irreversible damages that already had been done to the empire. To this was added the capture of Damascus and Jerusalem by the Persians. This event marked the historic ascent of Islam. The Ottoman armies proceeded to conquer even more Byzantine land in the name of Allah. Fortunately, the territorial loss that resulted was in Asia Minor and so less than vital to the Byzantines. They regarded the Balkans as their primary territory, and one that was now under threat from the Avars. In 617 the barbarians succeeded in capturing Heracleia (a short distance from Constantinople) and forced Heraclius to pay them in exchange for temporary peace. Given that there was a lull in military activities in the Balkans he was able to withdraw his army from there and proceed to liberate Jerusalem from the Persian occupation.

But in 626 the Persians engaged the Avars to besiege Constantinople thus allowing them to land troops on the eastern shore of the Bosporus. Both of these attacks were successfully repelled by Heraclius. He also scored a major victory the following year against the Persians at Nineveh when he personally killed their General Rhahzadh in a duel. King Khustro II fled and was subsequently assassinated.

Replicating the Persian tactic of tricking nomads into fighting on their behalf Heraclius encouraged the Serbian tribes to settle in the Balkans if they agreed to fight the Avars. It was a brilliant diversion and very convenient at the time. But, in the long run it was extremely damaging since it encouraged still another massive barbarian entity to carve out a part of the empire and claim it for them.

Overall, Heraclius's victories were considerable. He was able to reconquer Jerusalem in 629 when he prohibited the Jews from entering the city just like Emperor Hadrian (r. 117-138) had done 400 years earlier. He succeeded to keep Anatolia and restored Constantinople to a position of dominance in the Balkans. His legacy was that he was the first emperor to fight against an Islamic army. Since he was of Armenian origin he changed his royal title from the Roman *Augustus* (semi-devine) to *Basileus* (sovereign). He also dropped Latin in favor of Greek as the official language of the Empire.

Many of the other measures Heraclius introduced began to shape what would eventually become the Byzantine Empire's own unique form of government and identity. This religious emperor believed that once the invading Bulgars, Serbs, and Croats converted to Christianity and were allowed to settle in former the Dacian Moesia between the Danube and the Haemus (Balkan) Mountains, they will integrate in the Byzantine Empire.

Because Heraclius believed that once the barbarians would become Orthodox Christians they would be grateful and loyal subjects. It was an emperor's error in judgment which later had major adverse and irreversible historical consequences.

Now, the baptized pagan chieftains demanded to be crowned kings and even emperors. They expected to be given an equal share of the Byzantine lands with deserving privileges until the First Crusade in 1099.

✠

The Byzantine Empire began to decline in the year 638 in the distant Near East after Muslim troops re-occupied Jerusalem. The city was regarded as sacred by both Christian worlds the Orthodoxy and Catholicism. But the armies of the caliphate under Omar the Great (r. 634-644) conquered Palestine, Byzantine Armenia, Egypt, Libya, Mesopotamia and Syria. The Muslim armies also took over the southern section of Anatolia. At this point the majority of the empire's lands in Asia Minor seemed to be lost forever by the Byzantine Empire, included the Holy Land.

The beginning of the eighth century was marked by the firm rule of Justinian II (r. 685-695 and 705 – 711). He used the army from what was now the reduced Anatolian province to discipline the Slavic hordes as they swarmed over the Balkan Peninsula. By the end of 689 he had expelled the Bulgars from Macedonia and retaken Thessaloniki from the Slavic tribes. Justinian relocated the Slavs that he had captured to Anatolia and forced them to fight the Arabs whom he defeated in Armenia. However, in 694 the revolting Bulgars allied with the Muslim enemy and Armenia again came under Islam. Little did Justinian know that he would have to rely on these same Bulgars and Slavs to regain his throne in 705 after he had executed the emperors Leontius and Tiberius.

Justinian's second reign (705-711) was a costly one as he needed the assistance of this former barbarian enemy to survive politically. Khan Tervel of the First Bulgarian Empire sent 15,000 horsemen to help Justinian to regain his throne for the second time. In exchange Tervel was named Caesar and received from Justinian many gifts of gold, silver and silk along with the Byzantine region of Zagora, a land of Trace. Three years later the repentant Justinian tried to take back Zagora by invading Bulgaria, and to restore his imperial rule over it but was only badly defeated.

The emperor hardly escaped by boarding a ship to go back to Constantinople, and he was forced to accept a less than glorious peace. The Arabs took advantage of this situation and invaded Cappadocia. Justinian was then confronted with an internal revolt. Hastening back from the campaign in Armenia, he was executed by a rival faction as he approached Constantinople before he had a chance to reclaim his royal scepter. His six year old son who was co-emperor at the time was dragged from the church altar, where his mother had taken him for shelter, and murdered. Thus, the Heraclian dynasty came to an abrupt and brutal end.

By the spring of 717 the Muslims had succeeded in invading the Iberian Peninsula, and taking full advantage of the internal turmoil in Byzantium the Arab armies staged a second invasion of Constantinople. They possessed a fleet of some twenty five hundred ships, and an army of two hundred thousand. They forced Leo III (r. 717-741) to ally with the savage Bulgars to repel the invasion by land, and at the same time have his navy use the deadly Greek fires to destroy the enemy ships on the sea.

An unusually harsh winter decimated the ranks of the Arabs as they were ill adapted to the climate and they simply gave up the siege. As they retreated they were battered by a fierce storm that sank all but five of their ships and killed most of their troops. Once again, the prayers of the Constantinopolitans (many of whom were now sheltered inside Hagia Sofia) had been answered. This humiliating defeat of the Arab armies set a precedent for an Islamic Jihad (Holy War) and also defined the agenda of the future sultans.

The next ten Byzantine emperors, all of whom were tormented by countless inner court intrigues, were confronted with international dangers of no less significance. Nicephorus I had to confront the Venetians and Franks while losing a war against the Arabs in Asia Minor, and to buy their peace with an annual tribute. The Bulgars took full advantage of the hard pressed emperor and attacked southward conquering Serdica (Sofia) only to be pushed back and lose their own capital of Pliska in 811. As it happened, while the Byzantine army was on its way back home it was ambushed by the Bulgarians and Nikephoros was killed in the battle. Khan Krum the Czar of the Bulgarians celebrated his victory by drinking wine from the emperor's skull. This marked one of the lowest points in the empire's history of vulnerability.

By 865 even the remotely located Russians had attacked Constantinople. They would do so again in 907, 941, 944 and 1043 only

> to plunder their treasures. The events varied but the motives, means, and the objective were the same in all of these naval expeditions. The Russian traders had seen the magnificence,

and tasted the luxury of the city of the new Caesars. A marvelous tale along with a scanty supply excited the desires of their savage countrymen. They envied the gifts of nature which their climate denied, and they coveted the works of art which they were too lazy to imitate and too indigent to purchase.[3]

These together with other barbarian invasions led to large foreign settlements and unfavorable military outcomes. This caused Byzantium to lose nearly half of its territory, and its population in the course of two centuries. Nevertheless, the Eastern Empire still appeared large and powerful since it encompassed most of Greece, the region that had formerly been Thracia south of the Rhodope Mountains, most of Anatolia all the way to Cyprus, and the area extending from the northeast coast of the Black Sea all the way to Crimea.

With a mammoth bureaucracy and the state treasury now taking in only one fourth of its previous revenues the empire could only afford to pay fewer than eighty thousand soldiers.[4] Clearly this was not enough to maintain its authority and enforce the will of the emperors. The military discipline that had been a hallmark of the Roman army was now only a distant memory. Of increasing importance was the incipient religious dispute with Rome over the worship of icons. It became a reason for the division between Eastern and Western Europe.

The tenth century began with Arab pirates plundering Thessaloniki in 904, and in occupying Cyprus until 965. It was through the bravery of two Armenian generals later known as the emperors Nicephorus II (r. 963-969) and John I (r. 969-976), that the large territories of Mesopotamia, Palestine, and Syria were returned to being under Byzantine control. These soldier emperors destroyed the supremacy of the Arab fleet, and restored the power of the Byzantine navy in the eastern Mediterranean. However, attacks from marauding Slavs continued to plague the empire and even to threaten its existence.

The religious issue of iconoclasm was meanwhile settled in favor of the Orthodox Church, but with little consolation compared to the impact of the barbarian invasions and the hordes of unwanted migrants. They created irreversible cultural and demographic changes that initiated the process of a slow death for the Byzantine Empire.

✝

By the beginning of the eleventh century Basil II had succeeded in restoring the Eastern Empire to its previous dignity. His reign was initially marked by personal and imperial humiliations. He was overshadowed by powerful relatives and blackmailed by enemies while also dealing with mutiny and a civil war. He repeatedly lost military expeditions against the land hungry Bulgarians who ruled the Byzantine regions from the Danube River to the Adriatic and Black seas, and also controlled central Greece. He learned precious lessons from all of this and after the year 1000 made a spectacular comeback.

He proved his first class generalship by regaining Macedonia (his homeland) and part of Moesia including Preslav which was the former Bulgarian capital. In 1014 he firmly defeated the Bulgarians at Kleidon in Macedonia, and blinded some fifteen thousand prisoners to teach them a lesson in respect for imperial authority.

When they returned to their homeland (led by a few one-eyed comrades) the spectacle of their mass punishment caused Czar Samuil to collapse and die of a heart attack. In spite of all this it took Basil *Boulgaroktons* (the Bulgar Slayer) four more years to subdue the Bulgars and Serbs.

Once again, the northern border of the Byzantine Empire was the line formed by the Danube River as it flowed from Belgrade eastward to its delta on the Black Sea. Under his rule of 49 years the Byzantine Empire reached the zenith of its medieval power and territorial size. It extended from the heel and toe of the boot of Italy to Crete and Cyprus. It encompassed the areas of Syria and Anatolia all the away to the foothills of the Caucasus Mountains, and also included part of the Crimean Peninsula. All of this was the result of the emperor's skillful rule.

Basil was a soldier's soldier who lived and thought like his men. He provided for the children of his deceased officers who had served him well. Later, his troops became fanatically loyal to this adopted "Father of the Army". This army numbered as many as three hundred thousand men and protected eighteen million Byzantines.

He also re-conquered Armenia, Syria, and Southern Italy and repeatedly forced the Arabs and Turks back until they no longer posed a threat. Each time he reached a peace accord its terms were imposed with an iron fist. In doing so he duplicated the grand achievement of Charlemagne who two hundred years earlier had united Central and Western Europe into the Holy Roman Empire.

At this point in history the Orthodox Empire seemed to be rising to great heights. It was on its way to a new golden age. Constantinople, as opposed to either Athens or Rome (all of which were built on seven hills) was the ultimate European metropolis. However, its cultural splendors and riches also made it the ultimate target for the ever increasing numbers of barbarian attacks.

Unfortunately, Basil never married and therefore did not leave any children. Instead, he left 90 tons of gold for the imperial treasury, and this was never matched by any Byzantine emperor before or after him. Since Basil's close relatives had only daughters the throne was succeeded by a number of inferior and weak sovereigns.

It began with his brother Constantine VIII (r. 1025-1028) who proved to be decadent and incompetent, and he passed the scepter to his two daughters Zoe and Theodora. They were bitterly jealous of each other, and they killed three emperor husbands. They kept fighting each other while recklessly emptying the empire's treasury, diminishing the size of the regular imperial army, and hiring mercenaries to repel invaders.

A sudden schism in 1054 between the Catholic and Orthodox churches severed the Byzantine Empire from the rest of Europe.

This forced the Eastern Empire to do battle on their own against the increasing numbers of enemies attacking from all directions. Its borders continued to shrink while Constantinople separated from Asia Minor by less than one mile of water was increasingly vulnerable to Muslim attacks from Anatolia.

Thus far the Turks had been busy fighting their own wars, but now they were strong enough to raid and occupy the empire's many provinces in Asia Minor. Emperor Romanus IV carried out some successful campaigns against them and contemptuously refused to aid the Seljuks in their fight against the Shiites in Egypt.

He decided instead to again conquer Armenia and led his army into Anatolia when in 1071 he suffered a surprising but catastrophic defeat at Manzikert. The overconfident emperor was himself taken prisoner and humiliated by Sultan Alp Arslan. He forced Romanus to kiss the ground and triumphantly planted his foot on the emperor's neck.

This symbolic gesture destroyed the myth of the invincibility of the imperial army and opened the floodgates for Muslim incursions into Anatolia along with the occupation of Jerusalem by the Seljuks. Yet, the sultan treated Romanus with understanding and even released him to continue his emperorship in exchange for a friendly treaty and ransom. This made him the enemy of his own nation. He could not suppress an imminent civil war, and after being blinded by a throne contender, the emperor was exiled or executed.

From any standpoint, the next emperors who engaged in reckless spending and lavish living were all in political trouble and needed help, even if they still had the power to crown barbarian kings of Slavic nations. In a brief paragraph, Anna Comnena described how:

> great disorders and wave on wave of confusion united to afflict our affairs. For the Scyths from the north, the Kelts from the west and the Ishmaelites from the east were simultaneously in turmoil. Whenever they find an opportunity, all of them, by land or sea, flock from all quarters to attack us.[5]

Desperation forced her father Emperor Alexius I (r. 1081-1118) to turn to the West for assistance. By this point they understood the increasingly menacing Turkish presence as a threat to the future of Europe. Pope Urban II took advantage of the religious pathos associated with liberating the Holy Land from Muslim occupation and set in motion the first crusade. This established the Kingdom of Jerusalem in 1099.

During his long reign Manuel I (r. 1143-1180) continued the policy of his father John II, and he sought to correct the damages done by previous emperors. He succeeded in ruling over most of the Balkan Peninsula (less Croatia and Slovenia) by battling the Hungarians and Sicilians while at the same time subduing the rebel Serbs. Because he anticipated the rising military power of Islam in Anatolia and was unable to defeat the Turks the emperor stimulated hostilities among their leaders, and he befriended Sultan Kilidj Arslan.

The latter spent eighty days in Constantinople as a royal guest. In a characteristic imperial manner aimed to impress. Manuel dazzled the primitive Seljuk with rich displays of the culture of Constantinople and bestowed lavish gifts on him. This only attracted the sultan's envy and greed. It implanted in his mind thoughts of how much wealth could be plundered from the glamorous metropolis. An unrealistic myth was developed about the colossal wealth that was waiting for the right conqueror in the Byzantine capital, or in the megalopolises of Adrianople, Athens, Thessaloniki and others.

Up to this point in time, the popes from Rome and the emperors from Constantinople competed in anointing the kings and other rulers in the Balkans as well as throughout most of Eastern Europe. The Byzantines soon would lose that supreme privilege as they faced domestic and international challenges they could not solve, and thus saw their ruling status diminished.

Most of the problems proved to be internal to the royal family. The eleven year old Emperor Alexius II who followed his father to the purple was dominated and manipulated by his uncle Andronicos the first cousin of Manuel I. During his short reign, in 1182, the envious Greeks massacred many of the sixty thousand Italian Latins of Constantinople. They were Catholic and the majority of them were merchants from Venice. This bloody event triggered the ceaseless wrath of Western Europe.

As an immediate punishment the Normans sacked Thessalonica the empire's second city. This opened a path for more retaliatory attacks that would culminate with the Crusaders' conquest of Constantinople in 1204.

Meanwhile, Andronicos kept a jealous eye on his teenage nephew whom he ended up strangling. He then installed a reign of terror (1183-1185) which was aimed at diminishing the power of the highborn nobility (who unwillingly defended the peasants from predatory landlords) and so prevented them from making any claim to the throne. In an attempt to avenge the twelve years he spent in prison for conspiring against Manuel he relished his hold on power, and did not hesitate to fulfill his enormous appetite for cruelty and revenge done in the name of the people.

Ironically, this tyrant's removal from power was the result of a popular rebellion. He was tortured for three days, his eyes were pulled out, his teeth and hair were pulled out, his right hand was cut off, and his handsome face burned with boiling water. After all of this he was hung between two large pillars of the Hippodrome. His co-emperor son was executed by his own troops in Thracia.

It was in this bloody manner that the Comnenus dynasty came to an end. The last reserves of the treasury (twelve hundred pounds of gold, three thousand pounds of silver, and twenty thousand pounds of copper coins) were stolen by the revolting mob. According to Niketas who was the source of these historic details, the victorious rebels plundered the royal armories, and the palace, including its icons.

As a consequence of all this, the next emperor Isaac II Angelos (r. 1185-1195 and 1203-1204) had to deal with the contemptuous Normans whom he had defeated. He had taken back Thessaloniki but could do little about the Vlachians' tax rebellion in the former Dacian Moesia which now was referred to as Bulgaria. They united with the Cumans and Wallachians from north of the Danube River and pillaged Thracia and other imperial regions.

In the meantime, Isaac spent the funds from the state treasury recklessly. He gave overly generous donations to the churches and his people at the same time as he was engaged in massive construction projects. He financed mercenary armies to maintain order inside the empire and to fight off the increasingly aggressive Vlachians.

Eventually, in order to refill the imperial treasury he had to mint coins that had essentially no monetary value. He was also forced to offer imperial positions to the highest bidders regardless of their qualifications. Niketas is also the source of information on what followed.

Overwhelmed by his responsibilities Isaac transferred them to his uncle Theodore Kastamonitis who assumed royal powers while the emperor indulged in a life of luxury. He became an addict of refined cuisine, pleasurable baths, hunting trips, and other expensive pastimes. He was renowned for not wearing the same clothes twice. This lifestyle attracted the envy of his brother Alexius whom the emperor had treated exceptionally well but to no avail.

After ambushing his naively overconfident brother and blinding him during a hunting trip Alexius III became his successor (r. 1195-1203). He was an emperor with a still greater capacity for self-destruction. He emptied what remained of the treasury and the emperor enriched himself by acts of wholesale bribery that extended even to the commoners. His ultimate aim was also to enjoy the good life. Alexius paid little attention to the affairs of state and the Bulgars, Hungarians, Serbs, Vlachians and other nationalities could practically dictate their territorial demands to Constantinople. Naturally, this further weakened the feeble empire.

✠

A series of unsuccessful crusades ensued ultimately doing more harm than good to the Byzantines who were now increasingly subject to Turkish threats. Yet, Constantinople continued to be referred to as the "Queen of the Cities" and it retained its enviable maritime power. Situated on the Bosporus Strait (Greek for "ox ford") it controlled the commercial traffic from the Marmora Sea and the Black Sea. Constantinople also controlled the isthmus of the Golden Horn, which was the natural moat for the safety of the sailing ships.

Whenever the city blocked its harbors the troops involved in a land assault were doomed to linger around its massive fortified walls and starve or give up altogether. The often cited rule of thumb, "He who controls the seas controls the world." This certainly was played out in Constantinople the vital center of what was now *Imperium Graecorum* (the Empire of the Greeks).

In reality, this region was a land of many new ethnicities that revolted against existing authority and unsuccessfully attacked the city. Such conflicts occurred continually until 1204 when the capital was sacked not by Asian pagans but by its Christian Western European allies.

✜

In an irony of history, the army of the fourth crusade under the octogenarian Enrico Dandalo the blind Venetian doge did not sail to Egypt but instead to Constantinople. His purpose was to reinstate Emperor Isaac II and his son Alexius IV who promised in exchange a huge reward in gold and military aid. Alexius, who visited the French and German royalty, also assured the Latin Crusaders that he would subordinate the Orthodox Church to the Roman papacy. To prove his pledge he adopted Catholicism a gesture that must have been insulting to the Orthodox Byzantines.

True to their word the Crusaders arrived with their ships in the harbor of Constantinople at the end of May 1203. They were "greeted" by torrents of arrows and other missiles launched from atop the city walls. Greek fire prevented the ships from landing troops and forced the assailants to change tactics. Since they encountered no resistance from land the knights challenged the massive walls with stone-throwing engines. When the defenders ventured outside the fortifications the cavalry charges were loosed upon them. In mid-July Emperor Alexius III also failed to make good with his promised payments. Finally, he decided to break the line around the city only to be chased back by the superior Latin forces.

With the Seljuk Turks attacking from the east and the Vlachians raiding Bulgaria, Macedonia, and Thracia the emperor was running out of options. In desperation, Alexius decided to take whatever was left of the depleted treasury (one thousand pounds of gold and precious gems) and abdicate his responsibility to the city. His brother Isaac II whom he had imprisoned and blinded was re-seated on the throne along with his son Alexius IV.

Unable to deliver the substantial payments he had promised the eager Crusaders, Alexius essentially robbed the provinces he had control over. He still could not meet the demands of his benefactors. They entered the city and set punitive fires in many districts which triggered a mass revolt against the Crusaders and the two emperors. The blind elderly emperor was again thrown into prison. Alexius IV who had reigned a mere six months and eight days was strangled by Alexius Doukas the general whom both the old and young emperors had trusted would save them from the angry crowd and the fury of the Crusaders.

At this dramatic juncture the great imperial capital of one hundred fifty thousand citizens witnessed a civic upheaval. Unfortunately, their thirty thousand soldiers who were dispersed to all provinces of the empire were in no position to repel the powerful western Christian army, which would prove to be more savage than any barbarians. Alexius V was elected by the Constantinopolitans to fight the Latin invaders who asked for five thousand pounds of gold. This was a demand that was impossible to meet.

In their frustration the Crusaders began plundering the outskirts of the capital and on April 9, 1204 (the year 6712 on the Byzantine calendar) they stormed the city. While this was happening the new emperor was sailing away to safety. His bravery was not in question since none of the Greek citizens wanted to join his battle against the invaders. The city was captured while numerous citizens were inside the churches praying to sacred icons for their deliverance from the swords of the Crusaders. Instead of deliverance they experienced an appalling fate at the hands of their co-religious occupiers. The Crusaders were now on a mission to confiscate any valuables they could as "they plundered with impunity and stripped their victims shamelessly, beginning with their carts. Not only did they rob them of their substance but also the articles consecrated to God," wrote the eye-witness historian Niketas. He had reason to lament:

> O, the shameful dashing to earth of the venerable icons and the flinging of the relics of the saints, who had suffered for Christ's sake, into defiled places!...These forerunners of Anti-Christ, chief agents and harbingers of his anticipated ungodly deeds, seized as plunder the precious chalices and patens; some they smashed, taking possession of the ornaments embellishing them, and they set the remaining vessels on their tables to serve as bread dishes and wine goblets.[6]

Mules were led inside St. Sophia Cathedral where their excrement would soil the polished marble floors, while they removed the gold, silver, and precious stones from the altars. In addition, to considering that it was their legitimate right to plunder the city. The invaders were also seeking revenge and retribution for the prior massacre and destruction carried out by the Greeks on the Latin colony of Galata.

A large portion of Constantinople was set on fire. In the stormy winds it literally became a city of light as the flames illuminated the acts of plunder and rape as they were being committed in apocalyptic proportions by the Catholic Crusaders.

Only a few survivors were able to escape to Greece. The Saint Sophia cathedral was further stripped of its sacred objects wrought in silver and gold, and even the frames of paintings, and the moldings on the walls were removed. The four large bronze horses that had beautified the hippodrome since the time of Constantine were confiscated and transported to Venice to adorn Saint Mark's Basilica.

The last Byzantine Emperor Alexius V who reigned two months and sixteen days during the siege of Constantinople escaped and sought shelter with his father-in-law Alexius III. The latter eliminated his competition for the throne by blinding him. Totally helpless, Alexius V was captured by the Crusaders during a raid in Thracia and brought back to Constantinople to stand trial for imprisoning and killing Alexius IV. His death sentence was carried out to satisfy the mob. He was thrown from the top of a high column in the Forum of the Bull. His body crashed on the stone pavement ending the life of the only Byzantine emperor who had dared to fight the Crusaders. Constantinople and Rome were no longer impenetrable centers of civilization. Their legendary days of being a superpower were now a faded memory.

✠

The sacking of Constantinople marked the beginning of the end of the Byzantine Empire. A new Latin Empire would be created on the two mini-peninsulas of the Straits of the Bosporus which were ruled first by Baldwin of Flanders, and subsequently (over the next six decades) by five other western emperors. The rest of the land was partitioned into small states under the aegis of the most prominent knights and Venetians. The same thing was done in Western Europe.

Almost overnight there appeared the Despotate of Epirus and the subsidiary empires of Nicaea and Trebizond which also followed the Byzantine traditions. The kingdoms of Cyprus and Thessalonica, the Principality of Achaea along with other small provinces were organized under both Latin and Greek rulers. The Venetians controlled roughly one-third of the former empire's islands. The Seljuks occupied part of Anatolia now referred to as the Sultanate of Rum (Sultanate of Romans *sic*).

Beginning in 1220 this area came to be known by westerners as Turchia (the modern English pronunciation is Turkey). Yet, Nicaea remained strong enough to keep the Turks at bay and so ensured Greek supremacy along the eastern shores of the Aegean and Black seas. Personal quarrels and feudal tensions between the Greek and Latin rulers eventually escalated into new disasters as the power of the empire continued to wane.

The old divisions within the Balkan region were further undermined by the increased strength of the Vlachs who were helped by their co-nationalist Wallachians from north of the Danube River, and by the opportunistic Cuman cavalrymen. Their leader Ioannitsa, a king of Moesian Vlachia was called by the self-exiled Byzantines of Thracia to defend them against the Latin army. It was commanded by Emperor Baldwin I with the assistance of Count Louis I of Blois and Doge Enrico Dandolo. The battle took place near Adrianople on April 14, 1205.

The Crusaders were so badly defeated by the Vlachs that the emperor was taken prisoner (and later executed). The count was killed in action and the old blind doge died of exhaustion while making his escape. Ioannitsa crushed another Latin army at Serres (Syar) and also successfully stormed Philippopolis (Plovdiv). Proclaiming himself Emperor of the Vallachian lands Kaloyan (meaning Ioannitsa the Handsome) occupied much of the territory of the Latin Empire in Thrace, Macedonia, and "Thessaly which now are called Great Vlachia and ruled over the inhabitants there"[7] (the Vlachs).

Yet, another barbarian power came to the forefront when a Mongolian ruler changed his name from Temuchin to Genghis Khan (r. 1189-1227). The title meaning the Universal Ruler reflected the fact that he had conquered vast territories in central Asia. He laid waste to Persia, and thus spared the Byzantines from further devastation at the hands of another mortal enemy. After his death the Blue Horde of Batu Khan descended into Eastern Europe. There they raided Russia and Poland, occupied Bulgaria, and after almost entirely eliminating the Hungarians concluded their mission with an attack on Vienna. After pillaging the rest of the Balkan states, a splinter group of the Golden Horde ended up in Anatolia when in 1243 they crushed the Seljuks of Rum. Thus, the Mongols had unwittingly annihilated the primary enemies of Constantinople, and had ensured the Byzantine Empire's survival for the next two hundred years.

This enfeebled the Latin Empire which was reduced to patches of land surrounding Constantinople, and they continued to fight off numerous assaults from their former Balkan vassals which now were its dangerous neighbors. Taking advantage of the fact that the Latin troops were away on a mission of conquest, a Greek army entered the city in July 1261 almost unopposed, and forced Emperor Baldwin II into exile. In desperate need of money he had stripped even the lead roofing from his palace. The Venetian borough was once again plundered, and mostly reduced to ashes in an effort to confirm that the period of Latin domination was over.

The royal scepter then passed to Michael VIII (r. 1259-1282) who was able to retrieve a few glowing embers of the Byzantine Empire from what remained around Constantinople. He quickly restored Orthodoxy and the Greek language as official state institutions. His coat of arms featuring the double-headed eagle became the symbol of his bicentennial Paleologus dynasty.

For the remainder of his reign he was unsuccessful in his attempt to reconcile with Catholicism, and so keeping Rome aligned with him and against the Ottomans. Given that the last crusade had failed in Asia Minor in 1272 he concluded that any further help was not likely to be forthcoming from the West. For the most part, Michael was preoccupied with fighting the Greek states that refused to submit to the restored Byzantine Empire. He also recaptured lands south of the Balkan Mountains and throughout Greece.

His son Andronikos II (r. 1282-1328) understood the importance of the Orthodox Church, and also of taxation. He fully exploited the former but failed at the latter because his empire had become almost totally impoverished by wars and unsustainable economic pressures. He was desperate to pay his mercenary army so he disbanded the Byzantine fleet in 1284.

This proved to be a blunder of incredible proportions. One from which the empire would never recover. For all practical purposes it made Constantinople dependent on a foreign navy (mainly the Genoese and Venetian fleets) as far as it being able to receive supplies by water. It also made it unable to defend its two shores from maritime attacks. The only option was that non-Greek war ships would come to the rescue.

Many of Constantinople's beloved art treasures were pawned or sold in the West to pay its bloated and inept bureaucracy, and subsidize its pitifully weak mercenary army. The official coinage of the empire was the *hyperpyra*. Once in great demand it was now being minted with only 50 percent gold. To make matters worse a royal feud developed between Andronici II and III, which degenerated into a bloody civil war, one that divided the already shrunken empire. Eventually, Andronicus III (r. 1328-1341) replaced his grandfather. The latter was renamed Antony and died as a monk.

The young Andronicus took the recklessness and lavishness of the imperial lifestyle to new heights. His reduced and impoverished empire had hardly survived the recent onslaughts, and was in no position to repel the destructive advances of the invading Slavs and Turks. He tried to make a career for himself as a warrior but "pleasure rather than power was his aim; and maintaining a thousand hounds, a thousand hawks, and a thousand huntsmen was sufficient to sully his fame and disarm his ambition." As he put it, "my grandsire will leave me nothing to lose."[8] The empire was clearly in a state of free fall and its emperors seemed to be enjoying the ride.

✠

Thus far in the history of the empire the Turks of Anatolia who lived in isolated emirates (states) had been kept in check by western mercenary armies hired by the Byzantines. But, in 1300 the warlord of one tribe named Osman I (r. 1299-1326) decided to take advantage of the diminished Byzantine military presence in Asia Minor and form his own kingdom. His timing was perfect as countless numbers of Turks pulverized by the Golden Horde were in search of a safe place to live, and a ruler to lead them.

His warriors quickly defeated the Byzantines at Nicea in 1301 and after conquering Ephesus (today's Izmir) and Brusa (renamed Bursa) they became familiar with tactics for besieging fortified cities. In the course of a royal feud between the two Andronici's the Turks were invited to end the civil war. This gave them an opportunity to see firsthand how weak and vulnerable the Byzantine Empire was.

By the time of his death Osman occupied much of Anatolia which now stood for the new Ottoman (a Western mispronunciation of Osman) Empire. His son Orhan I (r. 1326-1362) inherited it with its capital in Bursa.[9] The Ottomans called Constantinople by its Turkish name Kostantiniyye and called their sultan, son of Gazi, the "Warrior of Allah."

Many Anatolian Byzantines had taken refuge across the Bosporus in the Balkans so it was only a short time before Orhan would conquer Nicea (Iznik) and Nicomedia (Izmit). This most capable leader is credited with the formation of the Janissary (a word derived from *Yeni Tscheri*, meaning "new soldiers"). From this point on it became the personal army of every sultan. It was a sort of Praetorian Guard formed of the enlisted boys kidnapped from conquered tribes and nations. In the absence of their parents or country they became fanatically loyal to their sultan. Ironically, this elite corps was formed from non-Turkish fighters and most of them were born Christian.

Orhan's wisdom combined with his military force allowed him to considerably extend his realm. Many Turkish areas readily joined this growing Islamic Empire. Byzantine military campaigns succeeded in retaining some control over Asia Minor thereby preventing the Turks from surrounding the Sea of Marmara. However, the Ottomans were a menace that could not be ignored particularly since they were united by both the Islamic religion and capable leadership.[10]

Still, the primary threat to the Byzantine Empire was to be found within it. In 1320 it encompassed only 9 percent of the land and 12 percent of the population that it formerly had in the year 457. Its army was now only seven thousand strong, a mere symbol for ceremonial duties. Western mercenaries who were hired to battle the Turks often plundered the Balkan lands because the Byzantine emperors were not able to pay them.

A case in point was the Catalans who took over the Gallipoli Peninsula and after occupying Athens in 1311 established their own Duchy of Athens and Thebes. Given that they were short of manpower they often relied on the Turks to help them plunder the remainder of Greece. It was under these sad circumstances that the Byzantines lost Anatolia in 1331. The Ottomans arrayed themselves on the east side of the Straits of the Bosporus. They were to gaze greedily at the magnificent city across the waters.

The Turks who were related to the Huns and Mongols (and by now were Muslims) did not have a legitimate claim to any of the Byzantine lands, and they were treated accordingly by the Europeans. However, since they had already settled in Anatolia the former home of the Thracians they also felt entitled to cross into the Balkan Peninsula as migrants. If they were not allowed to do so just like the ancient Thracians they would conquer it. This was a predictable and inescapable fact of history.

The civil war during the years 1341-1347 between the contenders to the Byzantine throne brought even more mercenaries to restore order inside the empire. Hence, the first Ottoman soldiers entered the Balkans by invitation. They helped Emperor John VI (r. 1347-1354) to gain power. The grateful emperor then married his daughter Theodora to Orhan and recognized him as the only Turkish ruler.

By 1355 the Turks were allowed to visit Constantinople where they defiantly and openly displayed their ethnicity on the streets. They were most probably also allowed to build the first mosque in the city. Their presence caused Czar Stephen Dusan (r. 1331-1355) to suspend his plans to attack Constantinople. He nevertheless took advantage of the civil war that was raging there and extended his Serbian Empire into Macedonia, Epirus, and Thessaly (Thessaloniki having been exempted). Thus, he created his own empire, one of the largest in Europe and one that seemed to be reflective of his massive frame (he was seven feet tall) and he had a great zest for power.

Unfortunately for the Byzantines, accepting military help from the Ottomans inevitably led to the Turkish settlement of the Gallipoli Peninsula. In 1354 Orhan's son Suleyman Pasha occupied the city of Callipolis after an earthquake crumbled its defensive walls. This was the first Turkish conquest in the Balkans and it served as their bridgehead into mainland Europe. Eventually, they were forced out (in 1366) but by this point the Ottomans already occupied Adrianople as well as part of Bulgaria and much of Greece. Their planted horsetail flags sent an unmistakable message that the Turks were there to stay, and that they intended to expand.

Their victory on the Maritza River (1371) and their capture of Niss and Sofia caused the Serbians to have to pay a yearly tribute. Czar Alexander of Bulgaria avoided this by committing his sister to the sultan's harem.

The Turkish presence in the Balkans had three crucial historic developments: the outbreak of the Black Death, the creation of weapons ignited by gun powder, and the Ottoman expansion north and west of the Danube River. The latter triggered opposition from the free Balkan nations and the Byzantines remained neutral. In 1389 in Kosovo, the combined armies of Albanians, Bosnians, and Serbians received assistance from the semi-Roman population of Wallachia and from the Magyars of Hungary, who, like their kinsmen the Ottoman Turks, had won by force a settlement in

Europe. However, unlike the Turks, adopted the creed and the civilization of European Christendom and became for ages its chivalrous defenders. Sclavonic Poland also sent aid to her sister Sclavonic kingdom of the South...The great kingdoms of western Christendom heard with indifference the sufferings and the perils, to which its eastern portions were exposed by the new Mahomedan power.[11]

In the end it was a military coalition of twelve thousand men from Eastern Europe who valiantly fought the powerful army of twenty-seven thousand of Sultan Murat I (r. 1362-1389). He scored a major victory against Christian forces. During this conflict a Serbian nobleman who was taken prisoner and pretended to beg for his life jumped up from kneeling and stabbed the benevolent sultan to death.

The heroics did not save King Lazar of Serbia who was a prisoner of war from execution. All three of them died in the same tent. The son of the sultan, Bayezid I, instantly became the new ruler of the Ottomans and in a pre-emptive action executed his other brother who had also fought at Kosovo. The province was now renamed the Field of Blackbirds.

When Serbia succumbed to these Ottoman onslaughts the new Despot Lazarevich gifted his sister the daughter of Lazar to the new sultan. Like any other minor rulers who continue to hold onto power he pledged unconditional loyalty to the Porte, and truly honored his commitment. He was first tested during the Ottoman invasion of Wallachia when Lazarevich's army of eight thousand supplemented the Ottoman expeditionary force of forty thousand, ended defeated by a Christian coalition led by Mircea the Elder at Rovine in 1395. It had severely crippled Bayezid's army.

Despite his dubious success in engagements north of the Danube, Sultan Bayezid (r. 1389-1402) settled territorial matters with Bosnia to his advantage and took control of Greece. In his view, the Byzantine Empire was identical to the City of Constantinople where he established a Turkish merchants' quarter.

Since Bayezid was threatened by the many royal intrigues and clandestine contacts which Emperor Manuel II maintained with western powers the ambitious sultan conducted the longest ever siege of Constantinople from 1394 to 1401. He began by building the fortress of Anadolu Hisar on the Asiatic side of the Bosporus. This Turkish military base across the narrow passageway from their city frightened the Constantinopolitans into requesting a new crusade from the Christian world.

Their cry for help and the threat of ongoing Ottoman expansion convinced the rest of Europe to respond. Western contingents of British, French, and Germans lined up with Bulgars, Hungarians, Poles and Wallachians to form an international contingent some fifteen thousand strong. They faced slightly more numerous Turkish and Serbian armies which had proved victorious in 1396 at Nicopolis on the southern bank of the Danube River.

This military confrontation ended with the unnecessary and tragic death or capture of the overconfident French and German knights. Most of the captives were massacred in front of the sultan while he drank wine. A few were kept alive to be paraded throughout the streets of the empire, and released for substantial ransoms.

This was a lesson to the rest of the world not to challenge Bayezid whose epithet was "Thunderbolt." The only positive outcome of this conflict was that Bayezid was forced to remove his army from Constantinople. Once again the great city was temporarily saved because an Ottoman war was taking place elsewhere. However, the siege of Constantinople later resumed and the arrogant Bayezid demanded that a mosque be built there, and that he receive an annual tribute of ten thousand gold ducats. Additionally, he decreed that the imperial crown had to be surrendered to him or all of its citizens would be put to death when the city was conquered.

Emperor Manuel refused these demands and was forced to leave the city and look for help from as far away as England. The sultan was now in control of the Balkans, and he moved the Turkish capital to Adrianople after renamed it Edirne. For all practical purposes Constantinople had been cut off by the Turks from the rest of the Balkan Peninsula. Predictably, its days were numbered.

However, in 1400 it once again escaped a brutal fate because of a distant happening. In remote Central Asia the formidable Timur Lenk (r. 1370-1405) also known as the "Earth Shaker" drew on the remnants of the Golden Horde, and the discontented Turkish tribes who had been subjugated by the Ottomans, to build a military machine that was unsurpassable. Under his invincible leadership the battle-hardened hordes clashed with the Ottoman army on July 20, 1402.

Bayezid I was captured at Angora (Ankara), and his empire was almost destroyed. The once haughty and merciless "Thunderbolt sultan" was carried inside a cage, and forced to kneel in front of his captor. Having been given a taste of his own medicine he would die of a broken heart.

This ironic twist of history ensured the survival of the Lilliputian Byzantine Empire which was now reduced for the next half century to only a shadow of what it was. In 1261, when Michael VIII (r.1259-1282) was reinstated as the emperor in Constantinople was the Byzantine Empire re-established to its former glory. Nevertheless, Constantinople remained unconquered and the undisputable capital of Orthodoxy.

The able and diplomatically gifted Manuel II (r. 1391-1425), who in his younger years had spent time as a hostage at the court of Bayezid I, became involved in the civil war among the sultan's sons. This consumed all of the military energy of the Ottoman Empire which had descended into a state of chaos.

Because of this inner turmoil, Constantinople was safe and the Byzantine Empire seemed to have regained its power and prestige especially after the advantageous treaty of Gallipoli in 1403. There, Suleiman (the oldest son of Bayezid) agreed to return Thessaloniki and many other Greek possessions to the Byzantine Empire. He cancelled the tribute which since 1379 had accumulated to 345,000 ducats to be paid in a lump sum by Constantinople to the Turks.

This was a huge accomplishment for the Byzantines but an outrage for the other sons of Bayezid. They now engaged in fratricidal wars over the right to rule the divided Ottoman Empire.

Once again Manuel rose to the occasion by disciplining the ambitious Musa who tried to pull a rank on him. The emperor endorsed his brother Mehmed who defeated Issa the brother who united with the fourth Suleiman, and invaded Anatolia. Musa killed Suleiman who had offered in vain all the Turkish provinces in the Balkans in exchange for the emperor's support. Musa then tried to besiege Constantinople but was killed by his own Janissaries.

The cautious runner-up Mehmed blinded another brother who was not even a contender to the throne. Manuel wisely endorsed Mehmed considering him to be a more reliable peacemaker than the others. The new sultan called Manuel his "father and overlord," and by ratifying the treaty of Gallipoli provided an enormous reversal of power over the early years when Manuel had been the vassal of Bayezid I.

Mehmed I (1413-1421) carried out successful campaigns in Asia Minor and re-united the Ottoman Empire by using his strength and clear thinking. Because of his integrity, his willingness to forgive, his love of the arts and his good taste in architecture he was given the epithet "The Gentleman." Before he died at the age of forty-seven he entrusted his two young sons to Emperor Manuel. He was aware that the third older one Murad would kill them to secure his throne.

However, another royal pretender Mustafa (or possibly an impersonator) who went missing in action in the Battle of Angora appeared out of nowhere to make a bid for the royal title. He was a strong contender who bitterly fought to claim his rights in the Balkans. He was defeated by Murad and executed by his own troops because of their doubts about his royal credentials.

In spite of Manuel's wish Murad II (r. 1404-1444) and (r. 1446-1451) ascended to the throne and quickly sought revenge by besieging

Constantinople. Once more Manuel attempted to create a distraction by helping another Mustafa (Murad's teenager brother) to become a sultan. The Turkish army subsequently suspended its siege of Constantinople to go to Bursa where they defeated the newly installed thirteen year old ruler. He was captured and a group of officers hung him.

Suddenly, the emperor was faced with a serious political problem. Sultan Murad forced a new treaty on Manuel and required him to pay a new annual tribute of one hundred thousand *hyperpyra* of 4.45 grams of gold per coin. These replaced the traditional but devaluated *solidus,* which was the standard gold coinage for seven centuries.

Health problems forced the physically disabled Manuel II to relinquish most of his official duties to his son John who immediately seized the throne. Strapped for financial resources the father and son sold Thessaloniki (the second city of the empire) to Venice. History revealed this to have been a very shrewd deal since it was conquered by Murad in 1430.

John VIII (r. 1425-1448) followed in his father's diplomatic footsteps when he visited Pope Eugene IV and tried to create an anti-Ottoman coalition. He succeeded in having the union of the Orthodox and Catholic churches ratified in 1439. A master of public relations he traveled to Florence with an entourage of seven hundred to demonstrate his imperial power. The priesthood of Constantinople resented this union, and it proved to be a decision that later would cost the stubborn Byzantines their empire.

On the brighter side, the Western diplomatic bluff worked on Murad who maintained his distance from Constantinople and diligently extended his rule into Serbia. He then turned his attention to the unruly Balkans in an effort to settle his territorial claims north of the Danube River. After Murad II's army failed to conquer Belgrade it invaded Transylvania in 1442 where it again failed to conquer the fortress of Sibiu (Hermannstadt).

The city was saved in time by John Hunyadi who had already

won against the Ottomans in Serbia. The Transylvanian Christian general continued his string of victories at Niss and Serdica (Sofia), in an attempt to reverse the Turkish ambition to dominate Albania, Bosnia, Bulgaria, Herzegovina, Serbia and Wallachia. The latter two countries served as the negotiating point for a ten year peace deal that ensured their independence from Ottoman vassalage.

The sultan's defeat in the Battle of Jalowaz left him with a diminished and exhausted army unwilling to face the "White Knight" as Hunyadi was referred to in recognition of for his glorious victories. Murad II decided to abdicate. Next in line for the throne and the sword of Islam was his twelve year old son Mehmed II. He was born in Edirne of a Christian mother from Hum/Hercegovina.

As it turned out the youngster who was catapulted into this most important position was not up to the imperial task, so Murad remained in power. He scored a brilliant victory in Varna in 1444 against a Christian coalition of Albanians, Hungarians, Germans, Poles, Serbs, and Wallachians. These stormy events resulted in a second crushing Ottoman victory at Kosovo in 1448 against the power-hungry Hungarians.

Three years later Murad II died in Edirne. Mehmed II and now a teenager was ready to succeed him. He demonstrated a limitless determination to be the next Alexander the Great and Caesar. He was to score victory upon victory on all the battlefields, and to raise the empire to its zenith.

✣

By 1450 the Byzantine Empire had lost so much land and revenue that it's economic and military power were only nominal. Constantinople seemed to be sustained by Orthodoxy which ruled the spiritual life of most of the Balkan nations and Eastern Europe. What really kept the great metropolis in one piece was its impregnable Theodosian Wall. It had been repaired in 1434 and was one of the defensive land lines that protected the triangular shaped peninsular city. It successfully held off sieges carried out by Arabs, Avars, Bulgars, Persians, Russians, Turks and others over the course of approximately one thousand years.

Up to this point in the history of the empire only internal treachery and turmoil could cause its gates to open and allow the enemy inside. Its massive towering walls were otherwise able to withstand just about any punishment conceived by any aggressor. Now, the past era was gone.

Militaries had new methods for gaining victory. The walls were rammed or attacked from mobile towers with stones and incendiary devices catapulted over them. The only way to get inside was by tunneling under the walls. These old fashioned methods would be replaced by the demolishing power of the cannon. Thus far it had been of marginal use in battle, but it was destined to markedly change the way wars were conducted.

✣

Certainly Mehmed II studied and understood the value of artillery and portable firearms as these had been successfully used in the battles at Varna and Kosovo. Since he was determined to conquer Constantinople the sultan decided to create a large military base for supplies and for shelter for his troops. One already existed on the Anatolian shore, the former Anadolu Hisar (Anatolian Castle) had been converted into the fort of Guzelce Hisar.

In 1452 Mehmed built a sister fortress Rumeli Hisar (Roman Fortress). Constructed over a period of only four months on the European shore it was instantly termed "the Throat Cutter." It had cannons on its fortified walls which were capable of destroying any enemy ship or contingent of troops incoming between the 660 meter (less than a half mile) wide shores of the Bosporus. This unmistakable military action indicated the sultan's intensions to besiege Constantinople.

Emperor Constantine XI (r.1449-1453) in turn planned every conceivable political maneuver to save the city and prevent the empire from its final collapse. He proclaimed the days of the Antichrist had arrived. He issued a plea for military help to all whom he believed would positively respond, from Pope Nicholas to Hunyadi, Alfonso of Aragon, the Venetians, the Genoese, and the people of Dubrovnik. However, the kingdoms of western Christendom did not respond to his desperate pleas even though their eastern borders were dangerously exposed to the near encroaching Ottoman power.

To westerners the problem was a strategic and economic one. The Throat Cutter was blocking the entrance to the Bosporus so they all depended on the sultan's permission to move their ships and cargo from the Mediterranean into the Black Sea. At one point when a Venetian ship defied warnings to stop it was sunk by a volley of cannon fire from the new fortress. Its crew was impaled as a lesson to future trespassers. Given these ominous signs seven Cretan and Venetian ships carrying hundreds of would be defenders from the Latin districts of the city departed from Constantinople.

Yet, another problem developed when Constantine tried to reconcile the differences between his own Orthodox Church and the Church of Rome as part of an attempt to attract the help of the Catholic world. As expected the effort intended to save the once glorious city:

> …alienated his own subjects from him, and the bigoted priests of Byzantium, when called on by the Emperor to contribute their treasures and to arm in the defense of their national independence, replied by reviling him as a heretic. The lay leader of the Orthodox Greeks, the Grand Duke Notaras, openly avowed that he would rather see the turban of the sultan than the tiara of the pope in Constantinople. Only six thousand Greeks, out of a population of one hundred thousand, took any part in the defense of the city; and the Emperor was obliged to leave even these under the command of the factious Nataras, whose ecclesiastical zeal showed itself in violent dissensions instead of cordial military co-operation with the chiefs of the Latin auxiliaries.[12]

Sadly, the emperor could not even count on his own people to defend their city. In fact he could not rely on his own brothers who were both despots of Morea (Peloponnese Peninsula of the Greek heartland). They fought bitterly against each other until they both became Ottoman vassals. In desperation Constantine tried to duplicate the diplomatic tactics of his father Manuel. He blackmailed Mehmed with another contender for the throne, the Prince Orhan, who now resided in Constantinople. His impudence backfired and this uncalled for action was met with outrage from Vizier Halil who was a top adviser to Mehmed:

> You stupid Greeks, I have had enough of your devious ways. The last sultan was a lenient and conscientious friend to you. The present sultan is not of the same mind...You are fools to think you can frighten us with your fantasies... If you want to proclaim Orhan as sultan in Thrace go ahead. If you want to bring the Hungarians across the Danube, let them come... All that you will achieve is to lose what little you still have.[13]

The lenient sultan mentioned here was Murad II. He had approved Constantine's coronation in 1449, and when he died he was still on friendly terms with the emperor. His son Mehmed II (r.1444-1446) and (1451-1481) was of a different mind. He had the Throat Cutter Byzantines from a nearby village massacred when they opposed his soldiers' acts of pillage.

Constantine sent an imperial envoy to Mehmed with a message. He announced that if the sultan continued to bring in troops and demonstrate hostility toward the empire he would have to close the gates of Constantinople. Mehmed executed the envoy and sent back a brief but non-negotiable message, "Either surrender the city or stand ready to do battle."[14] Both rulers stood their ground and were now committed to a war. At this point in time, many of the 350,000 inhabitants unwilling to risk dying began to evacuate Constantinople looking for safety in other lands.

✟

As previously mentioned for Mehmed II the key to military success was the cannon that was not produced by the Turks. Luckily, the best cannon maker was Orban a Wallachian expert from the city of Brasov who specialized in smelting and casting cannons of different sizes. His opportunism caused him to sell his expertise to the highest bidder, the Turks. His sample cannons were built at the foundry in Edirne. They easily passed the firing tests and were immediately transported to Constantinople 225 kilometers/140 miles away.

The sultan was pleased and ordered the largest bronze cannon ever to be built. It measured twenty-seven feet long and had a barrel diameter of thirty inches. It was capable of firing a half-ton stone projectile over more than a mile. This royal gun was respectfully named "Basilica", and being pulled by sixty oxen it arrived on the perimeter of Constantinople within six weeks. Its maker, who was not even a field artillerist, arrived there as well. Many other smaller super cannons produced at Orban's foundry were also brought there.

Some seventy of them were divided into fifteen batteries of different calibers. They were able to shoot stone projectiles weighing 200-400 kilograms/400-800 hundred pounds. Most were positioned to face the Saint Romanus Gate which was located in the middle of the city wall. The Basilica was placed in front of the royal tent guarded by Janissaries so it could be seen by the sultan and everyone else. Each cannon was dug in and protected by a parapet with a shelter for the artillerists and munitions. This was the first occasion in recorded warfare in which entrenched artillery contributed to a siege.

While Mehmed prepared meticulously for the war that would change the history of Europe the remaining 50,000 Constantinopolitans continued to believe that some heavenly power would eliminate their immediate danger. Indeed, they hated their pro-western emperor believing he was pro Catholic, who in reality was doing everything possible trying to save them. The fighting spirit that had created their empire had vanished by now as had the time when:

> ...the primitive Romans would have drawn their swords in the resolution of death or conquest. The primitive Christians might have embraced each other and awaited in patience and charity the stroke of martyrdom. However, the Greeks of Constantinople were animated only by the spirit of religion and that spirit was productive only of animosity and discord.[15]

It was under these circumstances that Mehmed arrived near Constantinople on April 6, 1453. There, he inspected his 80,000 troops and assessed their positions for attacking the twelve miles of Constantinople's walls. The walls were defended by only eight thousand soldiers under the command of Emperor Constantine XI making the fighting ratio 10 to 1.

A heavy iron chain lay across the entrance to the Golden Horn which harbored twenty-six ships which prevented a Turkish naval attack along the northeast wall. Some one hundred fifty small Turkish war galleys built at the shipyards of Gallipoli arrived on April 12 to oppose the much larger ships sailing under Byzantine, Genoese and Venetian flags. This was also the day when the cannons opened fire on the 6.5 kilometer/4 mile Theodosian Wall that protected the city.

✝

For six days a non-stop assault consisting of 70 cannons firing each seven minutes along with the traditional catapults pummeled the area of the Saint Romanus Gate. Then the wall and towers began to crumble. The damage that was incurred during the day was repaired at night with surprising efficiency by the city's defenders. The Basilica delivered a fifteen hundred pound deafening shot seven times a day producing the anticipated damage to the wall while terrifying the city's population.

But, with each volley the newly forming cracks in the super cannon's cast multiplied and became enlarged. Too much loaded gun powder caused the explosions inside the bronze barrel to exceed the metal's power of resistance. Orban kept bracing the damaged barrel with iron hoops before each shot, and he asked for permission to recast it before it split open.

The furious Mehmed denied his request, and the inevitable happened. On April 15th the eighteen ton gun fired and the barrel exploded killing everyone in its proximity including its maker, Orban (so legend has it).

☩

By now hundreds of cannon shots were fired each day at the same spot on the wall until the breach was so large that the nightly repairs could not handle the patching. On April 18th Mehmed ordered an all out assault on the city. It was bravely carried out by his troops, but equally brave defenders repelled the attack for over four hours. The defenders used their artillery, handguns, Greek fire (a kind of flame throwing device), rains of arrows, spears, stones, hot water or oil, and even the dead bodies of enemies to halt the attackers climbing the ladders under their shields.

When the intruders made it as far as the parapets hand-to-hand combat with swords and daggers, axes and maces, or even deadly wrestling matches took place. The defenders who were continually reinforced by the reserve detachment of one thousand men clearly had the advantage. The Latin auxiliaries formed from small groups of Aragonese, Catalans, and Genoese soldiers sent by friendly cities proved to be excellent fighters. In fact, their leader John Giustiniani was appointed by the emperor to be the commander-in-chief of the defense.

In the meantime, wave after wave of Janissaries climbed the ladders under the rain of boulders, thrown lances, arrows and hot water wounding or killing the brave Turks who fell 50 feet to the ground. Yet, each wave was inching its way to the top of the crumbling walls. The defenders claimed to have killed eighteen thousand enemy besiegers, and the Turkish survivors retreated in good order.

The attackers were wounded and along with the dead fell off the ladders and lay in piles at the base of the walls. They were covered by broken ladders and weapons, and blood and debris from the wall. To their brave merit the Turkish medics were being wounded and killed while trying to carry their wounded and dead to safety. Not one disabled fighter was left behind, unattended, or to rot. Mehmed's army took heavy loses each day but the massive walls began to fall apart.

The Christians also lost many men while repelling the enemies off the walls. Unfortunately, there were no reserves to fill the ranks of the missing defenders. Worse yet, each day the supplies of food, weapons, ammunition and other necessities ran lower and lower. Still, the fighting spirit was high and their trust in victory was intact in spite of the vast superiority of the Turkish attackers. As usual, after each fight the Constantinopolitans headed to the churches to thank God for their victory.

God seemed to be pleased because four Genoese and one Greek transport ship fought their way into the city's harbor, thereby renewing the hope of the ammunition deprived and under nourished defenders. To his dismay, Mehmed witnessed how the slow moving Christian sailing ships crashed into and sank each of the fast Turkish vessels that tried to halt them. The sultan who stood on the shore, and then rode his horse into the waves shouting orders could not believe how badly his fleet (which was powered by rowers) had performed.

Along the city's walls the cheerful Constantinopolitans saw the five tall ships majestically cruising over the lowered chain into the safety of the Golden Horn. The unlucky Turkish admiral faced punishment by impalement, but instead he received one hundred lashes delivered by Mehmed himself using his cudgel.

In spite of all of these salutary efforts a military rescue from outside remained an illusory hope, and one that would never materialize for the besieged Constantinople. The Venetians alone were willing to send a fleet to join the fight, but first they had to be paid by the pope for the naval help they had provided in 1444 in conjunction with the Varna Crusade. There were also persistent rumors that an Italian and a Hungarian army were on the way to Constantinople.

This led Mehmed to offer peace in exchange for seventy thousand gold ducats. The city's residents also had to convert to Islam. When his proposal was rejected the sultan ordered his sailors to bypass the heavy chain between Galata and Acropolis Point and carry their warships overland into the waters of the Golden Horn. The fleet of seventy small galleys had to be rolled there on wooden logs by the *Christea Turris* (Tower of Christ) of the Genoese fortress that allowed the transport. While inside Constantinople seven hundred Genoese fought under their commander Giustiniani.

This tactical maneuver was executed on Sunday April 22nd when many of the city's defenders were attending mass or enjoying a day of rest. They expected any sort of attack to be on the opposite side of the city where the Turkish cannons had opened a deceptive cannonade. In a single day, each warship was pulled a quarter of a mile on dry land by oxen and oarsmen until it reached the waters behind the chain that secured the city's other shoreline.

This entire water to land and then land to water operation was successfully carried out under the astonished eyes of the city's residents. They were intimidated by a second cannonade that encompassed the entire pharaonic task. The boat movers were urged forward by the roar of drums, shouts of encouragement, and the crack of whips. By nightfall the Turkish navy controlled both shores of the Straits of the Bosporus, and now both the eastern and western sides of Constantinople. The city's 50,000 people were now deprived of a safe harbor, and supplies were prevented from being ferried across from Galata the Genoese citadel. The encirclement of Constantinople was complete and deadly.

✢

The presence of the Turkish fleet in the bay of the Golden Horn forced Constantine to move precious troops and cannons from the Theodosian Wall to a second defensive area. The survival of the city's defenders depended on the elimination of this new front. During the night of April 28th Genoese and Venetian tall ships, followed by smaller and faster ones armed with the Greek fire, attacked the Turkish ships, all of which measured less than one hundred feet and were powered by oarsmen. Both adversaries had anticipated an easy victory, and both were disappointed.

The battle degenerated into a furious series of cannonades from both sides complicated by handgun and sword attacks among the sailors of the rammed ships. It ended with Byzantine prisoners being impaled by the Turks on the shore. The Turkish prisoners were being butchered along the city walls, all in full view of each other. Regardless of the outcome, the reduced Turkish fleet was still left to cruise the Golden Horn. The red, crescent flags on the Turkish mini fleet waved in dangerous proximity to the city walls.

☩

The first massive artillery duel took place on May 3$^{rd}$, and for the next ten days the Byzantine and Turkish cannons fired at each other across the massive walls and the Golden Horn. Four days later the Romanus Gate having the most damaged walls was attacked by successive waves of Janissaries along with the regular troops. The defenders held on in spite of hunger, lack of sleep and their many losses.

Cannon coverage allowed the Turkish engineers to build a pontoon bridge across the Golden Horn. The mercenary Saxon miners from Serbia dug tunnels under the wall. There was nothing those being besieged could do to fight back.

So far, all seemed to go well for the Byzantine defenders, and their few international allies until the last week of May when there was a partial eclipse of the moon (which left a crescent shape). This was followed by an incident in which the Virgin Mary's icon was dropped during a church service. Also, violent rainstorms pummeled the city and the sky over Hagia Sophia glowed with prolonged lightening bolts. All of these chilling revelations were taken by Constantinopolitans to prepare for their inevitable doom. For the Turks, all signs indicated their coming victory.

Mehmed rejoiced with confidence but was worried about the hot summer days when his camps would be transformed into an infested open sewer. He renewed his offer to the Byzantines that they should surrender in exchange for certain conditions. It would save the city from the three day long ritualistic plunder (something the sultan never wanted to happen). There would be an annual tribute paid of one hundred thousand bezants (gold coins) to conclude the pact. Constantine once again refused this offer. His decision was an agonized one. He was faced with an impossible task but he still believed that some military power from the East or the West would come to rescue the city of Christian Orthodoxy.

As if there was not enough bad news for the emperor, a small Venetian ship made its way into the city harbor and announced that no Venetian fleet was on the way. Peering out from the high wall by night the defenders saw a sea of lights on the horizon and believed that a Hungarian army was approaching to aid them.

In fact, it was the Turks marching toward the city for a final assault on it. Seeking refuge in churches the residents sang chants of *Alleluia* in Latin and *Kyrie Eleison* in Greek, and similar choirs prayed all across the city for salvation. During moments of silence, they were able to hear the roaring sound of the drums from the Turkish camp, and their calls for prayer to Allah. A thousand years of the city's defensive triumph were at stake. Its fate depended only on the condition of its massive walls.

On May 28th Hagia Sophia which could normally accommodate close to 20,000 worshipers was now double packed with nobility, military leaders and devoted Christians listening to the Greek mass.

They were interrupted at midnight by the news of the final Turkish assault on the city. Emperor Constantine who had already received the Holy Sacrament rushed to the breached wall where Giustiniani and his Latin fighters showed their savage tenacity in defense, and bravely held their fighting positions. As was customary on such occasions the bells of the city's churches began to toll unceasingly imploring God for victory, or at least protection.

The successive waves of attack began with the bashi-bazouks (sacrificial troops) and then with Anatolians storming the moat and outer walls. They eventually arrived at the battered much weakened Blachernae Gate that led to the imperial palace. It was through this same gate that the Crusaders had invaded the city in 1204.

Simultaneously, with this assault on the city the Turkish flotilla from the Golden Horn launched an attack on the eastern side. The defenders had to split their forces. Still, so far they proved victorious even against the third wave of Janissaries who assaulted the inner wall.

Unfortunately, the commander of the Genoese contingent the best armed and armored of all the units was mortally wounded. His men carried Giuseppianni to their ships where they lay anchored in the Golden Horn. Their departure left Emperor Constantine and his Greek soldiers alone to battle an increased number of attackers.

Worse yet, the tearful retreat of the Latins conveyed the message of a lost fight and induced a vast wave of panic in the cities population. As had often been the case in similar battles a small gate of Kerkoporta (leading to the royal palace) was found by the Turks to have been left unlocked. They rushed in and planted a few of their red, crescent flags on the wall's crenels. Chaos erupted among the weary defenders and many ran home to defend their families. Those who continued to fight back the Turks saw their Emperor Constantine throwing off his purple mantle to engage in hand to hand combat.

However, victory was a mathematical impossibility for the Byzantines as their numbers were insufficient. The few hundred of their remaining fighters were unable to prevent the Turkish army from entering the eight main gates of the city, or to maintain control of its ninety-six towers.

In no time the city was flooded with Ottoman warriors eager to enrich themselves at its expense. Constantine heroically vanished without a trace in the heat of the street battles. He was forty nine years old. His protégé Prince Orhan dressed as a Greek tried to escape the slaughter only to be recognized. He committed suicide by jumping off the wall. His head was presented to the laughing Mehmed.

As the battle died down the invaders took over Constantinople. The siege had lasted fifty-three days. In its entire history of 2,138 years the "Queen City" had been besieged twenty-eight times, but had been captured only eight times. It had now reached the end of its legendary existence. The Byzantine Empire existed no longer.

✠

The three days of looting promised to the victorious soldiers turned into an orgy of systematical plunder, rape and the massacre of both soldiers and civilians. Even the Turkish sailors joined the pillage inadvertently giving the surviving defenders a rare opportunity to escape by sea. Particularly to the non Greeks who sailed away from the Golden Horn in their ships.

Nevertheless, Mehmed did not wish to rule a ghost city and so he decided at least to save the churches and other valuable landmarks. He could not do anything about the symbol of Orthodoxy the majestic Hagia Sophia which was packed with horrified civilians. Its five inch thick doors were broken open, and the fighters of Allah savagely punished the "enemies of the Faith" also called the "infidels" while the priests were still at the altar chanting their prayers for mercy. Most of the women and children were instantly enslaved and dragged to various collection points for ransom evaluation in the once "God-protected city."

As the streets became streams of blood the religious artifacts were brutally stripped away. Many of them were made of gold and silver and studded with precious gems. What the victors of Allah could not take, they destroyed. In their search for hidden treasure they smashed the tomb of Enrico Dandalo. He was the blind Venetian Dodge who two hundred and fifty years earlier had allowed his Crusaders to similarly desecrate the Hagia Sophia. When they found only his bones the soldiers threw them to the dogs on the streets.

Thus, an act of justice that was long past due took place under images of the wide eyed saints painted on the walls. The entire city became a scene of indescribable horror. Mehmed was aware of his soldiers' barbarism and after two days ordered all looting to stop. He immediately posted armed guards around the churches and other important landmarks of the city. Then he sent his troops back outside the walls of the city which he did not want destroyed. However, some 30,000 inhabitants of Constantinople became instant prisoners to be sold at the slave markets.

When the sultan, a historian and art connoisseur in his own right entered the Holy Wisdom Church (a building that was of a size that no medieval mind could comprehend and whose domed architecture seemed to reach into the sky) he bowed in front of the biblical figures on the walls and prayed from the pulpit.

From the main dome above the Virgin Mary and Baby Jesus were lit by windows as if the angels illumined them with spotlights. They appeared to witness the historic scene in a way that made the twenty one year old monarch shiver under the weight of his responsibility. After 1,123 years and 27 days Hagia Sophia ceased to be a Christian church.

✝

Walking on the dilapidated streets now emptied of their last fifty thousand inhabitants Mehmed reviewed the monumental buildings, statues and other imperial symbols and saw Constantinople as his future capital.

On June 2nd the magnificent cathedral now renamed Aya Sofya Mosque held the first Islamic service. Soon wooden minarets would frame above its huge contours. The sultan never touched the Phanar quarter which was the commercial center of Orthodoxy and Byzantium. It was soon to become "the Mecca" of any and all important dealings within the Ottoman Empire.

It was the powerful marketplace in which everything including future positions of leadership in the Balkan nations was sold to the highest bidder. It produced the famous Phanariotism that dictated the future developments of the Balkan nations which recognized the Ottoman suzerainty from then on.

After more than 1,100 years, the empire that had made and destroyed other empires, countries, kingdoms and nations had been replaced by another. It was one that had nothing to do with the "City of Lights" of the European heritage, but it was strongly anchored in two continents. Finally, Mehmed II the Conqueror had achieved his ultimate dream for the Roman Empire to be now historically and literally at his feet. A commemorative coin was minted with the inscription *Islambol* (full of Islam).[16]

Thus, the momentous year of 1453 marked the beginning of a new Islamic era in the history of Europe. Eight years later, the minuscule but free "Byzantine Empire" which was left in Trebizont, was conquered and occupied by Sultan Mehmed II.

✝

Although the Ottoman Empire was totally unknown three hundred years prior to this conquest, it took fewer than ten sultans for it to become a world power, and to gain control over almost the entire Balkan Peninsula. Along with the Hellenic, Macedonian, Roman, Byzantine civilization, and many Slavic and other layers of paganism all wrapped in the religious influence of Orthodoxy, now a final new layer of Islamic culture was added to the history of Balkanization.

This ancient land persisted by simply accruing new influences as time went on. Not unlike a dying parent who leaves behind both biological and adopted children, the Byzantine Empire left a multi-ethnic family to a foster parent who spoke a different language and prayed to a different god. This new Turkish parent was despised and feared by all Christian nations for its brutality and corruption. Although it was initially perceived as a strong master it would come to be referred to as the "sick man of Europe."

At various levels of influence all this was germinating the seeds of a complicated Balkan life in which only bribery and sheer terror (of men or saints) brought an unwilling respect for a brutal social order. Needless to say, this legacy found fertile ground in Eastern Europe, sowing its seeds into an already competitive and corruptive cultural and historical process. The result was what has come to be known as *Balkanization*.

# REFERENCE NOTES

1. Warren Treadgold, *A Concise History of Byzantium* (New York: Palgrave/St. Martins, 2001), 236.
2. Michael Whitby, *The Emperor Maurice and His Historian: Theophylact Simocatta on Persian and Balkan Warfare* (Oxford: Clarendon Press, 1988), 89.
3. Edward Gibbon, *The Decline and Fall of the Roman Empire* (New York: Modern Library, 2003), 1015.
4. Treadgold, *Concise History*, 236.
5. Anna Comnena, *The Alexiad of Anna Comnena*, trans. E. R. A. Sewter (London: Penguin
6. Books, 1969), 458.
7. Niketas Choniatēs, *O City of Byzantium, Annals of Niketas Choniates*, trans. Harry J. Magoulias (Detroit: Wayne State University Press, 1984), 314-315.
8. Choniatēs, *O City*, 350.
9. Gibbon, *Decline and Fall*, 1145.
10. The family dynasty of the Osmans continued uninterrupted until 1923 when the Turkish Republic was proclaimed and the entire family expelled. The last sultan's grandson His Imperial Highness Prince Ertugrul Osman immigrated to the United States where he lived in New York City until September 23, 2009. He died there at the age of 97 leaving no survivors. Fred A. Bernstein, "Ertugrul Osman, Link to Ottoman Dynasty, Dies at 97," *New York Times*, September 24, 2009, B16.
11. Treadgold, *Concise History*, 236.
12. Edward S. Creasy, *History of the Ottoman Turks* (Beirut: Khayats, 1961), 27.
13. Creasy, *History of Ottoman Turks*, 78.
14. Roger Crowley, *1453: The Holy War for Constantinople and the Clash of Islam and the West* (New York: Hyperion, 2005), 55.

15. Gibbon, *Decline and Fall*, 1205.
16. The new capital Istanbul (pronounced "Istanbolin" by the Greeks and "Stamboul" in English) served as the Turkish capital until 1923 when it was relocated to Ankara in Anatolia. Today, the city in which vestiges of Byzantine and Ottoman history speak for its glorious centuries is one of the main tourist attractions. It is still the epicenter of the process of Balkanization. Most of its houses are built without permits polluting the medieval image of the city. The famous Phanar district has now been overtaken by Anatolian immigrants who have no interest in preserving its past or enhancing its future. The misappropriation of international funds for maintaining the city's unique architectural landmarks (including the famous walls whose cheap repairs crumbled in a 1999 earthquake while the old structure held on) defies the rules of concerned organizations, yet the city remains vibrant. It is reflective of life in both the modern and the old worlds as evidenced by the immense variety of colorful and tasteful goods to be found in its famous Grand Bazaar that was founded in 1461 by Sultan Mehmed II. As for the present day Turks take pride in reviving "Ottomania" which reminds them of the glorious legacy of the Ottoman Empire that ended in 1922 after a long string of lost wars.

# EPILOG

Balkanization began with the fall of the Roman Empire when the barbarian hordes from Eurasia invaded the Balkan Peninsula to plunder and terrorize the prosperous Byzantine Empire. Moreover, these barbarians invited other barbarians to ravage the Balkan Peninsula. They extensively looted and ruined the native population that hosted them. All of the pagan hordes attacked one single target, Constantinople, which paid them tribute to pacify them. Ultimately, the barbarians settled, and demanded from the emperors subsidies in exchange for a peaceful coexistence. Even so, they continued to join other barbarian invaders who attacked the same capital of the empire hoping to pillage it.

Over 2-3 generations the barbarians' birth rate multiplied so rapidly that they made the original inhabitants the minority. They were unable to oppose the superior numbers of the aliens who by now took over the lands and formed their own countries. They lived within the borders of the Byzantine Empire, which had to deal with the barbarian chieftains, when they asked to be elevated to the titles of princes, kings, tsars and even emperors. Moreover, after they became Orthodox Christians they wanted to be a state inside the empire and share all the benefits Constantinople had reserved for the Byzantine citizens.

Many times, the strongest and most numerous barbarians such as the Bulgarians and Serbians occupied so much land that with their population they formed their own empires. These were powerful enough to force the Byzantine emperors to ask for their military help fighting against different attacking barbarians. Often these attacks ended up with the barbarians occupying regions of the Byzantine Empire. This reduced its size, weakened its defense and increased its vulnerability all of which affected having the native population less prosperous, and it increased the low moral of the citizens. The empire without enough money to pay the necessary military force grows weaker and weaker until it collapses under its own inability to survive.

As the wars and revolutions are not won by the brave and courageous soldiers, but by the enemy who destroyed the most and killed the greatest numbers. This fits the definition of the victorious barbarians. The rule of the rise and fall of the empire and their civilization never changed until the invading barbarians with their superior numbers overpowered the Byzantines.

However, after the Sultan Mehmed II conquered Constantinople in the year 1453, the Ottoman domination of the Balkan Peninsula inherited so many distinctive and belligerent ethnic populations, who were forced to live together. It was like a "powder keg" ready to explode at anytime, because they wanted to be independent from Turkish control. They used wars to grab more land now from the Ottoman Empire, like they did with Byzantine Empire.

✣

The passage of time has only intensified the process of balkanization when the great powers of Europe tried to impose their will about how the land should be divided and owned. This reached new peaks before the end of the XIX century with the ethnic territorial disputes between Russia and the Ottoman Empire, ending up with the Crimean War (1853-1856). Why did Great Britain side with the Ottomans instead of the Russians? This was because the British did not want Moscow to dominate the Balkans, which had traditionally been ruled by the

Ottoman Empire, and was in control of the Bosporus Straits. Helping the Turks to win the war, the British would have a free commercial and military access to the Black and Azov seas. However, Russia recovered their lost territories after the Crimean War.

Another conflict arose between Russia and the Ottoman Empire and was renewed in the Russo-Romanian Turkish War of 1877- 1878. This time the Orthodox Russians wanted the Balkan Peninsula free of Islamic control, and eventually for Russia to dominate the Orthodox Balkan nations. A balkanization saga increased when the Ottomans increased taxes and used their irregular troops of "Bashi Bazouks" to crush the Bulgarian revolt. They massacred 30,000 civilians in 1876.

Serbia and Montenegro declared war on the Ottomans before the Russo-Romanian troops crossed the Danube River into Bulgaria to fight the Turks. After many bloody battles, the Ottomans were defeated and were pushed back to the vicinity of Constantinople. The Balkan Peninsula seemed to be under the Christian flags of many Balkan nations, but only Romania, Serbia and Montenegro gained total independence from the Ottoman Empire. The Balkan populations divided into Orthodox and Muslim, and kept being shifted around leaving each nation unhappy. They had each peace treaty being dictated by the great powers of Europe.

However, to prevent the Turkish domination of the Balkan Peninsula, an attack of a military coalition of Bulgaria, Greece, Montenegro and Serbia aimed in 1912 to push the Turks out of the Balkan Peninsula and Europe to eliminate their balkanization. Instead, they aggravated and increased balkanization. The defeated Turks lost more territories plus Albania and Macedonia. Yet, the unhappy Bulgaria which lost territories to Greece and Serbia, one year later in 1913, declared war on those two former allies to regain their lost territories. Defeated, Bulgaria lost even more land.

✢

Those bellicose events reminded of the balkanization during the last leg of the Byzantine Empires existence. It created a geographical and political instability based on the old flames of ethnic and nationalistic revenge in all of the other equally frustrated nations in the entire Balkans. Among others, the Slavic nationalists wanted their Greater Serbia and they did not want to be a province of the Austro Hungarian Empire.

One year later, such a nationalist found himself in front of the open car that turned on a wrong street, and it was carrying the imperial Archduke Franz Ferdinand and his wife who were there to visit Sarajevo. The Bosnian Serb revolutionary fired his pistol, and killed the two royal visitors, igniting the "powder keg" that exploded into World War I (1914-1918).

More than 100 nations including Luxemburg, Monaco, Cuba and Guinea joined the war, and four years later the military coalition of Germany, Austria Hungary, Italy, Bulgaria also joined. The Ottoman Empire was defeated by the Triple entente of Britain, France and only Russia withdrew from the war because of the Bolshevik Revolution.

The word "Balkanization" was coined by the British to describe the difficulty in understanding the perplexing situations of the two Balkan wars. Especially during WWI, after they were defeated by the Turks in The Battle of Gallipoli, which left 300,000 ally casualties including more that 56,000 Brits and allies dead.

The aftermath of WWI when Europe went up in flames left perhaps up to 90 million people dead worldwide. Four lasting empires were dissolved because of the outcome of WWI, namely Austro Hungarians, the British, the Russians and the Ottoman Empire all ceased to exist. If that was not enough, the revolutionary ideas of Marx (who despised the Russians) didn't take root in the western proletarian countries as he had predicted. But it took place in Russia where serfdom prevailed and the people still lived in the Dark Ages.

The balkanization in Russia provided fertile ground for the development of Communist ideals, mainly for the Red poor revolutionaries to plunder and murder the well to do people who were declared to be the "enemies of the working class." The violent and bloody balkanization of the Russian Empire into a Soviet Union ended in 1922 under the red flag of the communist dictatorship. Suddenly the Russians of the Slavic heritage became Soviet people of the new Communist heritage, blaring "Proletarians of the world, unite!"

In the 1930s two more empires immerged, the Communist Empire of the USSR, and the Nationalist Socialist Empire of the Third Reich. Soon both would collide in World War II.

It is little known that Hitler lost his "blitzkrieg" in the East, because of a balkanization reason. He delayed the German invasion of Soviet Russia from May to the end of June in 1941. Hitler was forced to rescue Mussolini's armies that were failing to occupy Albania and Yugoslavia which were being defended by the nationalist partisans. He had to divert precious panzer and infantry divisions to battle the local Tito's insurgents who were well nestled in the mountains, with no chance for the Germans to eliminate them. Thus, Hitler lost two of the most vital months for his armies to conquer Moscow, defeat the Red Empire of Russia, and eliminate Communism from the world.

The same impossible geographic circumstances faced the Soviet and American troops fighting in the mountains of Afghanistan. After 10 years with no final victory the cost of the war in Afghanistan collapsed the Communist Empire. After 20 years of fighting in vain the American troops withdrew leaving behind to their enemies, the Taliban, their entire heavy war equipment and base worth over $7 billion. Balkanization seems to win again and again.

✣

After WWII one of the main effects of Hitler's defeat was that the Soviet Union and its main ally, and the most helpful for them to win the war was the United States of America, only later to become bitter enemies. The former enemies, Germany and Japan became the best allies of America and were ready to fight the Cold War. It could easily be called balkanization regarding how their alliances changed.

The next effect was a peaceful one, when the United States and Western Europe adopted a most liberal attitude to spread a global freedom, equality, compassion and anti-racial doctrine. They wanted to prove how Hitler's ideology was wrong, and why he and the Third Reich needed to be destroyed. Suddenly, the theory of the "melting pot" was adopted among all cohabitant ethnicities and religions. The "global village" myth began that the rich and poor nations would live at the same level of progress and prosperity. It was a noble proclamation with huge predicted misuses when the old reality defied the ambitious politically correct intentions.

✛

After WWII, nothing was the same. Backed up by Soviet bayonets the Marxist doctrine was brought by Stalin to take over societies and their economies throughout the Eastern European nations which became the satellites of Moscow. It required those feudal people who had never experienced the Renaissance, the Age of Enlightenment, or the Industrial Revolution, to build an ideal and equalitarian communist society. Stalin, Tito, and other dictators understood how to exploit the mentality of balkanization that was also used by the Ottomans. Balkanization helped Communist domination there for three generations. Applying the principles of "divide and conquer," followed by that of "subjugate and rule," the communist tyrants forced countless millions of people from various ethnic groups to "relocate" and co-exist with many different ethnicities.

The new political order preached brotherhood, yet there was an ongoing and official policy of genocide. More than five hundred thousand nationalists in the relatively small country of Yugoslavia, and more than twenty million people in the Soviet Union were murdered, and paid the ultimate price for this proletarian experiment.

Broz Tito of Yugoslavia and Georgi Dimitrov of Bulgaria planned to build a Pan Slavic state south of the Danube River. They wanted to separate their nations from other Balkan Slavs they considered to be inferior, but they had a superior Communist status. Stalin discovered the plot at which point Dimitrov died in Moscow, and Tito broke away from the Communist block. It was the same international Communist leader Dimitrov whom Herman Goring failed to accuse for setting the Reichstad (German parliament building in Berlin) in a fire in 1933.

In other words, Communist dictatorship was merely an extension of the balkanization rule that prevailed in the Dark Ages. The brutal political leaders would go to any extent, including conducting inquisition type trials to hold onto absolute power and eliminate any opposition. Regrettably, Orthodoxy continued to preach "the bowed head avoids the striking sword" and prayed in public for the good health and long life of the Communist leaders. This is how it had been done in the past with the Balkan rulers.

In exchange for this, godless political chieftains promoted the zealous clergy to ever higher church positions. An impressive number of priests became informers for the Secret Communist Services to advance their careers. Thus, countless numbers of people who trusted their pastors with confessions ended up in interrogation rooms, and died at the hands of torturers, or in prison. The Communist dictatorship of Eastern Europe essentially exploited the medieval theocracy, and duplicated the terror of the czars of the Middle Ages.

The old meaning of the term "balkanization" resurfaced and was applied draconically in the Soviet occupied nations that were suffering from hunger, practiced bribery, corruption and nepotism and lied in order to survive.

To their credit, the Catholic Czechs, East Germans, Hungarians, and Poles refused to be dominated by the "Orthodoxy" of Moscow and revolted. They would not allow themselves to be swallowed up politically by these Eastern illiterate leaders who used terror to stay in power. They revolted against Communism. Ironically, it was the effect of balkanization that proved to have a boomerang effect when the Soviet tanks crushed all the anti-communist revolts, except for the victorious Polish solidarity movement.

Yet, history works its doings without taking orders from Moscow, and in the late 1980s and beginning of the 1990s each communist dictator was toppled from power, and the Communist Empire vanished forever.

✙

However, the free nations established a form of democracy to which they could not relate. They could not relate because they copied Americanism in the wrong way, balkanization style. While contact with Western culture created euphoria at all levels, instinctively the Balkan people clung more than ever to their heritage, and to their native habits which had helped them survive the constant turmoil that marked their convoluted history.

Indeed, in the Balkans the loss of one's ethnic identity is considered worse than dying, and clan dominance over a territory is still the main force that unites ethnic groups. This is the main root of the balkanization process. The term actually means the continual division, and re-division of a land and its homogenous individuals, where the people keep their identity and refuse to accept the presence of different ethnic groups within their territory. What they want is to stay in the comfort zone that they are familiar with.

For more than fifteen hundred years, no victorious nation would enjoy peace in Eastern Europe because of its unhappy and belligerent neighbors. They had an unquenchable thirst for bloody revenge, and were determined to repeatedly re-draw the map to their advantage. The same type of "balkanization" was taking place in the anti-colonial movement in Africa, and the dictatorial regimes in South America.

✙

In the meantime, after the dissolution of the Soviet Union and the fall of the Communist Empire, when freedom was allowed in the former communist countries it did not dissolve the inherited differences among the Balkan nations. To the contrary, they renewed medieval disputes and thus proved that tribal homogeneous was alive and well, in spite of the influence of the melting pot and globalization trumpeted by the democrats and liberal leaders from the West. In no time at all, the dismemberment of the former Communist states triggered ethnic conflicts in the Eastern block, especially in the former Yugoslavia.

When they were territorially challenged, the Orthodox Serbs tried to maintain their regional dominance, and resorted to military force to settle century old blood feuds with their neighbors. One of the cleansing aims of the Serbs was to expel all non-Serbs and non-Orthodox persons from their territories.

An ethnic civil war from 1991 to 2001 resulted in millions of refugees to run for safety, hundreds of mosques were destroyed or damaged, and some three hundred Catholic churches and monasteries were closed by the Orthodox Serbs. They also suffered massive human and material damage as a result of NATO bombings.

Supervised by international troops and under pressure from economic measures only intensified Serbia's sense of humiliation. When Kosovo declared its independence in 2008 the United States Embassy in Belgrade was surrounded by one hundred fifty thousand violent protestors and went up in flames. Even a McDonald's restaurant (considered a symbol of Americanism) was ransacked. Serbians could not understand how Americans who were fighting the Muslim Taliban movement in Afghanistan and Iraq could support the Muslims in the Balkans.

When Vice President Joseph R. Biden Jr. visited Sarajevo in May 2009, he was fully aware of the area's hate-filled past and spoke out against "the sharp and dangerous rise in nationalistic rhetoric" that followed "old patterns and ancient animosities." Evidently, now that American troops have fought in the Middle East, Washington D.C. has begun to understand the dangers of balkanization. Still, a full grasp and the unavoidable strong effect of its roots still remain elusive to many western experts and leaders.

The superpowers may have settled the ethnic dispute in Cyprus between the Greeks and Turks, or in Kosovo between the Albanians and the Serbs. The Greeks will never give up the hope of taking back Istanbul and forcing the Turks out of the Balkan Peninsula. Nor, will they admit that Alexander the Great was Macedonian. For that matter, they object to the name of the Republic of Macedonia, since they consider it to be the name of their own territory as it existed during Byzantine times.

In the same spirit, it is unlikely that the Serbians will ever recover from the loss of their iconic Kosovo to the Albanians, and from the humiliating 78 days of bombing by the NATO Air Force (striking without the approval of the United Nations), mainly the U.S. Air Force with 41 times more combat aircraft, and with 214 times more attack helicopters than Serbia had.

The air raids killed some 500 civilians, and destroyed military installations, factories, institutions, hospitals, private businesses, cultural centers, schools, bridges and main highways until the Serbians withdrew from Kosovo. The Serbians refused to give up.

✛

On the ground, the Serbians took full revenge and unleashed a true balkanization onslaught and committed unpardonable war crimes. They were later accused of crimes against humanity, massacres, genocide, wartime rape, ethnic cleansing and breach of the Geneva Convention. The total victims of this balkanization conflict, according to the International Criminal Tribunal for the former Yugoslavia Demographic Unit, were 104,732 casualties. According to the International Center for Transitional Justice, the number of dead was 140,000. The Humanitarian Law Center estimated at least 130,000 casualties, and the International Committee of the Red Cross, gave the number at 200,000 people having been killed during the Yugoslav Wars, in which 500,000 women were raped, and two million people were displaced. Countless people left the war areas, many asking political asylum abroad.

The Serbian ethnic strike was considered the deadliest military action since World War II. An International Criminal Tribunal for the former civil war in Yugoslavia at Hague, Netherlands was instituted ad hoc, to duplicate the Nuremberg Trials of the Nazi war criminals. Some 160 individuals were indicated, staring Slobodan Milosevik the former Serbian president. He was the first sitting head of state charged with war crimes.

To everybody's relief he conveniently died in his court cell of a heart attack in 2006 before the trial was over. Nevertheless, in Eastern Europe the Russians still occupied the German seaport of Königsberg, the citadel of the Prussian militarissm, and is now a Russian land. It is now surrounded by the free countries of Belarus, Lithuania, and Poland.

Certainly, the Russians have no thoughts of handing over the Crimean Peninsula to the Ukrainians or to the Muslim Tartars who were once deported by Stalin. The heart shaped peninsula was annexed to the Russian Empire since 1783 by Catherine the Great. In 1793 she included the present southern Ukraine in her empire as well.

Since President Putin wanted a land corridor for the Russians to reach Crimea (just like Hitler was asking Poland for the Dantzig corridor to travel to East Prussia), and being refused, a Russo-Ukrainian war erupted in February 2014. Obviously, the post Communism shifted borders renewed the balkanization solution to correct the Eastern border of Ukraine.

On the other hand, the Ukrainians are not willing to give up their occupation of the Romanian territory of Buceac/Budjak which belongs to the Republic of Moldova, also a Romanian territory since the ancient times of the Dacians. That non-Slavic region of the Romanian Bessarabia was taken by the Soviets before and after WWII, and now after the fall of Communism it is part of Ukraine. In fact, all of the minorities in Ukraine (which became a country in

1918) want to be independent as do the millions of Ukrainians who currently live in Poland.

The political implications affect Moldova that cannot join the European Union like Romania, because its Eastern border is framed by another former Romanian territory of Transnistria (beyond the Dnister River), a long strip of land of an independent semi-presidential republic. The tiny unrecognized state of 1,607sq. miles /4,163 sq. kilometers and a population of almost 368,000, is watched by a "peacekeeper" presence of 1,500 Russian troops. It is the main reason Transnistria cannot belong to the European Union. Balkanization cannot get more complicated than what happens in this forgotten little corner of the world.

✣

Slovenia and Croatia bisects the property. Patrons can "eat roast pork dinners in Slovenia, step a few yards across the room to Croatia to use the bathroom, saunter back to Slovenia to pay the bill and end their meal on Croatian soil over a game of billiards and a shot of local pear brandy." The owner concluded that in the Balkans, "every little piece of land counts." This is a centuries-old motto in the Balkans.

However, an issue which is even more complicated than that of land ownership in any country is the right of minorities to use their own language regardless of where they live. A case in point is the small Republic of Slovakia. It has approved the right to education in Czech, German, Hungarian, Polish, and Ukrainian (Ruthenian), add to this list Bulgarian, Croatian, and Romany (most known as Gypsy). Tiny Albania is the most densely populated country of the region, and has more than ten minorities, each of which speaks a different language, and all of them have dialects and sub-dialects. Needless to say, this reflects the mix of populations that has defined its past, and again demonstrates the revival of Middle Age Balkanization.

For more than forty years, the Russian language, imposed by Kremlin dictators, remained the *lingua franca* of all the former Soviet republics. They are now free to teach their own ethnic language in schools. This does not alleviate their heavy dependence on the natural resources of Russia. It is therefore next to impossible to mitigate against the omnipresence of the Russian language. Moreover, it has obvious benefits among them the "soul healing" curse words.

In our time, Balkanization was also used to describe forced colonization of unhappy native ethnic groups, and their separatist desire leading to their revolts for independence. On a larger scale, the Afghan and Iraq civil wars, the never-ending Palestinian Israeli conflict, and the genocides throughout Africa demonstrate that primitive and aggressive thinking about right and wrong. It has not by any means receded from the human consciousness. Nor, are nationalism and patriotism out of fashion in the modern world.

✣

Certainly, it is very hard to move everyone onto the same page when they have different points of view concerning ones own peace and prosperity. A telling example is the way the European Union decided in 1993 to create a single European market, and absorb part of Eastern Europe into its sphere of influence. Doing this required that certain borders be eliminated and ethnic tensions be brought to an end. These efforts have had a history of failure in the Balkans. At the time of this writing Western Europe continues to overlook many patterns of political and economic behavior that have their balkanization roots in the history of the Balkans and Eastern Europe.

At the core of continental political thoughts the idea is that a European Union will eventually be able to offer the Eastern nations an opportunity to be integrated into the better life of the Western culture, economy and civilization. This hope was built on the assumption that each nation's troubled past would be healed by a new prosperous economy, and a political future focused on the common European good. After all, Greece was the cradle of western civilization, and the Hellenic culture still fascinates the world.

The overwhelming enthusiasm and the public display of joy that marked the fall of Communism was sufficient reason to justify the revival of nations that had long been oppressed. Little attention was paid to the phenomenon of balkanization, with its seismic mosaic of people who had never experienced the capitalist system, and had no concept of a democratic constitution. What the well intended, but politically naive western leaders expected was, that as long as money was pumped into the regions all would go well. No one seemed to remember that the Byzantines also subsidized the barbarians in an effort to keep the peace, but no gratitude followed.

On the contrary, since the Middle Ages any governmental donors have become a hated enemy when their generosity did not increase, when it was halted altogether or ceased, or worse yet when payback time arrived. Now, centuries later an ambitious European Union was trying to teach new ethics and financial discipline to people who retain the centuries old habits of balkanization. The Greek example of owing Euro 329 billion/US $353.9 billion to foreign investors stands out.

The immense amount of money allowed the Greeks to live beyond their means until they were unable to repay or refinance the loans. In no time, hundreds of thousands of businesses went bankrupt, and a global recession from 2007 to 2012 produced a massive 25% rate of unemployment in Greece. Since tax evasion and low productivity continued, the Greek government went bankrupt in 2015, and the loan was up to US $382.04 billion in 2023. When the Greek economy recovered in 2024, the government promised to repay the entire national debt by the year 2028. The loans which were supposed to make the Greeks richer created an economic disaster, and made their country the next to last poorest after Bulgaria in the Euro zone. Somehow, balkanization was still strong in Greece which was at one time the strongest cornerstone of the ancient civilization of the Balkan Peninsula.

Yet curiously, it took very little time for the "happy" integration that was brought about in the name of cooperation to evolve into an enormous confrontation between the Western and Eastern European nations. This time it was not caused by a Church schism, nor was it the result of a Cold War. Instead, the trouble came about because of the former communist "gray countries" that had been elevated into the "Euro zone". They persisted in holding their hands out for free benefits while stubbornly remaining fiscally unsustainable and unreliable as productive workers. On top of this their sudden integration into the economic sphere of Central Europe resulted in a non-welcomed mass migration to the western countries. Yet, the flood of unwanted and un-needed immigrants continues to pour into the developed countries mainly to rip off their generous welfare systems.

☨

In the heated arguments, especially in the European Union debates about illegal immigrants flooding Europe, one name stands out to be criticized or praised: Viktor Orban, the longest elected prime-minister of Hungary. Considered to be a defender of Christianity, a national conservationist, a right wing populist, even a nationalist or a fascist, but also a Trump and Israeli supporter. He is also known to be defiant of the European Communities rules and "commands of foreign powers" to be imposed on other nation members. Most explicitly was the immigration and refugee quota for each country. He rejected it to be applied to Hungary which cannot be a diverse or a mixed nation. Orban's other reasons are that the Hungarians are to preserve their language, religion, traditions, national culture, morality, not having same sex families, and the nation to birth only Hungarian children.

On the other flip side of the coin, Orban is an active advocate and money provider for the Hungarian communities in other countries for them to maintain their heritage, especially Transylvania in Romania. The tendency is to re-establish the historical "Szekely land" (which in fact was founded by the German Saxons in the late 12$^{th}$ century) where now 312,043 Hungarians live. Now, in the 2024 census they are looking to have their own territorial autonomy with their local government. According to Romanian law, it is unconstitutional to claim the right to self-determination for the Hungarians to create their own state within the country of Romania.

Orban is the surname coming from Latin, meaning "citizen of a city." His first name Victor in Latin means "conqueror," and it is a very popular name for boys in Romania, and the feminine version Victoria, is also very common. President Victor Orban may be of Romanian origin himself, like King Matthias, considering that the Hungarian language is part of the Asiatic Ob-Ugric, and the present Hungarian vocabulary has a minimum of Latin roots.

Somehow, it is unlikely that the Hungarians have come from the former Magyars which are considered to be barbarian Huns, who in the 9$^{th}$ and 10$^{th}$ centuries crossed each border to raid and pillage Europe. Even now, the Hungarians are still proud to be "Attila's people" (a common name for baby boys). The Hungarians have erected guarded border fences to stop the illegal and unwanted foreign migrants from entering Hungary. Another good reason for the fence is that with almost ten million people and a low fertility birth rate, with the presence of millions of illegal residents, the Hungarians will soon be outnumbered. If this occurs, the once proud Hungarian nation will speak a different language and appear racially different. Put in another way, Hungary is not like the United States of America having almost 350 million people to absorb roughly the same number of undocumented and illegal invaders. Prime-minister Victor Orban can be called many names, but he is an old fashioned pragmatist and a down-to-earth visionary.

✣

In the early twenty-first century, a modern nation is expected to be free of internal ethnic conflicts. A society that aims at political correctness must embrace multi-cultural races, skin colors, and origins, and all of these need to be held together by common ideals.

Yet today, Eastern European and the Balkan cultures retain the same basic values they developed in the Middle Ages, regardless of what the western world considers moral and right.

The definition of "Balkanization" applied to unwanted illegal and poor immigrants to move into rich countries where they try to abuse the generous welfare systems while trashing the host societies. Right after communism fell, massive floods of Eastern Europeans, especially the ever opportunistic Gypsies now renamed Romas, and those from poor African and the Middle Eastern nations took advantage of them having no enforced borders. They flooded into the rich western countries of the European Union.

Millions of unauthorized and therefore illegal new immigrants, uprooted from their lands even if now by choice, live a dual life in their host nations. They are physically present in their new country, but mentally they are still back home. This causes them to resist assimilation and display habits which, from the Western point of view, are uncivilized. They have the sleazy opportunism to cheat governments, show disregard for personal and public hygiene, drink into comas, display public rudeness, and many are committing crimes, or are busy trafficking illegal drugs.

Defying work or education, their self-esteem is based on the fact that they look down on the taxpayers who support them. They take pleasure in the misinforming of immigration officials, and to them, co-existence means "let me have what you have." Such habits are stamped with the term Balkanization, a term that has now come to mean acting in ways that are diametrically opposed to Western standards of civilization.

However, the true meaning of balkanization was soon discovered by the eager western industrialists and businesses who ventured into Eastern Europe. Lured by the prospect of cheap labor (the average monthly salary in many of these nations is only a few hundred euros), optimistic speculators entered what they believed to be a second China boom.

However, in a short time they found themselves what a local balkanization was when they were facing the staggering reality of rampant corruption from the top down. The authorities and local leaders, who were groomed in the Communist era to lie and steal, are easily bribed, and even bought. The consequences of this prolonged mismanagement and these mafia-like activities was that the hundreds of billions of euros invested in the Eastern European economies from the 1990s onward produced little or no profit. They only created a new nomenclature a "kleptocracy," the new super-rich strata and the officials high above the law.

After foreign investors built or modernized factories and helped the local population with charity missions, they were confronted with argumentative workers who only felt exploited and demanded salary increases. When they surmised that a business was becoming prosperous, they wanted a larger share of the profit, while internal theft increased and production decreased. The Balkan work ethic, "promise everything, get the money, and deliver nothing" that had bankrupted the Communist system, surfaced once again, was now in full display. After a great deal of puzzlement and fruitless analysis of such situations, the investors realized they were risking the loss of their established clientele.

Because of local sabotage the buyers noticed a decline in the quality of their products, and the ruined investors took their businesses back home. Once again, the Byzantine, Russian, and Turkish legacy of bribery and corruption as an indispensable part of the "work ethic" was reinforced with the Balkan practices of "bite the hand that feeds it" and "kill the golden goose." In the Western style of bribery and corruption, the entrepreneur Hunter Biden, the son of US vice president and later the President Joe Biden, was allegedly paid millions of dollars by the Ukrainians, Romanians and Chinese for them to be directly connected with the second, then the first most powerful man in America.

In the meantime, massive unemployment created hardships that pressed the younger generation from undeveloped countries to migrate across the open European borders in search of a better life. When their welfare expired they moved to the next country, and under a different name started to collect any government subsidy, only to move on to the next country to do the same, "collecting" from the naïve governments, or compassionate charitable agencies. In doing so they brought with them the effects of balkanization.

In case they decided to work for a living, their labor may be cheap, but it is often tainted by a faulty sense of duty and lucrative trickery, all aimed at making fast money by trying to get something for nothing. They exaggerate any truth, make any wrongdoing someone else's fault, and a have passion for revenge.

Since they are unable to get, or to hold a job, many migrants live parasitically on the host society while engaging in unlawful activities, and soon they may become a public danger. When they are caught, they scream "discrimination." This is not to say that westerners do not practice deceitful behaviors. Some individuals or government employees certainly have similar traits, but as a whole Western culture does not encourage this sort of behavior. Moreover, it deliberately discourages breaking the law. All in all, instead of contributing something to the elevation of the lifestyle of the Eastern European people, the West is finding itself dealing with the reality of the everlasting historic process of the mighty balkanization.

Ironically, with so many Germans killed in the war, the West Germans invited five million Turks to immigrate to help them rebuild the German industries. Hitler may turn in his grave, when after a second and third generation of former "guest workers," they succeeded to bring balkanization. This is demonstrated by the Little Istanbuls that flourish in each major German city. Similarly, London is sometimes wryly called Londonistan after its Pakistani and Indian population. In Dublin, with its numerous Polish migrants, it could be nicknamed Dublinski. France, Italy, and Spain also have taken in millions of new settlers, including migrants from the Balkans. In many

Swedish schools the native children are in the minority because of the immigrants from the third world. Most numerous are the ones which bring the Islamism traditions from the lands and societies rooted in the balkanization traditions.

Oddly enough, the present migration has produced a labor vacuum in Eastern Europe, so in turn these countries have attracted poorer immigrants from China, Mongolia, Vietnam, and other Asian countries, all of whom are in search of a better life. Attila the Scourge and the Golden Horde failed to "mongolize" Europe, which now is invaded not by the savage horsemen, but by Asians arriving on comfortable planes in search of profitable jobs.

In fact, they prove to be disciplined and industrious workers playing a productive role during the economic booms. These new settlers enrolled their children in local schools aiming to follow the good examples of the Algerians and Turks in France and Italy. However, hundreds of thousands of Asians also found themselves living in a parallel world, exploited and unwanted by their host nations.

Although, during the economic crisis like in 2008, the non-integrated Asian migrants were unemployed, homeless, riddled with debt, and subject to helpless depression. Often they were offered a one-way plane ticket back home. To them, the much acclaimed process of globalization had turned into a doomed nomadic venture in the continent of Michelangelo, Shakespeare, Balzac, Monet and Wagner. Due to all of these adverse economic and social changes in the lives of the Asian migrants, they could call the Eastern European a vast land of "delusionism."

✢

While they are certainly not responsible for the global recession of 2009, the Eastern European nations are now heavily in debt as a result of an excessive use of credit. They are quick to blame their problems on foreign capitalists who closed the banks and businesses in their neighborhoods. However, The European Union promptly came to help in the form of financial rescue plans, emergency funds, reconstruction and development loans, and rescue packages from the International Monetary Fund, the European Central Bank, and other lending institutions.

As usual, those needy nations mostly riddled by colossal debt considered these trillions of euros merely another gift in disguise. If they had to be accountable for repayment Russia could always bail them out in exchange for their entering into an anti-western alliance. It had been done before. This would once again demonstrate that Western capitalism does not work, nor does its democracy; otherwise it was a political scheme which Eastern countries neither understand nor value. What is undeniable is that the Kremlin continues to replace the Phanar of Constantinople, as Balkanization contaminated all the rest of Europe.

Vice President Biden visited Ukraine and Georgia in July 2009 when he realized the threat posed by Moscow in the region. He commented on the troubled Russian economy. It is one which is based on a corrupt ridden banking system and inept judicial system. "The reality is the Russians...have a withering economy, they have a banking sector and structure that is not likely to be able to withstand the next 15 years. They're in a situation where the world is changing before them and they're clinging to something in the past that is not sustainable." In reality, Russia covers 1/7 of the dry surface of the world while underground harboring the richest minerals, and natural gas and oil whose export will cover any expense of its 144 million people for what they may need.

With this statement, he confirmed what many observers of Eastern Europe and of the Balkan history were aware of. The same economic and political conditions persist there today as they did five hundred years ago. The laws are not subject to enforcement, everything is negotiable and relative, and everyone interprets rules to their own advantage. Once again, this entire chaotic and inherited system is often portrayed by the people of the Balkans as a *talmesh-balmesh,* a dish whose contents cannot be described.

What nobody knew at that time was that the Vice President Biden was contaminated by balkanization, when his son Hunter became a director of Burisma the Ukraine's largest private gas producer, even though he never had any experience in that field, nor could he speak the Ukranian language. Since he would be paid $83,000 a month Hunter accepted the job, and also presumably took millions in bribes.

Obviously, the Balkanization of the Bidens was acting in the same ways it worked in the Balkan Peninsula during the early Middle Ages. In the modern time, the Eastern European nations revived balkanization and applied it in Western Europe. Now, in the 21$^{st}$ century Balkanization was ready to cross the Atlantic Ocean into the United States.

✜

In summary, no kings, emperors, or political regimes, such as Communism or Nazism, have been able to change the old habits of the Phanariotism, Turkocracy and Russianism, all products of Balkanization. It is based on epidemic corruption to sustain their financial and political power, their fixed elections, and a cherished brutal sense of patriotism. Politeness is rare and artificial, wheedling, cursing, and gossiping have long remained a favorite entertainment, and any promise is subject to change if there is some advantage in it. Shrewdness prevails over sound judgment, and there is virtually no interest in knowing how all of this might be viewed by the rest of the world which does not exist for them.

All these bad behavior patterns have survived the ravages of time and created a unique and uniquely troubled social system based on mistrust. Ironically, the ultimate influence in most European countries is still Russia, which can cut the gas and oil supplies in a flash, regardless of what the western world may think about the entire situation.

When Putin heard that the Western world will not cooperate with Russia, and does not need its oil and natural gas, President Putin replied that indeed that was possible, but then the westerners would need firewood, which he will be happy to supply from Siberia. In fact, a large portion of the financial aid given to the Eastern European countries ends up in Russia as payment for supplies from them.

Communism was murderous, but dictatorship brought order to the Balkan societies. In fact, many people look back ruefully on the time when everyone was taken care of by the state. A time period and set of conditions that brought democracy, and a new set of economic opportunities that has turned into a quagmire of problems no one can handle or solve. Prosperity meant either inflicting poverty on others or borrowing money that could not be repaid. The influx of western capital and the importation of its culture challenged tens of millions of people to live differently, and they became something they had no interest in becoming: to change with the times.

Despite the laudable efforts on the part of the advanced nations, the obscure and backward eastern nations will continue to play the role of victim, and jump at any opportunity to prove the superpowers wrong. The relationship between rich and poor nations has only superficially improved.

Globalization intended to erase ethnic differences at all levels, and create an ideal international society with the same goals. Yet the religious differences and inherited habits including different languages and customs, intensifies the difference among nations and races. Ideas of socialism and communism were good theory, not in reality. Above all, aggressive nationalism remains unchanged among hostile Balkan neighbors, and tribal rules supersede modern international laws. To them the past which they can brag about is more important than the future which seems to be against their way of life.

The process of balkanization has also preserved precious fruits in the form of some truly splendid human traits. The most common and most appreciated habit is that of hospitality. A host displays his or her best nature, and always tries to pleasantly impress a guest. Western tourists are often moved by the genuine welcome, compassion, and readiness to help displayed by people throughout Eastern Europe. These attitudes and behaviors point to a good inner core in the otherwise tortured souls, and to their sincere desire to be acknowledged, praised and be liked. Above all, the people of the Balkans display an enviable physical and mental endurance when it comes to pain and deprivation.

Their unadulterated belief in the possibility of a better life for their loved ones makes them willing to be tremendously self sacrificing. The belief in "God will give and God will take" is supreme and a mark of their obedient nature. The tribal like environment they create gives them great comfort and strength.

Certain taboos and family values are fiercely enforced in these Balkan cultures, as are a set of rules which are valued only locally. Patriarchal societies (men still dance with men), keep women in an inferior position even though they are the real achievers and leaders in the family, and do the best in school. The honor of an unmarried woman or a widow is always firmly defended by her family. Family clans take precedence over any other social organization. Overall, tribal life has remained strong and offers many therapeutic benefits, including abundant and genuine collective support. Children are a common good and protected by everyone, and the elderly are venerated and well cared for.

Since the Balkan people are deeply religious they rigorously observe all traditional rituals and holidays. Their deceased family members are honored and mourned for a long period of time with memorial feasts and offerings. But, spirituality also leads them to believe in dreams, omens, and other superstitions, and these can trigger irrational decisions or sudden mood swings.

Balkan people tend to laugh at everything, humorous or morbid, and they often use philosophical jokes that reflect surprisingly accurate thinking about the surrounding world. Their ethnic jokes mirror their prejudices and true opinions about other people, but their sense of irony and humor amounts to a form of therapy, one that is too often absent from life in the West. However, the person who laughs at everything usually ends up being the object of the laughter, and the joker often becomes the joke.

Lastly, to identify the true Balkan mentality one need only to listen to the way people of different ethnicities curse. Their imaginative curses are directed at everyone and everything, from God to the devil, personal relatives, friends and foes, the dead and the living, sacred holidays, objects, animals, and food. Cursing and joking are more than a national sport, and together with wailing a way of venting frustration, and healing their grievances by letting the negativity out of one's system.

Heavy drinking of alcohol is considered a proud challenge for strong men, and it is also believed to cure mental and physical problems. It is a must when it comes to socializing. It has been said that a bottle of wine contains more philosophy than all the libraries in the world. Medieval thinking is reflected in all aspects of life. An obese person is regarded as healthy and prosperous, as he obviously lived well even during years of famine, pellagra, and other starvation related epidemics in the past.

Eastern Europeans tend to be both witty and wise when it comes to practical matters and their ability to survive. Proud to a fault, fighters display incredible stamina and bravery for the sake of heroics. They are savage when victorious and woefully angry in defeat. Given that they have so little hope for the future, they eulogize the good old days, even though they were no better in the past. The history of each small and otherwise obscure nation is presented in a glamorous light. The Folk heroes' faults are dismissed and they are heralded for their inflated achievements that never happened, but led to their canonization. However, they proudly go to their Orthodox churches to see and to be seen in their communities.

As a rule, national pride involves showing contempt to others whose history seems to be of no account unless it supports a flattering point of view or justifies a valued event. Again, their painful past and unpredictable future makes these people difficult to trust. They cannot give up their bickering, set aside grievances, or get beyond their collective illusions. Their rich fantasy life creates a land of make-believe with a pathologic sense of humor, and a perverted feeling of optimism. All of this is based on the wisdom that "the less truth that is known, the better it is for everyone."

✢

Centuries of civilization have wrought little change in Eastern Europe, and now the ambitious European Union is trying to teach the people of the Balkans to stop turning back the clock, and begin to enjoy a better present and future. This is not easy. Inherited traditions are stronger than any outside influence even though they are curious about what is on the television and the internet. They are the most ardent soccer fans, and each game locally or internationally is an event to endlessly talk about.

However, the Balkanized nations will probably continue to lag behind the rest of Europe politically and economically regardless of any progress they claim to make. To them, "a kick in the butt means a step forward," but that is not the way success comes about. Their ongoing desire to craftily cheat each other, and collectively try to cheat any system, while the oligarchs dictate the governments, can only make their national prosperity a distant dream.

Can Westerners succeed in changing such old mentalities? Or, will they follow the Byzantines, Russians, and Turks by merely adding new layers to the historic process of balkanization? Most of the answers are provided by the legacy of Byzantine intrigue. One fact of life is not likely to change: the hegemony of the European Union will attract an increased number of Eastern European immigrants to the developed countries. In the Roman and Byzantine empires, this pattern resulted in the end of economic power, and brought down whole civilizations. Over time, it will become clear whether the broom of history erases present differences, or if the inherited roots of balkanization will be grafted onto those of Western culture under the patronage of global brotherhood. It remains to be seen if the melting pot of the Balkans will once again boil over into a social and political disaster that is reminiscent of past history.

☩

Certainly, the Balkanization of the Soviet Union was practiced on a large scale, based on the Slavic reputation of bribery and corruption, and well accomplished by the local Communist leaders. After the fall of the Soviet Empire, the independent Russia faced a Great Recession, due to the newly rich business oligarchs who took ownership of the state by stripping it of most of its natural resources. They bought factories and other productive institutions at the maximum discounted price, and became tycoons.

They were also enriching the new politicians who for substantial bribes approved their bids. As expected, the other former Communist countries, among them Romania, experienced the same balkanization of enrichment due to politicians who signed any ownership papers for a good bribe.

Certainly, the Russian President Dimitri A. Medvedev is fully aware of needed major changes. On November 12, 2009, he delivered a speech from the Kremlin in which he called for "…our contribution to lift up Russia to a new, higher stage in the development of our civilization…. resolve the problems we inherited." He concluded that "Any attempts to shatter the situation, destabilize the government and split society under demographic slogans will be prevented." Leaders of the former Communist nations echoed the ending of the corruption by the thriving balkanization system.

The five times elected president of Russia, the former KGB colonel Vladimir Putin, by now considered to be a lifetime dictator fluent in the German language, tried to stop the endemic corruption and human rights violations. Even he was accused of vote-rigging his elections and arrested his opponents, some of them died under dubious circumstances.

But, being a true Russian nationalist, and an ardent patriot, Putin who receives a salary of $140,000 a year, is considered to be one of the wealthiest persons in the world. Having 20 mansions and palaces, 43 aircrafts, 700 cars (not all in his name) and several yachts, some are the President Putin is dedicated to accomplishing the restoration of Russia, and being short of a labor force, today there are 10.5 million migrants, mainly from Central Asia, to fill that need. Some of them overstated their working visas and many brought their relatives and friends.

For once, Balkanization may have a good point to exist, and the Russian president may be worth $200 billion. (Source: Internet.)

✟

Over the centuries, the world saw the rise and fall of many powerful empires which were believed would last forever. Or, at the very least they used wars trying to destroy each other. In spite of that the global population increased from 500 million with the life expectancy of 35 years of age, during the Roman Empire.

If at the end of the nineteenth century the world population was one billion and life expectancy was 35-years-old, today the world's population is over 8 billion and the life expectancy is over 70 years of age, which drastically diminishes the food and other vital resources. While the white Europeans experience a very low birth rate, the black population of Africa numbering 1.5 billion, in the year 2050, their numbers will increase to 3.9 billion.

In 2000 almost one billion people worldwide lived in extreme poverty mostly in Africa and South Asia. Their poor were seeking refuge in Western Europe, and millions of poor from South and Central America wanted to migrate to Northern America.

The majority is non-white, uneducated and unskilled, and they are always hungry to abuse the generous welfare of civilized nations. They represent the modern migrant barbarians, which is the modern version of the barbarians invading the Byzantine Empire. The politicians who are looking for more votes to be elected as leaders encourage the illegal immigration.

They totally forget that wasting the taxpayer's money to subsidize the newly poor millions, affect the budgets for the domestic poor, while encouraging the balkanization of the host nation who for hundreds of years worked hard to enjoy the benefits of an advanced cultura society. The modern barbarians keep invading and ripping off the prosperous nations, with the blessings of the democrats and liberal politicians and leaders.

✢

## THE BALKANIZATION OF THE WESTERN WORLD

After the fall of Communism in Eastern Europe, and wars in the Middle East and Africa, there became an endless source of millions of desperate immigrants, including the Gypsies flooding into Western Europe. Due to the human policy of compassion, and being much publicized since the end of WWII, it is important not to behave like the Nazis. Combined with the selfish interests of the democratic and liberal leaders has allowed more than five million unwanted and undocumented illegal immigrants from third world countries to flood into the borderless European Union between the years 2014 to 2017.

They aimed first for the countries with the most generous welfare systems including France, Belgium, Germany, Denmark and Scandinavia. They were to rip off their benefits, abuse their hospitality, and take any possible advantage to plunder them by using their balkanization tricks of deceiving, begging, playing victim and making demands. They tried to milk as much money and benefits as possible and then return home and pretend to be rich. Tempted by the charitable incentives, other unauthorized invaders were seeking asylum, or using bribes and fake marriages because they wanted to become lifetime "retainers" of the government subsidies. They faked accidents, disabilities and other reasons not to work. They only collected money that they did not earn, or do not deserve.

✣

Until the end of the last century, the United States of America was mostly "invaded" by the Mexicans. Most of them preferred to be seasonable workers, especially in California, where farmers needed to hire more workers to harvest their crops. Some of them even paid income tax to the American government, and have proved to be disciplined and productive.

So far, the young America founded on the Anglo-Saxon civic laws and work ethics, had its own form of "balkanization" from within. This included people who cheat on their income tax, businesses cooking their books, fake bankruptcies, local "mafias," and falsely claimed disabilities. This is together with the corrupt local leaders that take bribes for favors, and even form a sort of mafia in fixing prices, extortions, and other illegal infractions.

One may wonder why a lawyer making a $300,000 a year salary wants to work in the US government for one half of that salary. It is because the political power is usually intoxicating, and is always translated into making more money, legally or illegally.

Once in a while scandals erupt when top politicians are heavily involved in bribery, corruption, or spending the tax payers' money for their personal benefits. Unchecked they waste billions of dollars for laughable reasons, with no regard for the national debt which currently runs at $37 trillion dollars, with $2 trillion being added each year. It made President Regan to declare in his Inaugural Address in

1981 that "government is not the solution to the problem: government is the problem."

Each administration under a new president has had many issues with spending the budget money recklessly. Since 2004 to 2024, an estimated 2.7 trillion was spent by the US government, the last time under the Biden Administration. In plain English, many unnecessary and illegal financial grants are given by governmental agencies to both private and business projects domestically and foreign. These include for research and to charities, many of them are nonexistent, but they give the kick backs to the official grantors.

It was reported that it spent "…an estimated $236 billion in 'improper payments' during the recently completed fiscal year (FY 2023). Such payments are essentially payments in errors that can be the result of many things including overpayments, inaccurate recordkeeping, or even fraud." (U.S. Government Accountability office's WatchBlog March 26, 2024)

The last $236 billion mentioned took place during the Joe Biden administration, when in four years, the old president took 577 vacation days, and Kamala Harris would remain in history as the most inefficient, do nothing vice-president. Obviously, the entire Biden cabinet members and tens of thousands of employees never had any supervision of how billions of dollars were spent on mostly illegitimate and unnecessary "demands."

The Biden family is known for their corruption and self-enrichment, as they seem to have instituted the official road to balkanization in America. It started with Biden's liberal policies, a decision to have the borders open for millions of undocumented and illegal immigrants to enter the country unchecked and unvetted, and they settled in the "sanctuary cities."

Once, all former pearls in the crown of America, wonderful places like San Francisco, Chicago and New York, which attracted millions of visitors from all over the world, were now reduced to dangerous and dirty cities by the illegal immigrants. The same thing happened during the Roman and Byzantine empires when the savage barbarians destroyed what they could never build themselves. The American Empire now lives under a similar danger because of the unwanted and unnecessary illegal immigrants.

Officially, the foreign free loaders claim to come to live in freedom that they imagine to be without limits. As the history of civilization has demonstrated, total freedom unchecked by laws is the most damaging to any society. Little did the Washington Democrats and Liberals know (or maybe they tolerated) that the massive torrents of millions of illegal immigrants crossing the southern and northern borders were controlled by the criminal cartels. They also smuggle the criminals and traffickers who bring prostitution, pedophilia and deadly drugs into the American communities. The cartels by charging on average US $10,000 per illegal immigrant have made $13 billion in 2021 alone.

The difference between the hordes of barbarians invading the Byzantine Empire in the Dark Ages, and the illegal immigrants invading the United States, is that now a military force was not at the border to stop the alien avalanche of the unwanted poor being rejected by their native countries. Most of them were unemployable, criminals, escapees from prisons, mental asylums, thugs, child molesters, drug dealers, sex traffickers and planted anti-American terrorists, all being hosted by the "sanctuary" cities. Those cities used the taxpayers' money to house them in expensive hotels, gave them free clothes, telephones, meals, credit cards, even a car and a house.

At the same time, when the Trump administration took over in January 2025, more than 770,000 American citizens were homeless on any given night, many with entire families. (PBS NewsHour, interview on December 27, 2024 with Shaun Donovan, former secretary of Housing and Urban Development.) The National Low Income Housing Coalition reported a shortage of 7.3 million units of affordable and available rental homes in the U.S. in 2024. Yet, there were hundreds of billion of dollars spent by the Biden administration to take care of the illegal immigrants, by providing the unwanted and unnecessary millions of foreign handouts.

✢

## DEBALKANIZATION OF THE UNITED STATES

Yet, the American spirit which gave the world most of the modern technical inventions which began in the repair shops and home garages, proving to succeed regardless of what calamities happen. This again prevailed on the November 5, 2024 voting for the presidential election. A number of 9,946,764 of aliens, felons and other ineligible voters in Michigan, and 25,975 dead registrants were on the voters rolls were removed from the voters list by the Public Interest Legal Foundation, according to Ken Blackwell, the former Ohio Secretary of State.

The 47th presidential election was won by the former 45th President Donald J. Trump, whom the American voters entrusted with a 312 Electoral College victory, and the biggest Republican popular vote with more than 77 million votes.

At the same time, the illegal and undocumented immigrants also received free education, medical and hospital expenses, and attorneys paid for by the Biden government (taxpayers) to bail them out of the jails after committing robberies, and rapes. This included beating up and murdering policemen, and terrorizing the people who hosted them.

Estimated to be only 3.5 million, in reality their numbers may well pass 10 million and be closer to 30 million, according to Tom Homan, the border Czar named by President Trump. (The Ingram Angle Show, Fox News 27/2/2024) These illegal new handouts are costing the tax payers over $150 billion a year just to shelter them. Most of them are unable to speak English, are uneducated and do not have any job skills.

In exchange, they bring with them a disorderly subculture and are trashing and burning parts of the most beautiful American cities. Because of their faulty hygiene, unknown diseases, and selling deadly drugs it is killing some 100,000 Americans a year, mostly young people. They are involved in criminal activities they undermine the local economies, rob the commercial outlets, defy the cultural traditions, upset the school systems, and create an unsafe environment of balkanization for the now fearful American citizens.

Roughly three months after President Trump's inauguration 60,000 of the most dangerous criminals were already deported (Fox News 4/8/ 2025) from the U.S.. President Trump kept his word to the American people and has continued to build the wall to stop the flood of illegal non vetted immigrants. Moreover, he authorized the U.S. military to take control of the public strip along the wall, and for the U.S. Navy to collaborate with the U.S. Coast Guard to secure the American territorial waters.

With the borders safely sealed, a good unexpected event happened, when tens of thousands of foreign cartel members, gang leaders, sex traffickers, rapists and deadly drug dealers, has now found themselves unable to escape back over the border. The same thing has occurred with the criminals, pedophiles, children and prostitute traffickers along with dangerous outlaws of all kinds. They have all trapped themselves on the wrong side of the American border. Now, being hunted by Tom Homan and his ICE agents, they are arrested and deported to their native countries to face their laws and penalties.

Ironically, the most daring criminals who came to rip off and terrorize America, ended up to be "terrorized," themselves, for being hunted, caught, handcuffed and forced to be expelled from the society, they believed they could exploit and control. What no other government could do about the criminals and their organizations to bring them to justice, the Trump Administration did in a few months. It will continue to do so until all of the illegal foreign lawbreakers are removed from the United States of America.

Starting with the first week of his term, Trump signed 73 presidential orders re-establishing law and order in the disrupted America which is in increasing peril. He will reduce business regulations to boost the economy, while rebuilding the U.S. military. Therefore, this will avoid the United States from turning itself into a third world nation.

Trump will prevent "the land of opportunity" from becoming a victim of Balkanization. This includes freeing the judicial system from politicizing, of which the ex-president Trump and many of his loyalists were victims of under the Biden Administration. They were harassed and even imprisoned without any proven fault or of any wrong doing.

Trump began to shake up the FBI by naming a new director and deputy director. To regain the public trust 1,500 federal FBI agents will be removed from the headquarters. Weeks later, $500 million was found to be misplaced. He also intends to purge many of the senior Pentagon leaders and many armchair generals from the Armed Forces. They were responsible for reaching a low military level, while spending the largest budget in the world, and it is riddled with inflated and unnecessary expenses.

✜

In contrast, President Trump and magnate Elon Musk both immensely successful and experienced businessmen, want to run American affairs as a business in an efficient fashion in order to lead the world. President Trump is asking for accountability from all government agencies' as to their spending since he intends to reduce the government deficit by cutting the federal work force. Running the Department of Government Efficiency (DOGE), Musk and his professional team wasted no time to discover the appalling inefficiencies of the bureaucrats who even do not come to work in their offices. DOGE will not be tolerating wasting billions of dollars, and committing fraud and theft of the taxpayers' money. More than 10,000 government employees were gone in one week.

Trump wants to overhaul the Department of Defense by cutting the budget by $50 billion and firing 5,000 employees. Trump wants to cut funds and even eliminate FEMA (Federal Emergency Management Agency), which proved almost useless to help the homeless citizens during many natural disasters, despite having a $25.5 billion budget, and $61.8 billion in discretionary funds for the Fiscal year 2024. Yet, FEMA ran out of money with not much to show as to how it was spent. No wonder some Government officials become millionaires overnight.

Also, Musk and his team were officially empowered by Trump to consolidate the number of federal agencies, and to eliminate numerous wasteful and unnecessary government run fraudulent charities. This is being done to bring accountability as to how the American taxpayers' money is being spent. Elon Musk believes he can cut $700 billion in fraud and waste from the year 2024, from Social Security ($1.3 trillion,) Medicare ($912 billion,) Medicaid ($626 billion,) which accounts for one quarter of all federal spending.

On March 4, 2025, addressing a joint session of a bitterly divided Congress in Washington, DC, after only six weeks into his second term, President Trump collected applause and ovations only from the Republican section for his many, and major achievements, such as cutting taxes for Social Security.

He also collected laughter on April 10, 2025 during an Emergency Cabinet Meeting when it was revealed that the Biden administration sent Social Security benefits of $59 million to almost 25,000 people older than 115 year old. Even the known oldest American person is 114 years old. $254 million was collected by children from the ages of 1 to 5 years old, and $69 million was received by 10,000 babies who were not yet born.

Of the people who collect Social Security checks, 40% of them are fraudulent. They change their addresses and their bank account numbers to avoid identification. Elon Musk eliminating this fraud will cause each legitimate Social Security check to be increased.

✢

When President Trump was assisted by Elon Musk, the richest man on the planet (with an estimated net worth of US $402 billion), the magnate became the presidential senior adviser. Both men are working for free to restructure the U.S. government. Musk was put in charge of the Department of Government Efficiency, and was authorized by Trump to downsize the number of employees not needed in the Federal Governments Administration.

Many thousands of them (the American government employs 2.4 million) are probably some of the main representatives of the American Balkanization. It was estimated that 521 billion dollars of the taxpayers' money per year is wasted by the government (Fox News Channel 2/14/25). Federal workers continue their habit of not showing up at their offices since the Covid 19 epidemic, and some are "pretending" to work from home. However, the federal government spent 4.6 billion dollars for new office furniture since 2020 at the time when less than half of the employees were showing up for work. (Fox News on 4/8/25 featuring President Trump in front of the House panel.)

Under the Trump Administration when giving these government employees a dead line, thousands of them could not describe what they do in a week. Yet, they are being paid on an average of $144,000 a year in salary, plus benefits. To eliminate such a waste of money 8,000 of them will also retire each month. Many of them are resigning with a more than generous severance pay for the next eight months. Reducing the federal government by only 10% of non-needed employees, $25 million annually from the tax payers' money will be saved, and not wasted. Also, millions of dollars will be saved by reducing the Department of Agriculture by the elimination of 6,000 jobs.

Government employees spent $4.6 million on credit cards which were paid for by the taxpayers. $300 million small businesses were owned by children and received grants, and babies received loans from government programs. All of this has happened because more than 500 executive agencies which distributed these funds never verified their activities, or checked on the validities of each contract presented.

Also, Elon Musk and his team have to down size, or eliminate unnecessary departments in the U.S. government, such as the Department of Education in Washington D.C.. It has succeeded to rank the U.S. educational system at the 40$^{th}$ place in the world, while ranking first in the cost per pupil. Over $100 million will be put back in the taxpayers pockets, and each state will run its own school system. What President Trump intends to do is to create a huge shift of funds from the centralized government to the individual states where they can be distributed according to the needs of their local American people.

The president ordered the Consumer Financial Protection Bureau to stop working. By his executive order, the Department of Labor's Office of Federal Contract Compliance Programs was shut down. The Pentagon and other military spending will also be reviewed and revised. All of this is necessary in order to reduce payrolls, and increase the efficiency of most of the government institutions which have too many unnecessary employees.

Musk's task is to eliminate agencies which in the past spent billions of dollars for imaginary tasks like environmental studies. He believes there are some 420 Government and federal agencies spending $2 billion for programs which have a zero benefit for the tax payers. Actually, $42 billion is spent with no interest for the American tax payers. Unchecked expensive funds have been sent abroad to help the supposed climate change, along with other unaccounted for wasteful spending on failed programs. In February 2025 there was $2 billion found stashed in a phony climate package for a charity organization founded in 2023, with only a $100.00 donation in it. (Fox News Sunday Morning Futures 2/23/2025)

A $1.9 billion misplaced fund was reported by Scott Turner, the new Secretary of Housing and Urban Department. (Fox News, Special Report 3/17/2025) Obviously, someone from the Biden-Harris Administration was too late to cash and use it, maybe for paying democratic and liberal "spontaneous" loud street protestors against Trump's policies. All of this waste of billions happened during the Biden Administration. It is believed that $200 billion was mishandled or stolen by the previous administration which hopefully may be returned to the American taxpayers. This is the shortest and most expensive Balkanization in the world history

On March 27, 2025, Fox News Channel hosted a special report with Bret Baier who interviewed Elon Musk and his DOGE team of seven investigators, all reputable, and the world's best software engineers. They agreed to work without pay for 130 days to oversee and discover, and then to correct the fraudulent spending of the taxpayers' money handled by the U.S. government in previous years. President Trump assured the public that Musk "He's not gaining anything from this."

So far, the Musk team has collected about $1 billion a day, seven days a week. Their goal is to reduce the domestic deficit by 1 trillion dollars when they are finished with their investigation into the governments spending of the taxpayers' money. After all these faulty findings the Balkanization of the American government has to stop.

☦

Trump's revolutionary statements and actions produced a tsunami of protests and accusations against both the president and his staff, by the Democratic Party leaders who are trying to justify their political positions. Their faulty bureaucracy which already has negatively impacted the majority of American people will have to stop. Fighting back, the same leaders came up with an accusatory

"Trump Derangement Syndrome," not to be found in the medical books, but used to accuse Trump's decisions and actions as those of a mad irrational leader acting only to destroy the American democracy. What Trump is doing is replacing the fraudulent bureaucracy with a true and transparent democracy. The qualified and competent members of his cabinet have been chosen to help the American citizens, and not to scam them as has been done in the past.

After five months in the office, Trump's DOGE team succeeded to recover $1,6 trillion from the previous wasteful Biden Administration. (Reported by Karoline Leavitt, President Trump's press secretary, May 21, 2025.)

However, if Trump is successful to "Make America Great Again" he will increase the current Trump movement in the future. It is possible that the country could elect Republican presidents for the next 100 years. Since the democratic leaders often call Trump "Hitler," if his presidency proves to be very successful, the democrats, without realizing it will put Hitler in a good light.

The president promised to defeat the inflation inherited from the Biden administration. It will happen by reducing the cost of energy, lowering mortgage rates, car payments and grocery prices, thus helping taxpayers to save money and "make America affordable again." He will never approve sending billions of dollars abroad for imaginary charities and fictional grants to countries nobody probably ever heard of. He already imposed tariffs against Canada, China, Mexico, and many other countries. He believes he will bring back 2 billion per day with his tariffs. He is bringing back and protecting American jobs, which will make America rich again.

Donald J. Trump confidently declared that he "...accomplished more in 43 days than most administrations accomplished in four years, or eight years and we are just getting started." That vote of confidence made the president to open on March 4, 2025 the longest joint address to Congress in history, with "America is Back."

✞

On July Fourth, 2025, President Trump signed his "One Big Beautiful Bill Act" into Law during a ceremony at the White House. At the same time, a stealth bomber escorted by fighter jets flew above the celebration picnic on the lawn below.

The signed Act is unique in American history, consisting of the biggest and permanent tax cuts ever, no tax on tips and overtime, an increase in small business tax deduction, and to boost child Tax Credit for more than 40 million American families. Also, there will be an increase in the budget for border and national security, hikes for defense spending, including the development of the "Golden Dome" above the U.S. territories.

At the same time, the Act will eliminate fraud in Medicare, a reduction in the size of the government for welfare programs, climate change organizations, and cuts for education funds for diversity and inclusion programs. Drastic cuts are made in foreign programs on climate and clean energy, and credit cuts for domestic solar power and clean Electricity Production. President Trump justified his "One Big Beautiful Bill Act" as a reminder that his promises made were now promises kept, to make America Great Again.

His achievements are based on drastic and necessary changes being done by the Trump administration. These changes are necessary to keep the American government from becoming bankrupt in a short period of time. Also, it is necessary to reduce the national debt which is currently over $33 trillion, and could reach $50 trillion in the next 10 years, according to the Congressional Budget Office.

Indeed, printing more money to cover the expenses of a nation with already trillions of dollars in debt would be another form of balkanization which America does not need to experience. What Trump wants is to successfully rebuild the American economy and military might. By achieving this it will again make the U.S. a global stabilizer and regain the international respect of the entire world. This will all lead to President Donald J. Trump's promise of "The Golden Age of America."

✛

In summary, the reason I wrote "The Roots of Balkanization" was to remind the readers that over many centuries, those roots have spread out from the Balkan Peninsula into Western Europe, and now into the United States. I have focused on how it was possible in our modern times that the Western civilization now finds itself in no better shape than the Roman and Byzantine empires which collapsed under the barbarian invasions. The final blow was delivered by the Islamic army which conquered Constantinople in 1453, allowing the Ottoman Empire to extend into the Balkan Peninsula and Eastern Europe. This was the amplification of balkanization for hundreds of years in a land that could be named "Absurdistan."

Restrained by natural and political barriers the Western world has waited the same hundreds of years while enduring many wars to keep balkanization at bay. In exchange, it was the Communist regime that efficiently used it to remain in power. They kept the masses believing in the "golden age of communism" which has never materialized. After Communism fell, balkanization seemed to continue to thrive in the poor Middle Eastern and South American nations. So far, the United States has not succumbed to Balkanization, and that is a good thing for its citizens.

I tried hard not to write a scholarly dry book, but to involve the reader as a part of the complicated and amazing reality of balkanization, which I hope will not be repeated.

Thank you interested reader,

Ion Grumeza Ph.D.
Metaphysical Sciences

# BIBLIOGRAPHY

Anastasoff, Christ. *The Bulgarians*. Hicksville, NY: Exposition Press, 1977.

Arnott, Peter. *The Byzantines and Their World*. New York: St. Martin's Press, 1973.

Aries, Philippe, Georges Duby, and Paul Veyne, eds. *A History of Private Life: From Pagan Rome to Byzantium*. Translated by Arthur Goldhammer. Cambridge, MA: Harvard University Press, 1997.

Atiya, Aziz Suryal. *The Crusade of Nicopolis*. London: Methuen, 1934.

Bachman, Ronald D. *Romania: A Country Study*. Lanham, MD: Bernan Press Federal Research Division, 1991.

Barraclough, Geoffrey, ed. *Harper Collins Atlas of World History*. Ann Arbor, Ml: Borders Press, 1998.

Barford, Paul. *The Early Slavs: Culture and Society in Early Medieval Eastern Europe*. Ithaca: Cornell University Press, 2001.

Bartha, Antal. *Hungarian Society in the 9th and 10th Centuries*. Budapest: Akademiai Kiado, 1975.

Bartusis, C. Mark. *The Late Byzantine Army: Arms and Society, 1204-1453*. Philadelphia: University of Pennsylvania Press, 1992.

Biel, Timothy Levi. *The Crusades*. San Diego: Lucent Books, 1996.

Bishop, Morris. *The Middle Ages*. New York: American Heritage Press, 1970.

Bunson, Matthew. *Encyclopedia of the Middle Ages*. New York: Facts on File, 1995.

Bury, J. B. *History of the Later Roman Empire*, Vol. 1, *From the Death of Theodosius I to the Death of Justinian*. New York: Dover, 1958.

—*History of the Later Roman Empire*. Vol. 2, *From Arcadius to*

*Irene*. London and New York: Macmillan, 1889.

Cadzow, John F., Andrew Ludanyi, and Louis J. Elteto, eds. Transylvania: The Roots of Ethnic Conflict. Kent, OH: Kent State University Press, 1983.

Cambell, John C. *The Balkans: Heritage and Continuity*. Berkeley: University of California Press, 1963.

Chesterton, G. K. *The Collective Works of G. K. Chesterton*. Introduction by James V. Schall. San Francisco: Ignatius Press, 2001.

Cirkovic, Sima M. *The Serbs*. Translated by Yuk Tosic. Oxford: Blackwell Publishing, 2004.

Comnena, Anna. *The Alexiad of Anna Comnena*. Translated by E. R. A. Sewter. London: Penguin Books, 1969.

Choniates, Niketas. *O City of Byzantium: Annals of Niketas Choniates*. Translated by Harry J. Magoulias. Detroit: Wayne State University Press, 1984.

Cornej, Petr, and Jiri Pokorny. *A Brief History of the Czech Lands to 2004*. Translated by Anna Bryson. Prague: Prah Press, 2004.

Creasy, Edward S. *History of the Ottoman Turks*. Beirut: Khayats, 1961.

Crowley, Roger. 1453: *The Holy War for Constantinople and the Clash of Islam and the West*. New York: Hyperion, 2005.

Cuppy, Will. *The Decline and Fall of Practically Everybody*. New York: Henry Holt, 1950.

Curtis, Glenn E., ed. *Bulgaria: A Country Study*. Lanham, MD: Bernan Press Federal Research Division, 1993.

Devries, Kelly, Iain Dickie, Phyllis G. Jestice, Christer Jorgensen, and Michael E. Pavkovic. *Battles of the Crusades 1097-1444: From Dorylaeum to Varna*. London: Amber Books, 2007.

Dienes, Istvan. *The Hungarians Cross the Carpathians*. Budapest: Corvina Press, 1972.

Dogaru, Mircea. *Dracula: mit și realitate istoricâ*. Bucharest: Editura Ianus, 1993.

Dragan, Josif Constantin. *Istoria Romanilor*. Bucuresti: Editura

Europa Nova, 1994.

Duichev, Ivan. *Kiril and Methodius: Founders of Slavonic Writing*. Boulder: East European Monographs, 1985.

Dunlop, D. M. *The History of the Jewish Khazars*. Princeton: Princeton University Press, 1954.

Dvornik, Francis. *Byzantine Missions Among the Slavs: SS. Constantine-Cyril and Methodius*. New Brunswick, NJ: Rutgers University Press, 1970.

Fine, John V. A. *The Early Medieval Balkans: A Critical Survey from the Sixth to the Late Twelfth Century*. Ann Arbor: University of Michigan Press, 1991.

—.*The Late Balkans: A Critical Survey from the Late Twelfth Century to the Ottoman Conquest*. Ann Arbor: University of Michigan Press, 1994.

Florescu, Radu R., and Raymond T. McNally. *Dracula: Prince of Many Faces, His life and His Times*. Boston: Little, Brown, 1989.

Georgescu, Vlad. *The Romanians: A History*. Columbus: Ohio State University Press, 1991.

Gibbon, Edward. *The Decline and Fall of the Roman Empire*. Edited by Hans-Friedrich Mueller. New York: Modern Library, 2003.

Goffart, Walter, and Barbarian Tides. *The Migration Age and the Later Roman Empire*. Philadelphia: University of Pennsylvania Press, 2006.

Grant, Michael. *A Guide to the Ancient World: A Dictionary of Classical Place Names*. New York: Barnes & Noble, 1986

Halberstadt, Hans. *The World's Great Artillery: From the Middle Ages to the Present Day*. New York: Barnes & Noble, 2002.

Hale, William Harlan, and The Editors of Horizon Magazine. *The Horizon Cookbook and Illustrated History of Eating and Drinking through the Ages*. New York: American Heritage Publishing, 1968.

Hall, John Whitney, and John Grayson Kirk, eds. *History of the World: Earliest Times to the Present Day*. North Dighton, MA:

World Publications Group, 1958, 2002.

Hammond, N. G. L. *A History of Macedonia*. New York: Oxford University Press, 1972.

Hartman, Gertrude. *Medieval Days and Ways*. New York: Macmillan, 1965.

Hristov, Hristo. A *History of Bulgaria*. Sofia: Sofia Press, 1985.

lvelja-Dalmatin, Ana. *Dubrovnik*. Translated by Zivan Filippi. Zagerb: Turisticka naklada, 2005.

Jelavich, Barbara. *History of the Balkans*. 2 vols. Cambridge: Cambridge University Press, 1997.

Jotischky, Andrew, and Caroline Hull. *Historical Atlas of the Medieval World*. London: Penguin Books, 2005.

Judah, Tim. *The Serbs: History, Myth and the Destruction of Yugoslavia*. New Haven, CT: Yale University Press, 1997.

Kann, Robert A. *The Multinational Empire*. New York: Octogon Books, 1970.

Kinross, Lord. *The Ottoman Centuries: The Rise and Fall of the Turkish Empire*. New York: Morrow Quill, 1977.

Kolsti, John. *Albanism: From the Humanism to Hoxha*. Boulder: East European Monographs, 1981.

Konecny, Zdenek, and Frantisek Mainus. *Stopami Minulosti: Kapitol z Dejin Moravy a Slezkal Traces of the Past: Chapters From the History of Moravia and Silesia*. Brno: Blok, 1979.

Jones, A. H. M. *The Later Roman Empire: 264-602*. Norman, OK: University of Oklahoma Press, 1964.

Lengyel, Emil. *1,000 Years of Hungary*. New York: John Day, 1958.

Lyttle, Richard B. *Land Beyond the River: Europe in the Age of Migration*. New York: Atheneum, 1986.

Makkai, Laszlo, and Andras Mocsy, eds. *History of Transylvania*. New York: Columbia University Press, 2001.

Martin, Edward J. *A History of the Iconnoclastic Controversy*. London: Ams Pr, 1930.

Martis, A. Nikos. *The Macedonians and Their Contribution to Western Civilization*. Athens: Diachronikes Ekdoseis, 2002.

McNally, Raymond T., and Radu Florescu. *In Search of Dracula*. Boston: Houghton Mifflin, 1994.

Mills, Dorothy M.A. *The Middle Ages*. New York: Putnam, 1935.

Norwich, John Julius. *Byzantium: The Apogee*. New York: Knopf, 1992.

—. *Byzantium: The Early Centuries*. New York: Knopf, 1989.

Perl, Lila. *Yugoslavia, Romania, Bulgaria*. Camden, NJ: Thomas Nelson, 1970.

Poulton, Hugh. *The Balkans: Minorities and States in Conflict*. London: Minority Rights Publication, 1991.

Procopius. *History of the Wars: Secret History and Buildings*. Edited by H. R. Trever Roper. New York: Washington Square Press, 1967.

Riasanovsky, Nicholas V., Gleb Struve, and Thomas Eekman, eds. *California Slavic Studies*. Berkeley and Los Angeles: University of California Press, 1967.

Shepard, Jonathan, ed. *The Expansion of Orthodox Europe: Byzantium, the Balkans and Russia*. Burlington, VT: Ashgate, 2007.

Sisa, Stephen. T*he Spirit of Hungary: A Panorama of Hungarian History and Culture*. Morristown, NJ: Vista Books, 1990.

Soulis, George C. *The Serbs and Byzantium During the Reign of Tzar Stephen Dusan, 1331-1335, and His Successors*. Washington, DC: Dumbarton Oaks Library and Collection, 1984.

Spinka, Matthew. *A History of Christianity in the Balkans: A Study in the Spread of Byzantine Culture Among the Slavs*. Hamden, CT: Archon Books, 1968.

Stevens, Rick, and Cameron Hewitt. *Eastern Europe*. Berkeley: Avalon Travel, 2008.

Stoicescu, N. *Vlad Tepes*. Bucharest: Editura Academiei, 1978.

Sugar, Peter F., ed. *A History of Hungary*. Bloomington, IN: Indiana University Press, 1990.

Tanner, Marcus. *Croatia: A Nation Forged in War*. New Haven, CT:

Yale University Press, 1997.

Tappan, Eva March. *When Knights Were Bold*. Boston: Houghton Mifflin, 1939.

Treadgold, Warren: *A Concise History of Byzantium*. New York: Palgrave Publishers: 1991.

—. *A History of the Byzantine State and Society*. Stanford: Stanford University Press, 1997.

Vekony, Gabor. *Dacians Romans Romanians*. Hamilton and Buffalo: Matthias Corvinus Publishing, 2000.

Veyne, Paul, ed., Philippe Aries and Georges Duby, general eds. *A History of Private Life: From Pagan Rome to Byzantium*. Translated by Arthur Goldhammer. Cambridge, MA: Harvard University Press, 1997.

Ware, Timothy. *The Orthodox Church*. New York: Penguin Books, 1985.

Warner, Philip. *The Medieval Castle: Life in a Fortress in Peace and War*. New York: Taplinger, 1971.

Whitby, Michael. *The Emperor Maurice and His Historian: Theophylact Simocatta on Persian and Balkan Warfare*. Oxford: Clarendon Press, 1988.

Whitlow, Mark. *The Making of Byzantium 600-1025*. Berkeley: University of California Press, 1996.

Woosnam-Savage, Robert C., and Anthony Hall. *Brassey's Book of Body Armor*. Washington, DC: Brassey, 2001.

Zickel, Raymond, and Walter R. Iwaskiw, eds. *Albania: A Country Study*. Lanham, MD: Beman Press Federal Research Division, 1994.

www.ingramcontent.com/pod-product-compliance
Lightning Source LLC
Chambersburg PA
CBHW060105170426
43198CB00010B/776